Stanley Gibbons
COLLEC
Channel Islands
and Isle of Man
STAMPS

D1077373

A STANLEY GIBBONS CHECKLIST

1998 Edition

30130 101156148

STANLEY GIBBONS LTD
London and Ringwood

By Appointment to
Her Majesty The Queen,
Stanley Gibbons Ltd., London,
Philatelists

Published by **Stanley Gibbons Publications**
Editorial, Sales Offices and Distribution Centre:
5 Parkside, Christchurch Road, Ringwood,
Hants BH24 3SH

FOURTEENTH COMBINED EDITION (1998)

ISBN: 0-85259-438-0

© Stanley Gibbons Ltd 1998

Item No. 2855 (98)

Text assembled by Black Bear Press Limited, Cambridge
Printed in Great Britain by The Alden Press Ltd., Oxford

Introductory Notes

Scope. The listing of **stamps** for Guernsey and Jersey comprises German Occupation issues, the 1958–69 Regionals and the issues of the Independent Postal Administrations from their inception in 1969. Isle of Man sections cover the 1958–71 Regionals and the issues of the Independent Postal Administration from 1973 onwards.

Information is given on:

- Designers and printers
- The different printings for definitives and postage dues
- Distinctive papers
- Such varieties as imperforates and missing colours
- Phosphors
- Cylinder and plate numbers
- Sheet sizes and imprints
- Quantities sold
- Withdrawal and invalidation dates

The 'Notes' on page 1 may be found helpful in further explanation.

The checklist also covers:

- Miniature sheets
- First-day covers
- Presentation packs and Yearbooks
- Gutter pairs
- Stamp booklets
- Stamp sachets (listed, but unpriced)
- Postal stationery commemorative cards and covers

Items outside the scope and therefore *omitted* are: cylinder and plate varieties; non-postage stamps, such as revenues; and other classes of postal stationery.

Layout. Stamps are set out chronologically by date of issue. In the catalogue lists the first numeral is the Stanley Gibbons catalogue number; the black (boldface) numeral alongside is the type number referring to the respective illustration. The denomination and colour of the stamp are then shown. Before February 1971 British currency was:

£1=20s One Pound = twenty shillings *and* 1s=12d One shilling = twelve pence.

Upon decimalisation this became:

£1=100p One pound = one hundred (new) pence.

The catalogue list then shows two price columns. The left-hand is for unused stamps and the right-hand for used.

Our method of indicating prices is:

Numerals for pence, e.g. 5 denotes 5p (5 pence). Numerals for pounds and pence, e.g. 4.25 denotes £4.25 (4 pounds and 25 pence). For £100 and above, prices are in whole pounds and so include the £ sign and omit the zeros for pence.

Size of illustrations. To comply with Post Office regulations illustrations of stamps and booklets are three-quarters linear size. Illustrations of watermarks are actual size.

Prices. Prices quoted in this catalogue are our selling prices at the time the book went to press. They are for stamps in fine average condition; in issues where condition varies we may ask more for the superb and less for the sub-standard. With unused stamps prices are for unmounted mint (though where not available unmounted, stamps are often supplied at a lower price). Used prices are normally for stamps postally used but may be for stamps cancelled-to-order where this practice exists. All prices are subject to change without prior notice and we give no guarantee to supply all stamps priced, since it is not possible to keep every catalogue item perpetually in stock. Commemoratives may, at times, only be available in complete sets. Individual low value stamps sold at 399, Strand are liable to an additional handling charge.

Perforations. The 'perforation' is the number of holes in a length of 2 cm, as measured by the Gibbons *Instanta* gauge. The stamp is viewed against a dark background with the transparent gauge put on top of it. Perforations are quoted to the nearest half. Stamps without perforation are termed 'imperforate'.

Se-tenant combinations. *Se-tenant* means 'joined together'. Some sets include stamps of different design arranged *se-tenant* as blocks or strips and, in mint condition, these are usually collected unsevered as issued. Where such combinations exist, the individual stamps are priced normally as mint and used singles. The set price for mint refers to the unsevered combination plus singles of any other values in the set. The used set price is for single stamps of all values.

First day covers. Prices for first day covers are for complete sets used on special covers, the stamps of which bear an official postmark for first day of issue. Where the stamps in a set were issued on different days, prices are for a cover from each day.

Catalogue numbers used. The checklist uses the same catalogue numbers as the Stanley Gibbons *British Commonwealth* catalogue, 1998 edition.

Latest stamps recorded in this edition appeared in November 1997.

CONTENTS

Stanley Gibbons Holdings Plc Addresses

STANLEY GIBBONS LIMITED, STANLEY GIBBONS AUCTIONS

399 Strand, London WC2R 0LX

Auction Room and Specialist Stamp Departments. Open Monday–Friday 9.30 a.m. to 5 p.m.
Shop. Open Monday–Friday 8.30 a.m. to 6 p.m. and Saturday 10 a.m. to 4 p.m.
Telephone 0171 836 8444 and Fax 0171 836 7342 for all departments.

STANLEY GIBBONS PUBLICATIONS

5 Parkside, Christchurch Road, Ringwood, Hants BH24 3SH. **Telephone** 01425 472363 (24-hour answer phone service), **Fax** 01425 470247 and **E-mail** info@stangib.demon.co.uk

Publications Showroom (at above address). Open Monday–Friday 9 a.m. to 3 p.m.
Publications Mail Order. COLLECTORS' FREEPHONE 0800 611622 and TRADE DESK 01425 478776 Monday–Friday 8.30 a.m. to 5 p.m.

URCH HARRIS & CO

(a division of Stanley Gibbons Ltd)

1 Denmark Avenue, Bristol BS1 5HD
Telephone 0117 9349333 and **Fax** 0117 9273037 Monday–Friday 8.30 a.m. to 5 p.m.

CHANNEL ISLANDS
& ISLE OF MAN
BUYER'S GUIDE

◉ **The Channel Islands & Isle of Man Suppliers**
The Channel Islands & Isle of Man Suppliers guide is your comprehensive, *at-a-glance* guide to the philatelic industry. Broken down by classifications, the Suppliers guide is an invaluable information service covering many dealers.
Whatever you require, simply turn to the guide for a selection of names, addresses and telephone numbers covering your specialist area.

◉ **Compilation**
The Channel Islands & Isle of Man Suppliers guide is compiled and published by Stanley Gibbons Publications. Every effort has been made to ensure the accuracy of all the entries in the directory, however, Stanley Gibbons Publications cannot in any circumstances be responsible for or accept any liability for any loss or damage of any kind which may arise or result from any errors or omissions in any entry, whether relating to wording, space, position, artwork or telephone number.

◆ CHANNEL ISLANDS

AURIGNY AUCTIONS
Occasional Sales of Stamps, postal history and postcards of the Channel Islands including the smaller islands of Herm, Jethou and Sark. Free Catalogue.

PO Box 210, Coventry Warwickshire, CV6 6HU   **Tel: 01203 686613 Fax: 01203 667428**

Hudson Roger
PO Box 172, Coventry, Warwickshire,
CV6 6NF, ENGLAND .Tel: 01203 686613
Fax: 01203 667428

◆ GENERAL

AJH Stamps (Auctions)
The Laurels, 243 Manchester Road,
Accrington, Lancs, Bl35 2PF ENGLAND
. . . . .Tel: 01254 393740
Fax: 01254 382274

Bartlett R H
La Roberge, Le Bigard Forest, Guernsey
GY8 0HT CHANNEL ISLANDS
. . . . .Tel: 01481 64757
Fax: 01481 64757

Bradford Stamp Centre
390 Dudley Hill Road, Undercliffe,
Bradford, West Yorks, BD2 3AA,
ENGLAND . . . . .Tel: 01274 630331

Channel Island Stamp Co
4 Havilland St. St. Peter Port, Guernsey,
CHANNEL ISLANDS .Tel: 01481 725560
Fax: 01481 711012

EPHEMERA
Guernsey, Jersey and Isle of Man. Mint, used first day covers & occupation stamps available. Shop open daily 10am-5pm.
**21B Contree Mansell,
St Peter Port, Guernsey
CHANNEL ISLANDS,
GY1 1LZ**   **Tel: 01481 714424
Fax: 01481 714424**

The Collectors Centre
Sausmarez Street, St. Peter Port,
Guernsey, CHANNEL ISLANDS
. . . . .Tel: 01481 725209

D.J. Russell
2 Brunswick Square, Herne Bay, Kent,
ENGLAND, CT6 5QF

Guernsey Post Office
Postal Headquarters, St. Peter Port,
Guernsey, GY1 1AA, CHANNEL ISLANDS
. . . . .Tel: 01481 726241
Fax: 01481 712082

Isle of Man Post Office
Post Office HQ, Circular Road, Douglas,
Isle of Man, IM1 1AA .Tel: 01624 686130
Fax: 01624 686132

Map Collectables
69 Fulbeck Road, Netherfields,
Middlesbrough, ENGLAND, TS3 0RE
. . . . .Tel: 01642 318388
Fax: 01642 320739
e-mail:maptrading@lineone.net

Ringdale Philatelics
242 Stroud Road, Gloucester, GL4 0AU,
ENGLAND . . . . .Tel: 01452 411942

Philatelic Software Limited,
Valley View, Colemans Lane, Nazeing,
Essex, EN9 2EA . . . .Tel: 01992 893086
Fax: 01992 892729

Stanley Gibbons Limited
399 Strand London WC2R 0LX
ENGLAND . . . . .Tel: 0171 836 8444
Fax: 0171 836 7342
e-mail:shop@stangiblondon.demon.co.uk

ISLE OF MAN POST OFFICE

Philatelic Bureau,
P.O. Box 10M,
Circular Road,
Douglas,
Isle of Man,
IM99 1PB,
Tel (01624) 686130,
Fax (01624) 686132.

MANX COLLECT STAMPS

Collecting Isle of Man stamps could not be easier. Simply open a standing order account with the Philatelic Bureau and we will send you your stamps as soon as they become available. Manx stamps over a wide range of topics including **Cats, Dogs, Motorcycles and Motorcars, Aeroplanes and Boats.** There are stamps for the young and the old in fact there is something for everyone at The Isle of Man Post Office. Other items available from the Philatelic Bureau include First Day Covers, Presentation Packs, our **Island Treasures range** and **a Limited Edition Year Book Priced @ £21.00**

The 1997 Limited Edition Year Book is a complete album in itself, it makes an attractive and inexpensive way of collecting Manx stamps on an annual basis. Finished in a deep maroon durable linen cover and slipcase it contains detailed information about the stamps and their designers. Issues featured this year include **OWLS, GOLF, AVIATION, STORIES & LEGENDS, CHRISTMAS NATIVITY, THE ROYAL GOLDEN WEDDING**

NOTES ON THE CATALOGUE LISTINGS

Printings
For definitives and postage due stamps released by the independent Postal Administrations we give the dates of the printings as announced, and relate them in the listings to the actual stamps involved. Users will therefore be able to see at a glance how many printings have been made of any particular item.

Cylinder and Plate Numbers
Following the listing of each issue we give the printers' cylinder or plate numbers known to us.

Sheet Size
In describing the sheet arrangement we always give the number of stamps across the sheet first. For example, '50 (5×10)' indicates a sheet of fifty stamps in ten horizontal rows of five stamps each.

Paper
Only distinctive types are mentioned. Granite paper can be easily distinguished by the coloured lines in its texture. *Chalky* or *chalk-surfaced* applies to paper which shows a black line when touched with silver.

Perforations
Perforations are normally given to the nearest half and the *Instanta* gauge is our standard. In this checklist we state if a perforation is by a line (L) or a comb (C) machine. A line machine only perforates one line at a time and consequently it requires two operations to do the horizontal and vertical perforations and where these intersect an irregular-shaped hole often results. A comb machine perforates three sides at a time and therefore produces a single hole at all corner intersections. The differences are easily seen in blocks of four.

The various perforations in this checklist are expressed as follows:

Perf 14:   Perforated alike on all sides.
Perf 14×15: Compound perforation. The first figure refers to top and bottom, the second to left and right sides.

Abbreviations
des=designer, designed
eng=engraver, engraved
litho=lithographed
mm=millimetres
MS=miniature sheet
No.=number
perf=perforated
photo=photogravure
recess=recess-printed
typo=typographed
wmk(d)=watermark(ed)

Channel Islands

C **1** Gathering Vraic   C **2** Islanders gathering Vraic

Third Anniversary of Liberation
(Des J. R. R. Stobie (1d), or from drawing by E. Blampied (2½d). Photo Harrison and Sons)

1948 (10 MAY). *Wmk Mult* G VI R. *Perf* 15×14 (C)

C1	C **1**	1d scarlet	20	20
C2	C **2**	2½d ultramarine	30	30
		First Day Cover		25·00

These stamps were primarily intended for use in the Channel Islands although they were also available at eight head post offices in Great Britain.

Cylinder Nos.: 1d 2; 2½d 4
Sheets: 120 (6×20)
Quantities sold: 1d 5,934,000; 2½d 5,398,000

Guernsey

THE GERMAN OCCUPATION 1940—1945

The first German soldiers to arrive in Guernsey set foot on the island on 30 June, 1940 and an official notice appeared in the local newspaper the following day announcing the occupation.

The first evidence of the occupation, philatelically, came towards the end of the year when supplies of Great Britain 1d stamps then in use began to dry up. It was decided that the bisecting of 2d stamps for use as 1d's be allowed and this commenced on 27 December. The decision to print 1d stamps locally had been taken in October, but these were not ready and were eventually issued on 18 February, 1941. In the meantime the two currently available 2d stamps, the 1937 definitive and the 1940 Postal Centenary, were bisected and used, as were 2d stamps of the reign of George V which were in collectors' hands. Other values are also known to have been bisected and used, and were allowed to pass through the post in most instances without a postage due charge being made.

When the decision to bisect the 2d stamps was taken the German Commandant in Guernsey decided on adding a swastika to each half of the stamp. This overprint was applied to the Postal Centenary stamp and these were submitted to Berlin for approval, but this proposal was turned down. Another proposal, the overprinting of the 1937 1d with a number of small swastikas, would appear to have been dealt with in a similar way. Examples of both items exist though these are very rare.

As previously mentioned, the locally printed 1d stamps were issued on 18 February, 1941. The ½d stamp was released on 7 April, 1941 and the 2½d on 12 April, 1944. This last stamp was issued in an effort to economise on the use of paper as it was found that sealed letters were franked with two 1d stamps and one ½d or a larger number of ½d's, a gross waste in times of shortage. Many printings of these stamps were made, the most notable being on the French bank-note paper in 1942.

Shades of these issues abound, the more outstanding ones being the bluish green (4th) and olive-green (8th) printings of the ½d., and the pale vermilion (11th) printing of the 1d. These stamps continued to be used after the liberation in 1945 until 13 April, 1946.

The Swastika Overprints

1940. *Prepared for use but not issued. Stamps of Great Britain overprinted*

(a) 1937 *definitive overprinted with a number of small swastikas*

Cat. No.		Unused
SW1	1d scarlet....................	£800

(b) 1940 *Postal Centenary issue overprinted with a swastika on each half of the stamp*

SW2	2d orange....................	£800

Example of bisected 2d Postal Centenary stamp

The Bisects

1940 (27 DEC)–**1941** (24 FEB).

(a) Stamps of King George V

Cat. No.			Price on cover
BS1	1912–22	2d orange	£180
BS2	1924–26	2d orange	£180
BS3	1934–36	2d orange	£200

(b) Stamps of King George VI

BS4	1937	1d scarlet	£450
BS5	1938	2d orange	22·00
BS6	1940	Stamp Centenary 1d scarlet	£450
BS7	1940	Stamp Centenary 2d orange....	16·00
BS8	1940	Stamp Centenary 2½d ultramarine	£600
BS9	1940	Stamp Centenary 3d violet	

1 Arms of Guernsey

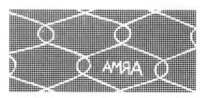

1a Loops

2

Stamps issued during the German Occupation

(Des E. W. Vaudin. Typo Guernsey Press Co Ltd)

1941–44. *Rouletted*

(a) *White paper. No wmk*

Cat. No.	Type No.		Unused	Used
1	1	½d light green (7.4.41)	2·75	2·00
		a. Emerald-green (6.41)	3·75	2·25
		b. Bluish green (11.41)	40·00	16·00
		c. Bright green (2.42)	24·00	10·00
		d. Dull green (9.42)	3·75	2·75
		e. Olive-green (2.43)	29·00	18·00
		f. Pale yellowish green (7.43 and later) (shades)	2·50	2·25
		g. Imperf (pair)	£150	
		h. Imperf between (horizontal pair)	£600	
		i. Imperf between (vertical pair)..	£700	
2		1d scarlet (18.2.41)	2·00	1·00
		a. Pale vermilion (7.43) (etc.)....	2·25	1·50
		b. Carmine (1943)............	2·50	2·75
		c. Imperf (pair)	£150	75·00
		d. Imperf between (horizontal pair)	£600	
		da. Imperf vert (centre stamp of horizontal strip of 3)		
		e. Imperf between (vertical pair)..	£700	
		f. Ptd double (scarlet shade)....	75·00	
3		2½d ultramarine (12.4.44)........	4·00	4·00
		a. Pale ultramarine (7.44)	4·00	4·00
		b. Imperf (pair)	£350	
		c. Imperf between (horizontal pair)	£800	
1		First Day Cover		6·50
2		First Day Cover		10·00
3		First Day Cover		6·50

(b) *Bluish French bank-note paper. Wmk loops (sideways)*

4	1	½d bright green (11.3.42)	18·00	19·00
5		1d scarlet (9.4.42)	9·00	21·00

The dates for the shades of Nos. 1/3 are the months in which they were printed as indicated on the printer's imprints (see below). Others are issue dates.

Printings and imprint: The various printings can be identified from the sheet imprints as follows:

½d 1st Printing 240M/3/41
2nd Printing 2×120M/6/41
3rd Printing 3×120M/6/41
4th Printing 4×120M/11/41
5th Printing 5×120M/2/42
6th Printing 6×240M/2/42
7th Printing 7×120M/9/42
8th Printing 8×120M/2/43
9th Printing 9×120M/7/43
10th Printing 10×120M/10/43
11th Printing Guernsey Press Co., (*stop and comma*)
12th Printing Guernsey Press Co. (*stop only, margin at bottom 23 to 27 mm*)
13th Printing Guernsey Press Co. (*stop only, margin at bottom 15 mm*)

1d 1st Printing 120M/2/41
2nd Printing 2×120M/2/41
3rd Printing 3×120M/6/41
4th Printing 4×120M/6/41
5th Printing 5×120M/9/41
6th Printing 6×240M/11/41
7th Printing 7×120M/2/42
8th Printing 8×240M/4/42
9th Printing 9×240M/9/42
10th Printing 10×240M/1/43
11th Printing 11×240M/7/43
12th Printing Guernsey Press Co.
13th Printing PRESS TYP.
14th Printing "PRESS" (*inverted commas unlevel*)
15th Printing "PRESS" (*inverted commas level, margin at bottom 28 mm*)
16th Printing "PRESS" (*inverted commas level, margin at bottom 12 mm*)

2½d 1st Printing Guernsey Press Co.,
2nd Printing "PRESS" (*inverted commas unlevel*)
3rd Printing "PRESS" (*inverted commas level, margin at bottom 22 mm*)
4th Printing "PRESS" (*inverted commas level, margin at bottom 15 mm*)

The numbered imprints occur in the left-hand corner, bottom margin on the 1st printing of the 1d, and central, bottom margin on all other printings of all three values.

In the numbered imprints, for example, 2×120M/6/41, the '2' indicates the number of the printing; '120M' denotes the number of stamps printed in thousands, in this case 120,000; and '6/41' denotes the date of the printing, June, 1941.

In the first ten printings of the ½d and the first eleven printings of the 1d the printing details are prefixed by the name of the printer, "Guernsey Press Co."

Sheets: 60 (6×10)

Quantities printed: ½d 1,772,160; 1d 2,478,000; 2½d 416,640

Withdrawn and invalidated: 13.4.46

REGIONAL ISSUES

Although specifically issued for regional use, these issues were initially valid for use throughout Great Britain. However, they ceased to be valid in Guernsey and Jersey from 1 October, 1969 when these islands each established their own independent postal administration and introduced their own stamps.

DATES OF ISSUE. Conflicting dates of issue have been announced for some of the regional issues, partly explained by the stamps being released on different dates by the Philatelic Bureau in Edinburgh or the Philatelic Counter in London and in the regions. We have adopted the practice of giving the earliest known dates, since once released the stamps could have been used anywhere in the U.K.

INVALIDATION. The regional issues of Guernsey were invalidated for use in Guernsey and Jersey on 1 November, 1969 (although Guernsey granted a further extension for British and regional stamps till the end of March 1970). The stamps continued to be valid for use in the rest of the United Kingdom until 29 February, 1972. Those still current remained on sale at philatelic sales counters until 30 September, 1970.

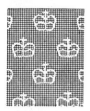

1*b* Multiple Crowns   **2**   **3**

4 Castle Cornet and Edward the Confessor

(Des E. A. Piprell. Portrait by Dorothy Wilding Ltd. Photo Harrison and Sons)

1958–67. *Wmk Type* **1***b*. *Perf* 15×14 (C)

6	**2**	2½d rose-red (8.6.64)	35	40
7	**3**	3d deep lilac (18.8.58)	35	30
		p. One centre phosphor band (24.5.67)	20	20
8		4d ultramarine (7.2.66)	25	30
		p. Two phosphor bands (24.10.67).	20	20
6/8*p*		*Set of 3*	70	75
6		*First Day Cover*		22·00
7		*First Day Cover*		17·00
8		*First Day Cover*		7·50

Cylinder Nos.: 2½d 1, 3; 3d (ord) 4, 5; 3d (phos) 5; 4d (ord) 1; 4d (phos) 1

Sheets: 240 (12×20)

Quantities sold (ordinary only): 2½d 3,485,760; 3d 25,812,360; 4d 4,415,040

Withdrawn: 31.8.66 2½d

Sold out: 6.3.68 3d and 4d (ordinary); 10.68 4d (phosphor); 11.68 3d (phosphor)

5 Map and William I

1968–69. *No wmk. Chalk-surfaced paper. One centre phosphor band (Nos.* 10/11*) or two phosphor bands (others). Perf* 15×14 (C)

9	**3**	4d pale ultramarine (16.4.68)	10	25
10		4d olive-sepia (4.9.68)	15	20
11		4d bright vermilion (26.2.69)	15	30
12		5d royal blue (4.9.68).	15	30
9/12		*Set of 4*	40	95
10, 12		*First Day Cover*		1·75

No. 9 was not issued in Guernsey until 22 April.

Cylinder Nos.: 4d (pale ultramarine) 1; 4d (olive-sepia) 1; 4d (bright vermilion) 1; 5d 1

Sold out: 3.69 4d ultramarine

Withdrawn: 30.9.69 (locally), 30.9.70 (British Philatelic Counters) 4d olive-sepia, 4d bright vermilion and 5d

6 Martello Tower and Henry II

INDEPENDENT POSTAL ADMINISTRATION

Guernsey established their own independent postal administration on 1 October, 1969 and introduced their own stamps.

NO WATERMARK. All the following issues are on unwatermarked paper.

7 Arms of Sark and King John

8 Arms of Alderney and Edward III

9 Guernsey Lily and Henry V

10 Arms of Guernsey and Elizabeth I

11 Arms of Alderney and Charles II

12 Arms of Sark and George III

13 Arms of Guernsey and Queen Victoria

14 Guernsey Lily and Elizabeth I

15 Martello Tower and King John

16 View of Sark

17 View of Alderney

18 View of Guernsey

Two types of 1d and 1s 6d

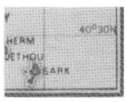
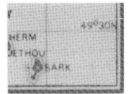

I Latitude inscr '40° 30' N'   II Corrected to '49° 30' N'

(Des R. Granger Barrett. Photo Harrison (½d to 2s 6d), Delrieu (others))

1969 (1 OCT)–**70.** *Perf* 14 (½d to 2s 6d) or 12½ (others), all comb

13	**4**	½d deep magenta and black (a) ..	10	10
		a. *Thin paper*	40	50
14	**5**	1d bright blue and black (I) (a) ..	10	10
		a. *Thin paper* (b)	50	50
14b		1d bright blue and black (*thin paper*) (II) (eg)	30	30
		c. *Booklet stamp with margins* (*thick paper*) (c).	40	40
15	**6**	1½d yellow-brown and black (a) ..	10	10
16	**7**	2d gold, brt red, dp blue & blk (a)	10	10
		a. *Thin paper* (g)	40	40
17	**8**	3d gold, pale greenish yellow, orange-red and black (a)	15	15
		a. *Error. Wmk Block CA*	£1100	
		ai. *Wmk inverted*	£800	
		b. *Thin paper* (g)	40	40
18	**9**	4d multicoloured (a)	25	25
		a. *Booklet stamp with margins* (c)	40	45
		ab. *Yellow omitted*.	£225	
		ac. *Emerald* (*stem*) *omitted*	£100	
19	**10**	5d gold, bright vermilion, bluish violet and black (a)	25	15
		a. *Booklet stamp with margins* (c)	50	50
		b. *Gold* (*inscription etc.*) *omitted* (*booklets*)	£450	
20	**11**	6d gold, pale greenish yellow, light bronze-green & black (a)	30	30
		a. *Thin paper* (g)	30	40
21	**12**	9d gold, brt red, crimson & blk (a)	40	30
		a. *Thin paper* (g)	3·25	3·25
22	**13**	1s gold, brt verm, bistre & blk (a)	30	30
		a. *Thin paper* (g)	1·00	1·00
23	**5**	1s 6d turquoise-grn & blk (I) (a) ..	30	30
		a. *Thin paper* (d)	1·75	3·25
23b		1s 6d turquoise-green and black (*thin paper*) (II) (eg)	2·25	1·75

24	**14**	1s 9d multicoloured (a)	1·25	1·50
		a. Emerald (stem) omitted	£300	
		b. Thin paper (g)	2·50	2·50
25	**15**	2s 6d brt reddish violet & black (a)	5·00	4·25
		a. Thin paper (g)	6·00	6·00
26	**16**	5s multicoloured (a)	3·25	3·25
27	**17**	10s multicoloured (a)	26·00	22·00
		a. Perf 13½×13 (f).	48·00	40·00
28	**18**	£1 multicoloured (a)	2·00	1·75
		a. Perf 13½×13 (fh)	2·00	2·00
13/28a		Set of 16	35·00	30·00
13/28		First Day Cover		32·00
13/28		Presentation Packs (incl. both		
		1d and 1s. 6d) (3) (9.70)	38·00	
13/25		Set of 13 Gutter Pairs	28·00	

Thinner paper – see note after Jersey No. 29.

There was no postal need for the ½d and 1½d values as the ½d coin had been withdrawn prior to their issue in anticipation of decimalisation. These values were only on sale at the Philatelic Bureau and at the Crown Agents as well as in the U.S.A.

Printings: (a) 1.10.69; (b) 24.11.69; (c) 12.12.69; (d) 1.70; (e) 4.2.70; (f) 4.3.70; (g) 18.5.70; (h) 7.71

Cylinder Nos.: ½d, 1½d, 2s 6d. 1A–1A, 1B–1B; 1d. (I) 1A–1A, 1B–1B, 2A–2A (b), 2B–2B; 1d. (II) 2A–2A, 2B–2B, 3A–3A (g), 3B–3B; 2d, 3d, 5d, 6d, 9d, 1s. 1A, 1B (each ×4); 4d, 1s 9d. 1A, 1B (each ×5); 1s 6d. (I) 1A–1A, 1B–1B, 1A–2A (d), 1B–2B; 1s 6d. (II) 1B–1B, 1A–2A, 1B–2B, 2A–3A (g), 2B–3B; 5s to £1 None

Sheets: 60 (2 panes 5×6) most sheets of the 5s, 10s and £1 were divided into two panes before issue

Imprint: Central, bottom margin (½d to 2s 6d)

Quantities sold: ½d 2,480,000; 1d (Nos. 14/14b) 1,560,971; 1½d 980,000; 2d 574,610; 3d 487,199; 4d 2,782,490; 5d 1,393,193; 6d 456,275; 9d 374,975; 1s 435,773; 1s 6d (Nos. 23/23b) 627,003; 1s 9d 255,111; 2s 6d 225,732; 5s 165,047; 10s (No. 27) 114,000; 10s (No. 27a) 55,200; £1 (No. 28) 120,000; £1 (No. 28a) 141,802

Sold out: 8.71 10 s (No. 27a)

Withdrawn: 6.10.69, ½d, 1½d; 4.2.70, 1d (No. 14), 1s 6d (No. 23); others 14.2.72 (except for No. 28a which remained on sale with decimal definitives until 31.3.76)

Although officially withdrawn the ½d, 1d (No. 14), 1½d and 1s 6d (No. 23) were subsequently included in Presentation Packs, whilst the ½d and 1½d remained on sale at the Philatelic Bureau until 14 February, 1972.

Invalidated: 14.2.72 (except £1)

19 Isaac Brock as Colonel

20 Sir Isaac Brock as Major-General

21 Isaac Brock as Ensign

22 Arms and Flags

Birth Bicentenary of Sir Isaac Brock

(Litho Format)

1969 (1 DEC). *Perf 13½×14 (2s 6d) or 14×13½ (others), all comb*

29	**19**	4d multicoloured	20	20
30	**20**	5d multicoloured	20	20
31	**21**	1s 9d multicoloured	1·40	1·25
32	**22**	2s 6d multicoloured	1·40	1·25
29/32		Set of 4	2·75	2·50
		First Day Cover		4·00
		Presentation Pack.	4·00	
		Set of 4 Gutter Pairs	£100	

Plate Nos.: 4d, 2s 6d 1A, 1B, 1C, 1D (each ×6); 5d 1A, 1B, 1C, 1D (each ×7); 1s 9d 1A, 1B, 1C, 1D (each ×5)

Sheets: 60 (2 panes 5×6) 2s 6d; (2 panes 6×5) others

Imprint: Right-hand corner, bottom margin

Quantities sold: 4d 940,956; 5d 732,658; 1s 9d 224,157; 2s 6d 218,955

Withdrawn: 30.11.70

Invalidated: 14.2.72

23 H.M.S. *L103* (landing craft) entering St. Peter's Harbour

24 British Warships entering St. Peter Port

25 Brigadier Snow reading the Proclamation

25th Anniversary of Liberation

(Des and photo Courvoisier)

1970 (9 MAY). *Granite paper. Perf* 11½ (C)

33	**23**	4d blue and pale blue	40	40
34	**24**	5d brown-lake and pale grey	40	40
35	**25**	1s 6d bistre-brown and buff	3·25	2·50
33/5		Set of 3	3·50	3·00
		First Day Cover		3·50
		Presentation Pack..........	4·75	

Cylinder Nos.: A1–1, B1–1 (all values)

Sheets: 25 (5×5)

Imprint: Left-hand corner, top margin (4d, 5d); bottom corner, left-hand margin (1s 6d)

Quantities sold: 4d 968,873; 5d 817,958; 1s 6d 248,532

Withdrawn: 8.5.71

Invalidated: 14.2.72

26 Guernsey 'Toms'

27 Guernsey Cow

28 Guernsey Bull

29 Freesias

Agriculture and Horticulture

(Des and photo Courvoisier)

1970 (12 AUG). *Granite paper. Perf* 11½ (C)

36	**26**	4d multicoloured	80	20
37	**27**	5d multicoloured	90	20
38	**28**	9d multicoloured	5·00	2·75
39	**29**	1s 6d multicoloured	6·00	3·00
36/9		Set of 4	12·00	5·50
		First Day Cover		5·50
		Presentation Pack..........	23·00	

Cylinder Nos.: A1–1–1–1, B1–1–1–1, C1–1–1–1, D1–1–1–1 (all values)

Sheets: 25 (5×5)

Imprint: Central, bottom margin

Quantities sold: 4d 1,082,608; 5d 1,000,000; 9d 237,685; 1s 6d 241,816

Withdrawn: 11.8.71

Invalidated: 14.2.72

30 St. Anne's Church, Alderney

31 St. Peter's Church, Guernsey

32 St. Peter's Church, Sark

33 St. Tugual Chapel, Herm

Christmas. Guernsey Churches (1st series)

(Des and photo Courvoisier)

1970 (11 NOV). *Granite paper. Perf* 11½ (C)

40	**30**	4d multicoloured	35	20
41	**31**	5d multicoloured	45	25
42	**32**	9d multicoloured	1·75	1·10
43	**33**	1s 6d multicoloured	2·00	1·50
40/3		Set of 4	4·00	2·75
		First Day Cover		3·25
		Presentation Pack..........	6·00	

See also Nos. 63/6.

Cylinder Nos.: A1–1–1–1 or B1–1–1–1 (all values)

Sheets: 50 (5×10) 4d, 5d; (10×5) others

Quantities sold: 4d 815,737; 5d 668,886; 9d 236,833; 1s 6d 223,907

Withdrawn: 10.11.71

Invalidated: 14.2.72

34 Martello Tower and King John

Decimal Currency

(Photo Harrison (½p to 10p), Delrieu (others))

1971 (6 JAN)–**73**. *Designs as Type* **4** *etc., but values inscribed in decimal currency as in Type* **34**. *Chalk-surfaced paper. Perf* 14 (½p to 10p) *or* 13½×13 *(others), all comb*

44	**4**	½p deep magenta and black (b) ..	10	15
		a. Booklet stamp with margins. Glazed, ordinary paper	15	20
		ab. Ditto. Chalk-surfaced paper (e)	15	20
45	**5**	1p bright blue and black (II) (b) ..	10	10
46	**6**	1½p yellow-brown and black (b) ..	15	15

36 Great Britain 4d of 1855–7

37 Italy 5c of 1862

38 Confederate States 5c of 1862

47	**9**	2p multicoloured (b)	15	15
		a. Booklet stamp with margins. Glazed, ordinary paper	20	20
		ab. Ditto. Chalk-surfaced paper (e)	20	20
		ac. Emerald (stem) omitted	£1100	
		b. Glazed, ordinary paper (b)	20	20
48	**10**	2½p gold, bright vermilion, bluish violet and black (be)	15	10
		a. Bright vermilion omitted	£450	
		b. Booklet stamp with margins. Glazed, ordinary paper	20	20
		ba. Ditto. Chalk-surfaced paper (e)	20	20
49	**8**	3p gold, pale greenish yellow, orange-red and black (be)	20	20
50	**14**	3½p mult (glazed, ordinary paper) (b)	25	25
51	**7**	4p multicoloured (b)	35	25
52	**5**	5p turquoise-green & black (II) (b)	30	25
53	**11**	6p gold, pale greenish yellow, lt bronze-green and black (b) . .	30	35
54	**13**	7½p gold, brt verm, bistre & blk (b)	40	45
55	**12**	9p gold, brt red, crimson & blk (b)	50	75
56	**34**	10p bright reddish violet & blk (a)	2·25	1·75
		a. Ordinary paper. Bright reddish violet and deep black (c)	1·75	1·75
57	**16**	20p mult (glazed, ordinary paper) (af)	1·00	1·00
		a. Shade* (d)	1·00	1·00
58	**17**	50p mult (glazed, ordinary paper) (adg)	2·00	2·00
44/58		Set of 15	7·00	7·00
		First Day Covers (2)		8·50
44/58, 28a		Presentation Packs (3)	8·00	
44/56		Set of 13 Gutter Pairs	15·00	

*No. 57 has the sky in a pale turquoise-blue; on No. 57a it is pale turquoise-green.

Printings: (a) 6.1.71; (b) 15.2.71; (c) 1.9.72; (d) 25.1.73; (e) 2.4.73; (f) 10.74; (g) 7.75

Cylinder Nos.: ½p, 1p, 1½p, 5p, 10p 1A–1A, 1B–1B; 2p, 3½p 1A, 1B (each ×5); 2½p, 3p, 4p, 6p, 7½p, 9p 1A, 1B (each ×4); 20p none; 50p 21–22–23–24. Sheets from ptg (g) have and additional S99 (reversed)

On the 3½p only four '1A' Nos. are shown in the margin, the black '1A' being omitted in error.

Sheets: 50 (2 panes 5×5) ½p to 10p; 30 (5×6) others

Imprint: Central, bottom margin (½p to 10p)

Quantities sold: ½p 980,959; 1p 568,509; 1½p 559,576; 2p 2,512,903; 2½p 4,469,578; 3p 2,245,564; 3½p 317,523; 4p 527,696; 5p 511,742; 6p 346,255; 7½p 322,905; 9p 349,211; 10p 538,153; 20p 630.888; 50p 258,150

Withdrawn: 1.4.75 ½p to 10p (½p, 9p, 10p and Presentation Packs sold out by 5.74); 31.3.76 20p, 50p

Thomas De La Rue Commemoration

(Des and recess De La Rue)

1971 (2 JUNE). Perf 14×13½ (C)

59	**35**	2p dull purple to brown-purple* . .	50	30
60	**36**	2½p carmine-red	50	30
61	**37**	4p deep bluish green	3·00	2·25
62	**38**	7½p deep blue	3·25	2·25
59/62		Set of 4	6·50	4·50
		First Day Cover		4·75
		Presentation Pack	7·00	

*These colours represent the extreme range of shades of this value. The majority of the printing, however, is an intermediate shade.

Plate Nos.: 1A, 1B each

Sheets: 25 (5×5)

Imprint: Central, bottom margin

Quantities sold: 2p 897,742; 2½p 1,404,085; 4p 210,691; 7½p 199,424

Withdrawn: 1.6.72

35 Hong Kong 2c of 1862

39 Ebenezer Church, St. Peter Port

40 Church of St. Pierre du Bois

41 St. Joseph's Church, St. Peter Port

42 Church of St. Philippe de Torteval

Christmas. Guernsey Churches (2nd series)

(Des and photo Courvoisier)

1971 (27 OCT). *Granite paper. Perf* 11½ (C)

63	**39**	2p multicoloured	. . . .	25	25
64	**40**	2½p multicoloured	. . . .	25	25
65	**41**	5p multicoloured	. . . .	2·50	2·00
66	**42**	7½p multicoloured	. . . .	2·75	2·00
63/6		Set of 4	. . . .	5·25	4·00
		First Day Cover	. . . .		4·50
		Presentation Pack.	. . . .	6·50	
		Set of 4 Gutter Pairs	. . . .	23·00	

Cylinder Nos.: A1–1–1, B1–1–1, C1–1–1, D1–1–1–1 (all values)

Sheets: 50 (2 panes 5×5)

Imprint: Central, bottom margin (2p, 2½p) or left-hand corner, bottom margin (5p, 7½p)

Quantities sold: 2p 991,155; 2½p 916,004; 5p 223,412; 7½p 215,768

Withdrawn: 26.10.72

43 *Earl of Chesterfield* (1794)

44 *Dasher* (1827)

45 *Ibex* (1891)

46 *Alberta* (1900)

Mail Packet Boats (1st series)

(Des and photo Courvoisier)

1972 (10 FEB). *Granite paper. Perf* 11½ (C)

67	**43**	2p multicoloured	. . . .	15	15
68	**44**	2½p multicoloured	. . . .	20	20
69	**45**	7½p multicoloured	. . . .	90	1·00
70	**46**	9p multicoloured	. . . .	1·50	1·40
67/70		Set of 4	. . . .	2·50	2·50
		First Day Cover	. . . .		4·00
		Presentation Pack.	. . . .	3·50	

See also Nos. 80/3

Cylinder Nos.: A1–1–1–1 or B1–1–1–1 (all values)

Sheets: 25 (5×5)

Imprint: Central, bottom margin

Quantities sold: 2p 973,503; 2½p 954,263; 7½p 288,929; 9p 289,340

Withdrawn: 9.2.73

47 Guernsey Bull

World Conference of Guernsey Breeders, Guernsey

(Photo Courvoisier)

1972 (22 MAY). *Granite paper. Perf* 11½ (C)

71	**47**	5p multicoloured	. . . .	75	60
		First Day Cover*	. . . .		1·75
		Gutter Pair	. . . .	14·00	

*Prepared by the Royal Guernsey Agricultural and Horticultural Society.

Cylinder Nos.: A1–1–1–1, B1–1–1–1

Sheets: 50 (2 panes 5×5)

48 Bermuda Buttercup

49 Heath Spotted Orchid

50 Kaffir Fig   **51** Scarlet Pimpernel

Wild Flowers

(Des and photo Courvoisier)

1972 (24 MAY). *Granite paper. Perf* 11½ (C)

72	**48**	2p multicoloured	....	15	20
73	**49**	2½p multicoloured	....	15	20
74	**50**	7½p multicoloured	....	90	90
75	**51**	9p multicoloured	....	1·25	1·25
72/5		Set of 4	....	2·25	2·25
		First Day Cover	....		3·25
		Presentation Pack	....	4·00	
		Set of 4 Gutter Pairs	....	8·00	

Cylinder Nos.: A1–1–1–1, B1–1–1–1, C1–1–1–1, D1–1–1–1 (all values)

Sheets: 50 (2 panes 5×5)

Imprint: 2p, 7½p Central, bottom margin; others left-hand corner, bottom margin

Quantities sold: 2p 1,006,041; 2½p 1,028,826; 7½p 249,471; 9p 244,839

Withdrawn: 23.5.73

52 Angels adoring Christ   **53** The Epiphany

54 The Virgin Mary   **55** Christ

Royal Silver Wedding and Christmas

(Des and photo Courvoisier)

1972 (20 NOV). *Designs show stained glass windows from Guernsey Churches. Granite paper. Perf* 11½ (C)

76	**52**	2p multicoloured	....	10	10
77	**53**	2½p multicoloured	....	15	15
78	**54**	7½p multicoloured	....	60	55
79	**55**	9p multicoloured	....	75	60
76/9		Set of 4	....	1·50	1·25
		First Day Cover	....		1·75
		Presentation Pack	....	2·00	
		Set of 4 Gutter Pairs	....	5·50	

Cylinder Nos.: A1–1–1–1, B1–1–1–1 each

Sheets: 50 (2 panes 5×5)

Imprint: Central, bottom margin of each pane

Quantities sold: 2p 878,893; 2½p 1,037,387; 7½p 314,972; 9p 313,367

Sold out: By 31.3.73

56 *St. Julien* (1925)

57 *Isle of Guernsey* (1930)

58 *St. Patrick* (1947)

59 *Sarnia* (1961)

Mail Packet Boats (2nd series)

(Des and photo Courvoisier)

1973 (9 MAR). *Granite paper. Perf* 11½ (C)

80	**56**	2½p multicoloured	. . . .	10	10
81	**57**	3p multicoloured	. . . .	30	20
82	**58**	7½p multicoloured	. . . .	90	60
83	**59**	9p multicoloured	. . . .	1·00	75
80/3		*Set of* 4	. . . .	2·00	1·50
		First Day Cover	. . . .		1·60
		Presentation Pack.	. . . .	2·75	
		Set of 4 *Gutter Pairs*		6·00	

Cylinder Nos.: All values A1–1–1–1, B1–1–1–1, C1–1–1–1, D1–1–1–1

Sheets: 50 (2 panes 5×5)

Imprint: Central, bottom margin of each pane

Quantities sold: 2½p 947,888; 3p 1,274,699; 7½p 278,998; 9p 263,569

Withdrawn: 8.3.74 (3p and Presentation Pack sold out earlier)

60 Supermarine Sea Eagle

61 Westland Wessex Trimotor

62 De Havilland D.H.89 Dragon Rapide

63 Douglas DC-3

64 Vickers Viscount 800 *Anne Marie*

50th Anniversary of Air Service

(Des and photo Courvoisier)

1973 (4 JULY). *Granite paper. Perf* 11½ (C)

84	**60**	2½p multicoloured	. . . .	10	10
85	**61**	3p multicoloured	. . . .	15	15
86	**62**	5p multicoloured	. . . .	30	25
87	**63**	7½p multicoloured	. . . .	80	50
88	**64**	9p multicoloured	. . . .	85	55
84/8		*Set of* 5	. . . .	2·00	1·40
		First Day Cover	. . . .		2·00
		Presentation Pack.	. . . .	2·50	
		Set of 5 *Gutter Pairs*		4·25	

Cylinder Nos.: A1–1–1–1, B1–1–1–1 each

Sheets: 50 (2 panes 5×5)

Imprint: Central, bottom margin of each pane

Quantities sold: 2½p 918,953; 3p 1,285,890; 5p 313,882; 7½p 294,369; 9p 288,225

Withdrawn: 3.7.74 (5p and Presentation Pack sold out earlier)

65 'The Good Shepherd'

66 Christ at the Well of Samaria

67 St. Dominic

68 Mary and the Child Jesus

Christmas

(Des and photo Courvoisier)

1973 (24 OCT). *Designs show stained glass windows from Guernsey Churches. Granite paper. Perf* 11½ (C)

89	**65**	2½p multicoloured	. . . .	10	10
90	**66**	3p multicoloured	. . . .	10	10

91	**67**	7½p multicoloured	. . . .	30	30
92	**68**	20p multicoloured	. . . .	60	60
89/92		Set of 4	. . . .	1·00	1·00
		First Day Cover	. . . .		1·00
		Presentation Pack.	. . . .	1·75	
		Set of 4 Gutter Pairs .	. . . . . .	3·00	

Cylinder Nos.: A1–1–1–1, B1–1–1–1 each

Sheets: 50 (2 panes 5×5)

Imprint: Central, bottom margin of each pane

Quantities sold: 2½p 1,284,342; 3p 1,285,851; 7½p 367,714; 20p 367,625

Withdrawn: 23.10.74

73 *Arun*, 1972

150th Anniversary of Royal National Life-boat Institution

(Des and photo Courvoisier)

1974 (15 JAN). *Granite paper. Perf* 11½ (C)

94	**70**	2½p multicoloured	. . . .	10	10
95	**71**	3p multicoloured	. . . .	10	10
96	**72**	8p multicoloured	. . . .	45	45
97	**73**	10p multicoloured	. . . .	45	45
94/97		Set of 4	. . . .	1·00	1·00
		First Day Cover	. . . .		1·00
		Presentation Pack.	. . . .	1·25	
		Set of 4 Gutter Pairs .	. . . . . .	2·00	

69 Princess Anne and Capt. Mark Phillips

Royal Wedding

(Des G. Anderson. Photo Courvoisier

1973 (14 NOV). *Granite paper. Perf* 11½ (C)

93	**69**	25p multicoloured	. . . .	1·00	75
		First Day Cover	. . . .		75
		Presentation Pack.	. . . .	1·40	
		Gutter Pair	. . . .	2·00	

Cylinder Nos.: A1–1–1–1, B1–1–1–1

Sheets: 50 (2 panes 5×5)

Imprint: Central, bottom margin of each pane

Quantity sold: 392,767

Withdrawn: 13.11.74

Cylinder Nos.: A1–1–1–1, B1–1–1–1 each

Sheets: 50 (2 panes 5×5)

Imprint: Central, bottom margin of each pane

Quantities sold: 2½p 1,016,058; 3p 1,162,020; 8p 393,660; 10p 393,668

Withdrawn: 14.1.75 (8p, 10p and Presentation Pack sold out earlier)

70 *John Lockett*, 1875

74 Private, East Regt., 1815

75 Officer, 2nd North Regt., 1825

76 Gunner, Guernsey Artillery, 1787

71 *Arthur Lionel*, 1912

77 Gunner, Guernsey Artillery, 1815

78 Corporal, Royal Guernsey Artillery, 1868

79 Field Officer, Royal Guernsey Artillery, 1895

72 *Euphrosyne Kendal*, 1954

80 Sergeant, 3rd Regt., 1867

81 Officer, East Regt., 1822

82 Field Officer, Royal Guernsey Artillery, 1895

83 Colour-Sergeant of Grenadiers, 1833

84 Officer, North Regt., 1832

85 Officer, East Regt., 1822

86 Field Officer, Rifle Company, 1868

87 Private, 4th West Regt., 1785

88 Field Officer, 4th West Regt., 1824

89 Driver, Field Battery, Royal Guernsey Artillery, 1848

90 Officer, Field Battery, Royal Guernsey Artillery, 1868

91 Cavalry Trooper, Light Dragoons, 1814

Militia Uniforms

(Photo Courvoisier (½p to 10p), Delrieu (others))

1974 (2 APR)–**78**. *Granite paper* (½p to 10p). *Perf* 11½ (½p to 10p), 13×13½ (20, 50p) *or* 13½×13 (£1), *all comb*

98	**74**	½p multicoloured (*aj*)	10	10
		a. Booklet strip of 8 (98×5 and 102×3)†	30	
		b. Booklet pane of 16 (98×4, 102×6 and 103×6)†	65	
99	**75**	1p multicoloured (*aci*)	10	10
		a. Booklet strip of 8 (99×4, 103, 105×2 and 105a) (8.2.77)† . .	80	
		b. Booklet strip of 4 (99, 101×2, and 105a) (7.2.78)†	50	
100	**76**	1½p multicoloured (*a*)	10	10
101	**77**	2p multicoloured (*ak*)	10	10
102	**78**	2½p multicoloured (*a*)	10	10
103	**79**	3p multicoloured (*a*)	10	10
104	**80**	3½p multicoloured (*a*)	10	10
105	**81**	4p multicoloured (*abc*)	15	15
105a	**82**	5p multicoloured (*f*)	15	15
106	**83**	5½p multicoloured (*a*)	20	25
107	**84**	6p multicoloured (*ae*)	20	25
107a	**85**	7p multicoloured (*f*)	25	25
108	**86**	8p multicoloured (*ag*)	25	30
109	**87**	9p multicoloured (*al*)	30	30
110	**88**	10p multicoloured (*ah*)	30	30
111	**89**	20p multicoloured (*d*)	55	40
112	**90**	50p multicoloured (*d*)	1·50	1·25
113	**91**	£1 multicoloured (*d*)	3·25	2·50
98/113		Set of 18	7·00	6·00
		First Day Covers (3)		7·50
		Presentation Packs (3)	8·00	
		Set of 15 Gutter Pairs (Nos. 98/110)	5·50	

†Nos. 98*a*/*b* come from a special booklet sheet of 88 (8×11), and Nos. 99*a*/*b* from booklet sheets of 80 (two panes 8×5). These sheets were put on sale in addition to the normal sheets. The strips and panes have the left-hand selvedge stuck into booklet covers, except for No. 99*b* which had the strip loose, and then folded and supplied in plastic wallets.

Printings: (*a*) 2.4.74; (*b*) 10.74; (*c*) 12.74; (*d*) 1.4.75; (*e*) 12.75; (*f*) 29.5.76; (*g*) 7.76; (*h*) 11.76; (*i*) 8.2.77; (*j*) 7.77; (*k*) 12.77; (*l*) 7.2.78

Plate Nos: 20p to £1 none; A1–1–1–1, B1–1–1–1 1½p, 2p, 6p; A1–1–1–1, B1–1–1–1 others

Sheets: 20p to £1, 25 (5×5); others, 100 (2 panes 10×5)

Imprint: Central, bottom margin of each page

Quantities sold: ½p 1,173,560; 1p 1,367,828; 1½p 525,248; 2p 1,098,053; 2½p 1,124,091; 3p 1,953,796; 3½p 1,891,493; 4p 3,435,614; 5p 2,920,246; 5½p 634,870; 6p 2,006,983; 7p 3,103,925; 8p 811,418; 9p 717,815; 10p 1,133,141; 20p 788,840; 50p 570,505; £1 464,428

Withdrawn: 12.2.80 ½p to 20p; 4.2.81 50p, £1

92 Badge of Guernsey and U.P.U. Emblem

93 Map of Guernsey

94 U.P.U. Building,
Berne, and Guernsey
Flag

98 'Au Bord de la Mer'   **99** Self-portrait

Renoir Paintings

(Des and photo Delrieu)

1974 (21 SEPT). *Perf* 13 (C)

118	**96**	3p multicoloured	....	10	10
119	**97**	5½p multicoloured	....	15	15
120	**98**	8p multicoloured	....	40	40
121	**99**	10p multicoloured	....	45	45
118/21		Set of 4	....	1·00	1·00
		First Day Cover	....		1·00
		Presentation Pack	....	1·25	

95 'Salle des Etats'

Sheets: 25 (5×5)

Imprint: Right-hand corner, top margin (3p and 5½p), and bottom corner, right-hand margin (others)

Centenary of Universal Postal Union

(Photo Courvoisier)

Quantities sold: 3p 670,648; 5½p 422,677; 8p 377,615; 10p 391,095

Withdrawn: 20.9.75

1974 (7 JUNE). *Granite paper. Perf* 11½ (C)

114	**92**	2½p multicoloured	....	10	10
115	**93**	3p multicoloured	....	10	10
116	**94**	8p multicoloured	....	45	45
117	**95**	10p multicoloured	....	45	45
114/17		Set of 4	....	1·00	1·00
		First Day Cover	....		1·00
		Presentation Pack	....	1·25	
		Set of 4 Gutter Pairs	......	2·00	

Cylinder Nos.:2½p, 8p A1–1–1, B1–1–1; 3p A1–1–1–1. B1–1–1–1; 10p A1–1–1–1–1, B1–1–1–1–1

Sheets: 50 (2 panes 5×5)

Imprint: Central, bottom margin

Quantities sold: 2½p 1,231,657; 3p 1,839,674; 8p 345,271; 10p 356,501

Withdrawn: 6.6.75

100 Guernsey Spleenwort   **101** Sand Quillwort

96 'Cradle Rock'

102 Guernsey Fern   **103** Least Adder's Tongue

Guernsey Ferns

(Des and photo Courvoisier)

1975 (7 JAN). *Granite paper. Perf* 11½ (C)

122	**100**	3½p multicoloured	....	15	10
123	**101**	4p multicoloured	....	15	10

97 'Moulin Huet Bay'

124	**102**	8p multicoloured	....	40	40
125	**103**	10p multicoloured	....	60	50
122/5		Set of 4	....	1·25	1·00
		First Day Cover	....		1·00
		Presentation Pack	....	1·50	
		Set of 4 Gutter Pairs	......	2·50	

Cylinder Nos.: 3½p, 4p, 8p each A1–1–1–1, B1–1–1–1, C1–1–1–1, D1–1–1–1; 10p A1–1–1–1, B1–1–1–1, C1–1–1–1, D1–1–1–1

Sheets: 50 (2 panes 5×5)

Imprint: Central, bottom margin

Quantities sold: 3½p 1,089,142; 4p 1,370,743; 8p 430,672; 10p 443,636

Withdrawn: 6.1.76

104 Victor Hugo House

106 United Europe
Oak, Hauteville

107 Tapestry Room,
Hauteville

Victor Hugo's Exile in Guernsey

(Des and photo Courvoisier)

1975 (6 JUNE). *Granite paper. Perf* 11½ (C)

126	**104**	3½p multicoloured	....	10	10
127	**105**	4p multicoloured	....	20	10
128	**106**	8p multicoloured	....	40	40
129	**107**	10p multicoloured	....	50	50
126/9		Set of 4	....	1·10	1·00
		First Day Cover	....		1·00
		Presentation Pack	....	1·25	
MS130		114×143 mm. Nos. 126/9	....	1·10	1·00

Cylinder Nos.: A1–1–1–1, B1–1–1–1 each

Sheets: 50 (5×10) 3½p, 10p; (10×5) others

Imprint: Central, left-hand margin (3½p, 10p) or central, bottom margin (4p, 8p).

Quantities sold: 3½p 810,327; 4p 1,346,628; 8p 377,637; 10p 369,282; miniature sheet 269,217.

Withdrawn: 5.6.76

108 Globe and Seal
of Bailiwick

109 Globe and
Guernsey
Flag

110 Globe, Guernsey Flag
and Alderney Shield

111 Globe, Guernsey Flag
and Sark Shield

Christmas

(Des and photo Delrieu)

1975 (7 OCT). *Perf* 13 (C)

131	**108**	4p multicoloured	....	10	10
132	**109**	6p multicoloured	....	15	15
133	**110**	10p multicoloured	....	45	35
134	**111**	12p multicoloured	....	50	50
131/4		Set of 4	....	1·10	1·00
		First Day Cover	....		1·00
		Presentation Pack	....	1·25	

Sheets: 25 (5×5)

Imprint: Central, left-hand margin (4p, 6p); central, bottom margin (10p, 12p).

Quantities sold: 4p 678,619; 6p 667,413; 10p 392,529; 12p 361,548

Withdrawn: 6.10.76

112 Les Hanois

113 Les Casquets

114 Quesnard

115 Point Robert

Lighthouses

(Des and photo Courvoisier)

1976 (10 FEB). *Granite paper. Perf* 11½ (C)

135	**112**	4p multicoloured	....	10	10
136	**113**	6p multicoloured	....	20	25
137	**114**	11p multicoloured	....	50	45
138	**115**	13p multicoloured	....	55	60
135/8		*Set of* 4	....	1·25	1·25
		First Day Cover	....		1·25
		Presentation Pack	....	1·50	
		Set of 4 *Gutter Pairs*	......	2·50	

Cylinder Nos.: A1–1–1–1, B1–1–1–1 each

Sheets: 50 (2 panes 5×5)

Quantities sold: 4p 846,362; 6p 900,899; 11p 366,468; 13p 348,358

Withdrawn: 9.2.77

116 Milk Can

117 Christening Cup

Europa

(Des and photo Courvoisier)

1976 (29 MAY). *Granite paper. Perf* 11½ (C)

139	**116**	10p brown and green	....	40	40
140	**117**	25p grey and blue	....	85	85
139/40		*Set of* 2	....	1·25	1·25
		First Day Cover	....		1·25
		Presentation Pack	....	1·40	

Sheets: 9 (3×3)

Quantities sold: 1,185,014 of each

Sold out: 4.6.76

118 Pine Forest, Guernsey

119 Herm and Jethou

120 Grand Greve Bay, Sark

121 Trois Vaux Bay, Alderney

Views

(Des and photo Courvoisier)

1976 (3 AUG). *Granite paper. Perf* 11½ (C)

141	**118**	5p multicoloured	....	15	10
142	**119**	7p multicoloured	....	15	20
143	**120**	11p multicoloured	....	55	45
144	**121**	13p multicoloured	....	55	65
141/4		*Set of* 4	....	1·25	1·25
		First Day Cover	....		1·25
		Presentation Pack	....	1·50	
		Set of 4 *Gutter Pairs*	......	2·50	

Cylinder Nos.: A1–1–1–1, B1–1–1–1 each
Sheets: 50 (2 panes 5×5)
Quantities sold: 5p 661,771; 7p 1,016,350; 11p 349,773; 13p 336,027
Withdrawn: 2.8.77

122 Royal Court House, Guernsey

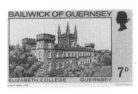

123 Elizabeth College, Guernsey

124 La Seigneurie, Sark

125 Island Hall, Alderney

Christmas. Buildings

(Des and photo Courvoisier)

1976 (14 OCT). *Granite paper. Perf* 11½ (C)

145	**122**	5p multicoloured	. . . .	15	10
146	**123**	7p multicoloured	. . . .	15	15
147	**124**	11p multicoloured	. . . .	55	50
148	**125**	13p multicoloured	. . . .	55	50
145/8		*Set of* 4	. . . .	1·25	1·25
		First Day Cover			1·25
		Presentation Pack	1·50	
		Set of 4 *Gutter Pairs*	2·50	

Cylinder Nos.: A1–1–1–1, B1–1–1–1 each
Sheets: 50 (2 panes 5×5)
Imprint: Central, bottom margin
Quantities sold: 5p 1,097,445; 7p 1,051,184; 11p 371,155; 13p 352,347
Withdrawn: 13.10.77

126 Queen Elizabeth II **127**

Silver Jubilee

(Des R. Granger Barrett. Photo Courvoisier)

1977 (8 FEB). *Granite paper. Perf* 11½ (C)

149	**126**	7p multicoloured	. . . .	25	25
150	**127**	35p multicoloured	. . . .	1·00	1·00
149/50		*Set of* 2	. . . .	1·25	1·25
		First Day Cover			1·25
		Presentation Pack	1·50	

Cylinder Nos.: 7p A1–1–1–1–1, B1–1–1–1–1; 35p A1–1–1–1–1–1
Sheets: 25 (5×5)
Imprint: Central, bottom margin
Quantities sold: 7p 1,004,250; 35p 536,971
Withdrawn: 7.2.78

128 Woodland, Talbots Valley

129 Pastureland, Talbots Valley

Europa

(Des and photo Courvoisier)

1977 (17 MAY). *Granite paper. Perf* 11½ (C)

151	**128**	7p multicoloured	. . . .	35	35
152	**129**	25p multicoloured	. . . .	90	90
151/2		*Set of* 2	. . . .	1·25	1·25
		First Day Cover			1·25
		Presentation Pack	1·50	
		Set of 2 *Gutter Pairs*	2·50	

Cylinder Nos.: A1–1–1–1, B1–1–1–1 each
Sheets: 50 (2 panes 5×5)
Imprint: Right-hand corner, bottom margin
Quantities sold: 7p 1,371,463; 25p 598,453
Withdrawn: 16.5.78

130 Statue-menhir, Castel

131 Megalithic Tomb, St. Saviour

132 Cist, Tourgis

133 Statue-menhir, St. Martin

Prehistoric Monuments

(Des and photo Courvoisier)

1977 (2 AUG). *Granite paper. Perf* 11½ (C)

153	**130**	5p multicoloured	10	10
154	**131**	7p multicoloured	15	15
155	**132**	11p multicoloured	55	55
156	**133**	13p multicoloured	60	60
153/6		*Set of* 4	1·25	1·25
		First Day Cover		1·25
		Presentation Pack	1·50	
		Set of 4 *Gutter Pairs*	2·50	

Cylinder Nos.: A1–1–1–1, B1–1–1–1 each

Sheets: 50 (2 panes 5×5)

Imprint: Central, right-hand margin (5p and 13p); Central, bottom margin (others)

Quantities sold: 5p 747,236; 7p 1,077,714; 11p 390,927; 13p 373,063;

Withdrawn: 1.8.78

134 Mobile First Aid Unit

135 Mobile Radar Unit

136 Marine Ambulance *Flying Christine II*

137 Cliff Rescue

Christmas. St John Ambulance Centenary

(Des P. Slade and M. Horder. Photo Courvoisier)

1977 (25 OCT). *Granite paper. Perf* 11½ (C)

157	**134**	5p multicoloured	10	10
158	**135**	7p multicoloured	15	15
159	**136**	11p multicoloured	55	55
160	**137**	13p multicoloured	60	60
157/60		*Set of* 4	1·25	1·25
		First Day Cover		1·25
		Presentation Pack	1·50	
		Set of 4 *Gutter Pairs*	2·50	

Cylinder Nos.: 5p A1–1–1–1, B1–1–1–1; others A1–1–1–1, B1–1–1–1

Sheets: 50 (2 panes 5×5)

Imprint: Right-hand corner, bottom margin (7p and 11p); top, right-hand margin (others)

Quantities sold: 5p 1,218,293; 7p 1,155,448; 11p 406,244; 13p 383,489

Withdrawn: 24.10.78

138 View from Clifton, *c* 1830

139 Market Square, St. Peter Port, *c* 1838

140 Petit-Bo Bay, *c* 1839

141 The Quay, St. Peter Port, *c* 1830

Old Guernsey Prints (1st series)

(Des, recess and litho De La Rue)

1978 (7 FEB). *Perf* 14×13½ (C)

161	**138**	5p black and light stone	10	10
162	**139**	7p black and cream	15	15
163	**140**	11p black and light pink	55	55
164	**141**	13p black and light azure	60	60
161/4		*Set of* 4	1·25	1·25
		First Day Cover		1·25
		Presentation Pack	1·50	
		Set of 4 *Gutter Pairs*	2·50	

See also Nos. 249/52.

Plate Nos.: All values 1A–1A, 1B–1B, 1C–1C, 1D–1D
Sheets: 50 (2 panes 5×5)
Imprint: Left-hand corner, bottom margin
Quantities sold: 5p 858,816; 7p 930,955; 11p 442,009; 13p 388,163
Withdrawn: 6.2.79

142 *Prosperity* Memorial

143 Victoria Monument

Europa. Monuments

(Des R. Granger Barrett. Litho Questa)

1978 (2 MAY). *Perf* 14½ (C)

165	**142**	5p multicoloured	35	35
166	**143**	7p multicoloured	40	40
165/6		*Set of 2*	75	75
		First Day Cover		1·00
		Presentation Pack	1·00	

Sheets: 20 (5p 5×4; 7p 4×5)
Quantities sold: 5p 2,581,345; 7p 2,370,766
Withdrawn: 1.5.79

144 Queen Elizabeth **145**

25th Anniversary of Coronation

(Des R. Granger Barrett from bust by Arnold Machin. Photo Courvoisier)

1978 (2 MAY). *Granite paper. Perf* 11½ (C)

167	**144**	20p black, grey and bright blue	75	75
		First Day Cover		1·00
		Presentation Pack	1·00	
		Gutter Pair	1·50	

Cylinder Nos.: A1–1–1, B1–1–1
Sheets: 50 (2 panes 5×5)
Imprint: Right-hand corner, bottom margin
Quantity sold: 488,466
Withdrawn: 1.5.79

Royal Visit

(Des R. Granger Barrett from bust by Arnold Machin. Photo Courvoisier)

1978 (28 JUNE). *Granite paper. Perf* 11½ (C)

168	**145**	7p black, grey and bright green	50	50
		First Day Cover		1·00
		Presentation Pack	1·00	
		Gutter Pair	1·00	

Cylinder Nos.: A1–1–1, B1–1–1
Sheets: 50 (2 panes 5×5)
Imprint: Top corner, right-hand margin
Quantity sold: 1,149,768
Withdrawn: 27.6.79

146 Northern Gannet   **147** Firecrest

148 Dartford Warbler   **149** Spotted Redshank

Birds

(Des John Waddington Ltd. Photo Courvoisier)

1978 (29 AUG). *Granite paper. Perf* 11½ (C)

169	**146**	5p multicoloured	. . . .	15	15
170	**147**	7p multicoloured	. . . .	25	25
171	**148**	11p multicoloured	. . . .	45	45
172	**149**	13p multicoloured	. . . .	55	55
169/72		*Set of* 4	. . . .	1·25	1·25
		First Day Cover			1·50
		Presentation Pack	1·50	
		Set of 4 *Gutter Pairs*	2·50	

Cylinder Nos.: All values A1–1–1–1, B1–1–1–1, C1–1–1–1, D1–1–1–1
Sheets: 50 (2 panes 5×5)
Imprint: Right-hand corner, bottom margin
Quantities sold: 5p 750,011; 7p 924,627; 11p 442,395; 13p 432,106
Withdrawn: 28.8.79

150 Solanum

151 Christmas Rose

152 Holly   **153** Mistletoe

Christmas

(Des and photo Courvoisier)

1978 (31 OCT). *Granite paper. Perf* 11½ (C)

173	**150**	5p multicoloured	. . . .	10	10
174	**151**	7p multicoloured	. . . .	20	20
175	**152**	11p multicoloured	. . . .	40	40
176	**153**	13p deep blue-green, grey and greenish yellow		50	50
173/6		*Set of* 4	. . . .	1·10	1·10
		First Day Cover			1·25
		Presentation Pack	1·40	
		Set of 4 *Gutter Pairs*	2·25	

Cylinder Nos.: 13p A1–1–1, B1–1–1; others A1–1–1–1, B1–1–1–1
Sheets: 50 (2 panes 5×5)
Imprint: 5, 7p central, bottom margin; others central, right-hand margin
Quantities sold: 5p 1,222,140; 7p 1,246,261; 11p 409,168; 13p 372,991
Withdrawn: 30.10.79

154 One Double, 1830   **155** Two Doubles, 1899   **156** Four Doubles, 1902

157 Eight Doubles, 1959   **158** Three Pence, 1956   **159** Five New Pence, 1968

160 Fifty New Pence, 1969

161 Ten New Pence, 1970

162 Half New Penny, 1971

163 One New Penny, 1971

164 Two New Pence, 1971

165 Half Penny, 1979

166 One Penny, 1977

167 Two Pence, 1977

168 Five Pence, 1977

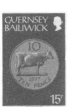

169 Ten Pence, 1977

170 Twenty-five Pence, 1972

171 Ten Shillings William I Commem, 1966

172 Silver Jubilee Commemorative Crown, 1977

173 Royal Silver Wedding Commemorative Crown, 1972

174 Seal of the Bailiwick

Coins

(Des R. Reid and Courvoisier (£5). Photo Courvoisier)

1979 (13 FEB)–**83**. *Granite paper. Perf 11½ (C)*

177	**154**	½p multicoloured (a)	10	10
		a. *Booklet pane. Nos. 177×2, 178×3, 179×2, 181, 183 and 187 (c)*	1·00	
		b. *Booklet pane. Nos. 177×2, 178, 179×2, 183×2 and 187×3 (c)*	1·25	
178	**155**	1p multicoloured (al)	10	10
		a. *Booklet strip of 4. Nos. 178×2, 179 and 182*	60	
179	**156**	2p multicoloured (a)	10	10
		a. *Booklet strip of 5. Nos. 179, 182×2 and 184×2* . .	1·25	
180	**157**	4p multicoloured (a)	10	10
		a. *Booklet pane of 10. Nos. 180 and 184, each ×5 (d)*	1·75	
		b. *Booklet pane of 15. Nos. 180, 184 and 190, each ×5 (d)*	2·75	
		c. *Booklet pane of 10. Nos. 180×2, 185×3 and 191×5 (k)*	3·00	
		d. *Booklet pane of 15. Nos. 180, 185 and 191, each ×5 (k)*	3·75	
181	**158**	5p grey-black, silver and chestnut (a)	15	10
		a. *Grey-black, silver and yellowish brown (f)*	30	30
		b. *Booklet pane of 10. Nos. 181a×5, 184×4 and 191 (f)*	2·25	
		c. *Booklet pane of 15. Nos. 181a, 184, and 191, each ×5 (f)*	3·75	

182	**159**	6p grey-black, silver and brown-red (a)	15	15
183	**160**	7p grey-black, silver & grn (a)	15	20
184	**161**	8p grey-blk, silver & brn (agij)	20	20
185	**162**	9p multicoloured (a)	25	20
186	**163**	10p mult (green background) (a)	50	50
187		10p mult (orge background) (b)	35	30
188	**164**	11p multicoloured (a)	25	30
189	**165**	11½p multicoloured (b)	25	30
190	**166**	12p multicoloured (a)	30	30
191	**167**	13p multicoloured (ah)	30	30
192	**168**	14p grey-blk, silver & dull bl (a)	30	30
193	**169**	15p grey-blk, silver & bistre (a)	35	35
194	**170**	20p grey-black, silver and dull brown (a)	50	45
195	**171**	50p grey-black, orange-red and silver (b)	1·00	75
196	**172**	£1 grey-black, yellowish green and silver (b)	2·00	1·50
197	**173**	£2 grey-black, new blue and silver (b)	4·00	2·50
198	**174**	£5 multicoloured (e)	10·00	7·50
177/98		Set of 22	19·00	14·50
		First Day Covers (4)		17·00
		Presentation Packs (4)	22·00	
		Set of 22 Gutter Pairs	38·00	

Nos. 177a/b, 178a, 179a, 180a/d and 181b/c come from special booklet sheets of 40 (80×5) (Nos. 177a and 178a), 30 (6×5) (Nos. 177b, 180a/b, 180d and 181b/c), 25 (5×5) (No. 179a) or 20 (4×5) (No. 180c). These were put on sale as complete sheets or separated into strips, folded and either affixed by the selvedge to booklet covers or supplied loose in plastic wallets.

The booklet sheets containing Nos. 177a/b show either four (No. 177a) or three (No. 177b) different arrangements of the same stamps.

Printings: (a) 13.2.79; (b) 5.2.80; (c) 6.5.80; (d) 24.2.81; (e) 22.5.81; (f) 2.2.82; (g) 4.82; (h) 5.82; (i) 7.82; (j) 11.82; (k) 14.3.83; (l) 6.83.

Cylinder Nos.: 5, 6, 7, 8, 14, 15, 20, 50p, £1, £2 A1–1–1, B1–1–1; others A1–1–1–1, B1–1–1–1

Sheets: ½ to 20p 100 (2 panes 10×5); 50p to £5 50 (2 panes 5×5)

Imprint: 50p top corner, left-hand margin; £1, £2 right-hand corner, bottom margin; £5 bottom corner, right-hand margin; others central margin

Quantities sold: ½p 1,285,162; 1p 1,888,850; 2p 1,249,506; 4p 650,195; 5p 1,110,783; 6p 1,678,775; 7p 1,683,430; 8p 3,059,366; 9p 1,952,892; 10p (No. 186) 484,956; 10p (No. 187) 1,751,126; 11p 711,268; 11½p 351,422; 12p 957,197; 13p 1,459,086; 14p 595,744; 15p 677,289; 20p 960,124; 50p 863,760; £1 537,871; £2 375,786

Withdrawn: 4.2.81 10p (No. 186); 22.7.85 (all other values except £5)

175 Pillar Box and Postmark, 1853, Mail Van and Postmark, 1979

176 Telephone, 1897 and Telex Machine, 1979

Europa. Communications

(Des R. Granger Barrett. Photo Courvoisier)

1979 (8 MAY). Granite paper. Perf 11½ (C)

201	**175**	6p multicoloured	30	30
202	**176**	8p multicoloured	30	30
201/2		Set of 2	60	60
		First Day Cover		1·00
		Presentation Pack	1·00	

Cylinder Nos.: Both values A1–1–1–1, B1–1–1–1

Sheets: 20 (5×4)

Quantities sold: 6p 1,863,564; 8p 2,293,379

Withdrawn: 7.5.80

177 Steam Tram, 1879

178 Electric Tram, 1896

179 Motor Bus, 1911

180 Motor Bus, 1979

184 'Philately'

History of Public Transport

(Photo Courvoisier)

1979 (7 AUG). *Granite paper. Perf 11½* (C)

203	**177**	6p multicoloured	. . . .	15	15
204	**178**	8p multicoloured	. . . .	20	20
205	**179**	11p multicoloured	. . . .	55	55
206	**180**	13p multicoloured	. . . .	60	60
203/6		Set of 4	. . . .	1·25	1·25
		First Day Cover			1·50
		Presentation Pack	1·50	
		Set of 4 Gutter Pairs	2·50	

Cylinder Nos.: 6p A1–1–1–1–1, B1–1–1–1–1; others A1–1–1–1, B1–1–1–1

Sheets: 50 (2 panes 5×5)

Imprint: Central, bottom margin

Quantities sold: 6p 676,046; 8p 981,431; 11p 384,701; 13p 371,882

Withdrawn: 6.8.80

181 Bureau and Postal Headquarters

182 'Mails and Telegrams'

183 'Parcels'

10th Anniversary of Guernsey Postal Administration

(Des R. Granger Barrett. Photo Courvoisier)

1979 (1 OCT). *Granite paper. Perf 11½* (C)

207	**181**	6p multicoloured	. . . .	15	15
208	**182**	8p multicoloured	. . . .	25	15
209	**183**	13p multicoloured	. . . .	50	55
210	**184**	15p multicoloured	. . . .	60	60
207/10		Set of 4	. . . .	1·25	1·25
		First Day Cover			1·25
		Presentation Pack	1·60	
		Set of 4 Gutter Pairs	2·50	
MS211		120×80 mm. Nos. 207/10	1·00	70
		First Day Cover			1·50

One copy of a pre-release sample as No. 210, but with a face value of 11p, is known. Such stamps were not sold for postal purposes

Cylinder Nos.: All values A1–1–1–1, B1–1–1–1

Sheets: 50 (2 panes 5×5)

Imprint: Central, bottom margin

Quantities sold: 6p 1,254,914; 8p 1,376,682; 13p 389,524; 15p 386,234; miniature sheet 398,443

Withdrawn: 30.9.80

185 Major-General Le Marchant

186 Admiral Lord De Saumarez

Europa. Personalities

(Des and photo Courvoisier)

1980 (6 MAY). *Granite paper. Perf 11½* (C)

212	**185**	10p multicoloured	. . . .	45	45
213	**186**	13½p multicoloured	. . . .	55	50
212/13		Set of 2	. . . .	1·00	1·00
		First Day Cover			1·00
		Presentation Pack	1·25	

Cylinder Nos.: Both values A1–1–1–1–1, B1–1–1–1–1, C1–1–1–1–1, D1–1–1–1–1

Sheets: 20 (5×4)

Quantities sold: 10p 2,794,871; 13½p 1,715,880

Withdrawn: 5.5.81

187 Policewoman with Lost Child

188 Police Motorcyclist escorting Lorry

189 Police Dog-handler

60th Anniversary of Guernsey Police Force

(Litho John Waddington Ltd)

1980 (6 MAY). *Perf* 13½×14 (C)

214	**187**	7p multicoloured	20	20
215	**188**	15p multicoloured	55	55
216	**189**	17½p multicoloured	65	65
214/16		*Set of 3*	1·25	1·25
		First Day Cover		1·50
		Presentation Pack	1·50	
		Set of 3 Gutter Pairs	2·50	

Plate Nos.: All values 1A, 1B, 1C, 1D (each ×4)

Sheets: 50 (2 panes 5×5)

Imprint: Central, bottom margin

Quantities sold: 7p 907,714; 15p 352,802; 17½p 337,551

Withdrawn: 5.5.81

190

191

192

193

T **190/3** show Golden Guernsey Goats.

Golden Guernsey Goats

(Des P. Lambert. Photo Delrieu)

1980 (5 AUG). *Perf* 13 (C)

217	**190**	7p multicoloured	20	20
218	**191**	10p multicoloured	30	35
219	**192**	15p multicoloured	55	45
220	**193**	17½p multicoloured	65	60
217/20		*Set of 4*	1·50	1·40
		First Day Cover		1·40
		Presentation Pack	1·75	
		Set of 4 Gutter Pairs	3·00	

Cylinder Nos.: 7p 598–599–600–601–602–603; 10p 578–580–581–583; 15p 605–606–607–608–609–610; 17½p 621–622–623–624–625–626

Sheets: 50 (2 panes 5×5)

Imprint: Bottom margin

Quantities sold: 7p 779,424; 10p 931,214; 15p 364,917; 17½p 329,133

Withdrawn: 4.8.81

194 'Sark Cottage'

195 'Moulin Huet'

196 'Boats at Sea'

201 *Aglais urticae*

202 *Lasiommata megera*

197 'Cow Lane'

198 'Peter le Lievre''

Butterflies

(Photo Harrison)

1981 (24 FEB). *Perf* 14 (C)
226	**199**	8p multicoloured	25	25
227	**200**	12p multicoloured	40	40
228	**201**	22p multicoloured	75	70
229	**202**	25p multicoloured	85	90
226/9		*Set of 4*	2·00	2·00
		First Day Cover.........		2·00
		Presentation Pack.......	2·50	
		Set of 4 Gutter Pairs......	4·00	

Cylinder Nos.: All values 1A, 1B (each ×5)

Sheets: 50 (2 panes 5×5)

Imprint: Right-hand corner, bottom margin

Quantities sold: 8p 986,229; 12p 971,801; 22p 438,478; 25p 438,575

Withdrawn: 23.2.82

Christmas. Peter le Lievre Paintings

(Photo Courvoisier)

1980 (15 NOV). *Granite paper. Perf* 11½ (C)
221	**194**	7p multicoloured	25	20
222	**195**	10p multicoloured	35	25
223	**196**	13½p multicoloured	40	30
224	**197**	15p multicoloured	50	40
225	**198**	17½p multicoloured	65	50
221/5		*Set of 5*	2·00	1·50
		First Day Cover		1·50
		Presentation Pack	2·25	
		Stamp-cards (set of 5)	2·00	5·50
		Set of 5 Gutter Pairs	4·50	

Cylinder Nos.: All values A1–1–1–1, B1–1–1–1

Sheets: 50 (2 panes 5×5)

Imprint: 15, 17½p top corner, right-hand margin; others right-hand corner, bottom margin

Quantities sold: 7p 1,199,280; 10p 1,159,622; 13½p 397,812; 15p 432,182; 17½p 359,116

Withdrawn: 14.11.81

203 Sailors paying respect to 'Le Petit Bonhomme Andriou' (rock resembling head of a man)

204 Fairies and Guernsey Lily

Europa. Folklore

(Des C. Abbott. Litho Questa)

1981 (22 MAY). *Perf* 14½ (C)
230	**203**	12p gold, red-brown & cinnamon	45	45
231	**204**	18p gold, indigo and azure	55	55
230/1		*Set of 2*	1·00	1·00
		First Day Cover.........		1·25
		Presentation Pack.......	1·40	
		Set of 2 Gutter Pairs......	2·00	

Plate Nos.: 12p 1B, 1F, 1G, 1H (each ×3); 18p 1B, 1D, 1F, 1G, 1H (each ×3)

Sheets: 20 (2 panes 5×2)

Imprint: Central, left-hand margin

Quantities sold: 12p 2,516,514; 18p 1,937,023

Withdrawn: 21.5.82

199 *Polyommatus icarus*

200 *Vanessa atalanta*

205 Prince Charles   **206** Prince Charles and Lady Diana Spencer   **207** Lady Diana

210 Britten Norman 'short nose' Trislander Airplane

211 Hydrofoil

208 Royal Family

212 Herm Catamaran

Royal Wedding

(Des C. Abbott. Litho Questa)

1981 (29 JULY). *Perf* 14½ (C)

232	**205**	8p multicoloured	. . . .	50	50
		a. Strip of 3. *Nos.* 232/4	. . . .	1·50	1·50
233	**206**	8p multicoloured	. . . .	50	50
234	**207**	8p multicoloured	. . . .	50	50
235	**205**	12p multicoloured	. . . .	90	90
		a. Strip of 3. *Nos.* 235/7	. . . .	2·75	2·75
236	**206**	12p multicoloured	. . . .	90	90
237	**207**	12p multicoloured	. . . .	90	90
238	**208**	25p multicoloured	. . . .	1·50	1·50
232/8		*Set of* 7	. . . .	5·00	5·00
		First Day Cover	. . . .		5·50
		Presentation Pack	. . . .	6·00	
		Stamp-cards (*set of* 7)	. . . .	3·50	12·00
MS239		104×127 mm. Nos. 232/8. P 14 (C)		6·50	6·50
		First Day Cover	. . . .		7·00

213 *Sea Trent* (coaster)

Plate Nos.: 8p 1A, 1C (each ×6); 12p 1B (×6); 25p 1A (×6)

Sheets: 8p, 12p 60 (6×10) each value in *se-tenant* strips of 3 across sheet, 25p 30 (3×10)

Imprint: Bottom corner, right-hand side margin

Quantities sold: 8p 2,115,103; 12p 2,235,005; 25p 510,608; miniature sheet 432,743

Withdrawn: 28.7.82

Inter-island Transport

(Des and photo Courvoisier)

1981 (25 AUG). *Granite paper. Perf* 11½ (C)

240	**209**	8p multicoloured	. . . .	20	20
241	**210**	12p multicoloured	. . . .	40	40
242	**211**	18p multicoloured	. . . .	60	50
243	**212**	22p multicoloured	. . . .	75	65
244	**213**	25p multicoloured	. . . .	90	75
240/4		*Set of* 5	. . . .	2·50	2·25
		First Day Cover	. . . .		2·25
		Presentation Pack	. . . .	2·75	
		Set of 5 *Gutter Pairs*	. . . . . .	5·00	

Cylinder Nos.: All values A1–1–1–1, B1–1–1–1

Sheets: 50 (2 panes 5×5)

Imprint: Right-hand corner, bottom margin

Quantities sold: 8p 790,215; 12p 785,488; 18p 457,763; 22p 469,315; 25p 466,112

Withdrawn: 24.8.82

209 Sark Launch

214 Rifle Shooting

215 Riding

216 Swimming

217 Circuit Construction

International Year for Disabled Persons

(Des P. le Vasseur. Litho Questa)

1981 (17 NOV). *Perf* 14½ (C)

245	**214**	8p multicoloured	20	20
246	**215**	12p multicoloured	35	35
247	**216**	22p multicoloured	65	55
248	**217**	25p multicoloured	75	60
245/8		*Set of* 4	1·75	1·50
		First Day Cover		1·50
		Presentation Pack	2·00	
		Set of 4 *Gutter Pairs*	3·50	

Plate Nos.: All values 1A, 1B, 1C, 1D, 1E, 1F, 1G, 1H (each ×4)
Sheets: 50 (2 panes 5×5)
Imprint: Foot of right-hand margin on each pane
Quantities sold: 8p 912,908; 12p 910,614; 22p 280,882; 25p 287,725
Withdrawn: 16.11.82

218 Jethou

219 Fermain Bay

220 The Terres

221 St. Peter Port

Old Guernsey Prints (2nd series)

(Des, recess and litho De La Rue)

1982 (2 FEB). *Perf* 14×13½ (C)

249	**218**	8p black and pale blue	20	20
250	**219**	12p black & pale turquoise-grn	35	35
251	**220**	22p black and pale yellow-brown	65	65
252	**221**	25p black and pale rose-lilac	75	75
249/52		*Set of* 4	1·75	1·75
		First Day Cover		2·25
		Presentation Pack	2·00	
		Set of 4 *Gutter Pairs*	3·50	

Plate Nos.: All values 1A–1A, 1B–1B, 1C–1C, 1D–1D
Sheets: 50 (2 panes 5×5)
Imprint: Left-hand corner, bottom margin
Quantities sold: 8p 350,198; 12p 346,515; 22p 346,661; 25p 244,669
Withdrawn: 1.2.83

222 Sir Edgar MacCulloch
(founder-president)
and Guille-Allès
Library, St. Peter Port

223 Norman Invasion Fleet
crossing English
Channel, 1066
('history')

224 H.M.S. *Crescent,*
1793 ('history')

225 Dragonfly
('entomology')

226 Common Snipe
caught for Ringing
('ornithology')

227 Samian Bowl 160–200
A.D. ('archaeology')

Centenary of La Sociètè Guernesiaise

(Des G. Drummond. Photo Courvoisier)

1982 (28 APR). *Granite paper. Perf* 11½ (C)

253	**222**	8p multicoloured	20	20
254	**223**	13p multicoloured	35	35
255	**224**	20p multicoloured	45	45
256	**225**	24p multicoloured	70	70
257	**226**	26p multicoloured	80	80
258	**227**	29p multicoloured	85	85
253/8		*Set of 6*	3·00	3·00
		First Day Cover		3·00
		First Day Cover (Nos. 254/5)		1·50
		Presentation Pack	3·50	
		Presentation Pack (Nos. 254/5)	1·75	
		Stamp-cards (set of 6)	1·50	5·50

The 13p and 20p (Nos. 254/5) also include the Europa C.E.P.T. emblem in the designs

Cylinder Nos.: 24p A1–1–1–1, B1–1–1–1; C1–1–1–1; D1–1–1–1; others A1–1–1–1–1; B1–1–1–1–1, C1–1–1–1–1, D1–1–1–1–1

Sheets: 20 (5×4)

Quantities sold: 8p 921,095; 13p 2,820,311; 20p 1,491,351; 24p 315,735; 26p 309,919; 29p 298,761

Withdrawn: 27.4.83

228 Sea Scouts

229 Scouts

230 Cub Scouts

231 Air Scouts

75th Anniversary of Boy Scout Movement

(Des W.L.G. Creative Services Ltd. Litho Questa)

1982 (13 JULY). *Perf* 14½×14 (C)

259	**228**	8p multicoloured	20	25
260	**229**	13p multicoloured	50	50

261	**230**	26p multicoloured	70	70
262	**231**	29p multicoloured	85	80
259/62		*Set of 4*	2·25	2·25
		First Day Cover		2·50
		Presentation Pack	2·50	
		Set of 4 Gutter Pairs	4·50	

Plate Nos.: 8p 1A, 1B, 1C, 1D (each ×6); others 1A, 1B, 1C, 1D (each ×7)

Sheets: 50 (2 panes 5×5)

Imprint: Bottom corner, right-hand margin

Quantities sold: 8p 796,018; 13p 930,924; 26p 237,958; 29p 233,204

Withdrawn: 12.7.83

232 Midnight Mass

233 Exchanging Gifts

234 Christmas Meal

235 Exchanging Cards

236 Queen's Christmas Message

Christmas

(Des Lynette Hammant. Photo Harrison)

1982 (12 OCT). *Perf* 14½ (C)

263	**232**	8p multicoloured	20	20
		a. Black (*Queen's head, value and Inscr*) omitted		
264	**233**	13p multicoloured	30	30
265	**234**	24p multicoloured	75	75
266	**235**	26p multicoloured	75	75
267	**236**	29p multicoloured	80	80
263/7		*Set of 5*	2·50	2·50
		First Day Cover		3·00
		Presentation Pack	3·50	
		Set of 5 Gutter Pairs	5·00	

Cylinder Nos.: All values 1A, 1B (each ×5)

Sheets: 50 (2 panes 5×5)

Imprint: Right-hand corner, bottom margin

Quantities sold: 8p 944,560; 13p 927,844; 24p 227,145; 26p 249,110; 29p 232,323

Withdrawn: 11.10.83

237 Flute Player and Boats

238 Cymbal Player and Tug 'o' war

239 Trumpet Player and Bible Class

240 Drummer and Cadets marching

 241 Boys' Brigade Band

Centenary of Boys' Brigade

(Des Sally Stiff. Photo Harrison)

1983 (18 JAN). *Perf* 14 (C)

268	**237**	8p multicoloured	. . . .	25	25
269	**238**	13p multicoloured	. . . .	40	40
270	**239**	24p multicoloured	. . . .	85	85
271	**240**	26p multicoloured	. . . .	90	90
272	**241**	29p multicoloured	. . . .	95	95
268/72		*Set of* 5	. . . .	3·00	3·00
		First Day Cover			3·75
		Presentation Pack	3·25		
		Set of 5 *Gutter Pairs*	6·00		

Cylinder Nos.: All values 1A, 1B (each ×5)

Sheets: 50 (2 panes 5×5)

Imprint: Bottom margin, right-hand corner

Quantities sold: 8p 671,921; 13p 538,257; 24p 223,069; 26p 234,482; 29p 214,723

Withdrawn: 17.1.84

242 Building Albert Pier Extension, 1850s

243 St. Peter Port Harbour, 1983

244 St. Peter Port, 1680

245 Artist's Impression of Future Development Scheme

Europa. Development of St. Peter Port Harbour

(Des C. Abbott. Photo Courvoisier)

1983 (14 MAR). *Granite paper. Perf* 11½ (C)

273	**242**	13p multicoloured	. . . .	35	35
		a. *Horiz pair. Nos.* 273/4	. . . .	70	70
274	**243**	13p multicoloured	. . . .	35	35
275	**244**	20p multicoloured	. . . .	75	75
		a. *Horiz pair. Nos.* 275/6	. . . .	1·50	1·50
276	**245**	20p multicoloured	. . . .	75	75
273/6		*Set of* 4	. . . .	2·00	2·00
		First Day Cover			2·50
		Presentation Pack	3·00		

Cylinder Nos.: Both values A1–1–1–1–1, B1–1–1–1–1

Sheets: 20 (4×5). The two designs of each value were printed together, *se-tenant*, in horizontal pairs throughout

Quantities sold: 13p 1,884,714; 20p 1,676,250

Withdrawn: 13.3.84

246 'View at Guernsey'

247 'Children on the Seashore'

248 'Marine, Guernesey'

249 'La Baie du Moulin Huet à travers les Arbres'

250 'Brouillard à Guernesey'

Centenary of Renoir's Visit to Guernsey

(Des and photo Courvoisier)

1983 (6 SEPT). *Granite paper. Perf* 11×11½ (13p) *or* 11½ (*others*), *all comb*

277	**246**	9p multicoloured	. . . .	25	25
278	**247**	13p multicoloured	. . . .	45	45
279	**248**	26p multicoloured	. . . .	80	80
280	**249**	28p multicoloured	. . . .	1·10	1·10
281	**250**	31p multicoloured	. . . .	1·25	1·25
277/81		Set of 5	. . . .	3·50	3·50
		First Day Cover.			4·25
		Presentation Pack		4·00	
		Stamp-cards (set of 5)		1·10	5·00
		Set of 5 Gutter Pairs		7·00	

Cylinder Nos.: 13p A1–1–1–1–1, B1–1–1–1–1, C1–1–1–1–1, D1–1–1–1–1; others A1–1–1–1–1, B1–1–1–1–1

Sheets: 40 (2 panes 4×5)

Quantities sold: 9p 547,148; 13p 757,838; 26p 185,045; 28p 219,830; 31p 305,219

Withdrawn: 5.9.84

251 Launching *Star of the West*, 1869, and Capt. J. Lenfestey

252 Leaving St. Peter Port

253 Off Rio Grande Bar

254 Off St. Lucia

255 Map of 1879–80 Voyage

Guernsey Shipping (1st series). Star of the West (brigantine)

(Des R. Granger Barrett. Litho Questa)

1983 (15 NOV). *Perf* 14 (C)

282	**251**	9p multicoloured	. . . .	25	25
283	**252**	13p multicoloured	. . . .	40	40
284	**253**	26p multicoloured	. . . .	80	80
285	**254**	28p multicoloured	. . . .	1·10	1·10
286	**255**	31p multicoloured	. . . .	1·25	1·25
282/6		Set of 5	. . . .	3·50	3·50
		First Day Cover.			4·00
		Presentation Pack.		4·00	
		Set of 5 Gutter Pairs		7·00	

See also Nos. 415/19

Plate Nos.: 26p, 31p 1C, 1D (each ×5); others 1A, 1B (each ×5)

Sheets: 50 (2 panes 5×5)

Imprint: Bottom corner, right-hand margin

Quantities sold: 9p 706,809; 13p 974,736; 26p 236,974; 28p 216,279; 31p 218,647

Withdrawn: 14.11.84

256 Dame of Sark as Young Woman

257 German Occupation, 1940–45

258 Royal Visit, 1957

259 Chief Pleas

260 Dame of Sark Rose

Birth Centenary of Sibyl Hathaway, Dame of Sark

(Des Jennifer Toombs. Litho Questa)

1984 (7 FEB). *Perf* 14½ (C)

287	**256**	9p multicoloured	. . . .	25	25
288	**257**	13p multicoloured	. . . .	40	45
289	**258**	26p multicoloured	. . . .	90	90

290	**259**	28p multicoloured	. . . .	95	95
291	**260**	31p multicoloured	. . . .	1·10	1·10
287/91		Set of 5	. . . .	3·25	3·25
		First Day Cover	. . . .		4·00
		Presentation Pack	. . . .	4·00	
		Set of 5 Gutter Pairs	. . . . . .	6·50	

Plate Nos.: 13p 1A, 1B, 1C, 1D (each ×5); others 1A, 1B, 1C, 1D, (each ×7)

Sheets: 50 (2 panes 5×5)

Imprint: Bottom margin, right-hand corner

Quantities sold: 9p 637,566; 13p 836,270; 26p 315,561; 28p 293,716; 31p 270,742

Withdrawn: 6.2.85

261 C.E.P.T. 25th Anniversary Logo

Europa

(Des J. Larrivière. Litho Questa)

1984 (10 APR). Perf 15×14½ (C)

292	**261**	13p cobalt, dull ultramarine & blk	65	65
293		20½p emerald, deep dull grn & blk	85	85
292/3		Set of 2	1·50	1·50
		First Day Cover		2·25
		Presentation Pack	2·00	

Plate Nos.: Both values 1A, 1B (each ×3)

Sheets: 20 (4×5)

Imprint: Bottom corner, right-hand margin

Quantities sold: 13p 1,680,033; 20½p 903,972

Withdrawn: 9.4.85

262 The Royal Court and St. George's Flag

263 Castle Cornet and Union Flag

Links with the Commonwealth

(Des C. Abbott. Litho Questa)

1984 (10 APR). Perf 14×14½ (C)

294	**262**	9p multicoloured	. . . .	40	40
295	**263**	31p multicoloured	. . . .	1·10	1·10
294/5		Set of 2	. . . .	1·50	1·50
		First Day Cover		2·00
		Presentation Pack	2·25	

Plate Nos.: Both values 1A, 1B, 1C, 1D (each ×6)

Sheets: 20 (4×5)

Imprint: Bottom corner, right-hand margin

Quantities sold: 9p 1,419,845, 31p 285,099

Withdrawn: 9.4.85

264 Little Chapel

265 Fort Grey

266 St. Apolline Chapel

267 Petit Port

268 Little Russel

269 The Harbour, Herm

270 Saints

271 St. Saviour

272 New Jetty (inscr 'Cambridge Berth')

273 Belvoir, Herm

GUERNSEY 11ᴾ

274 La Seigneurie, Sark

GUERNSEY 12ᴾ

275 Petit Bot

GUERNSEY 13ᴾ

276 St. Saviour's Reservoir

GUERNSEY 14ᴾ

277 St. Peter Port

GUERNSEY 15ᴾ

278 Havelet

GUERNSEY 16ᴾ

279 Hostel of St. John

GUERNSEY 18ᴾ

280 Le Variouf

GUERNSEY 20ᴾ

281 La Coupee, Sark

GUERNSEY 21ᴾ

282 King's Mills

GUERNSEY 26ᴾ

283 Town Church

GUERNSEY 30ᴾ

284 Grandes Rocques

GUERNSEY 40ᴾ

285 Torteval Church

GUERNSEY 50ᴾ

286 Bordeaux

GUERNSEY £1

287 Albecq

GUERNSEY £2

288 L'Ancresse

Views

(Des C. Abbott. Litho Questa)

1984 (18 SEPT)–**91.** *Perf* 14½ (C)

296	**264**	1p multicoloured (c)	20	10
297	**265**	2p multicoloured (c)	20	10
		a. *Booklet pane. Nos. 297×2, 299×4, 300×2 and 305×2 (d)*	2·75	
298	**266**	3p multicoloured (a)	20	10
		a. *Booklet pane. Nos. 298, 299×2, 306×4 and 309×3 (f)*	4·25	
299	**267**	4p multicoloured (a)	20	10
		a. *Booklet pane. Nos. 299×2, 304×3 and 307×5*	4·00	
		b. *Booklet pane. Nos. 299, 304 and 307, each ×5*	4·75	
		c. *Booklet pane. Nos. 299×4, 306b×3 and 309c×3 (g)* ..	4·00	
		d. *Booklet pane. Nos. 299, 301, 306b×3 and 309d×3 (h)* ..	4·50	
		e. *Black ptg double*		
300	**268**	5p multicoloured (c)	20	10
		a. *Booklet pane. Nos. 300×2, 301×2, 309×3 and 310b×3 (j)*	4·00	
301	**269**	6p multicoloured (c)	20	15
		a. *Booklet pane. Nos. 301×4, 308×4 and 310×2 (i)*......	4·25	
		b. *Uncoated paper*		
		c. *Black ptg double*		
302	**270**	7p multicoloured (c)	20	20
303	**271**	8p multicoloured (c)	20	20

304	**272**	9p multicoloured (a)	20	25
		a. Booklet pane. Nos. 304×4		
		and 308×6 (b)	4·75	
		b. Booklet pane. Nos. 304×2		
		and 308×8 (b)	4·50	
305	**273**	10p multicoloured (a)	25	25
		a. Booklet pane. Nos. 305 and		
		308, each ×5 (e)	4·50	
306	**274**	11p multicoloured (c)	25	25
		a. Booklet pane. Nos. 306 and		
		309, each × 5 (f)	4·50	
306b	**275**	12p multicoloured (g)	40	30
		ba. Booklet pane. Nos. 306b and		
		309c, each ×5	4·25	
		bb. Booklet pane. Nos. 306b and		
		309d, each ×4 (h)	4·75	
		bc. Black ptg double		
307	**276**	13p multicoloured (a)	30	30
308	**277**	14p multicoloured (a)	30	35
		a. Booklet pane. Nos. 308 and		
		310, each ×5 (i)	4·75	
		b. Uncoated paper		
309	**278**	15p multicoloured (c)	30	35
		a. Booklet pane. Nos. 309 and		
		310b, each ×5 (j)	5·25	
		b. Imperf at sides and foot		
		(horiz pair)		
309c	**279**	16p multicoloured (g)	30	35
		ca. Black and red ptgs double . .		
309d	**280**	18p multicoloured (h)	35	40
		da. Black ptg double		
310	**281**	20p multicoloured (a)	50	45
		a. Uncoated paper		
310b	**282**	21p multicoloured (j)	50	45
310c	**283**	26p multicoloured (j)	70	55
		ca. Imperf at sides and foot		
		(horiz pair)	£800	
311	**284**	30p multicoloured (c)	60	65
312	**285**	40p multicoloured (a)	80	85
313	**286**	50p multicoloured (a)	1·00	1·10
314	**287**	£1 multicoloured (a)	2·00	2·10
315	**288**	£2 multicoloured (c)	4·25	4·25
296/315		Set of 25	12·50	12·50
		First Day Covers (5)		17·00
		Presentation Packs (3)	12·50	
		Stamp-cards (set of 25)	4·50	21·00
		Set of 25 Gutter Pairs	25·00	

For 11p, 12p, 15p and 16p stamps in a smaller size see Nos. 398/9a.

Booklet panes Nos. 297a, 298a, 299a/c, 304a/b, 305a, 306a and 306ba have margins all round and were issued, folded and loose, within the booklet covers.

Booklet panes Nos. 299d, 300a, 301a, 306bb, 308a and 309a have the outer edges imperforate on three sides and were also issued loose within the booklet covers.

Nos. 299e, 301c, 306bc and 309da come from an example of booklet pane No. 299d.

Nos. 301b, 308b and 310a come from examples of booklet panes Nos. 301a and 308a.

Printings: (a) 18.9.84; (b) 19.3.85; (c) 23.7.85; (d) 2.12.85; (e) 1.4.86; (f) 30.3.87; (g) 28.3.88; (h) 28.2.89; (i) 27.12.89; (j) 2.4.91

Plate Nos.: All values 1A, 1B, 1C, 1D (each ×5)

Sheets: 1p, 3p, 8p, 12p, 14p, 15p, 18p, 26p, 40p, 100 (2 panes 10×5): others 100 (2 panes 5×10)

Imprint: Bottom, right-hand margin of each pane

Withdrawn: 21.5.93

289 'A Partridge in a Pear Tree' **290** 'Two Turtle Doves' **291** 'Three French Hens'

292 'Four Colly Birds' **293** 'Five Gold Rings' **294** 'Six Geese a-laying'

295 'Seven Swans a-swimming' **296** 'Eight Maids a-milking' **297** 'Nine Drummers drumming'

298 'Ten Pipers piping' **299** 'Eleven Ladies dancing' **300** 'Twelve Lords a-leaping'

'The Twelve Days of Christmas'

(Des R. Downer. Litho Questa)

1984 (20 NOV). *Perf* 14½ (C)

316	**289**	5p multicoloured	20	20
		a. *Sheetlet of* 12. *Nos.* 316/27	2·50	
317	**290**	5p multicoloured	20	20
318	**291**	5p multicoloured	20	20
319	**292**	5p multicoloured	20	20
320	**293**	5p multicoloured	20	20
321	**294**	5p multicoloured	20	20
322	**295**	5p multicoloured	20	20
323	**296**	5p multicoloured	20	20
324	**297**	5p multicoloured	20	20
325	**298**	5p multicoloured	20	20
326	**299**	5p multicoloured	20	20
327	**300**	5p multicoloured	20	20
316/27		*Set of* 12	2·50	2·50
		First Day Cover		3·00
		Presentation Pack	3·75	

Sheets: 12 (4×3) containing Nos. 316/27 *se-tenant*

Imprint: Bottom, left-hand margin

Quantity sold: 271,168 sheetlets

Withdrawn: 19.11.85

301 Sir John Doyle and Coat of Arms

302 Battle of Germantown, 1777

303 Reclaiming Braye du Valle, 1806

304 Mail for Alderney, 1812

150th Death Anniversary of Lieutenant-General Sir John Doyle

(Des E. Stemp. Photo Courvoisier)

1984 (20 NOV). *Granite paper. Perf* 11½ (C)

328	**301**	13p multicoloured	40	40
329	**302**	29p multicoloured	1·00	1·00
330	**303**	31p multicoloured	1·25	1·25
331	**304**	34p multicoloured	1·25	1·25
328/31		*Set of* 4	3·50	3·00
		First Day Cover		4·00
		Presentation Pack	4·00	
		Set of 4 *Gutter Pairs*	7·00	

Cylinder Nos.: All values A1–1–1–1–1, B1–1–1–1–1, C1–1–1–1–1, D1–1–1–1–1

Sheets: 50 (2 panes 5×5)

Quantities sold: 13p 642,178; 29p 460,535; 31p 450,051; 34p 465,982

Withdrawn: 19.11.85

Yearbook 1984

1984 (1 DEC). *Comprises Nos.* 287/95, 298/9, 304/5, 307/8, 310, 312/14, 316/31 *and* A13/17

	Yearbook	40·00

Withdrawn: 29.3.86

305 Cuckoo Wrasse

306 Red Gurnard

307 Red Mullet

308 Mackerel

309 Sunfish

Fishes

(Des P. Barrett. Photo Courvoisier)

1985 (22 JAN). *Granite paper. Perf* 11½ (C)

332	**305**	9p multicoloured	40	40
333	**306**	13p multicoloured	60	60
334	**307**	29p multicoloured	1·50	1·10
335	**308**	31p multicoloured	1·50	1·10
336	**309**	34p multicoloured	1·60	1·25
332/6		*Set of* 5	5·00	4·00
		First Day Cover		5·00
		Presentation Pack	5·25	
		Set of 5 *Gutter Pairs*	10·00	

Cylinder Nos.: 13p, 29p A1–1–1–1–1, B1–1–1–1–1, C1–1–1–1–1, D1–1–1–1–1; others A1–1–1–1, B1–1–1–1, C1–1–1–1, D1–1–1–1

Sheets: 50 (2 panes 5×5)

Quantities sold: 9p 465,322; 13p 724,941; 29p 221,392; 31p 174,948; 34p 157,422

Withdrawn: 21.1.86

310 Dove

40th Anniversary of Peace in Europe

(Des C. Abbott. Litho Questa)

1985 (9 MAY). *Perf* 14×14½ (C)

337	**310**	22p multicoloured	. . . .	1·10	1·10
		First Day Cover			1·50
		Presentation Pack		1·50	
		Gutter Pair		2·25	

Plate Nos.: 1A, 1B, 1C, 1D (each ×4)

Sheets: 50 (2 panes 5×5)

Imprint: Bottom. right-hand margin of each pane

Quantity sold: 246,024

Withdrawn: 8.5.86

311 I.Y.Y. Emblem and Young People of Different Races

312 Girl Guides cooking over Fire

International Youth Year

(Des Suzanne Brehaut (9p), Mary Harrison (31p). Litho Questa)

1985 (14 MAY). *Perf* 14 (C)

338	**311**	9p multicoloured	. . . .	40	40
339	**312**	31p multicoloured	. . . .	1·00	1·00
338/9		*Set of 2*	. . . .	1·40	1·40
		First Day Cover			2·00
		Presentation Pack (with No. 342)		3·25	

Plate Nos.: Both values 1A, 1B, 1C, 1D, 1E, 1F (each ×6)

Sheets: 20 (5×4)

Imprint: Bottom, right-hand margin

Quantities sold: 9p 1,246,421; 31p 264,938

Withdrawn: 13.5.86

313 Stave of Music enclosing Flags

314 Stave of Music and Musical Instruments

Europa. European Music Year

(Des Fiona Sloan (14p), Katie Lillington (22p). Litho Questa)

1985 (14 MAY). *Perf* 14×14½ (C)

340	**313**	14p multicoloured	. . . .	45	40
341	**314**	22p multicoloured	. . . .	95	1·00
340/1		*Set of 2*	. . . .	1·40	1·40
		First Day Cover			2·00
		Presentation Pack		2·25	

Plate Nos.: Both values 1A, 1B, 1C, 1D, 1E, 1F (each ×6)

Sheets: 20 (4×5)

Imprint: Bottom, right-hand margin

Quantities sold: 14p 1,742,651; 22p 879,421

Withdrawn: 13.5.86

315 Guide Leader, Girl Guide and Brownie

75th Anniversary of Girl Guide Movement

(Des Karon Mahy. Litho Questa)

1985 (14 MAY). *Perf* 14 (C)

342	**315**	34p multicoloured	. . . .	1·50	1·50
		First Day Cover			2·00

Plate Nos.: 1A, 1B, 1C, 1D (each ×6)

Sheets: 20 (5×4)

Imprint: Bottom, right-hand margin

Quantity sold: 182,426

Withdrawn: 13.5.86

316 Santa Claus

317 Lussibruden (Sweden)

318 King Balthazar

319 Saint Nicholas (Netherlands)

320 La Befana (Italy)

321 Julenisse (Denmark)

322 Christkind (Germany)

323 King Wenceslas (Czechoslovakia)

324 Shepherd of Les Baux (France)

325 King Caspar

326 Baboushka (Russia)

327 King Melchior

Christmas. Gift-bearers

(Des C. Abbott. Photo Courvoisier)

1985 (19 NOV). *Granite paper. Perf 12½ (C)*

343	**316**	5p multicoloured	25	25
		a. Sheetlet of 12. Nos. 343/54.	4·25	
344	**317**	5p multicoloured	25	25
345	**318**	5p multicoloured	25	25
346	**319**	5p multicoloured	25	25
347	**320**	5p multicoloured	25	25
348	**321**	5p multicoloured	25	25
349	**322**	5p multicoloured	25	25
350	**323**	5p multicoloured	25	25
351	**324**	5p multicoloured	25	25
352	**325**	5p multicoloured	25	25
353	**326**	5p multicoloured	25	25
354	**327**	5p multicoloured	25	25
343/54		*Set of 12*	4·25	4·00
		First Day Cover		4·00
		Presentation Pack	4·75	

Sheets: 12 (4×3) containing Nos. 343/54 *se-tenant*

Imprint: Central, bottom margin

Quantity sold: 236,937 sheetlets

Withdrawn: 18.11.86

328 'Vraicing'

329 'Castle Cornet'

330 'Rocquaine Bay'

331 'Little Russel'

332 'Seaweed-gatherers'

Paintings by Paul Jacob Naftel

(Des and photo Harrison)

1985 (19 NOV). *Perf 15×14 (C)*

355	**328**	9p multicoloured	30	30
356	**329**	14p multicoloured	40	40
357	**330**	22p multicoloured	90	90
358	**331**	31p multicoloured	1·40	1·40
359	**332**	34p multicoloured	1·50	1·50
355/9		*Set of 5*	4·00	4·00
		First Day Cover		5·50
		Presentation Pack	5·25	
		Set of 5 Gutter Pairs	8·00	

Cylinder Nos.: All values 1A, 1B (each ×5)

Sheets: 50 (2 panes 5×5)

Imprint: Left-hand margin of each pane

Quantities sold: 9p 398,472; 14p 452,728; 22p 164,922; 31p 197,422; 34p 173,428

Withdrawn: 18.11.86

Yearbook 1985

1985 (DEC). *Comprises Nos.* 296/7, 300/3, 306, 309, 311, 315, 332/59 *and* A18/27

Yearbook . . . . 60·00

Withdrawn: 31.12.86

333 Squadron off Nargue Island, 1809

334 Battle of the Nile, 1798

335 Battle of St. Vincent, 1797

336 H.M.S. *Crescent* off Cherbourg, 1793

337 Battle of the Saints, 1782

150th Death Anniversary of Admiral Lord De Saumarez

(Des T. Thompson. Photo Courvoisier)

1986 (4 FEB). *Granite paper. Perf* 11½ (C)

360	**333**	9p multicoloured	. . . .	40	40
361	**334**	14p multicoloured	. . . .	50	50
362	**335**	29p multicoloured	. . . .	1·25	1·25
363	**336**	31p multicoloured	. . . .	1·40	1·40
364	**337**	34p multicoloured	. . . .	1·40	1·40
360/4		Set of 5	. . . .	4·50	4·00
		First Day Cover	. . . .		5·50
		Presentation Pack	. . . .	5·75	
		Set of 5 Gutter Pairs	. . . . . .	9·00	

Cylinder Nos.: All values A1–1–1–1–1, B1–1–1–1–1

Sheets: 40 (2 panes 5×4)

Quantities sold: 9p 456,518; 14p 706,727; 29p 157,693; 31p 163,612; 34p 160,724

Withdrawn: 3.2.87

338 Profile of Queen Elizabeth II (after R. Maklouf)

60th Birthday of Queen Elizabeth II

(Des C. Abbott. Litho Questa)

1986 (21 APR). *Perf* 14 (C)

365	**338**	60p multicoloured	. . . .	2·50	2·50
		First Day Cover	. . . .		3·75
		Presentation Pack	. . . .	4·00	
		Gutter Pair	. . . .	5·00	

Plate Nos.: 1A, 1B, 1C, 1D (each ×4)

Sheets: 40 (2 panes 5×4)

Imprint: Bottom, right-hand margin of each pane

Quantity sold: 169,661

Withdrawn: 20.4.87

339 Northern Gannet and Nylon Net ('Operation Gannet')

340 Loose-flowered Orchid

341 Guernsey Elm

Europa. Nature and Environmental Protection

(Des P. Newcombe. Photo Courvoisier)

1986 (22 MAY). *Granite paper. Perf* 11½ (C)

366	**339**	10p multicoloured	. . . .	45	45
367	**340**	14p multicoloured	. . . .	75	75
368	**341**	22p multicoloured	. . . .	1·00	1·00
366/8		Set of 3	. . . .	2·00	2·00
		First Day Cover	. . . .		3·25
		Presentation Pack	. . . .	3·00	

Cylinder Nos.: All values A1–1–1–1–1–1, B1–1–1–1–1–1,
C1–1–1–1–1–1, D1–1–1–1–1–1

Sheets: 20 (4×5)

Quantities sold: 10p 977,212; 14p 995,123; 22p 662,565

Withdrawn: 21.5.87

342   Prince Andrew and Miss Sarah Ferguson   **343**

Royal Wedding

(Des C. Abbott. Litho Questa)

1986 (23 JULY). *Perf 14 (14p) or 13½×14 (34p), both comb*

369	**342**	14p multicoloured	75	75
370	**343**	34p multicoloured	1·50	1·50
369/70		Set of 2	2·25	2·25
		First Day Cover		3·50
		Presentation Pack	3·25	
		Set of 2 Gutter Pairs	4·50	

Plate Nos.: Both values 1A, 1B, 1C, 1D, 1E, 1F (each ×5)

Sheets: 50 (2 panes 5×5)

Imprint: Bottom right-hand margin of each pane

Quantities sold: 14p 292,018; 34p 199,297

Withdrawn: 22.7.87

344 Bowls   **345** Cricket

346 Squash   **347** Hockey

348 Swimming   **349** Shooting

Sport in Guernsey

(Des R. Goldsmith. Litho Questa)

1986 (24 JULY). *Perf 14½ (C)*

371	**344**	10p multicoloured	30	30
372	**345**	14p multicoloured	50	50
		a. Black (face value, inscr etc.) printed treble		
373	**346**	22p multicoloured	75	75
		a. Black (face value, inscr etc.) printed treble		
374	**347**	29p multicoloured	1·25	1·25
375	**348**	31p multicoloured	1·40	1·40
376	**349**	34p multicoloured	1·50	1·50
371/6		Set of 6	5·00	5·00
		First Day Cover		5·75
		Presentation Pack	6·00	
		Set of 6 Gutter Pairs	10·00	

Plate Nos.: All values 1A, 1B, 1C, 1D (each ×4)

Sheets: 50 (2 panes 5×5)

Imprint: Bottom right-hand margin of each pane

Quantities sold: 10p 399,897; 14p 985,699; 22p 212,203; 29p 141,882; 31p 157,751; 34p 156,164

Withdrawn: 23.7.87

350 Guernsey Museum   **351** Fort Grey Maritime
and Art Gallery,   Museum
Candie Gardens

352 Castle Cornet   **353** National Trust of
                                Guernsey Folk
                                Museum

Centenary of Guernsey Museums

(Des Sir Hugh Casson. Litho Questa)

1986 (18 NOV). *Perf* 14 (C)

377	**350**	14p multicoloured	. . . .	60	60
378	**351**	29p multicoloured	. . . .	1·10	1·10
379	**352**	31p multicoloured	. . . .	1·10	1·10
380	**353**	34p multicoloured	. . . .	1·40	1·40
377/80		*Set of* 4	. . . .	3·75	3·75
		First Day Cover			5·50
		Presentation Pack		4·75	
		Set of 4 *Gutter Pairs*		7·50	

Plate Nos.: All values 1A, 1B, 1C, 1D (each ×5)

Sheets: 50 (2 panes 5×5)

Imprint: Bottom right-hand margin of each pane

Quantities sold: 14p 796,879; 29p 141,974; 31p 159,326; 34p 144,074

Withdrawn: 17.11.87

354 'While Shepherds Watched their Flocks by Night'

355 'In the Bleak Mid-Winter'

356 'O Little Town of Bethlehem'

357 'The Holly and the Ivy'

358 'O Little Christmas Tree'

359 'Away in a Manger'

360 'Good King Wenceslas'

361 'We Three Kings of Orient Are'

362 'Hark the Herald Angels Sing'

363 'I Saw Three Ships'

364 'Little Donkey'

365 'Jingle Bells'

Christmas. Carols

(Des Wendy Bramall. Photo Courvoisier)

1986 (18 NOV). *Granite paper. Perf* 12½ (C)

381	**354**	6p multicoloured	40	40
		a. Sheetlet of 12. *Nos.* 381/92	4·00	
382	**355**	6p multicoloured	40	40
383	**356**	6p multicoloured	40	40
384	**357**	6p multicoloured	40	40
385	**358**	6p multicoloured	40	40
386	**359**	6p multicoloured	40	40
387	**360**	6p multicoloured	40	40
388	**361**	6p multicoloured	40	40
389	**362**	6p multicoloured	40	40
390	**363**	6p multicoloured	40	40
391	**364**	6p multicoloured	40	40
392	**365**	6p multicoloured	40	40
381/92		*Set of* 12	4·00	4·00
		First Day Cover		4·25
		Presentation Pack	4·25	

Sheets: 12 (4×3) containing Nos. 381/92 *se-tenant*

Imprint: Central bottom margin

Quantity sold: 226,119 sheetlets

Withdrawn: 17.11.87

Yearbook 1986

1986 (DEC). *Comprises Nos.* 360/92 *and* A28/31

	Yearbook	40·00

Withdrawn: 31.12.87

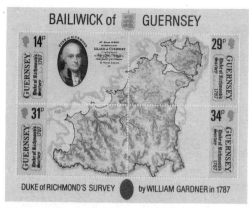

366a Duke of Richmond and Map of 1787
(illustration reduced to half size)

Bicentenary of Duke of Richmond's Survey of Guernsey

(Des J. Cooter. Litho Questa)

1987 (10 FEB). Perf 14½×14 (C)
MS393 134×103 mm **366a** 14p, 29p, 31p,
           34p multicoloured . . . .   4·00   4·00
           First Day Cover . . . .   5·00
           Presentation Pack . . . .   5·00

Quantity sold: 176,655
Withdrawn: 9.2.88

367 Post Office
Headquarters

368 Architect's Elevation
of Post Office
Headquarters

369 Guernsey Grammar
School

370 Architect's Elevation
of Grammar School

Europa. Modern Architecture

(Des R. Reed. Litho Cartor)

1987 (5 MAY). Perf 13×13½ (C)

394	**367**	15p multicoloured	55	55
		a. Horiz pair. Nos. 394/5	1·10	1·10
395	**368**	15p multicoloured	55	55
396	**369**	22p multicoloured	80	80
		a. Horiz pair. Nos. 396/7	1·75	1·75
397	**370**	22p multicoloured	80	80
394/7		Set of 4	2·50	2·50
		First Day Cover		4·00
		Presentation Pack	4·00	

Plate Nos.: Both values 1A, 1B, 1C, 1D (each ×4)
Sheets: 20 (4 × 5), the two designs for each value printed together, se-tenant, in horizontal pairs throughout the sheets
Quantities sold: 15p 595,661 pairs; 22p 434,886 pairs
Withdrawn: 4.5.88

Coil Stamps

(Photo Harrison)

1987 (15 MAY)–**88.** As Nos. 306, 306b, 309 and 309c, but
smaller. 22×18 mm (11p, 16p) or 18×22 mm (12p, 15p).
Perf 14×14½ (11p, 16p) or 14½×14 (12p, 15p), all comb

398	**274**	11p multicoloured (a)	30	40
398a	**275**	12p multicoloured (b)	25	25
399	**278**	15p multicoloured (a)	45	55
399a	**279**	16p multicoloured (b)	35	35
398/9a		Set of 4	1·40	1·25
		First Day Covers (2)		3·00

Printings: (a) 15.5.87; (b) 28.3.88
Coils: Rolls of 1000 (a) or 500 (b)
Withdrawn: 26.12.89 11p, 15p; 22.5.92 12p, 16p

371 Sir Edmund Andros
and La Plaiderie,
Guernsey

372 Governor's Palace,
Virginia

373 Governor Andros in
Boston

374 Map of New Amsterdam
(New York), 1661

350th Birth Anniversary of Sir Edmund Andros (colonial administrator)

(Des B. Sanders. Photo Courvoisier)

1987 (7 JULY). *Granite paper. Perf* 12 (C)

400	**371**	15p multicoloured	45	45
401	**372**	29p multicoloured	1·00	1·00
402	**373**	31p multicoloured	1·10	1·10
403	**374**	34p multicoloured	1·40	1·40
400/3		Set of 4	3·50	3·50
		First Day Cover		4·25
		Presentation Pack	4·50	
		Set of 4 Gutter Pairs	7·00	

Cylinder Nos.: All values A1–1–1–1–1–1, B1–1–1–1–1–1

Sheets: 40 (2 panes 5×4)

Quantities sold: 15p 707,843; 29p 129,462; 31p 136,308; 34p 129,527

Withdrawn: 6.7.88

375 The Jester's Warning to Young William

376 Hastings Battlefield

377 Norman Soldier with Pennant

378 William the Conqueror

379 Queen Matilda and Abbaye aux Dames, Caen

380 William's Coronation Regalia and Halley's Comet

900th Death Anniversary of William the Conqueror

(Des P. le Vasseur. Litho Cartor)

1987 (9 SEPT). *Perf* 13½×14 (C)

404	**375**	11p multicoloured	45	35
405	**376**	15p multicoloured	50	50
		a. Horiz pair. Nos. 405/6	1·00	1·00
406	**377**	15p multicoloured	50	50
407	**378**	22p multicoloured	80	75
		a. Horiz pair. Nos. 407/8	1·60	1·50

408	**379**	22p multicoloured	80	80
409	**380**	34p multicoloured	1·25	1·25
404/9		Set of 6	4·00	3·75
		First Day Cover		5·00
		Presentation Pack	5·00	
		Set of 4 Gutter Pairs	8·00	

Plate Nos.: All values 1A, 1B, 1C, 1D (each ×4)

Sheets: 40 (2 panes 4×5), The two designs for the 15p and 22p values were printed together, *se-tenant*, in horizontal pairs throughout the sheets

Imprint: Bottom, left-hand margin

Quantities sold: 11p 639,904; 15p 241,572 pairs; 22p 142,718 pairs; 34p 131,655

Withdrawn: 8.9.88

381 John Wesley preaching on the Quay, Alderney

382 Preaching at Mon Plaisir, St. Peter Port

383 Preaching at Assembly Rooms

384 Wesley and La Ville Baudu (early Methodist meeting place)

385 Wesley and first Methodist Chapel, St. Peter Port

Bicentenary of John Wesley's Visit to Guernsey

(Des R. Geary. Litho Questa)

1987 (17 NOV). *Perf* 14½ (C)

410	**381**	7p multicoloured	30	30
411	**382**	15p multicoloured	45	45
412	**383**	29p multicoloured	1·25	1·25
413	**384**	31p multicoloured	1·25	1·25
414	**385**	34p multicoloured	1·25	1·25
410/14		Set of 5	4·00	4·00
		First Day Cover		5·00
		Presentation Pack	5·00	
		Set of 5 Gutter Pairs	8·00	

Plate Nos.: All values 1A, 1B, 1C, 1D (each ×4)

Sheets: 50 (2 panes 5×5)

Imprint: Bottom, right-hand margin of each pane

Quantities sold: 7p 762,772; 15p 887,797; 29p 122,322; 31p 126,591; 34p 125,863

Withdrawn: 16.11.88

Yearbook 1987

1987 (DEC). *Comprises Nos.* **MS**393/7, 400/14 *and* A32/6

Yearbook . . . . 40·00

Withdrawn: 31.12.88

386 *Golden Spur* off St. Sampson Harbour

387 Entering Hong Kong Harbour

388 Anchored off Macao

389 In China Tea Race

390 *Golden Spur* and Map showing Voyage of 1872–74

Guernsey Shipping (2nd series). Golden Spur *(full- rigged ship)*

(Des R. Granger Barrett. Litho B.D.T.)

1988 (9 FEB). *Perf* 13½ (C)

415	**386**	11p multicoloured	. . . .	35	35
416	**387**	15p multicoloured		50	50
417	**388**	29p multicoloured	. . . .	1·25	1·25
418	**389**	31p multicoloured		1·25	1·25
419	**390**	34p multicoloured	. . . .	1·25	1·25
415/19		Set of 5	. . . .	4·00	4·00
		First Day Cover	. . . .		5·00
		Presentation Pack	. . . .	5·00	
		Set of 5 Gutter Pairs	. . . . . .	8·00	

Plate Nos.: All values 1A, 1B, 1C, 1D (each ×4)

Sheets: 50 (2 panes 5×5)

Imprint: Central, side margins of each pane

Quantities sold: 11p 213,291; 15p 214,048; 29p 136,246; 31p 143,815; 34p 141,177

Withdrawn: 8.2.89

391 Rowing Boat and Bedford 'Rascal' Mail Van

392 Rowing Boat and Vickers Viscount 800 Mail Plane

393 Postman on Bicycle and Horse-drawn Carriages, Sark

394 Postmen on Bicycles and Carriage

Europa. Transport and Communications

(Des C. Abbott. Litho Questa)

1988 (10 MAY). *Perf* 14½ (C)

420	**391**	16p multicoloured	. . . .	60	60
		a. Horiz pair. Nos. 420/1	. . . .	1·25	1·25
421	**392**	16p multicoloured		60	60
422	**393**	22p multicoloured	. . . .	95	95
		a. Horiz pair. Nos. 422/3	. . . .	1·90	1·90
423	**394**	22p multicoloured	. . . .	95	95
420/3		Set of 4	. . . .	2·75	2·75
		First Day Cover	. . . .		4·00
		Presentation Pack	. . . .	3·75	

Plate Nos.: Both values 1A, 1B, 1C, 1D (each ×5)

Sheets: 20 (4×5), the two designs for each value printed together, *se-tenant*, in horizontal pairs throughout the sheets

Imprint: Top, right-hand margin

Quantities sold: 16p 387,699 pairs: 22p 359,634 pairs

Withdrawn: 9.5.89

395 Frederick Corbin Lukis and Lukis House, St Peter Port

396 Natural History Books and Reconstructed Pot

397 Lukis directing Excavation of Le Creux ès Faies and Prehistoric Beaker

398 Lukis House Observatory and Garden

399 Prehistoric Artifacts

Birth Bicentenary of Frederick Corbin Lukis (archaeologist)

(Des Wendy Bramall. Photo Courvoisier)

1988 (12 JULY). *Granite paper. Perf* 12½ (C)

424	**395**	12p multicoloured	. . . .	40	40
425	**396**	16p multicoloured	. . . .	50	50
426	**397**	29p multicoloured	. . . .	1·10	1·10
427	**398**	31p multicoloured	. . . .	1·25	1·25
428	**399**	34p multicoloured	. . . .	1·25	1·25
424/8		Set of 5	. . . .	4·00	4·00
		First Day Cover			5·25
		Presentation Pack		5·00	
		Set of 5 Gutter Pairs		8·00	

Cylinder Nos.: 29p, 34p, A1–1–1, B1–1–1, C1–1–1, D1–1–1–1; others A1–1–1–1, B1–1–1–1, C1–1–1–1, D1–1–1–1

Sheets: 40 (2 panes 5×4)

Quantities sold: 12p 634,056; 16p 510,713; 29p 120,538; 31p 114,192; 34p 134,358

Withdrawn: 11.7.89

400 Powerboats and Westland Wessex Rescue Helicopter off Jethou

401 Powerboats in Gouliot Passage

402 Start of Race at St. Peter Port

403 Admiralty Chart showing Course

World Offshore Powerboat Championships

(Des and photo Courvoisier)

1988 (6 SEPT). *Granite paper. Perf* 12 (C)

429	**400**	16p multicoloured	. . . .	60	60
430	**401**	30p multicoloured	. . . .	1·10	1·10
431	**402**	32p multicoloured	. . . .	1·25	1·25
432	**403**	35p multicoloured	. . . .	1·50	1·50
429/32		Set of 4	. . . .	4·00	4·00
		First Day Cover			5·00
		Presentation Pack		5·00	
		Set of 4 Gutter Pairs		8·00	

Cylinder Nos.: 16p, 32p A1–1–1–1, B1–1–1–1; 30p, 35p C1–1–1–1, D1–1–1–1

Sheets: 40 (2 panes 5×4) 16p, 30p or (2 panes 4×5) others

Quantities sold: 16p 582,190; 30p 127,183; 32p 166,804; 35p 128,552

Withdrawn: 5.9.89

404 Joshua Gosselin and Herbarium

405 Hares-tail Grass

406 Dried Hares-tail Grass

407 Variegated Catchfly

408 Dried Variegated Catchfly

409 Rock Sea Lavender

Bicentenary of Joshua Gosselin's Flora Sarniensis

(Des M. Oxenham. Litho Cartor)

1988 (15 NOV). *Perf* 13½×14 (C)

433	**404**	12p multicoloured	. . . .	40	40
434	**405**	16p multicoloured	. . . .	55	55
		a. Horiz pair. Nos. 434/5	. . . .	1·10	1·10
435	**406**	16p multicoloured	. . . .	55	55
436	**407**	23p multicoloured	. . . .	80	80
		a. Horiz pair. Nos. 436/7	. . . .	1·60	1·60
437	**408**	23p multicoloured	. . . .	80	80
438	**409**	35p multicoloured	. . . .	1·40	1·40
433/8		*Set of* 6	. . . .	4·00	4·00
		First Day Cover	. . . .		5·00
		Presentation Pack	. . . .	4·25	
		Set of 4 Gutter Pairs	. . . . . .	8·00	

Plate Nos.: All values 1A, 1B, 1C, 1D (each ×4)

Sheets: 40 (2 panes 4×5), the two designs for the 16p and 23p values printed together, *se-tenant*, in horizontal pairs throughout the sheets

Imprint: Bottom, left-hand margin

Quantities sold: 12p 562,702; 16p 378,679 pairs; 23p 141,152 pairs; 35p 133,205

Withdrawn: 14.11.89

410 Coutances Cathedral, France

411 Interior of Notre Dame du Rosaire Church, Guernsey

412 Stained Glass, St. Sampson's Church, Guernsey

413 Dol-de-Bretagne Cathedral, France

414 Bishop's Throne, Town Church, Guernsey

415 Winchester Cathedral

416 St. John's Cathedral, Portsmouth

417 High Altar, St. Joseph's Church, Guernsey

418 Mont Saint-Michel, France

419 Chancel, Vale Church, Guernsey

420 Lychgate, Forest Church, Guernsey

421 Marmoutier Abbey, France

Christmas. Ecclesiastical Links

(Des R. Downer. Litho Questa)

1988 (15 NOV). *Perf* 14½ (C)

439	**410**	8p multicoloured	. . . .	25	25
		a. Sheetlet of 12. *Nos.* 439/50		3·50	
440	**411**	8p multicoloured	. . . .	25	25
441	**412**	8p multicoloured	. . . .	25	25
442	**413**	8p multicoloured	. . . .	25	25
443	**414**	8p multicoloured	. . . .	25	25
444	**415**	8p multicoloured	. . . .	25	25
445	**416**	8p multicoloured	. . . .	25	25
446	**417**	8p multicoloured	. . . .	25	25
447	**418**	8p multicoloured	. . . .	25	25
448	**419**	8p multicoloured	. . . .	25	25
449	**420**	8p multicoloured	. . . .	25	25
450	**421**	8p multicoloured	. . . .	25	25
439/50		*Set of* 12		3·50	3·50
		First Day Cover	. . . .		4·50
		Presentation Pack	. . . .	4·00	

Sheets: 12 (4×3) containing Nos. 439/50 *se-tenant*
Imprint: Bottom, left-hand margin
Quantity sold: 185,939 sheetlets
Withdrawn: 14.11.89

Yearbook 1988

1988 (DEC). *Comprises Nos.* 306*b*, 309*c* and 415/50
Yearbook . . . . 26·00

Withdrawn: 31.12.89

422 Lé Cat (Tip Cat)

423 Girl with Cobo Alice Doll

424 Lé Colimachaön (hopscotch)

Europa. Children's Toys and Games

(Des P. le Vasseur. Litho Cartor)

1989 (28 FEB). *Perf* 13½ (C)
451	**422**	12p multicoloured	40	40
452	**423**	16p multicoloured	60	60
453	**424**	23p multicoloured	1·25	1·25
451/3		*Set of 3*	2·00	2·00
		First Day Cover		2·75
		Presentation Pack	2·75	

Plate Nos.: All values 1A, 1B, 1C (each ×4)
Sheets: 20 (4×5)
Imprint: Top, right-hand margin
Quantities sold: 12p 839,111; 16p 829,156; 23p 448,761
Withdrawn: 27.2.90

425 Outline Map of Guernsey

Coil Stamps

(Photo Harrison)

1989 (3 APR–27 DEC). *No value expressed. Perf* 14½×14 (C)
454	**425**	(–) ultramarine (*b*)	40	40
455		(–) emerald (*a*)	60	60
454/5		*Set of 2*	1·00	1·00
		First Day Covers (2)		2·00

No. 454 is inscribed 'MINIMUM BAILIWICK POSTAGE PAID' and No. 455 'MINIMUM FIRST CLASS POSTAGE TO UK PAID'. They were originally sold at 14p. and 18p., but this was changed in line with postage rate rises.

Printings: (*a*) 3.4.89; (*b*) 27.12.89
Coils: Rolls of 500, numbered on the reverse of every fifth stamp
Withdrawn: 30.6.96

426 Guernsey Airways De Havilland D.H.86 Dragon Express and Mail Van

427 Supermarine Southampton II Flying Boat at Mooring

428 B.E.A. De Havilland D.H.89 Dragon Rapide

429 Short S.25 Sunderland Mk V Flying Boat taking off

430 Air U.K. British Aerospace BAe 146

431 Avro Shackleton M.R.3

50th Anniversaries of Guernsey Airport (Nos. 456, 458 and 460) and 201 Squadron's Affiliation with Guernsey (Nos. 457, 459 and 461)

(Des N. Foggo. Litho B.D.T.)

1989 (5 MAY). *Perf* 13½ (C)
456	**426**	12p multicoloured	50	40
		a. Booklet pane. No. 456×6	2·00	
457	**427**	12p multicoloured	50	40
458	**428**	18p multicoloured	75	75
		a. Booklet pane. No. 458×6	3·00	
459	**429**	18p multicoloured	75	75

460	**430**	35p multicoloured	. . . .	1·25	1·25
		a. Booklet pane. No. 460×6		6·00	
461	**431**	35p multicoloured	. . . .	1·25	1·25
456/61		Set of 6	. . . .	4·50	4·50
		First Day Cover	. . . .		5·50
		Presentation Pack	. . . .	5·00	
		Set of 6 Gutter Pairs	. . . . . .	9·00	

Each booklet pane has margins all round with text printed at the foot.

Plate Nos.: All values 1A, 1B (each ×4)

Sheets: 50 (2 panes 5×5)

Imprint: Central, side margins of each pane

Quantities sold: No. 456, 461,080; No. 457, 362,154; No. 458, 436,134; No. 459, 388,274; No. 460, 172,574; No. 461, 149,134

Withdrawn: 4.5.90

432 'Queen Elizabeth II' (June Mendoza)

Royal Visit

(Des A. Theobald. Litho B.D.T.)

1989 (23 MAY). Perf 15×14

462	**432**	30p multicoloured	. . . .	1·25	1·25
		First Day Cover	. . . .		2·25
		Presentation Pack	. . . .	2·25	

Plate Nos.: 1A (×5)

Sheets: 20 (5×4)

Imprint: Top, right-hand margin

Quantity sold: 180,900

Withdrawn: 22.5.90

433 Ibex at G.W.R. Terminal, St. Peter Port

434 Great Western (paddle-steamer) in Little Russel

435 St. Julien passing Casquets Light

436 Roebuck off Portland

437 Antelope and Boat Train at Weymouth Quay

Centenary of Great Western Railway Steamer Service to Channel Islands

(Des C. Jaques. Litho B.D.T.)

1989 (5 SEPT). Perf 13½ (C)

463	**433**	12p multicoloured	. . . .	30	30
464	**434**	18p multicoloured	. . . .	65	65
465	**435**	29p multicoloured	. . . .	90	90
466	**436**	34p multicoloured	. . . .	1·25	1·25
467	**437**	37p multicoloured	. . . .	1·40	1·40
463/7		Set of 5	. . . .	4·00	4·00
		First Day Cover	. . . .		5·50
		Presentation Pack	. . . .	4·75	
		Set of 5 Gutter Pairs	. . . . . .	8·00	
MS468		115×117 mm. Nos. 463/7	. . . .	4·00	4·00
		First Day Cover	. . . .		5·50

Plate Nos.: All values 1A, 1B (each ×4)

Sheets: 50 (2 panes 5×5)

Imprint: Central, side margins of each pane

Quantities sold: 12p 741,870; 18p 666,520; 29p 223,570; 34p 202,570; 37p 209,020; miniature sheet 74,127

Withdrawn 4.9.90

GUERNSEY 18ᴾ

438 Two-toed Sloth

GUERNSEY 29ᴾ

439 Capuchin Monkey

GUERNSEY 32ᴾ

440 White-lipped Tamarin

GUERNSEY 34ᴾ

441 Common Squirrel-Monkey

GUERNSEY 37ᴾ

442 Common Gibbon

10th Anniversary of Guernsey Zoological Trust. Animals of the Rainforest

(Des Anne Farncombe. Litho Cartor)

1989 (17 NOV). *Perf* 13½×14 (C)

469	**438**	18p multicoloured	. . . .	1·00	90
		a. *Strip of 5. Nos.* 469/73	. . . .	4·50	
470	**439**	29p multicoloured	. . . .	1·00	90
471	**440**	32p multicoloured	. . . .	1·00	90
472	**441**	34p multicoloured	. . . .	1·00	90
473	**442**	37p multicoloured	. . . .	1·00	90
469/73		*Set of 5*	. . . .	4·50	4·00
		First Day Cover			5·50
		Presentation Pack	6·00	
		Stamp-cards (*set of* 5)	1·00	6·00

Plate Nos.: 1B (×4)

Sheets: 20 (5×4). Nos. 469/73 were printed in *se-tenant* strips of 5 across the sheet

Imprint: Top, right-hand margin

Quantities sold: 148,505 of each value

Withdrawn: 16.11.90

443 Star

444 Fairy

445 Candles

446 Bird

447 Present

448 Carol-singer

449 Christmas Cracker

450 Bauble

451 Christmas Stocking

452 Bell

453 Fawn

454 Church

Christmas. Christmas Tree Decorations

(Des Wendy Bramall. Litho B.D.T.)

1989 (17 NOV). *Perf* 13 (C)

474	**443**	10p multicoloured	. . . .	30	30
		a. *Sheetlet of* 12. *Nos.* 474/85	4·00		
475	**444**	10p multicoloured	. . . .	30	30
476	**445**	10p multicoloured	. . . .	30	30
477	**446**	10p multicoloured	. . . .	30	30
478	**447**	10p multicoloured	. . . .	30	30
479	**448**	10p multicoloured	. . . .	30	30
480	**449**	10p multicoloured	. . . .	30	30
481	**450**	10p multicoloured	. . . .	30	30
482	**451**	10p multicoloured	. . . .	30	30
483	**452**	10p multicoloured	. . . .	30	30
484	**453**	10p multicoloured	. . . .	30	30
485	**454**	10p multicoloured	. . . .	30	30
474/85		*Set of* 12	4·00	4·00
		First Day Cover		4·75
		Presentation Pack	4·50	

Sheets: 12 (3×4) containing Nos. 474/85 *se-tenant*

Imprint: Central, left-hand margin

Quantity sold: 229,000 sheetlets

Withdrawn: 16.11.90

Yearbook 1989

1989 (17 NOV). *Comprises Nos.* 309*d*, 451/3, 456/62, **MS**468/85 *and* A37/41

Yearbook . . . . 28·00

Withdrawn: 31.12.90

455 Sark Post Office, *c* 1890

456 Sark Post Office, 1990

457 Arcade Post Office Counter, St. Peter Port, *c* 1840

47

458 Arcade Post Office Counter, St. Peter Port, 1990

Europa. Post Office Buildings

(Des C. Abbott. Litho Enschedé)

1990 (27 FEB). *Perf* 13½×14 (C)

486	**455**	20p blackish brown, sepia and pale cinnamon	60	60
487	**456**	20p multicoloured	60	60
488	**457**	24p blackish brown, sepia and pale cinnamon	75	75
489	**458**	24p multicoloured	75	75
486/9		*Set of 4*	2·50	2·50
		First Day Cover		3·50
		Presentation Pack	3·50	

Plate Nos.: Nos. 486 and 488 1A, 1B (each ×3); Nos. 487 and 489 1A, 1B (each ×4)

Sheets: 20 (4×5)

Imprint: Central, side margins

Quantities sold: No. 486, 498,819; No. 487, 398,759; No. 488, 495,039; No. 489, 397,759

Withdrawn: 26.2.91

459 Penny Black and Mail Steamer off St. Peter Port, 1840

460 Penny Red, 1841, and Pillar Box of 1853

461 Bisected 2d., 1940, and German Army Band

462 Regional 3d., 1958, and Guernsey Emblems

463 Independent Postal Administration 1½d., 1969, and Queue at Main Post Office

150th Anniversary of the Penny Black

(Des Jennifer Toombs. Litho Questa)

1990 (3 MAY). *Perf* 14 (C)

490	**459**	14p multicoloured	45	45
491	**460**	20p multicoloured	60	60
492	**461**	32p multicoloured	1·00	90
493	**462**	34p multicoloured	1·10	95
494	**463**	37p multicoloured	1·10	1·00
490/4		*Set of 5*	3·75	3·50
		First Day Cover		5·00
		Presentation Pack	4·50	
		Set of 5 Gutter Pairs	7·50	
MS495		151×116 mm. Nos. 490/4	4·00	3·75
		First Day Cover		5·00

No. **MS**495 also commemorates 'Stamp World London 90' International Stamp Exhibition. It was reissued on 24 August 1990 overprinted for 'NEW ZEALAND 1990' and sold at this international stamp exhibition in Auckland.

Plate Nos.: 14p, 32p 1A, 1B (each ×4); 20p, 34p 1C, 1D (each ×4); 37p 1A, 1B, 1C, 1D (each ×4)

Sheets: 50 (2 panes 5×5)

Imprint; Bottom corner, right-hand margin of each pane

Quantities sold: 14p 687,850; 20p 662,800; 32p 155,960; 34p 143,850; 37p 174,830; miniature sheet 92,701

Withdrawn: 2.5.91

464 Lt. Philip Saumarez writing Log Book

465 Anson's Squadron leaving Portsmouth, 1740

466 Ships at St. Catherine's Island, Brazil

467 H.M.S. *Tryal* (sloop) dismasted, Cape Horn, 1741

468 Crew of H.M.S. *Centurion* on Juan Fernandez

250th Anniversary of Anson's Circumnavigation

(Des R. Granger Barrett. Litho Enschedé)

1990 (26 JULY). *Perf* 13½×14 (C)

496	**464**	14p multicoloured	. . . .	45	45
497	**465**	20p multicoloured	. . . .	60	60
498	**466**	29p multicoloured	. . . .	1·00	90
499	**467**	34p multicoloured	. . . .	1·10	95
500	**468**	37p multicoloured	. . . .	1·10	1·00
496/500		Set of 5	. . . .	3·75	3·50
		First Day Cover			5·00
		Presentation Pack		4·50	
		Stamp-cards (set of 5)		2·00	5·00
		Set of 5 Gutter Pairs		7·50	

Plate Nos.: 14p, 20p, 29p 1A, 1B, 1C, 1D (each ×4); 34p, 37p 1A, 1B (each ×4)

Sheets: 50 (2 panes 5×5)

Imprint: Central, side margins of each pane

Quantities sold: 14p 985,850; 20p 481,400; 29p 162,800; 34p 143,500; 37p 138,450

Withdrawn: 25.7.91

469 Grey Seal and Pup

470 Bottle-nosed Dolphin

471 Basking Shark

472 Common Porpoise

Marine Life

(Des Jennifer Toombs. Litho Questa)

1990 (16 OCT). *Perf* 14½ (C)

501	**469**	20p multicoloured	. . . .	60	60
502	**470**	26p multicoloured	. . . .	1·10	1·10
503	**471**	31p multicoloured	. . . .	1·10	1·10
504	**472**	37p multicoloured	. . . .	1·40	1·40
501/4		Set of 4	. . . .	3·75	3·75
		First Day Cover			4·50
		Presentation Pack		4·50	
		Set of 4 Gutter Pairs		7·50	

Plate Nos.: 20p, 31p 1A, 1B (each ×4); 26p, 37p 1C, 1D (each ×4)

Sheets: 50 (2 panes 5×5)

Imprint: Top, right-hand margin of each pane

Quantities sold: 20p 973,900; 26p 478,200; 31p 328,650; 37p 303,600

Withdrawn: 15.10.91

473 Blue Tit and Great Tit

474 Snow Bunting

475 Common Kestrel

476 Common Starling

477 Greenfinch

478 European Robin

479 Winter Wren

480 Barn Owl

481 Mistle Thrush

482 Grey Heron

483 Chaffinch

484 Common Kingfisher

Christmas. Winter Birds

(Des Wendy Bramall, Litho B.D.T.)

1990 (16 OCT). *Perf* 13 (C)

505	**473**	10p multicoloured		25	25
		a. Sheetlet of 12. *Nos.* 505/16		4·00	
506	**474**	10p multicoloured		25	25
507	**475**	10p multicoloured		25	25
508	**476**	10p multicoloured		25	25
509	**477**	10p multicoloured		25	25
510	**478**	10p multicoloured		25	25
511	**479**	10p multicoloured		25	25
512	**480**	10p multicoloured		25	25
513	**481**	10p multicoloured		25	25
514	**482**	10p multicoloured		25	25
515	**483**	10p multicoloured		25	25
516	**484**	10p multicoloured		25	25
505/16		*Set of* 12		4·00	4·00
		First Day Cover..........			4·75
		Presentation Pack		4·75	

Sheets: 12 (3×4) containing Nos. 505/16 *se-tenant*

Imprint: Central, left-hand margin

Quantity sold: 237,602 sheetlets

Withdrawn: 15.10.91

Yearbook 1990

1990 (1 NOV). *Comprises Nos.* 486/9, **MS**495, 496/516, A12*a and* A42/6

	Yearbook	24·00

Withdrawn: 31.12.91

485 Air Raid and 1941
½d. Stamp

486 1941 1d. Stamp

487 1944 2½d Stamp

50th Anniversary of First Guernsey Stamps

(Des C. Abbott. Litho B.D.T.)

1991 (18 FEB). *Perf* 13½ (C)

517	**485**	37p multicoloured		1·25	1·25
		a. Booklet pane. Nos. 517/19		4·00	
518	**486**	53p multicoloured		1·60	1·60
519	**487**	57p multicoloured		1·60	1·60
517/19		*Set of* 3		4·00	4·00
		First Day Cover..........			5·50
		Presentation Pack		5·00	
		Set of 3 *Gutter Pairs*		8·00	

Booklet pane No. 517*a* exists in three versions, which differ in the order of the stamps from left to right and in the information printed on the pane margins.

Plate Nos.: 37p, 53p 1A, 1B (each ×4); 57p 1A, 1B, 1C, 1D (each ×4)

Sheets: 40 (2 panes 5×4)

Imprint: Central, side margins

Quantities sold: 37p 260,015; 53p 250,536; 57p 250,219

Withdrawn: 17.2.92

488 Visit of Queen Victoria to Guernsey, and Discovery of Neptune, 1846

489 Visit of Queen Elizabeth II and Prince Philip to Sark, and Flight of 'Sputnik' (1st artificial satellite, 1957)

490 Maiden Voyage of *Sarnia* (ferry), and 'Vostok 1' (first manned space flight), 1961

491 Cancelling Guernsey Stamps, and First Manned Landing on Moon, 1969

Europa. Europe in Space

(Des Jennifer Toombs. Litho Enschedé)

1991 (30 APR). *Perf* 13½×14 (C)

520	**488**	21p multicoloured	....	65	65
521	**489**	21p multicoloured	....	65	65
522	**490**	26p multicoloured	....	90	75
523	**491**	26p multicoloured	....	90	75
520/3		*Set of* 4	....	2·75	2·50
		First Day Cover	....		4·00
		Presentation Pack	....	3·75	

Plate Nos.: Both values 1A, 1B (each ×5)

Sheets: 20 (4×5)

Imprint: Central, side margins

Quantities sold: No. 520, 390,924; No. 521, 390,834; No. 522, 369,404; No. 523, 370,244

Withdrawn: 29.4.92

492 Children in Guernsey Sailing Trust 'GP14' Dinghy

493 Guernsey Regatta

494 Lombard Channel Islands' Challenge Race

495 Rolex Swan Regatta

496 Old Gaffers' Association Gaff-rigged Yacht

Centenary of Guernsey Yacht Club

(Des C. Abbott. Litho B.D.T.)

1991 (2 JULY). *Perf* 14 (C)

524	**492**	15p multicoloured	....	50	50
525	**493**	21p multicoloured	....	80	80
526	**494**	26p multicoloured		90	90
527	**495**	31p multicoloured	....	1·00	1·00
528	**496**	37p multicoloured	....	1·25	1·25
524/8		*Set of* 5	....	4·00	4·00
		First Day Cover	....		4·75
		Presentation Pack	....	4·75	
		Set of 5 *Gutter Pairs*	......	8·00	
MS529	163×75 mm. Nos. 524/8		....	4·00	4·00
		First Day Cover	....		4·75

Stamps from No. **MS**529 show 'GUERNSEY' and the face value in yellow.

Plate Nos.: 37p 1C, 1D (each ×5); others 1A, 1B (each ×5)

Sheets: 50 (2 panes 5×5)

Imprint: Top corner, right-hand margin of each pane

Quantities sold: 15p 711,043; 21p 708,743; 26p 188,894; 31p 158,938; 37p 138,543; miniature sheet 81,012

Withdrawn: 1.7.92

497 Pair of Oystercatchers

498 Three Turnstones

499 Dunlins and Turnstones

500 Curlew and Turnstones

501 Ringed Plover with Chicks

502 Gull, Sea Campion and Sea Radish

503 Yellow Horned Poppy

504 Pair of Stonechats, Hare's Foot Clover and Fennel

505 Hare's Foot Clover, Fennel and Slender Oat

506 Sea Kale on Shore

Nature Conservation. L'Eree Shingle Bank Reserve

(Des Wendy Bramall. Litho Questa)

1991 (15 OCT). *Perf* 14½ (C)

530	**497**	15p multicoloured	....	40	40
		a. *Horiz strip of* 5. *Nos.* 530/4		3·00	
531	**498**	15p multicoloured	....	40	40
532	**499**	15p multicoloured	....	40	40
533	**500**	15p multicoloured	....	40	40
534	**501**	15p multicoloured	....	40	40
535	**502**	21p multicoloured		50	50
		a. *Horiz strip of* 5. *Nos.* 535/9		3·00	
536	**503**	21p multicoloured	....	50	50
537	**504**	21p multicoloured	....	50	50
538	**505**	21p multicoloured	....	50	50
539	**506**	21p multicoloured	....	50	50
530/9		*Set of* 10	....	5·50	4·00
		First Day Cover	....		5·50
		Presentation Pack	....	6·00	
		Stamp-cards (set of 10)	....	2·00	6·25

Plate Nos.: Both values 1A, 1B, 1C, 1D (each ×4)

Sheets: 20 (5×4), the five designs for each value printed together, *se-tenant*, in horizontal strips throughout the sheets.

Imprint: Bottom, left-hand margin

Quantities sold: 15p 270,830 strips; 21p 272,198 strips

Withdrawn: 14.10.92

507 'Rudolph the Red-nosed Reindeer' (Melanie Sharpe)

508 'Christmas Pudding' (James Quinn)

509 'Snowman' (Lisa Guille)

510 'Snowman in Top Hat' (Jessica Ede-Golightly)

511 'Robins and Christmas Tree' (Sharon Le Page)

512 'Shepherds and Angels' (Anna Coquelin)

513 'Nativity' (Claudine Lihou)

514 'Three Wise Men' (Jonathan Le Noury)

515 'Star of Bethlehem and Angels' (Marcia Mahy)

516 'Christmas Tree' (Laurel Garfield)

517 'Santa Claus' (Rebecca Driscoll)

518 'Snowman and Star' (Ian Lowe)

Christmas. Children's Paintings

(Litho B.D.T.)

1991 (15 OCT). *Perf* 13½×13 (C)

540	**507**	12p multicoloured	....	35	35
		a. *Sheetlet of* 12. *Nos.* 540/51		4·00	
541	**508**	12p multicoloured	....	35	35
542	**509**	12p multicoloured	....	35	35
543	**510**	12p multicoloured	....	35	35
544	**511**	12p multicoloured	....	35	35
545	**512**	12p multicoloured	....	35	35
546	**513**	12p multicoloured	....	35	35
547	**514**	12p multicoloured	....	35	35
548	**515**	12p multicoloured	....	35	35
549	**516**	12p multicoloured	....	35	35
550	**517**	12p multicoloured	....	35	35
551	**518**	12p multicoloured	....	35	35
540/51		*Set of* 12	....	4·00	4·00
		First Day Cover	....		5·50
		Presentation Pack	....	4·75	

Sheets: 12 (3×4) containing Nos. 540/51 *se-tenant*

Imprint: Central, left-hand margin

Quantity sold: 192,203 sheetlets

Withdrawn: 14.10.92

Yearbook 1991

1991 (1 NOV). *Comprises Nos.* 310*b/c*, 517/51, A12*b and* A47/51

Yearbook . . . . 30·00

Withdrawn: 31.12.92

519 Queen Elizabeth II in 1952

520 In 1977

521 In 1986

522 In 1991

40th Anniversary of Accession

(Des C. Abbott. Litho Questa)

1992 (6 FEB). *Perf* 14 (C)

552	**519**	23p multicoloured	. . . .	70	70
553	**520**	28p multicoloured	. . . .	75	75
554	**521**	33p multicoloured	. . . .	85	85
555	**522**	39p multicoloured	. . . .	1·10	1·10
552/5		*Set of* 4	. . . .	3·00	3·00
		First Day Cover			4·75
		Presentation Pack	4·00	
		Set of 4 *Gutter Pairs*	6·00	

Plate Nos.: All values 1A, 1B (each ×6)

Sheets: 50 (2 panes 5×5)

Quantities sold: 23p 773,200; 28p 479,095; 33p 212,446; 39p 219,900

Withdrawn: 5.2.93

523 Christopher Columbus

524 Examples of Columbus's Signature

525 Santa Maria

526 Map of First Voyage

Europa. 500th Anniversary of Discovery of America by Columbus

(Des R. Ollington. Litho Walsall)

1992 (6 FEB). *Perf* 13½×14 (C)

556	**523**	23p multicoloured	. . . .	60	60
557	**524**	23p multicoloured	. . . .	60	60
558	**525**	28p multicoloured	. . . .	1·10	1·10
559	**526**	28p multicoloured	. . . .	1·10	1·10
556/9		*Set of 4*	. . . .	3·00	3·00
		First Day Cover			3·75
		Presentation Pack	4·00	
MS560		157×77 mm. Nos. 556/9		3·00	3·00
		First Day Cover			4·00

No. **MS**560 was reissued on 22 May 1992 overprinted for 'WORLD COLUMBIAN STAMP EXPO 92' and sold at this international stamp exhibition in Chicago.

Plate Nos.: All values 1A, 1B, 1C (each ×4)

Sheets: 20 (4×5)

Imprint: Bottom, right-hand margin

Quantities sold: No. 556, 543,672; No. 557, 575,633; No. 558, 363,124; No. 559, 364,684; miniature sheet 157,166

Withdrawn: 5.2.93

527a Guernsey Calves

150th Anniversary of Royal Guernsey Agricultural and Horticultural Society

(Des R. Goldsmith. Litho Questa)

1992 (22 MAY). *Sheet* 93×71 *mm. Perf* 14 (C)
MS561 527*a* 75p multicoloured . . . . 2·00 2·00
First Day Cover . . . . 3·25
Presentation Pack . . . . 3·25

Quantity sold: 142,549
Withdrawn: 21.5.93

528 *Stephanotis floribunda*

529 Potted Hydrangea

530 Stock

531 Anenomes

532 Gladiolus

533 *Asparagus plumosus, Gypsophila paniculata*

534 Guernsey Lily

535 Enchantment Lily

536 Clematis 'Freckles'

537 Alstroemeria

538 Standard Carnation

539 Standard Rose

540 Spray Rose

541 Mixed Freesia

542 Standard Rose

543 Iris 'Ideal'

544 Freesia 'Pink Glow'

545 Lisianthus

546 Spray Chrysanthemum

547 Spray Carnation

548 Single Freesia

549 Floral Arrangement

550 Chelsea Flower Show Exhibit

551 'Floral Fantasia' (exhibit)

Horticultural Exports

(Des R. Gorringe. Litho Walsall (Nos. 572*a*, 572*ba*, 574*a*, 575*a*, 576*b* and 577*a*), Questa (No. 576*a*), Cartor (No. 582*a*) or B.D.T. (others))

1992 (22 MAY)–**97**. *Perf* 14 (£1, £2) *or* 13 (*others*), *all comb*

562	**528**	1p multicoloured (*b*)	10	10
563	**529**	2p multicoloured (*b*)	10	10
564	**530**	3p multicoloured (*a*)	10	10
565	**531**	4p multicoloured (*a*)	10	10
566	**532**	5p multicoloured (*a*)	10	15
567	**533**	6p multicoloured (*b*)	10	15
568	**534**	7p multicoloured (*b*)	15	20
569	**535**	8p multicoloured (*b*)	15	20
570	**536**	9p multicoloured (*b*)	20	25
571	**537**	10p multicoloured (*a*)	20	25
572	**538**	16p multicoloured (*a*)	30	35
		a. Perf 14 (*ab*)	50	50
		ab. Lavender ptg double		
		ac. Booklet pane. Nos. 572*a*×5		
		and 574*a*×3 (*a*)	4·00	
		ad. Booklet pane of 8 (*b*)	3·00	
572*b*	**539**	18p multicoloured (*e*)	35	40
		ba. Perf 14	35	40
		bb. Booklet pane of 8	3·00	
573	**540**	20p multicoloured (*a*)	40	45
574	**541**	23p multicoloured (*a*)	45	50
		a. Perf 14	60	60
		ab. Brownish grey ptg double ..		
		ac. Booklet pane of 8	4·50	
575	**542**	24p multicoloured (*b*)	50	55
		a. Perf 14	50	55
		ab. Booklet pane of 8	4·00	
576	**543**	25p multicoloured (*c*)	50	55
		a. Perf 14½×15	50	55
		ab. Booklet pane of 4	2·00	
576*b*	**544**	26p multicoloured (*e*)	55	60
		ba. Perf 14	55	60
		bb. Booklet pane of 4	2·10	
577	**545**	28p multicoloured (*b*)	55	60
		a. Perf 14	55	60
		ab. Booklet pane of 4	2·25	
578	**546**	30p multicoloured (*b*)	60	65
579	**547**	40p multicoloured (*a*)	80	85
580	**548**	50p multicoloured (*a*)	1·00	1·10
581	**549**	£1 multicoloured (*a*)	2·00	2·10
582	**550**	£2 multicoloured (*b*)	4·00	4·25
582*a*	**551**	£3 multicoloured (*d*)	6·00	6·25
562/82*a*		Set of 24	18·50	20·00
		First Day Covers (5)		23·00
		Presentation Packs (3)	21·00	
		Stamp-cards (set of 24)	5·00	27·00
		Set of 24 Gutter Pairs	40·00	

Nos. 572*a*, 572*ba*, 574*a*, 575*a*, 576*a*, 576*ba* and 577*a* were only issued in booklets with the upper and lower edges of the panes imperforate.

For No. 581 in miniature sheets see Nos. **MS**644 and **MS**681.

Printings: (*a*) 22.5.92; (*b*) 2.3.93; (*c*) 18.2.94; (*d*) 24.1.96; (*e*) 2.1.97, each with appropriate imprint date.
Plate Nos.: £1 1A, 1B (each ×8); £3 1A, 1B, 1C, 1D (each ×5); others 1A, 1B, 1C, 1D (each ×6)

Sheets: 1p, 2p, 3p, 4p, 5p, 6p, 7p, 8p, 9p, 10p, 18p, 20p, 40p 100 (2 panes 10×5); 16p, 23p, 24p, 25p, 26p, 28p, 30p, 50p (2 panes 5×10); £1, £2, £3 50 (2 panes 5×5)
Imprints: 1p, 2p, 3p, 4p, 5p, 6p, 7p, 8p, 9p, 10p, 18p, 20p, 40p, £1, £2 left-hand corner, top and bottom margin; £3 central, side margins; others top of side margin.

552 Building the Ship

553 Loading the Cargo

554 Ship at Sea

555 Ship under Attack

556 Crew swimming Ashore

"Operation Asterix" (excavation of Roman ship)

(Des Studio Legrain. Litho Cartor)

1992 (18 SEPT). *Perf* 13 (C)

583	**552**	16p multicoloured	45	45
		a. Booklet pane. Nos. 583/7		
		plus label	3·50	
584	**553**	23p multicoloured	60	60
585	**554**	28p multicoloured	80	80
586	**555**	33p multicoloured	95	95
587	**556**	39p multicoloured	1·10	1·10
583/7		Set of 5	3·50	3·50
		First Day Cover		4·75
		Presentation Pack	4·00	
		Set of 5 Gutter Pairs	7·00	

Booklet pane No. 583*a* has margins all round and exists with marginal inscriptions in either English, French, Italian or German.

Plate Nos.: All values 1A, 1B, 1C, 1D (each ×4)
Sheets: 50 (2 panes 5×5)
Imprint: Central, side margins
Quantities sold: 16p 904,428; 23p 743,228; 28p 308,091; 33p 281,941; 39p 291,841
Withdrawn: 17.9.93

557 Tram No. 10 decorated for Battle of Flowers

558 Tram No. 10 passing Hougue a la Perre

559 Tram No. 1 at St. Sampsons

560 First Steam Tram at St. Peter Port, 1879

561 Last Electric Tram, 1934

Guernsey Trams

(Des A. Peck. Litho Enschedé)

1992 (17 NOV). *Perf* 13½ (C)

588	**557**	16p multicoloured	....	45	45
589	**558**	23p multicoloured	....	60	60
590	**559**	28p multicoloured	....	80	80
591	**560**	33p multicoloured	....	95	95
592	**561**	39p multicoloured	....	1·10	1·10
588/92		*Set of* 5	....	3·50	3·50
		First Day Cover	....		4·75
		Presentation Pack	....	4·00	
		Set of 5 *Gutter Pairs*	......	7·00	

Plate Nos.: 39p 1A, 1B, 1C, 1D (each ×6); others 1A, 1B (each ×6)

Sheets: 50 (2 panes 5×5)

Imprint: Central, side margins of each pane

Quantities sold: 16p 366,400; 23p 282,520; 28p 181,670; 33p 130,920; 39p 156,170

Withdrawn: 16.11.93

562 Man in Party Hat

563 Girl and Christmas Tree

564 Woman and Balloons

565 Mince Pies and Champagne

566 Roast Turkey

567 Christmas Pudding

568 Christmas Cake

569 Fancy Cakes

570 Cheese

571 Nuts

572 Ham

573 Chocolate Log

Christmas. Seasonal Fayre

(Des Wendy Bramall. Litho B.D.T.)

1992 (17 NOV). *Perf* 13 (C)

593	**562**	13p multicoloured	....	35	35
		a. *Sheetlet of* 12. *Nos.* 593/604	4·00		
		ab. *Gold ptg double*	....		
594	**563**	13p multicoloured	....	35	35
595	**564**	13p multicoloured	....	35	35
596	**565**	13p multicoloured	....	35	35
597	**566**	13p multicoloured	....	35	35
598	**567**	13p multicoloured	....	35	35
599	**568**	13p multicoloured	....	35	35
600	**569**	13p multicoloured	....	35	35
601	**570**	13p multicoloured	....	35	35
602	**571**	13p multicoloured	....	35	35
603	**572**	13p multicoloured	....	35	35
604	**573**	13p multicoloured	....	35	35
593/604		*Set of* 12	....	4·00	4·00
		First Day Cover	....		5·00
		Presentation Pack	....	4·50	

Sheets: 12 (3×4) containing Nos. 593/604 *se-tenant*, forming a composite design showing family during Christmas meal

Imprint: Central, left-hand margin

Quantity sold: 183,550 sheetlets

Withdrawn: 16.11.93

Yearbook 1992

1992 (18 NOV). *Comprises Nos.* 552/61, 564/6, 571/4, 579/81, 583/604, A12c *and* A52/5

	Yearbook	32·00

Withdrawn: 31.12.93

24 GUERNSEY   **574** Rupert Bear, Bingo and Dog

574a Rupert and Friends
(illustration reduced. Actual size 116×97 mm)

Rupert Bear and Friends (cartoon characters created by Mary and Herbert Tourtel)

(Des J. Harold. Litho Walsall)

1993 (2 FEB). Perf 13½×13 (C)
605   **574**   24p multicoloured . . . .   1·00   1·00
                        First Day Cover . . . .   2·00
                        Gutter Pair . . . .   2·00
MS606   116×97 mm. **574a** 16p Airplane and castle; 16p Professor's servant and Autumn Elf; 16p Algy Pug; 16p Baby Badger on sledge; 24p Bill Badger, Willie Mouse, Reggie Rabbit and Podgy playing in snow; 24p Type **574**; 24p The Balloonist avoiding Gregory on toboggan; 24p Tiger Lily and Edward Trunk . . . .   5·00   5·00
                        a. Black ptg double . . . .
                        First Day Cover . . . .   5·50
                        Presentation Pack (Nos. 605/6) . . . .   6·50

The 24p values in No. **MS**606 are as Type **574**; the 16p designs are smaller, each 25½×26 mm.

Plate Nos.: 24p 1A, 1B (each ×4)
Sheets: 50 (2 panes 5×5)
Imprint: Top left-hand margin of each pane
Withdrawn: 1.2.94

24 GUERNSEY   **24**   GUERNSEY

575 Tapestry by Kelly Fletcher   **576** 'Le Marchi a Paissaon' (etching and aquatint, Sally Reed)

28 GUERNSEY   **28**   GUERNSEY

577 'Red Abstract' (painting, Molly Harris)   **578** 'Dress Shop, King's Road' (painting, Damon Bell)

Europa. Contemporary Art

(Des B. Bell. Litho Enschedé)

1993 (7 MAY). Perf 13½×14 (C)
607   **575**   24p multicoloured   80   80
608   **576**   24p multicoloured   80   80
609   **577**   28p multicoloured   90   90
610   **578**   28p multicoloured   90   90
607/10   Set of 4 . . . .   3·00   3·00
                        First Day Cover . . . .   3·50
                        Presentation Pack . . . .   3·25

Plate Nos.: 24p (No. 607) 1A, 1B, 1C, 1D (each ×5); others 1A, 1B (each ×5)
Sheets: 20 (4×5)
Imprint: Central, side margins
Withdrawn: 6.5.94

579 Arrest of Guernsey Parliamentarians, Fermain Bay

580 Parliamentary Ships attacking Castle Cornet

581 Parliamentary Captives escaping

582 Castle Cannon firing at St. Peter Port

583 Surrender of Castle Cornet, 19 December 1651

350th Anniversary of Siege of Castle Cornet

(Des C. Abbott. Litho Questa)

1993 (7 MAY). *Perf* 14½×14 (C)

611	**579**	16p multicoloured	. . . .	40	40
612	**580**	24p multicoloured	. . . .	65	65
613	**581**	28p multicoloured	. . . .	85	85
614	**582**	33p multicoloured	. . . .	95	95
615	**583**	39p multicoloured	. . . .	1·10	1·10
611/15		*Set of 5*	. . . .	3·50	3·50
		First Day Cover			4·25
		Presentation Pack	4·00	
		Set of 5 Gutter Pairs	7·25	
MS616		203×75 mm. Nos. 611/15	3·50	3·50
		First Day Cover			4·25

Plate Nos.: All values 1A, 1B (each ×5)

Sheets: 40 (2 panes 4×5)

Imprint: Central, right-hand margin

Withdrawn: 6.5.94

584 Playing Cards

585 Fountain Pens

586 Envelope-folding Machine

587 Great Britain 1855 4d Stamp

588 Thomas de la Rue and Mauritius £1 Banknote

Birth Bicentenary of Thomas de la Rue (printer)

(Des J. Stephenson. Litho (16, 24, 28p) or recess (33, 39p) Enschedé)

1993 (27 JULY). *Perf* 13½ (C)

617	**584**	16p multicoloured	. . . .	40	40
		a. Booklet pane of 4 with margins all round	1·25	
618	**585**	24p multicoloured	. . . .	65	65
		a. Booklet pane of 4 with margins all round	1·90	
619	**586**	28p multicoloured	. . . .	80	80
		a. Booklet pane of 4 with margins all round	2·25	
620	**587**	33p carmine-lake	. . . .	95	95
		a. Booklet pane of 4 with margins all round	2·75	
621	**588**	39p blackish green	. . . .	1·10	1·10
		a. Booklet pane of 4 with margins all round	3·00	
617/21		*Set of 5*	. . . .	3·50	3·50
		First Day Cover			4·25
		Presentation Pack	4·00	
		Set of 5 Gutter Pairs	7·25	

Plate Nos.: 16p, 24p 1A×4; 28p 1A, 1B (each ×4); 33p, 39p 1A

Sheets: 50 (2 panes 5×5)

Imprint: Central, side margins of each pane

Withdrawn: 26.7.94

589 'The Twelve Pearls'

590 'Healing Rays'

591 'Hand of God over the Holy City'

592 'Wing and Seabirds' (facing left)

593 'Christ the Healer'

594 'Wing and Seabirds' (facing right)

595 'The Young Jesus in the Temple'

596 'The Raising of Jairus' Daughter'

597 'Suffer Little Children to come unto Me'

598 'Pilgrim's Progress'

599 'The Light of the World'

600 'Raphael, Archangel of Healing, with Tobias'

Christmas. Stained Glass Windows by Mary-Eily de Putron from Chapel of Christ the Healer

(Des Jennifer Toombs. Litho B.D.T.)

1993 (2 NOV). *Perf* 13 (C)

622	**589**	13p multicoloured	. . . .	45	45
		a. Sheetlet. Nos. 622/33	. . . .	4·00	
623	**590**	13p multicoloured	. . . .	45	45
624	**591**	13p multicoloured	. . . .	45	45
625	**592**	13p multicoloured	. . . .	45	45
626	**593**	13p multicoloured	. . . .	45	45
627	**594**	13p multicoloured	. . . .	45	45
628	**595**	13p multicoloured	. . . .	45	45
629	**596**	13p multicoloured	. . . .	45	45
630	**597**	13p multicoloured	. . . .	45	45
631	**598**	13p multicoloured	. . . .	45	45
632	**599**	13p multicoloured	. . . .	45	45
633	**600**	13p multicoloured	. . . .	45	45
622/33		*Set of* 12	. . . .	4·00	4·00
		First Day Cover	. . . .		4·25
		Presentation Pack	. . . .	4·25	

Sheets: 12 (3×4) containing Nos. 622/33 *se-tenant*

Imprint: Central, left-hand margin

Withdrawn: 1.11.94

Yearbook 1993

1993 (2 NOV). *Comprises Nos.* 562/3, 567/70, 575, 577/8, 582, 605/33, A12*d/e* and A56/9

	Yearbook	38·00

Withdrawn: 30.12.94

601 Les Fouaillages (ancient burial ground)

602 Mounted Celtic Warrior

603 Jars, Arrow Heads and Stone Axe from Les Fouaillages

604 Sword, Spear Head and Torque from King's Road Burial

Europa. Archaeological Discoveries

(Des Miranda Schofield. Litho Cartor)

1994 (18 FEB). *Perf* 13½ (C)

634	**601**	24p multicoloured	....	60	60
635	**602**	24p multicoloured	....	60	60
636	**603**	30p multicoloured	....	80	80
637	**604**	30p multicoloured	....	80	80
634/7		Set of 4	....	2·50	2·50
		First Day Cover	....		2·75
		Presentation Pack	....	2·75	

Some sheets of No. 635 were overprinted with the 'Hong Kong '94' emblem on the left margin for sale at this philatelic exhibition.

Plate Nos.: All values 1A

Sheets: 10 (2×5) with large inscribed margin at left

Withdrawn: 17.2.95

605*a* Canadian Supermarine Spitfires Mk V over Normandy Beaches

50th Anniversary of D-Day

(Des N. Trudgian. Litho B.D.T.)

1994 (6 JUNE). *Sheet* 93×71 *mm. Perf* 14 (C)

MS638	**605***a*	£2 multicoloured	....	4·50	4·50
		First Day Cover	....		4·75
		Presentation Pack	....	4·75	

Withdrawn: 5.6.95

606 Peugeot 'Type 3', 1894

607 Mercedes 'Simplex', 1903

608 Humber Tourer, 1906

609 Bentley Sports Tourer, 1936

610 MG TC Midget, 1948

Centenary of First Car in Guernsey

(Des R. Ollington. Litho B.D.T.)

1994 (19 JULY). *Perf* 14½×14 (C)

639	**606**	16p multicoloured	....	45	45
		a. Booklet pane of 4 with margins all round	....	1·75	
640	**607**	24p multicoloured	....	70	70
		a. Booklet pane of 4 with margins all round	....	2·75	
641	**608**	35p multicoloured	....	1·00	1·00
		a. Booklet pane of 4 with margins all round	....	4·00	
642	**609**	41p multicoloured	....	1·10	1·10
		a. Booklet pane of 4 with margins all round	....	4·25	
643	**610**	60p multicoloured	....	1·75	1·75
		a. Booklet pane of 4 with margins all round	....	7·00	
639/43		Set of 5	....	4·50	4·50
		First Day Cover	....		5·00
		Presentation Pack	....	4·75	
		Set of 5 Gutter Pairs	......	9·00	

Plate Nos.: 60p 1A, 1B, 1C, 1D (each ×5); others 1A, 1B (each ×5)

Sheets: 50 (2 panes 5×5)

Imprint: Central, side margins of each pane

Withdrawn: 18.7.95

610a Floral Arrangement
(*illustration reduced. Actual size* 110×90 *mm*)

'Philakorea '94' International Stamp Exhibition, Seoul

(Des R. Gorringe and M. Whyte. Litho Cartor)

1994 (16 AUG). *Sheet* 110×90 *mm containing stamp as No.* 581 *with changed imprint date. Perf* 13 (C)

MS644	**610a**	£1 multicoloured	2·50	2·50
		First Day Cover		2·75
		Presentation Pack	2·75	

Withdrawn: 15.8.95

611 *Trident* (Herm Ferry)

612 Handley Page HPR-7 Super Dart Herald of Channel Express

613 Britten Norman Trislander G-JOEY of Aurigny Air Services

614 *Bon Marin de Serk* (Sark Ferry)

615 Map of Bailiwick

25th Anniversary of Guernsey Postal Administration

(Des A. Copp. Litho Questa)

1994 (1 OCT). *Perf* 14 (C)

645	**611**	16p multicoloured	....	35	35
646	**612**	24p multicoloured	....	55	55
647	**613**	35p multicoloured	....	75	75
648	**614**	41p multicoloured	....	85	85
649	**615**	60p multicoloured	....	1·40	1·40
645/9		*Set of* 5	....	3·75	3·75
		First Day Cover			4·25
		Presentation Pack	4·25	
		Stamp-cards (*set of* 5)	1·00	4·75
MS650		150×100 mm. Nos 645/9	3·75	3·75
		First Day Cover			4·25

Plate Nos.: All values 1A (×5)
Sheets: 20 (5×4)
Imprint: Central, left-hand margin
Withdrawn: 30.9.95

616 Dolls' House   **617** Doll   **618** Teddy in Bassinette

619 Sweets in Pillar Box and Playing Cards   **620** Spinning Top   **621** Building Blocks

622 Rocking Horse   **623** Teddy Bear   **624** Tricycle

625 Wooden Duck   **626** Hornby Toy Locomotive   **627** Ludo Game

Christmas. Bygone Toys

(Des A. Peck. Litho B.D.T.)

1994 (1 OCT). *Perf* 13 (C)

651	**616**	13p multicoloured	....	40	40
		a. *Sheetlet. Nos.* 651/6	......	2·00	
652	**617**	13p multicoloured	....	40	40
653	**618**	13p multicoloured	....	40	40
654	**619**	13p multicoloured	....	40	40
655	**620**	13p multicoloured	....	40	40
656	**621**	13p multicoloured	....	40	40
657	**622**	24p multicoloured	....	75	75
		a. *Sheetlet. Nos.* 657/62	....	3·50	
658	**623**	24p multicoloured	....	75	75
659	**624**	24p multicoloured	....	75	75
660	**625**	24p multicoloured	....	75	75
661	**626**	24p multicoloured	....	75	75
662	**627**	24p multicoloured	....	75	75
651/62		*Set of 12*	......	5·00	5·00
		First Day Covers (2)	.....		5·00
		Presentation Pack	....	5·25	

Sheets: 6 (3×2) containing Nos. 650/5 or 656/61 *se-tenant*

Imprint: Bottom, left-hand margin

Withdrawn: 30.9.95

Yearbook 1994

1994 (1 OCT). *Comprises Nos.* 576, 634/62 *and* A60/76

	Yearbook (softback)	...... 38·00
	Yearbook (hardback)	...... 60·00

Withdrawn: 29.12.95

628 Seafood 'Face'

629 Buckets and Spade 'Face'

630 Flowers 'Face'

631 Fruit and Vegetables 'Face'

632 Sea Shells and Seaweed 'Face'

633 Anchor and Life Belts 'Face'

634 Glasses, Cork and Cutlery 'Face'

635 Butterflies and Caterpillars 'Face'

Greetings Stamps. 'The Welcoming Face of Guernsey'

(Des R. Ollington. Litho Questa)

1995 (28 FEB). *Perf* 14 (C)

663	**628**	24p multicoloured	....	65	65
664	**629**	24p multicoloured	....	65	65
665	**630**	24p multicoloured	....	65	65
666	**631**	24p multicoloured	....	65	65
667	**632**	24p multicoloured	....	65	65
668	**633**	24p multicoloured	....	65	65
669	**634**	24p multicoloured	....	65	65
670	**635**	24p multicoloured	....	65	65
663/70		*Set of 8*	....	4·50	4·50
		First Day Cover	....		4·75
		Presentation Pack	....	5·00	
		Stamp-cards (set of 8)	....	1·60	5·25
		Set of 8 Gutter Pairs	......	9·50	
MS671		137×109 mm. Nos. 663/70	......	4·00	4·25
		First Day Cover	....		4·50

Plate Nos.: All values 1A, 1B (each ×5)

Sheets: 50 (2 panes 5×5)

Imprint: Central, left-hand margin

Withdrawn: 27.2.96

636 Winston Churchill and Wireless

637 Union Jack and Royal Navy Ships off St. Peter Port

638 Royal Arms and Military Band

639 *Vega* (Red Cross supply ship)

640 Rejoicing Crowd

50th Anniversary of Liberation

(Des M. Whyte. Litho Enschedé)

1995 (9 MAY). *Perf* 13½×14 (C)

672	**636**	16p multicoloured	50	50
673	**637**	24p multicoloured	75	75
674	**638**	35p multicoloured	1·00	1·00
675	**639**	41p multicoloured	1·00	1·00
676	**640**	60p multicoloured	1·75	1·75
672/6		*Set of* 5	4·50	4·50
		First Day Cover		5·00
		Presentation Pack	5·00	
		Set of 5 *Gutter Pairs*	9·50	
MS677	189×75 mm. Nos. 672/6		4·50	4·50
		First Day Cover		5·00

Plate Nos.: 60p 1A, 1B, 1C, 1D (each ×4); others 1A, 1B (each ×4)
Sheets: 50 (2 panes 5×5)
Imprint: Central, side margins
Withdrawn: 8.5.96

641 Silhouette of Doves on Ground

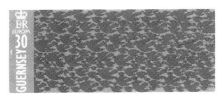

642 Silhouette of Doves in Flight

Europa. Peace and Freedom

(Des K. Bassford, Litho Walsall)

1995 (9 MAY). *Perf* 14 (C)

678	**641**	25p multicoloured	65	65
679	**642**	30p multicoloured	85	85
678/9		*Set of* 2	1·50	1·50
		First Day Cover		1·75
		Presentation Pack	1·75	

The designs of Nos. 678/9 each provide a stereogram or hidden three-dimensional image of a single dove designed by D. Burder.

Plate Nos.: Both values 1A, 1B, 1C (each ×4)
Sheets: 10 (2×5)
Imprint: Central, bottom margin
Withdrawn: 8.5.96

643 Prince Charles, Castle Cornet and Bailiwick Arms

Royal Visit

(Des C. Abbott. Litho Questa)

1995 (9 MAY). *Perf* 14 (C)

680	**643**	£1.50 multicoloured	4·00	4·00
		First Day Cover		4·25
		Presentation Pack	4·50	
		Gutter Pair	8·25	

Plate Nos.: 1A, 1B, 1C, 1D (each ×5)
Sheets: 40 (2 panes 5×4)
Imprint: Central, left-hand margin
Withdrawn: 8.5.96

643a (*illustration reduced. Actual size* 110×90 mm)

'Singapore '95' International Stamp Exhibition

(Des R. Gorringe and M. Whyte. Litho Cartor)

1995 (1 SEPT). *Sheet* 110×90 mm *containing stamp as No. 581 with changed imprint date. Perf* 13 (C)

MS681	**643**a	£1 multicoloured	2·50	2·50
		First Day Cover		2·75
		Presentation Pack	3·00	

Withdrawn: 31.8.96

644

645

646

647

50th Anniversary of United Nations

(Des K. Bassford. Litho and embossed Enschedé)

1995 (24 OCT). *Perf* 14×13½ (C)

682	**644**	50p pale new blue and gold	1·25	1·25
		a. *Block of* 4. *Nos.* 682/5	5·00	
683	**645**	50p pale new blue and gold	1·25	1·25
684	**646**	50p pale new blue and gold	1·25	1·25
685	**647**	50p pale new blue and gold	1·25	1·25
682/5		*Set of* 4	5·00	5·00
		First Day Cover		5·25
		Presentation Pack	5·25	

Plate Nos.: 1A–1A

Sheets: 36 (6×6). Nos. 682/5 were printed together, *se-tenant*, throughout the sheet with each block of 4 showing the complete United Nations emblem

Imprint: Central, side margins

Withdrawn: 23.10.96

648 "Christmas Trees for Sale in Bern" **649**
(Cornelia Nussbrum-Weibel)

650 "Evening Snowfall" **651**
(Katerina Mertikas)

652 "It came upon a Midnight Clear" **653**
(Georgia Guback)

654 "Children of the World" **655**

Christmas. 50th Anniversary of U.N.I.C.E.F.

(Adapted M. Whyte from U.N.I.C.E.F. Christmas Cards. Litho B.D.T.)

1995 (16 NOV). *Perf* 13 (C)

686	**648**	13p multicoloured	40	40
		a. *Horiz pair. Nos.* 686/7	80	80
687	**649**	13p multicoloured	40	40
688	**650**	13p + 1p multicoloured	40	40
		a. *Horiz pair. Nos.* 688/9	80	80
689	**651**	13p + 1p multicoloured	40	40
690	**652**	24p multicoloured	70	70
		a. *Horiz pair. Nos.* 690/1	1·40	1·40
691	**653**	24p multicoloured	70	70
692	**654**	24p + 2p multicoloured	70	70
		a. *Horiz pair. Nos.* 692/3	1·40	1·40
693	**655**	24p + 2p multicoloured	70	70
686/93		*Set of 8*	4·00	4·00
		First Day Cover		4·25
		Presentation Pack	4·25	

Sheets: 12 (4×3), the two designs for each value printed together, *se-tenant*, in horizontal pairs throughout the sheets, each pair forming a composite design

Withdrawn: 15.11.96

Yearbook 1995

1995 (1 DEC). *Comprises Nos. 663/93 and A77/84*

Yearbook .... 45·00

656 Princess Anne (President, Save the Children Fund) and Children

657 Queen Elizabeth II and People of the Commonwealth

Europa. Famous Women

(Des D. Miller. Litho B.D.T.)

1996 (21 APR). *Perf* 14 (C)

694	**656**	25p multicoloured	65	65
695	**657**	30p multicoloured	85	85
694/5		*Set of 2*	1·50	1·50
		First Day Cover		1·75
		Presentation Pack	1·75	

The background designs of Nos. 694/5 continue on to the vertical sheet margins.

Plate Nos.: Both values 1A, 1B (each ×4)

Sheets: 10 (2×5)

Withdrawn: 20.4.97

658 England v U.S.S.R., 1968 **659**

660 Italy v Belgium, 1972 **661**

662 Ireland v Netherlands, 1988 **663**

664 Denmark v Germany, 1992 Final **665**

European Football Championship

(Des M. Whyte. Litho Questa)

1996 (25 APR). *Perf* 14½×14 (C)

696	**658**	16p multicoloured	55	55
		a. *Horiz pair. Nos.* 696/7	1·10	1·10
697	**659**	16p multicoloured	55	55
698	**660**	24p multicoloured	75	75
		a. *Horiz pair. Nos.* 698/9	1·50	1·50
699	**661**	24p multicoloured	75	75
700	**662**	35p multicoloured	80	80
		a. *Horiz pair. Nos.* 700/1	1·60	1·60
701	**663**	35p multicoloured	80	80
702	**664**	41p multicoloured	95	95
		a. *Horiz pair. Nos.* 702/3	1·90	1·90
703	**665**	41p multicoloured	95	95
696/703		*Set of 8*	5·50	5·50
		First Day Cover		6·00
		Presentation Pack	6·00	
		Souvenir Folder (complete sheets)	22·00	

Plate Nos.: All values 1A (×4)

Sheets: 8 (2×4), the two designs for each value printed together, *se-tenant*, in horizontal pairs throughout sheets with illustrated margins, each pair forming a composite design

Withdrawn: 24.4.97

666a Maj-Gen. Brock meeting Tecumseh (Indian Chief) (24p); Maj-Gen. Isaac Brock on Horseback, 1812 (£1) (*illustration reduced. Actual size* 110×90 *mm*)

'CAPEX '96' International Stamp Exhibition, Toronto

(Des A. Peck. Litho Enschedé)

1996 (8 JUNE). *Sheet* 110×90 *mm. Perf* 13½ (C)

MS704	666a	24p, £1 multicoloured	.....	2·50	2·75
		First Day Cover	....		3·25
		Presentation Pack	....	3·25	

Withdrawn: 7.6.97

667 Runner

668 Throwing the Javelin

669 Throwing the Discus

670 Wrestling

671 Jumping

Centenary of Modern Olympic Games. Ancient Greek Athletes

(Des K. Bassford. Litho Questa)

1996 (19 JULY). *Perf* 14 (C)

705	**667**	16p black, orange-yellow & orge		50	50
706	**668**	24p black, orange-yellow & orge		95	95
707	**669**	41p black, orange-yellow & orge		1·10	1·10
708	**670**	55p black, orange-yellow & orge		1·40	1·40
709	**671**	60p black, orange-yellow & orge		1·60	1·60
705/9		*Set of* 5	....	5·00	5·00
		First Day Cover	....		5·50
		Presentation Pack	....	5·50	
		Set of 5 *Gutter Pairs*	......	10·50	
MS710		192×75 mm. Nos. 705/9	....	5·00	5·00

No. 708 also includes the 'OLYMPHILEX '96' International Stamp Exhibition, Atlanta, logo.

Plate Nos.: All values 1A, 1B (each ×3)

Sheets: 55p 50 (2 panes 5×5); others 100 (2 panes 10×5)

Imprint: Central, right-hand margin of top pane

Withdrawn: 18.7.97

672 Humphrey Bogart as Philip Marlowe

673 Peter Sellers as Inspector Clouseau

674 Basil Rathbone as Sherlock Holmes

675 Margaret Rutherford as Miss Marple

676 Warner Oland as Charlie Chan

Centenary of Cinema. Screen Detectives

(Des R. Ollington. Litho Enschedé)

1996 (6 NOV). *Perf* 15×14 (C)

711	**672**	16p multicoloured	30	35
		a. *Booklet pane. No.* 711×3 *with margins all round* . . .	90	
		b. *Booklet pane. Nos.* 711/15 *with margins all round*	3·50	
712	**673**	24p multicoloured	50	55
		a. *Booklet pane. No.* 712×3 *with margins all round*	1·50	
713	**674**	35p multicoloured	70	75
		a. *Booklet pane. No.* 713×3 *with margins all round*	2·10	
714	**675**	41p multicoloured	80	85
		a. *Booklet pane. No.* 714×3 *with margins all round*	2·40	
715	**676**	60p multicoloured	1·25	1·40
		a. *Booklet pane. No.* 715×3 *with margins all round*	3·75	
711/15		*Set of* 5	3·50	4·00
		First Day Cover		4·50
		Presentation Pack	4·50	
		Set of 5 *Gutter Pairs*	7·25	

Plate Nos.: All values 1A, 1B (each ×4)

Sheets: 50 (2 panes 5×5)

Imprint: Central, side margins

Withdrawn: 5.11.97

677 The Annunciation

678 Journey to Bethlehem

679 Arrival at the Inn

680 Angel and Shepherds

681 Mary, Joseph and Jesus in Stable

682 Shepherds worshipping Jesus

683 Three Kings following Star

684 Three Kings with Gifts

685 The Presentation in the Temple

686 Mary and Jesus

687 Joseph warned by Angel

688 The Flight into Egypt

689 Mary cradling Jesus

690 The Nativity

Christmas

(Des P. le Vasseur. Litho B.D.T.)

1996 (6 NOV). *Perf* 13 (C)

716	**677**	13p multicoloured	25	30
		a. *Sheetlet. Nos.* 716/27	3·00	
717	**678**	13p multicoloured	25	30
718	**679**	13p multicoloured	25	30
719	**680**	13p multicoloured	25	30
720	**681**	13p multicoloured	25	30
721	**682**	13p multicoloured	25	30
722	**683**	13p multicoloured	25	30
723	**684**	13p multicoloured	25	30
724	**685**	13p multicoloured	25	30
725	**686**	13p multicoloured	25	30
726	**687**	13p multicoloured	25	30
727	**688**	13p multicoloured	25	30
728	**689**	24p multicoloured	50	55
729	**690**	25p multicoloured	50	55
716/29		*Set of* 14	4·00	4·75
		First Day Cover		5·25
		Presentation Pack	5·25	
		Set of 2 *Gutter Pairs*	2·10	

Plate Nos.: 24p, 25p 1A, 1B (each ×4)

Sheets: 13p 12 (4×3) containing Nos. 716/27 *se-tenant*; 24p, 25p 100 (2 panes 5×10)

Imprint: 13p bottom, left-hand margin; 24p, 25p central, side margins

Withdrawn: 5.11.97

Yearbook 1996

1996 (1 DEC). *Comprises Nos. 582a, 694/729 and A85/95*
Yearbook . . . . 50·00

691 Holly Blue (*Celastrina argiolus*)

692 Hummingbird Hawk-moth (*Macroglossum stellatarum*)

693 Emperor Moth (*Saturnia pavonia*)

694 Brimstone (*Gonepteryx rhamni*)

695a Painted Lady (*Cynthia cardui*)

Endangered Species. Butterflies and Moths

(Des A. Peck. Litho B.D.T.)

1997 (12 FEB). *Perf* 14 (C)

730	**691**	18p multicoloured	. . . .	35	40
731	**692**	25p multicoloured	. . . .	50	55

732	**693**	26p multicoloured	. . . .	55	60
733	**694**	37p multicoloured	. . . .	75	80
730/3		*Set of 4*	. . . .	2·10	2·25
		First Day Cover	. . . .		3·00
		Presentation Pack	. . . .	3·00	
		Souvenir Folder (complete sheets)	. . . .	21·00	

MS734 92×68 mm. **695a** £1 multicoloured.
Perf 13½ (C) . . . . 2·00 2·10

		First Day Cover	. . . .		2·75
		Presentation Pack	. . . .	2·75	

No. **MS**734 includes the 'HONG KONG '97' International Stamp Exhibition logo on the sheet margin.

Plate Nos.: All values 1A, 1B (each ×4)

Sheets: 10 (2×5) with designs extending into side margins

26 **696** Gilliatt fighting Octopus

31 **697** Gilliatt grieving on Rock

Europa. Tales and Legends. Scenes from Les Travailleurs de la Mer by Victor Hugo

(Des M. Wilkinson. Litho Cartor)

1997 (24 APR). *Perf* 13½ (C)

735	**696**	26p multicoloured	. . . .	55	60
736	**697**	31p multicoloured	. . . .	60	65
735/6		*Set of 2*	. . . .	1·10	1·25
		First Day Cover	. . . .		2·00
		Presentation Pack	. . . .	2·00	

Plate Nos.: Both values 1A, 1B (each ×4)

Sheets: 10 (2×5) with enlarged inscribed margins at left

698 Shell Beach, Herm

699 La Seigneurie, Sark

703 Television, Video Camera and Satellite Dish

700 Castle Cornet, Guernsey

Guernsey Scenes

(Litho B.D.T)

1997 (24 APR). *Self-adhesive. Perf 9½* (C)

737	**698**	18p multicoloured	40	45
		a. *Booklet pane of 8*	3·00	
738	**699**	25p multicoloured	55	60
		a. *Booklet pane of 8*	4·25	
739	**700**	26p multicoloured	55	60
		a. *Booklet pane of 4*	2·10	
737/9		*Set of 3*	1·50	1·60
		First Day Cover		2·25
		Presentation Pack	2·25	

Nos. 737/9 were issued as stamp booklets or as rolls of 100 (18p and 25p).

704 Fax Machine, Telephones and Mobile Phone

705 Printing Press, Newspaper and Type

701*a* 19th-century Boatyard, St. Peter's Port (30p); *Costa Rica Packet* (coffee clipper) (£1) (*illustration reduced. Actual size* 110×90 *mm*)

706 Stamp, Coding Machine and Postbox

'PACIFIC '97' World Philatelic Exhibition, San Francisco

(Des C. Abbott. Litho Questa)

1997 (29 MAY). *Sheet* 110×90 *mm. Perf* 14 (C)

MS740	**701***a*	30p. brn-olive & gold; £1 mult. .	2·50	2·75
		First Day Cover		3·50
		Presentation Pack	3·50	

707 C.D., Computer and Disk

Methods of Communication

(Des Miranda Schofield. Litho Cartor)

1997 (21 AUG). *Perf* 13½×13 (C)

741	**702**	18p multicoloured	40	45
742	**703**	25p multicoloured	55	60
743	**704**	26p multicoloured	55	60
744	**705**	37p multicoloured	75	80
745	**706**	43p multicoloured	85	90
746	**707**	63p multicoloured	1·25	1·40
741/6		*Set of 6*	4·25	4·75
		First Day Cover		5·00
		Presentation Pack	5·00	
		Set of 6 Gutter Pairs	8·75	

702 Transistor Radio, Microphone and Radio Logos

Let us make your life a little easier

★ If you open a standing order account with us you'll find everything goes like clockwork.

★ You'll receive your order as soon as it is available.

★ Our friendly, helpful staff will answer any questions you might have.

★ Regular copies of our Philatelic News will give you full details of all issues with colour pictures.

★ There are no handling charges.

★ You will have the satisfaction and reassurance of dealing with us direct.

★ Single stamps, First Day Covers, Presentation Packs, Special Requirements.. we'll get them to you promptly and with no fuss.

You enjoy the simple life... well so do we.

Plate Nos.: All values 1A, 1B (each ×4)

Sheets: 50 (2 panes 5×5)

Imprint: Central, side margins

708 Teddy Bear
making Cake

709 Teddy Bears
decorating
Christmas Tree

710 Two Teddy Bears
in Armchair

711 Teddy Bear as
Father Christmas

712 Teddy Bears
unwrapping
Presents

713 Teddy Bears
eating Christmas
Dinner

Christmas. Teddy Bears

(Des Sally Diamond. Litho Walsall)

1997 (6 NOV). *Perf* 14½×14 (C)

747	**708**	15p multicoloured	. . . .	30	35
748	**709**	25p multicoloured	. . . .	50	55
749	**710**	26p multicoloured	. . . .	50	55
750	**711**	37p multicoloured	. . . .	75	80
751	**712**	43p multicoloured	. . . .	85	90
752	**713**	63p multicoloured	. . . .	1·25	1·40
747/52		Set of 6	. . . .	4·00	4·50
		First Day Cover		5·00
		Presentation Pack	5·00	
		Set of 6 Gutter Pairs	8·25	
MS753		123×107 mm. Nos. 747/52	4·00	4·50
		First Day Cover		5·00

Plate Nos.: All values 1A, 1B (each ×4)

Sheets: 50 (2 panes 5×5)

Imprint: Central, right-hand margin

714 Visiting Guernsey,
1957

715 Coronation Day,
1953 (inscr '1947')

716 Royal Family, 1957

717 On Royal Yacht,
1972

718 Queen Elizabeth
and Prince Philip at
Trooping the
Colour, 1987

719 Queen Elizabeth
and Prince Philip,
1997

71

Golden Wedding of Queen Elizabeth and Prince Philip

(Des M. Whyte. Litho Questa)

1997 (20 NOV). *Perf* 14½ (C)

754	**714**	18p multicoloured	35	40
		a. *Booklet pane. Nos. 754/5, each* ×3	2·50	
		b. *Booklet pane. Nos. 754/9* ..	4·25	
755	**715**	25p multicoloured	50	55
756	**716**	26p multicoloured	50	55
		a. *Booklet pane. Nos. 756/7, each* ×3	3·75	
757	**717**	37p multicoloured	75	80
758	**718**	43p multicoloured	85	90
		a. *Booklet pane. Nos. 758/9, each* ×3	6·25	
759	**719**	63p multicoloured	1·25	1·40
754/9		*Set of* 6	4·25	4·50
		First Day Cover..........		5·00
		Presentation Pack........	5·00	
		Set of 6 *Gutter Pairs*	8·75	

Plate Nos.: All values 1A, 1B (each ×6)

Sheets: 50 (2 panes 5×5)

Imprint: Central, right-hand margin

Yearbook 1997

1997 (1 DEC). *Comprises Nos.* 572*b*, 576*b*, 730/59, A70*b*, A72*b*/*c and* A96/101

	Yearbook	50·00

POSTAGE DUE STAMPS

D **1** Castle Cornet

D **2** Castle Cornet

(Des R. Granger Barrett. Photo Delrieu)

1969 (1 OCT). *Face value in black; background colour given.*
No wmk. Perf 12½×12 (C)

D1	D **1**	1d plum	. . . .	2·25	1·25
D2		2d bright green	. . . .	2·25	1·25
D3		3d vermilion	. . . .	3·75	4·00
D4		4d ultramarine	. . . .	5·00	5·00
D5		5d yellow-ochre	. . . .	5·50	5·50
D6		6d turquoise-blue	. . . .	6·50	6·00
D7		1s lake-brown	. . . .	17·00	17·00
D1/7		*Set of* 7	. . . .	35·00	35·00

Sheets: 60 (10×6)

Quantities sold: 1d 82,802; 2d 75,340; 3d 74,532; 4d 74,659; 5d
71,129; 6d 72,912; 1s 71,659

Withdrawn and Invalidated: 14.2.72

Decimal Currency

(Des R. Granger Barrett. Photo Delrieu)

1971 (15 FEB)–**76.** *No wmk. Perf* 12½×12 (C)

D8	D **2**	½p plum (*a*)	. . . .	10	10
D9		1p bright green (*a*)	. . . .	10	10
D10		2p vermilion (*a*)	. . . .	10	10
D11		3p ultramarine (*a*)	. . . .	10	15
D12		4p yellow-ochre (*a*)	. . . .	10	15
D13		5p turquoise-blue (*a*)	. . . .	10	15
D14		6p violet (*c*)	. . . .	15	20
D15		8p yellow-orange (*b*)	. . . .	25	20
D16		10p lake-brown (*a*)	. . . .	30	30
D17		15p grey (*c*)	. . . .	40	40
D8/17		*Set of* 10	. . . .	1·50	1·60
D1/13, 16		*Presentation Pack* (*a*)	. . . . . .	60·00	
D8/17		*Presentation Pack* (*c*)	. . . . . .	1·75	

Printings: (*a*) 15.2.71; (*b*) 7.10.75; (*c*) 10.2.76

Sheets: 60 (10×6)

Withdrawn: 14.2.72 Presentation Pack (Nos. D1/13 and D16); 1.8.78
½p to 15p (½p and 1p sold out by 6.78)

D **3** St. Peter Port

(Photo Delrieu)

1977 (2 AUG)–**80.** *Face value in black; background colour
given. Perf* 13 (C)

D18	D **3**	½p lake-brown (*a*)	. . . .	10	10
D19		1p bright purple (*a*)	. . . .	10	10
D20		2p bright orange (*a*)	. . . .	10	10
D21		3p vermilion (*a*)	. . . .	10	10
D22		4p turquoise-blue (*a*)	. . . .	15	15
D23		5p yellow-green (*a*)	. . . .	15	15
D24		6p turquoise-green (*a*)	. . . .	20	20
D25		8p brown-ochre (*a*)	. . . .	25	25
D26		10p ultramarine (*a*)	. . . .	30	30
D27		14p green (*b*)	. . . .	35	35
D28		15p bright violet (*a*)	. . . .	35	35
D29		16p rose-red (*b*)	. . . .	45	45
D18/29		*Set of* 12	. . . .	2·10	2·10
D18/26, 28		*Presentation Pack*	1·75	

Printings: (*a*) 2.8.77; (*b*) 5.2.80

Sheets: 50 (5×10)

Withdrawn: 12.7.83 (Presentation Pack sold out earlier)

D **4** Milking Cow

D **5** Vale Mill

D **6** Sark Cottage

D **7** Quay-side, St.
Peter Port

D **8** Well, Water Lane,
Moulin Huet

D **9** Seaweed
Gathering

D **10** Upper Walk,
White Rock

D **11** Cobo Bay

D **12** Saint's Bay

D **13** La Coupee, Sark

D **14** Old Harbour, St.
Peter Port

D **15** Greenhouse,
Doyle Road, St.
Peter Port

Guernsey Scenes, c. 1900

(Des C. Abbott. Litho Questa)

1982 (13 JULY). *Perf* 14½ (C)

D30	D **4**	1p indigo, blue-black & brt grn	10	10
D31	D **5**	2p yellow-brown, sepia & azure	10	10
D32	D **6**	3p blackish green, black & lilac	10	10
D33	D **7**	4p bottle green, blk & dull orge	10	10
D34	D **8**	5p deep violet-blue, blue-black and turquoise-green	10	10
D35	D **9**	16p dp grey-blue, dp bl & cobalt	30	35
D36	D **10**	18p steel bl, indigo & apple grn	35	40
D37	D **11**	20p brown-olive, agate & pale bl	40	45
D38	D **12**	25p Prussian blue, blue-black and rose-pink	50	55
D39	D **13**	30p deep bluish green, blackish olive and bistre-yellow	60	65
D40	D **14**	50p olive-brown, sepia and dull violet-blue	1·00	1·10
D41	D **15**	£1 lt brown, brown & pale brn	2·00	2·10
D30/41		*Set of 12*	5·25	5·75
		Presentation Pack.	5·75	

Sheets: 50 (5×10)

Imprint: Bottom corner, right-hand margin

STAMP BOOKLETS

PRICES given are for complete booklets. Booklets Nos. SB1/12 are stitched.

B **1** Military Uniforms

1969 (12 DEC). *White covers as Type* B **1**, *printed in black*
SB1   2s booklet containing 3×4d (No. 18*a*), 2×5d (No. 19*a*) and 2×1d (No. 14*c*) (*cover showing Trooper, Royal Guernsey Cavalry* (*Light Dragoons*), 1814) . . . .   2·00
SB2   4s booklet containing 6×4d (No. 18*a*), 4×5d (No. 19*a*) and 4×1d (No. 14*c*) (*cover showing Officer, St. Martin's Company* (*La Milice Bleue*), *Guernsey, 1720*) . . . .   2·75
SB3   6s booklet containing 9×4d (No. 18*a*), 6×5d (No. 19*a*) and 6×1d (No. 14*c*) (*cover showing Colour Sergeant of Grenadiers and Rifleman, East* (*Town*) *Regiment, Guernsey, 1833*) . . . .   5·00

Withdrawn: 14.2.72

1970 (29 JUNE). *White covers as Type* B **1**. *Printed in black* (SB4), *green* (SB5) *or red* (SB6). *Same composition as Nos. SB1/3*
SB4   2s booklet (*cover showing Officer, Royal Guernsey Horse Artillery, 1793*) . . . .   4·50
SB5   4s booklet (*cover showing Gunner, Royal Guernsey Artillery, 1743*) . . . .   14·00
SB6   6s booklet (*cover showing Sergeant, Royal Guernsey Light Infantry, 1832*) . . . .   13·00

Quantities sold: 2s (SB1, SB4), 81,928; 4s (SB2, SB5), 23,817; 6s (SB3, SB6), 25,123

Withdrawn: 14.2.72

Decimal Currency

1971 (15 FEB). *White covers as Type* B **1**. *Printed in black* (SB7), *green* (SB8) *or red* (SB9)
SB7   10p booklet containing 2×½p (No. 44*a*), 2×2p (No. 47*a*) and 2×2½p (No. 48*b*) (*cover showing Officer, Royal Guernsey Horse Artillery, 1850*)   2·50
SB8   20p booklet containing 4×½p (No. 44*a*), 4×2p (No. 47*a*) and 4×2½p (No. 48*b*) (*cover showing Sergeant, Guernsey Light Infantry* (*Grenadiers*), *1826*) . . . .   1·00
SB9   30p booklet containing 6×½p (No. 44*a*), 6×2p (No. 47*a*) and 6×2½p (No. 48*b*) (*cover showing Sergeant and Bandsman, Royal Guernsey Light Infantry* (*North Regiment*), *1866*) . . . .   2·00

Withdrawn: 27.6.73 (SB7); 12.3.75 (SB8); 15.1.75 (SB9)

1973 (2 APR). *White covers as Type* B **1**. *Printed in black* (SB10), *green* (SB11) *or red* (SB12)
SB10 10p booklet containing 2×½p (No. 44*ab*), 2×2p (No. 47*ab*) and 2×2½p (No. 48*ba*) (*cover showing Officer, Guernsey Horse Artillery, 1828*) . . . .   1·00
SB11 20p booklet containing 4×½p (No. 44*ab*), 4×2p (No. 47*ab*) and 4×2½p (No. 48*ba*) (*cover showing Grenadier, Guernsey Light Infantry, 1792*) . . . .   1·25
SB12 30p booklet containing 6×½p (No. 44*ab*), 6×2p (No. 47*ab*) and 6×2½p (No. 48*ba*) (*cover showing Insignia, Royal Guernsey Light Infantry*) . . . .   1·50

Nos. SB10/12 are inscribed 'January 1973' on back cover.

Withdrawn: 1.4.75

B **2** Arms of Guernsey

1974 (2 APR). *Silver* (SB13) *or gold cover* (SB14) *as Type* B **2**
SB13 10p booklet containing five ½p stamps and three 2½p in *se-tenant* strip (No. 98*a*)   60
SB14 35p booklet containing four ½p stamps, six 2½p and six 3p in *se-tenant* pane (No. 98*b*)   1·25

The strips and panes have the left-hand selvedge stuck into booklet covers and then folded and supplied in plastic wallets.

Withdrawn 6.2.79

1977 (8 FEB). *Green cover as Type* B **2**
SB15 20p booklet containing No. 99*a*   80

The note beneath SB14 also applies here.

Withdrawn: 12.2.80

BOOKLET PANES from Nos. SB16/18 are loose within card covers supplied in plastic sachets.

1978 (7 FEB). *Blue cover as Type* B **2**
SB16 10p booklet containing No. 99*b*   50

Withdrawn: 12.2.80

1979 (13 FEB). *Covers as Type* B **2**
SB17 10p booklet containing No. 178*a* (*black and green cover*)   60
SB18 30p booklet containing No. 179*a* (*black and red cover*) . . . .   1·25

Withdrawn: 23.2.82

B **3** Castle Cornet

B **4** View of Post Office Headquarters, St. Peter Port

1980 (6 MAY). *Horiz covers as Type B* **3**. *Folded*
SB19   30p booklet containing No. 177*a* (*blue printed
         cover, Type* C) . . . .   1·00
SB20   50p booklet containing No. 177*b* (*brown
         printed cover showing view from the sea*)   ..   1·25

Withdrawn: 4.5.83

1981 (24 FEB). *Covers similar to Type B* **3**, *but vert. Folded*
SB21   60p booklet containing No. 180*a* (*red printed
         cover showing Fort Grey*)   . . . .   1·75
SB22   £1.20 booklet containing No. 180*b* (*green
         printed cover showing Rokaine Castle*)   . . . .   2·75

Withdrawn 23.2.84

1982 (2 FEB). *Covers similar to Type B* **3** *showing Fort George.
Folded*
SB23   70p booklet containing No. 181*b* (*orange
         printed cover showing main entrance*) . . . . . .   2·25
SB24   £1.30 booklet containing No. 181*c* (*magenta
         printed cover showing aerial view of Citadel*)   3·75

Withdrawn: 22.7.85

1983 (14 MAR). *Covers similar to Type B* **3**. *Folded*
SB25   £1 booklet containing No. 180*c* (*new blue
         printed cover showing States Office, St. Peter
         Port*) . . . .   3·00
SB26   £1.30 booklet containing No. 180*d* (*sepia
         printed cover showing Constable's Office, St.
         Peter Port*) . . . .   3·75

Withdrawn: 22.7.85

BOOKLET PANES from Nos. SB27/38 are loose within card
covers.

1984 (18 SEPT). *Multicoloured covers as Type B* **4**
SB27   £1 booklet containing No. 299*a* . . . .   4·00
SB28   £1.30 booklet containing No. 299*b* (*cover
         showing Head Post Office, St. Peter Port*)   ..   4·75

Withdrawn 1.87

1985 (19 MAR). *Multicoloured covers as Type B* **4**
SB29   £1.20 booklet containing No. 304*a* (*cover
         showing French Halles, St. Peter Port*) . . . . . .   4·75
SB30   £1.30 booklet containing No. 304*b* (*cover
         showing Market Halls, St. Peter Port*) . . . . . .   4·50

Withdrawn: 8.87

1985 (2 DEC). *Multicoloured cover as Type B* **4**, *but vert*
SB31   50p booklet containing No. 297*a* (*cover
         showing Victoria Tower, St. Peter Port*)   . . . .   2·75

Withdrawn: 8.87

1986 (1 APR). *Multicoloured cover as Type B* **4**, *but vert*
SB32   £1.20 booklet containing No. 305*a* (*cover
         showing St. James-the-Less, St. Peter Port*)   4·50

Withdrawn: 2.89

1987 (30 MAR). *Multicoloured covers as Type B* **4**, *but vert*
SB33   £1 booklet containing No. 298*a* (*cover
         showing Lukis Observatory, St. Peter Port*)   ..   4·25
SB34   £1.30 booklet containing No. 306*a* (*cover
         showing Weighbridge, St. Peter Port*) . . . . . .   4·50

Withdrawn: 2.89

1988 (28 MAR). *Multicoloured covers as Type B* **4**, *but vert*
SB35   £1 booklet containing No. 299*c* (*cover
         showing North Pier Light, St. Peter Port*) . . . .   4·00
SB36   £1.40 booklet containing No. 306*ba* (*cover
         showing Castle Light, St. Peter Port*) . . . . . .   4·25

Withdrawn 2.90

1989 (28 Feb). *Multicoloured covers as Type B* **4**, *but vert*
SB37   £1 booklet containing No. 299*d* (*cover
         showing Town Church, St. Peter Port*) . . . . . .   4·50
SB38   £1.20 booklet containing No. 306*bb* (*cover
         showing St. Barnabas Church, St. Peter Port*)   4·75

Withdrawn: 12.90

B **5** Opening Ceremony, 1939
(*illustration reduced. Actual size* 163×97 *mm*)

50th Anniversary of Guernsey Airport

1989 (5 MAY). *Multicoloured cover, Type* B **5**. *Booklet contains text and illustrations on panes and interleaving pages. Stitched*
SB39   £3.90 booklet containing Nos. 456a, 458a and
         460a . . . .   11·00

Quantity sold: 38,025
Sold out: By 11.89

1989 (27 DEC). *Multicoloured covers as Type* B **4**, *but vert*
SB40   £1.20 booklet containing No. 301a (*cover
         showing Fish Market, St. Peter Port*) . . . . . .   4·25
SB41   £1.70 booklet containing No. 308a (*cover
         showing Lloyds Bank, St. Peter Port*) . . . . . .   4·75

Withdrawn: 21.5.92

B **6** Crown Hotel
(*illustration reduced. Actual size* 163×97 *mm*)

50th Anniversary of First Guernsey Stamps

1991 (18 FEB). *Multicoloured cover, Type* B **6**. *Booklet contains text on panes and text and illustrations on interleaving pages. Stitched*
SB42   £4.41 booklet containing No. 517a×3 . . . . . .   11·00

Quantity sold: 31,955
Withdrawn: 17.2.92

1991 (2 APR). *Multicoloured covers as Type* B **4**, *but vert*
SB43   £1.30 booklet containing No. 300a (*cover
         showing Golden Lion Inn, St. Peter Port*) . . . .   4·00
SB44   £1.80 booklet containing No. 309a (*cover
         showing National Trust Building, St. Peter
         Port*) . . . .   5·25

Withdrawn: 21.5.92

B **7** Carnations

1992 (22 MAY). *Multicoloured covers as Type* B **7**. *Panes attached by selvedge*
SB45   £1.45 booklet containing pane No. 572ac
         (*cover Type* B **7**) . . . .   3·00
SB46   £1.80 booklet containing pane No. 574ac
         (*cover showing mixed freesias*) . . . .   3·50

B **8** Bow of Ship and Relics
(*illustration reduced. Actual size* 163×97 *mm*)

"Operation Asterix"

1992 (18 SEPT). *Multicoloured cover, Type* B **8**. *Booklet contains text and illustrations on interleaving pages. Stitched*
SB47   £5.60 booklet containing No. 583a×4 . . . . . .   13·00

Quantity sold: 24,211
Withdrawn: 17.9.93

1993 (2 MAR)–**95**. *Multicoloured covers as Type* B **7**, *but different Guernsey Post Office logo. Without barcode on the reverse. Panes attached by selvedge*
SB48   £1.12 booklet containing pane No. 577ab
         (*cover showing Lisianthus*) . . . .   2·25
SB49   £1.28 booklet containing pane No. 572ad
         (*cover Type* B **7**) . . . .   3·25
         a. With barcode sticker on reverse (6.95) . . . .   3·25
         b. Barcode printed on reverse (10.95) . . . . . .   3·00

SB50 £1.92 booklet containing pane No. 575*ab*
(*cover showing standard roses*) . . . . 4·50
a. With barcode sticker on reverse (3.95) . . . . 4·50
b. Barcode printed on reverse (6.95) . . . . . . 4·00

B **9** Thomas de la Rue
(*illustration reduced. Actual size 163×97 mm*)

Birth Bicentenary of Thomas de la Rue (printer)

1993 (27 JULY). *Multicoloured cover as Type B* **9**. *Booklet contains text and illustrations on interleaving pages. Stapled*
SB51 £5.60 booklet containing panes Nos. 617*a*/21*a* 11·00

Withdrawn: 26.7.94

1994 (18 FEB). *Multicoloured cover as Type B* **7**, *but different Guernsey Post Office logo. With barcode on reverse. Pane attached by selvedge*
SB52 £1 booklet containing pane No. 576*ab* (*cover showing Iris "Ideal"*) . . . . 2·00

B **10** Guernsey View and 1936 Bentley
(*illustration reduced. Actual size 162×97 mm*)

Centenary of First Car in Guernsey

1994 (19 JULY). *Black and grey cover as Type B* **10**. *Booklet contains text and illustrations on labels attached to panes and on interleaving pages. Stitched*
SB53 £7 booklet containing panes Nos. 639*a*/43*a* 14·00

Withdrawn 18.7.95

B **11** Coins, Postbox and Stamps "Face"

Greetings Stamps. "The Welcoming Face of Guernsey"

1995 (28 FEB). *Multicoloured cover as Type B* **11**. *Miniature sheet folded and attached by selvedge*
SB54 £1.92 booklet containing No. **MS**671 . . . . . . 4·25

Withdrawn: 27.2.96

B **12** Stamps and Magnifying Glass

Centenary of Cinema. Screen Detectives

1996 (6 NOV). *Multicoloured cover as Type B* **12**. *Booklet contains text and illustrations on margins of panes and interleaving pages. Stitched*
SB55 £7.04 booklet containing panes Nos. 711*a*/15*a* 14·00

Withdrawn: 5.11.97

B **13** Freesia 'Pink Glow'

1997 (2 JAN). *Multicoloured covers as Type B* **13**. *Panes attached by selvedge.*

SB56	£1.04 booklet containing pane No. 576*bb* (*cover Type B* **13**)	2·10
SB57	£1.44 booklet containing pane No. 572*bb* (*cover showing Standard Rose*)	3·00
SB58	£2 booklet containing No. 576*ab*×2 (*cover showing Iris 'Ideal'*)	4·00

B **14** Castle Cornet, Guernsey

Guernsey Scenes

1997 (24 APR). *Multicoloured covers as Type B* **14**. *Self-adhesive.*

SB59	£1.04, booklet containing pane No. 739*a* (*cover as Type B* **14**)	2·10
SB60	£1.44, booklet containing pane No. 737*a* (*cover showing Shell Beach, Herm*)	3·00
SB61	£2 booklet containing pane No. 738*a* (*cover showing La Seigneurie, Sark*)	4·00

B **15** Queen Elizabeth and Prince Philip
(*illustration reduced. Actual size 162×95 mm*)

1997 (20 NOV). *Golden Wedding of Queen Elizabeth and Prince Philip. Multicoloured cover as Type B* **15**. *Booklet contains text and illustrations on panes and interleaving pages. Stitched*

SB62	£8.48 booklet containing Nos. 754*a*/*b*, 756*a* and 758*a*..........................	17·00

ALDERNEY

The following issues are provided by the Guernsey Post Office for use on Alderney. They are also valid for postal purposes throughout the rest of the Bailiwick of Guernsey.

A **1** Island Map

A **2** Hanging Rock

A **3** States' Building, St. Anne

A **4** St. Anne's Church

A **5** Yachts in Braye Bay

A **6** Victoria St, St. Anne

A **7** Map of Channel

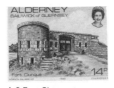

A **8** Fort Clonque

A **9** Corblets Bay and Fort

A **10** Old Tower, St. Anne

A **11** Golf Course and Essex Castle

A **12** Old Harbour

A **12***a* Quesnard Lighthouse

A **12***b* Braye Harbour

A **12***c* Island Hall

A **12***d* J. T. Daly (steam locomotive)

A **12***e* Louis Marchesi of Round Table (lifeboat)

Island Scenes

(Des G. Drummond. Litho B.D.T. (20p to 28p) or photo Courvoisier (others))

1983 (14 JUNE)–**93**. *Granite paper* (1p to 18p). *Perf* 15×14 (20p to 28p) *or* 11½ (*others*), *both comb*

A1	A **1**	1p multicoloured (*a*)	10	10
A2	A **2**	4p multicoloured (*a*)	10	10
A3	A **3**	9p multicoloured (*a*)	20	25
A4	A **4**	10p multicoloured (*a*)	25	25
A5	A **5**	11p multicoloured (*a*)	25	25
A6	A **6**	12p multicoloured (*a*)	25	30
A7	A **7**	13p multicoloured (*a*)	25	30
A8	A **8**	14p multicoloured (*a*)	30	35
A9	A **9**	15p multicoloured (*a*)	30	35
A10	A **10**	16p multicoloured (*a*)	30	35
A11	A **11**	17p multicoloured (*a*)	35	40
A12	A **12**	18p multicoloured (*a*)	35	40

A12a	A **12a**	20p multicoloured (b)	. . . .	80	80
A12b	A **12b**	21p multicoloured (c)	. . . .	80	80
A12c	A **12c**	23p multicoloured (d)	. . . .	70	70
A12d	A **12d**	24p multicoloured (e)	. . . .	1·75	1·75
A12e	A **12e**	28p multicoloured (e)	. . . .	2·00	2·00
A1/12e		*Set of 17*	. . . .	8·00	8·00
		First Day Covers (5)	. . . .		23·00
		Presentation Packs (2)	. .	10·00	
		Set of 17 Gutter Pairs	. . . .	16·00	

Printings: (a) 14.6.83; (b) 27.12.89; (c) 2.4.91; (d) 6.2.92; (e) 2.3.93

Plate and Cylinder Nos.: 1p, 12p, 13p, 17p, 20p to 28p 1A, 1B, 1C, 1D (each ×4); others 1A, 1B, 1C, 1D (each ×5)

Sheets: 40 (2 panes 5×4)

Imprint: Central, bottom margin

Withdrawn: 4.6.94

A **13** Oystercatcher

A **14** Turnstone

A **15** Ringed Plover

A **16** Dunlin

A **17** Curlew

Birds

(Des and photo Harrison)

1984 (12 JUNE). *Perf* 14½ (C)

A13	A **13**	9p multicoloured	. . . .	1·50	1·50
A14	A **14**	13p multicoloured	. . . .	1·50	2·00
A15	A **15**	26p multicoloured	. . . .	5·00	4·00
A16	A **16**	28p multicoloured	. . . .	5·00	4·00
A17	A **17**	31p multicoloured	. . . .	5·00	4·00
A13/17		*Set of 5*	. . . .	16·00	14·00
		First Day Cover	. . . .		14·00
		Presentation Pack	. . . .	20·00	
		Set of 5 Gutter Pairs	. . . . . .	32·00	

Cylinder Nos.: All values 1A, 1B (each ×5)

Sheets: 50 (2 panes 5×5)

Imprint: Bottom margin, right-hand corner

Quantities sold: 9p 285,931; 13p 360,619; 26p 246,916; 28p 261,370; 31p 334,484

Withdrawn: 11.6.85

A **18** Westland Wessex Hu Mk 5 Helicopter of the Queen's Flight

A **19** Britten Norman 'long-nose' Trislander

A **20** De Havilland D.H.114 Heron 1B

A **21** De Havilland D.H.89A Dragon Rapide *Sir Henry Lawrence*

A **22** Saro A.21 Windhover Flying Boat *City of Portsmouth*

50th Anniversary of Alderney Airport

(Des A. Theobald. Photo Courvoisier)

1985 (19 MAR). *Granite paper. Perf* 11½ (C)

A18	A **18**	9p multicoloured	. . . .	2·50	2·25
A19	A **19**	13p multicoloured	. . . .	2·50	3·00
A20	A **20**	29p multicoloured	. . . .	6·00	5·00
A21	A **21**	31p multicoloured	. . . .	6·50	5·50
A22	A **22**	34p multicoloured	. . . .	7·00	5·50
A18/22		*Set of 5*	. . . .	22·00	19·00
		First Day Cover	. . . .		19·00
		Presentation Pack	. . . .	25·00	

Cylinder Nos.: All values A1–1–1–1–1, B1–1–1–1–1

Sheets: 25 (5×5)

Quantities sold: 9p 294,437; 13p 321,276; 29p 231,422; 31p 171,528; 34p 162,429

Withdrawn: 18.3.86

A **23** Royal Engineers, 1890

A **24** Duke of Albany's Own Highlanders (72nd Highland Regt), 1856

A **25** Royal Artillery, 1855

A **26** South Hampshire Regiment, 1810

A **30** Fort Clonque

A **31** Fort Albert

A **27** Royal Irish Regiment, 1782

Regiments of the Alderney Garrison

(Des E. Stemp. Litho Harrison)

1985 (24 SEPT). *Perf* 14½ (C)

A23	A **23**	9p multicoloured	....	45	45
A24	A **24**	14p multicoloured	....	1·00	1·00
A25	A **25**	29p multicoloured	....	1·50	1·50
A26	A **26**	31p multicoloured	....	1·75	1·75
A27	A **27**	34p multicoloured	....	2·00	2·00
A23/7		Set of 5	....	6·00	6·00
		First Day Cover	....		8·00
		Presentation Pack	....	10·00	
		Set of 5 Gutter Pairs	......	12·00	

No. A24 shows the tartan and insignia of the 78th Highland Regiment in error.

Plate Nos.: All values 1A, 1B, 1C, 1D (each ×5)

Sheets: 50 (2 panes 5×5)

Imprint: Central, left-hand margin of each pane

Quantities sold: 9p 286,572; 14p 283,493; 29p 224,196; 31p 151,948; 34p 145,422

Withdrawn: 23.9.86

A **28** Fort Grosnez

A **29** Fort Tourgis

Alderney Forts

(Des R. Reed. Litho Cartor)

1986 (23 SEPT). *Perf* 13×13½ (C)

A28	A **28**	10p multicoloured	....	1·10	1·10
A29	A **29**	14p multicoloured	....	1·75	1·75
A30	A **30**	31p multicoloured	....	4·00	4·00
A31	A **31**	34p multicoloured	....	4·25	4·25
A28/31		Set of 4	....	10·00	10·00
		First Day Cover	....		12·00
		Presentation Pack	....	14·00	
		Set of 4 Gutter Pairs	......	20·00	

Plate Nos.: All values 1A, 1B, 1C, 1D (each ×5)

Sheets: 50 (2 panes 5×5)

Imprint: Left-hand margin of left-hand pane

Quantities sold: 10p 325,706; 14p 231,891; 31p 143,423; 34p 138,556

Withdrawn: 22.9.87

A **32** *Liverpool* (full-rigged ship), 1902

A **33** *Petit Raymond* (schooner), 1906

A **34** *Maina* (yacht), 1910

A **35** *Burton* (steamer), 1911

A **36** *Point Law* (oil tanker), 1975

Alderney Shipwrecks

(Des C. Jaques. Litho Questa)

1987 (5 MAY). *Perf* 14×14½ (C)

A32	A **32**	11p multicoloured	. . . .	2·00	1·50
A33	A **33**	15p multicoloured	. . . .	2·25	2·00
A34	A **34**	29p multicoloured	. . . .	5·50	5·00
A35	A **35**	31p multicoloured	. . . .	6·00	5·50
A36	A **36**	34p multicoloured	. . . .	6·50	6·00
A32/6		*Set of* 5	. . . .	20·00	18·00
		First Day Cover			18·00
		Presentation Pack		24·00	
		Set of 5 *Gutter Pairs*		40·00	

Plate Nos. All values 1A, 1B, 1C, 1D (each ×4)

Sheets: 50 (2 panes 5×5)

Imprint: Bottom, right-hand margin of each pane

Quantities sold: 11p 228,998; 15p 233,861; 29p 139,453; 31p 148,572; 34p 145,641

Withdrawn: 4.5.88

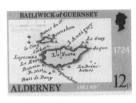

A **37** Moll's Map of 1724

A **38** Bastide's Survey of 1739

A **39** Goodwin's Map of 1831

A **40** General Staff Map of 1943

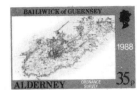

A **41** Ordnance Survey Map of 1988

250th Anniversary of Bastide's Survey of Alderney

(Des J. Cooter. Litho Enschedé)

1989 (7 JULY). *Perf* 13½×14 (C)

A37	A **37**	12p multicoloured	. . . .	40	40
A38	A **38**	18p blk, greenish blue & orge-brn		60	60
A39	A **39**	27p black, greenish blue and dull yellow-green		1·10	1·10
A40	A **40**	32p black, greenish blue & brt rose-red		1·25	1·25
A41	A **41**	35p multicoloured		1·40	1·40
A37/41		*Set of* 5		4·25	4·25
		First Day Cover			6·00
		Presentation Pack		6·50	
		Set of 5 *Gutter Pairs*		8·50	

Plate Nos.: 12p 1–1–1–1; 18p, 27p, 32p 1–1–1; 35p 1–1–1–1–1

Sheets: 50 (2 panes 5×5)

Imprint: Central, both side margins of each pane

Quantities sold: 12p 169,993; 18p 194,667; 27p 148,621; 32p 158,600; 35p 153,544

Withdrawn: 6.7.90

A **42** H.M.S. *Alderney* (bomb ketch), 1738

A **43** H.M.S. *Alderney* (frigate), 1742

A **44** H.M.S. *Alderney* (sloop), 1755

A **45** H.M.S. *Alderney* (submarine), 1945

A **46** H.M.S. *Alderney* (patrol vessel), 1979

Royal Navy Ships named after Alderney

(Des A. Theobald. Litho B.D.T.)

1990 (3 MAY). *Perf* 13½ (C)

A42	A **42**	14p black and olive-bistre	45	45
A43	A **43**	20p black and orange-brown . .	60	60
A44	A **44**	29p black and cinnamon	1·10	1·10
A45	A **45**	34p black & pale turquoise-blue	1·10	1·10
A46	A **46**	37p black and cobalt	1·25	1·25
A42/6		*Set of 5*	4·00	4·00
		First Day Cover		6·00
		Presentation Pack	5·00	
		Set of 5 Gutter Pairs	8·00	

Plate Nos.: 14p, 20p, 29p, 34p 1A–1A, 1B–1B; 37p 1A–1A, 1B–1B, 1C–1C, 1D–1D

Sheets: 50 (2 panes 5×5)

Imprint: Central, side margins of each pane

Quantities sold: 14p 290,801; 20p 291,996; 29p 142,011; 34p 146,711; 37p 151,711

Withdrawn: 4.5.91

A **47** Wreck of H.M.S. *Victory*, 1744

A **48** Lighthouse Keeper's Daughter rowing back to the Casquets

A **49** MBB-Bolkow Bo 105D Helicopter leaving pad on St. Thomas Tower

A **50** Migrating Birds over Lighthouse

A **51** Trinity House Vessel *Patricia* and Arms

Automation of the Casquets Lighthouse

(Des A. Theobald. Litho Cartor)

1991 (30 APR). *Perf* 14×13½ (C)

A47	A **47**	21p multicoloured	. . . .	1·60	2·00
A48	A **48**	26p multicoloured	. . . .	2·00	2·25
A49	A **49**	31p multicoloured	. . . .	2·50	2·75

A50	A **50**	37p multicoloured	. . . .	3·50	3·75
A51	A **51**	50p multicoloured	. . . .	6·00	5·00
A47/51		*Set of 5*	14·00	14·00
		First Day Cover		14·00
		Presentation Pack	17·00	
		Set of 5 Gutter Pairs	28·00	

Plate Nos.: All values 1A, 1B, 1C, 1D (each ×4)

Sheets: 50 (2 panes 5×5)

Imprint: Central, side margins

Quantities sold: 21p 280,555; 26p 164,155; 31p 158,465; 37p 158,375; 50p 238,825

Withdrawn: 29.4.92

A **52** Two French Warships on Fire

A **53** Crews leaving burning Ships

A **54** French Warship sinking

A **55** "The Battle of La Hogue"

300th Anniversary of Battle of La Hogue

(Des C. Abbott. Litho B.D.T.)

1992 (18 SEPT). *Perf* 14×15 (50p) *or* 13½ (others), *both comb*

A52	A **52**	23p multicoloured	. . . .	1·50	1·50
A53	A **53**	28p multicoloured	. . . .	2·25	2·25
A54	A **54**	33p multicoloured	. . . .	2·50	2·50
A55	A **55**	50p multicoloured	. . . .	3·75	3·75
A52/5		*Set of 4*	9·00	9·00
		First Day Cover		9·50
		Presentation Pack	10·00	
		Set of 4 Gutter Pairs	18·00	

Nos. A52/4 show details of the painting on the 50p value.

Plate Nos.: All values 1A, 1B (each ×5)

Sheets: 50 (2 panes 5×5)

Imprint: Central, right-hand margin (50p) or central, side margins (others)

Quantities sold: 23p 238,820; 28p 188,685; 33p 172,565; 50p 186,096

Withdrawn: 17.9.93

A **56** Spiny Lobster

A **57** Plumose Anemone

A **58** Starfish

A **59** Sea Urchin

Endangered Species. Marine Life

(Des A. Peck. Litho Questa)

1993 (2 NOV). *Perf* 14½ (C)

A56	A **56**	24p multicoloured	90	90
		a. *Horiz strip of* 4. *Nos.* A56/9	4·25	
A57	A **57**	28p multicoloured	1·00	1·00
A58	A **58**	33p multicoloured	1·25	1·25
A59	A **59**	39p multicoloured	1·60	1·60
A56/9		*Set of* 4	4·25	4·25
		First Day Cover		5·00
		Presentation Pack	5·00	

Plate Nos.: All values 1A, 1B (each ×5)

Sheets: 16 (4×4). Nos. A56/9 were printed together, *se-tenant*, in horizontal strips of 4 throughout the sheet

Imprint: Central, right-hand margin

Withdrawn: 1.11.94

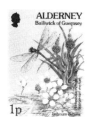

A **60** Blue-tailed Damselfly, Dark Hair Water Crowfoot and Branched Bur-reed

A **61** White-toothed Shrew and Flax-leaved St. John's Wort

A **62** Fulmar and Kaffir Fig

A **63** Clouded Yellow (butterfly) and Red Clover

A **64** Bumble Bee, Prostrate Broom and Giant Broomrape

A **65** Dartford Warbler and Lesser Dodder

A **66** Peacock (butterfly) and Stemless Thistle

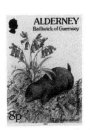

A **67** Mole and Bluebell

A **68** Great Green Grasshopper and Common Gorse

A **69** Six-spot Burnet (moth) and Viper's Bugloss

A **70** Common Blue (butterfly) and Pyramidal Orchid

A **70**a Small Tortoiseshell and Buddleia

A **75** Pale-spined Hedgehog and Pink Oxalis

A **76** Common Tern and Bermuda Grass

A **71** Common Rabbit and Creeping Buttercup

A **72** Great Black-backed Gull and Sand Crocus

A **77** Northern Gannet and *Fucus vesiculosus* (seaweed)

Flora and Fauna

(Des Wendy Bramall. Litho Questa)

A **72**a Rock Pipit and Sea Stock

A **72**b Sand Digger Wasp and Sea Bindweed

1994 (5 MAY)–**97**. Perf 14½ (C)

A60	A **60**	1p multicoloured (a)	10	10
A61	A **61**	2p multicoloured (a)	10	10
A62	A **62**	3p multicoloured (a)	10	10
A63	A **63**	4p multicoloured (a)	10	10
A64	A **64**	5p multicoloured (a)	10	10
A65	A **65**	6p multicoloured (a)	15	20
A66	A **66**	7p multicoloured (a)	15	20
A67	A **67**	8p multicoloured (a)	15	20
A68	A **68**	9p multicoloured (a)	20	25
A69	A **69**	10p multicoloured (a)	20	25
A70	A **70**	16p multicoloured (a)	30	35
		a. Perf 14×15	30	35
		ab. Booklet pane of 8	2·50	
A70b	A **70**a	18p multicoloured (c)	35	40
		ba. Perf 14×15	35	40
		bb. Booklet pane of 8	3·00	
A71	A **71**	20p multicoloured (a)	40	45
A72	A **72**	24p multicoloured (a)	50	55
		a. Perf 14×15	50	55
		ab. Booklet pane of 8	3·75	
A72b	A **72**a	25p multicoloured (c)	50	55
		ba. Perf 14×15	50	55
		bb. Booklet pane of 8	4·00	
A72c	A **72**b	26p multicoloured (c)	50	55
A73	A **73**	30p multicoloured (a)	60	65
A74	A **74**	40p multicoloured (a)	80	85
A75	A **75**	50p multicoloured (a)	1·00	1·10
A76	A **76**	£1 multicoloured (a)	2·00	2·10
A77	A **77**	£2 multicoloured (b)	4·00	4·25
A60/77		Set of 21	11·50	12·50
		First Day Covers (5)		17·00
		Presentation Packs (3)	14·00	
		Stamp-cards (set of 21) . .	4·50	18·00
		Set of 21 Gutter Pairs	24·00	

A **73** Puffin and English Stonecrop

A **74** Emperor (moth) and Bramble

Nos. A70a, A70ba, A72a and A72ba were only issued in booklets with the upper and lower edges of the panes imperforate.

Printings: (a) 5.5.94; (b) 28.2.95; (c) 2.1.97

Plate Nos.: 1p, 3p, 5p, 7p, 9p, 16p, 18p, 20p, 25p, 26p, 40p 1A, 1B (each ×4); 2p, 4p, 6p, 8p, 10p, 24p, 30p, 50p 1C, 1D (each ×4); £1, £2 1A, 1B, 1C, 1D (each ×4)

Sheets: 50 (2 panes 5×5)

Imprint: £1, £2 Central left margin of each pane; others central left or right margin of each pane

A **78** Royal Aircraft Factory SE5A

A **79** Miles Master II and other Miles Aircraft

A **80** Miles Aerovan and Miles Monitor

A **81** Miles Falcon Six winning King's Cup Air Race, 1935

A **82** Miles Hawk Speed Six winning Manx Air Derby, 1947

A **83** Miles Falcon Six breaking U.K.–Cape Record, 1936

Birth Centenary of Tommy Rose (aviator)

(Des C. Abbott. Litho B.D.T.)

1995 (1 SEPT). *Perf* 14×15 (C)

A78	A **78**	35p multicoloured	85	85
		a. Horiz strip of 3. Nos. A78/80	2·50	
A79	A **79**	35p multicoloured	85	85
A80	A **80**	35p multicoloured	85	85
A81	A **81**	41p multicoloured	1·00	1·00
		a. Horiz strip of 3. Nos. A81/3	3·00	
A82	A **82**	41p multicoloured	1·00	1·00
A83	A **83**	41p multicoloured	1·00	1·00
A78/83		Set of 6	5·50	5·50
		First Day Cover		6·00
		Presentation Pack	6·00	
		Gutter Strips of 6 (2)	11·00	

Plate Nos.: Both values 1A, 1B, 1C (each ×5)

Sheets: 12 (2 panes 3×2). Nos. A78/80 and A81/3 were printed together, *se-tenant*, as horizontal strips of 3 throughout the sheet

Imprint: Central, bottom margin

Withdrawn: 31.8.96

A **84**a Returning Islanders
(*illustration reduced. Actual size* 93×70 *mm*)

50th Anniversary of Return of Islanders to Alderney

(Des C. Abbott. Litho B.D.T.)

1995 (16 NOV). *Sheet* 93×70 *mm. Perf* 13½ (C)

MSA84	A **84**a	£1.65 multicoloured	4·00	4·00
		First Day Cover		4·25
		Presentation Pack	4·25	

Withdrawn: 15.11.96

A **85** Signallers training on Alderney

A **86** Communications Station, Falkland Islands

A **87** Dish Aerial and Land Rover, Gulf War

A **88** Service with United Nations

25th Anniversary of Adoption of 30th Signal Regiment by Alderney

(Des A. Theobald. Litho Walsall)

1996 (24 JAN). *Perf* 14 (C)

A85	A **85**	24p multicoloured	65	65
		a. Horiz strip of 4. Nos. A85/8	5·00	
A86	A **86**	41p multicoloured	1·10	1·10
A87	A **87**	60p multicoloured	1·50	1·50
A88	A **88**	75p multicoloured	1·75	1·75
A85/8		Set of 4	5·00	5·00
		First Day Cover		5·50
		Presentation Pack	7·00	
		Gutter Strip of 8	10·00	

Plate Nos.: All values 1A, 1B, 1C, 1D, 1E, 1F (each ×4)

Sheets: 16 (2 panes 4×2). Nos. A85/8 were printed in *se-tenant* strips of 4 across the sheet, each strip forming a composite design

Imprint: Central, bottom margin

Withdrawn: 28.1.97

A **91** Tabby Kitten grooming Blue and White Persian Kitten

A **92** Red Persian under Table

A **93** White Cat with Tortoiseshell and White in Toy Cart

A **94** Siamese playing with Wool

Cats

(Des P. le Vasseur. Litho B.D.T.)

1996 (19 JULY). *Perf* 13½ (C)

A89	A **89**	16p multicoloured	45	45
A90	A **90**	24p multicoloured	65	65
A91	A **91**	25p multicoloured	65	65
A92	A **92**	35p multicoloured	95	95
A93	A **93**	41p multicoloured	1·10	1·10
A94	A **94**	60p multicoloured	1·75	1·75
A89/94		Set of 6	5·00	5·00
		First Day Cover		5·50
		Presentation Pack	5·50	
		Set of 6 Gutter Pairs	10·00	
MSA95		144×97 mm. Nos. A89/94	5·00	5·00
		First Day Cover		5·50

Plate Nos.: All values 1A, 1B (each ×4)

Sheets: 50 (2 panes 5×5)

Imprint: Central, right-hand margin of top pane

Withdrawn: 18.7.97

A **89** Cat with Butterfly

A **90** Blue and White on Table

A **95** Harold Larwood

A **96** John Arlott

A **97** Pelham J. Warner

A **98** W. G. Grace

A **99** John Wisden

150th Anniversary of Cricket on Alderney

(Des R. Ollington. Litho Walsall)

1997 (21 AUG). *Perf* 13½ (C)

A96	A **95**	18p multicoloured	. . . .	40	45
A97	A **96**	25p multicoloured	. . . .	55	60
A98	A **97**	37p multicoloured	. . . .	75	80
A99	A **98**	43p multicoloured	. . . .	85	90
A100	A **99**	63p multicoloured	. . . .	1·25	1·40
A96/100		*Set of* 5	. . . .	3·75	4·00
		First Day Cover	. . . .		4·50
		Presentation Pack	. . . . . .	4·50	
		Set of 5 *Gutter Pairs*	. . . .	7·75	
MS101		190×75 mm. Nos. A96/100 and label	3·75	4·00
		First Day Cover	. . . .		4·50

Plate Nos.: All values 1A, 1B (each ×5)

Sheets: 50 (2 panes 5×5)

Imprint: Central, top and bottom margins

A **100** Railway under
Construction

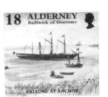

A **101** *Ariadne* (paddle
steamer) at
Anchor

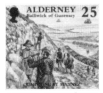

A **102** Quarrying Stone

A **103** Quarry Railway

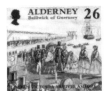

A **104** Queen Victoria
and Prince Albert
on Alderney

A **105** Royal Yacht
*Victoria and
Albert* and Guard
of Honour

A **106** Railway Workers
greet Queen
Victoria

A **107** Royal Party in
Railway Wagons

Garrison Island (1st series). 150th Anniversary of Harbour

(Des R. Carter. Litho Questa)

1997 (20 NOV). *Perf* 14½×14 (C)

A102	A **100**	18p multicoloured	. . . .	35	40
		a. Horiz pair. Nos. A102/3	. .	70	80
A103	A **101**	18p multicoloured	. . . .	35	40
A104	A **102**	25p multicoloured	. . . .	50	55
		a. Horiz pair. Nos. A104/5	. .	1·00	1·10
A105	A **103**	25p multicoloured	. . . .	50	55
A106	A **104**	26p multicoloured	. . . .	50	55
		a. Horiz pair. Nos. A106/7	. .	1·00	1·10
A107	A **105**	26p multicoloured	. . . .	50	55
A108	A **106**	31p multicoloured	. . . .	60	65
		a. Horiz pair. Nos. A108/9	. .	1·10	1·25
A109	A **107**	31p multicoloured	. . . .	60	65
A102/9		*Set of* 8	. . . .	3·75	4·25
		First Day Cover	. . . .		4·75
		Presentation Pack	. . . . . .	4·75	

Plate Nos.: All values 1A, 1B

Sheets: 20 (4×5), the two designs for each value printed together, *se-tenant*, in horizontal pairs throughout the sheets, each pair forming a composite design.

Imprint: Central, side margins

STAMP BOOKLETS

PRICES given are for complete booklets.

AB **1** Common Blue and Pyramidal Orchid
(*illustration reduced. Actual size 99×60 mm*)

1994 (5 MAY)–**95.** *Multicoloured covers as Type* AB **1**. *Without barcode on the reverse. Panes attached by selvedge*

ASB1	£1.28 booklet containing pane No. A70*ab* (cover Type AB **1**)	2·50
	a. With barcode sticker on reverse (1995) ..	2·50
ASB2	£1.92 booklet containing pane No. A72*ab* (cover showing Great Black-backed Gull and Sand Crocus	3·75

1997 (2 JAN). *Multicoloured covers as Type* AB **1**. *Panes attached by selvedge.*

ASB3	£1.44 booklet containing pane No. A70*bb* (cover showing Small Tortoiseshell (butterfly) and Buddleia)	3·00
ASB4	£2 booklet containing pane No. A72*bb* (cover showing Rock Pipit and Sea Stock)	4·00

Isle of Man

REGIONAL ISSUES

Although specifically issued for regional use, these issues were initially valid for use throughout the U.K. Regional issues ceased to be valid in the Isle of Man from 5 July, 1973 when the island established its own independent postal administration and introduced its own stamps.

DATES OF ISSUE. Conflicting dates of issue have been announced for some of the regional issues, partly explained by the stamps being released on different dates by the Philatelic Bureau in Edinburgh or the Philatelic Counter in London and in the regions. We have adopted the practice of giving the earliest known dates, since once released the stamps could have been used anywhere in the U.K.

INVALIDATION. Nos. 1/7 were invalidated as from 1 March, 1972 in common with other British 'fsd' stamps. Nos. 8/11 were invalidated for use in the Isle of Man on 5 July, 1973, but, together with other British stamps, were accepted for the prepayment of postage on letters from the island until 5 August, 1973. The Manx Regionals remained valid for use in the rest of the United Kingdom and were withdrawn from sale at the British Post Office Philatelic Sales counters on 4 July, 1974.

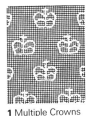

1 Multiple Crowns

2

3

(Des J. Nicholson. Portrait by Dorothy Wilding Ltd. Photo Harrison)

1958–68. *Wmk Type* **1.** *Perf* 15×14 (C)

1	**2**	2½d carmine-red (8.6.64)	45	80
2	**3**	3d deep lilac (18.8.58)	20	10
		a. *Chalk-surfaced paper* (17.5.63)	10·00	8·50
		p. *One centre phosphor band* (27.6.68)	20	40
3		4d ultramarine (7.2.66)	1·50	1·10
		p. *Two phosphor bands* (5.7.67)	20	25
1/3p		*Set of 3*	75	1·00
1		*First Day Cover*		28·00
2		*First Day Cover*		28·00
3		*First Day Cover*		7·50

Cylinder Nos.: 2½d 1; 3d (ord and phos) 1; 4d (ord and phos) 1
Sheets: 240 (12×20)
Quantities sold (ordinary only): 2½d 4,298,160; 3d 35,959,420 (up to 31.3.68 and including 1,080,000 on chalky paper); 4d 4,353,840
Withdrawn: 31.8.66 2½d
Sold out: 11.67 4d ordinary; 12.68 3d ordinary, 4d phosphor; 4.69 3d phosphor

1968–69. *No wmk. Chalk-surfaced paper. One centre phosphor band* (Nos. 5/6) *or two phosphor bands* (others). *Perf* 15×14 (C)

4	**3**	4d blue (24.6.68)	20	25
5		4d olive-sepia (4.9.68)	20	30
6		4d bright vermilion (26.2.69)	45	60
7		5d royal blue (4.9.68)	45	60
4/7		*Set of 4*	1·00	1·60
5,7		*First Day Cover*		2·00

Cylinder Nos.: 4d (blue) 1; 4d (olive-sepia) 1; 4d (bright vermilion) 1; 5d 1
Sheets: 240 (12×20)
Sold out: 16.7.69 4d blue
Withdrawn: 14.3.71 (locally), 25.11.71 (British Philatelic Counters) 4d

4

Decimal Currency

(Des J. Matthews. Portrait after plaster cast by Arnold Machin. Photo Harrison)

1971 (7 JULY). *Chalk-surfaced paper. One centre phosphor band* (2½p) *or two phosphor bands* (others). *Perf* 15×14 (C)

8	**4**	2½p bright magenta	20	15
9		3p ultramarine	20	15
10		5p reddish violet	40	50
11		7½p chestnut	40	65
8/11		*Set of 4*	1·10	1·25
		First Day Cover		2·50
		Presentation Pack	2·00	

All values were originally issued on ordinary cream paper, but the 2½p and 3p later appeared on white fluorescent paper.

Cylinder Nos.: (dot and no dot): 2½p 3, phos 5; 3p 1, phos 4; 5p 4, phos 12; 7½p 4, phos 10
Sheets: 200 (10×20)
Withdrawn: 4.7.73 (locally), 4.7.74 (British Philatelic Counters)

INDEPENDENT POSTAL ADMINISTRATION

The Isle of Man established an independent postal administration on 5 July, 1973 and introduced its own stamps.

NO WATERMARK. All the following issues are on unwatermarked paper *unless otherwise stated.*

5 Castletown

6 Port Erin

7 Snaefell

8 Laxey

9 Tynwald Hill

10 Douglas Promenade

11 Port St. Mary

12 Fairy Bridge

13 Peel

14 Cregneish

15 Ramsey Bay

16 Douglas Bay

17 Manx Cat

20 Manx Loaghtyn Ram

18 Monk's Bridge, Ballasalla

19 Derbyhaven

21 Manx Shearwater

22 Viking Longship

(Des J. Nicholson. Photo Courvoisier)

1973 (5 JULY)–**75**. *Granite paper. Perf* 11½ (C)

12	**5**	½p multicoloured (*ab*)	10	10
13	**6**	1p multicoloured (*ae*)	10	10
14	**7**	1½p multicoloured (*ak*)	10	10
15	**8**	2p multicoloured (*aj*)	10	10
16	**9**	2½p multicoloured (*a*)	10	10
17	**10**	3p mult (*sage-green border*) (*ac*)	10	10
		a. Error. Olive-bistre border † . .	£150	£100
18	**11**	3½p mult (*olive-brown border*) (*ad*)	15	15
		a. Error. Grey-brown border † . .	£150	£100
19	**12**	4p multicoloured (*a*)	15	15
20	**9**	4½p multicoloured (*f*)	20	20
21	**13**	5p multicoloured (*ah*)	20	20
22	**10**	5½p multicoloured (*g*)	25	25
23	**14**	6p multicoloured (*ah*)	25	25
24	**8**	7p multicoloured (*g*)	30	30
25	**15**	7½p multicoloured (*a*)	25	25
26		8p multicoloured (*f*)	35	35

27	**16**	9p multicoloured (an)	30	35
28	**17**	10p multicoloured (an)	40	35
29	**18**	11p multicoloured (l)	30	30
30	**19**	13p multicoloured (l)	40	40
31	**20**	20p multicoloured (an)	50	50
32	**21**	50p multicoloured (an)	1·25	1·25
33	**22**	£1 multicoloured (am)	2·50	2·50
12/33		Set of 22	7·50	7·50
		First Day Covers (7)		9·00
		Presentation Packs (6)	10·00	

†These errors occur on printings (c) and (d). That on the 3p resembles the border colour of the ½p and that on the 3½p the 2p.

Printings: (a) 5.7.73; (b) 1.11.73; (c) 16.4.74; (d) 29.7.74; (e) 2.9.74; (f) 8.1.75; (g) 28.5.75; (h) 16.6.75; (i) 29.10.75; (j) 1.12.75; (k) 2.2.76; (l) 20.9.76; (m) 16.2.77; (n) 7.7.77

Printings (a) and (l) have thick shiny gum, but all the other printings have matt, almost invisible gum. Printings (f), (g) and (i) are inscribed "1975". The remainder are inscribed "1973".

Sheets: 50 (5×10) ½p to 9p, 11p, 13p; (10×5) 10p, 20p to £1

Withdrawn: 31.12.78 (except ½p, 3p and 3½p values in booklets withdrawn 15.5.79. In addition 2p and 3½p values were kept available for use on postal orders after 31.12.78 until finally withdrawn on 30.6.83 (2p) or 31.12.85 (3½p))

23 Landing of the Vikings on Man, A.D. 938

Inauguration of Postal Independence

(Des J. Nicholson. Photo Harrison)

1973 (5 JULY). Perf 14 (C)

34	**23**	15p multicoloured	60	60
		First Day Cover		1·75
		Presentation Pack	3·00	

For 15p inscr 'POST OFFICE DECENNIUM 1983' see No. 256

Cylinder Nos.: 1A (×4)
Sheets: 50 (10×5)
Quantity sold: 350,000
Sold out: Soon after issue

24 Sutherland

25 Caledonia

26 Kissack

27 Pender

Steam Railway Centenary

(Des J. Nicholson. Photo Harrison)

1973 (4 AUG). Perf 15×14 (C)

35	**24**	2½p multicoloured	20	20
36	**25**	3p multicoloured	20	20
37	**26**	7½p multicoloured	70	90
38	**27**	9p multicoloured	85	90
35/8		Set of 4	1·75	2·00
		First Day Cover		2·50
		Presentation Pack	3·00	

Cylinder Nos. All values 1A (×5)
Sheets: 50 (5×10)
Quantities sold: 2½p 617,122; 3p 808,173; 7½p 331,695; 9p 324,414
Withdrawn: 3.8.74

28 Leonard Randles, First Winner, 1923

29 Alan Holmes, Double Winner, 1957

Golden Jubilee of Manx Grand Prix

(Des J. Nicholson. Litho John Waddington)

1973 (4 SEPT). Perf 14 (C)

39	**28**	3p multicoloured	30	20
40	**29**	3½p multicoloured	30	20
39/40		Set of 2	60	40
		First Day Cover		1·00
		Presentation Pack	1·00	
		Set of 2 Gutter Pairs	2·00	

Plate Nos.: Both values 1A, 1B, 1C, 1D (each ×4)
Sheets: 50 (2 panes 5×5)
Imprint: Central, bottom margin
Quantities sold: 3p 550,347; 3½p 653,355
Withdrawn: 3.9.74

30 Princess Anne and
Capt. Mark Philips

Royal Wedding

(Des A. Larkins. Recess and litho De La Rue)

1973 (14 NOV). *Perf* 13½ (C)

41	**30**	25p multicoloured	. . . .	1·00	1·00
		First Day Cover	. . . .		1·50
		Presentation Pack.	. . . .	1·75	
		Gutter Pair	. . . .	2·25	

Plate Nos.: 1A, 1B (each ×4)

Sheets: 50 (2 panes 5×5)

Imprint: Right-hand corner, bottom margin

Quantity sold: 400,813

Withdrawn: 13.11.74

31 Badge, Citation and Sir
William Hillary (founder)

32 Wreck of *St. George*,
1830

33 Manchester & Salford,
1868–87

34 Osman Gabriel

150th Anniversary of Royal National Lifeboat Institution

(Des J. Nicholson. Photo Courvoisier)

1974 (4 MAR). *Granite paper. Perf* 11½ (C)

42	**31**	3p multicoloured	. . . .	10	10
43	**32**	3½p multicoloured	. . . .	15	15
44	**33**	8p multicoloured	. . . .	40	40
45	**34**	10p multicoloured	. . . .	45	45
42/5		*Set of 4*	. . . .	1·00	1·00
		First Day Cover	. . . .		1·50
		Presentation Pack.	. . . .	1·60	

Sheets: 100 (10×10)

Quantities sold: 3p 674,984; 3½p 849,990; 8p 374,941; 10p 375,043

Withdrawn: 3.3.75

35 Stanley Woods, 1935

36 Freddy Frith, 1937

37 Max Deubel and Emil
Horner, 1961

38 Mike Hailwood, 1961

Tourist Trophy Motor Cycle Races (1st issue)

(Des J. Nicholson. Litho De La Rue)

1974 (29 MAY). *Perf* 13×13½ (C)

46	**35**	3p multicoloured	. . . .	10	10
47	**36**	3½p multicoloured	. . . .	10	10
48	**37**	8p multicoloured	. . . .	45	45½
49	**38**	10p multicoloured	. . . .	60	45
46/9		*Set of 4*	. . . .	1·10	1·00
		First Day Cover	. . . .		1·40
		Presentation Pack.	. . . .	1·25	
		Set of 4 Gutter Pairs	. . . .	2·25	

See also Nos. 63/6

Plate Nos.: All values 1A, 1B, 1C, 1D (each ×6); 3p also 1A
(×4)–2A–2A, 1B (×4)–2B–2B, 1C (×4)–2C–2C, 1D (×4)–2D–2D; 8p
also 1A–1A–2A–1A (×3), 1B–1B–2B–1B (×3), 1C–1C–2C–1C (×3),
1D–1D–2D–1D (×3)

Sheets: 50 (2 panes 5×5)

Imprint: Right-hand corner, bottom margin

Quantities sold: 3p 578,045; 3½p 816,235; 8p 334,760; 10p 403,177

Withdrawn: 28.5.75

39 Rushen Abbey and Arms

40 Magnus Haraldson rows King Edgar on the Dee

41 King Magnus and Norse Fleet

42 Bridge at Avignon and Bishop's Mitre

Historical Anniversaries. Events described on stamps

(Des J. Nicholson, from ideas by G. Kneale. Litho Questa (3½p, 10p) or John Waddington (others))

1974 (18 SEPT). *Perf* 14 (C)

50	**39**	3½p multicoloured	....	10	10
51	**40**	4½p multicoloured	....	10	10
52	**41**	8p multicoloured	....	40	40
53	**42**	10p multicoloured	....	50	50
50/3		Set of 4	....	1·00	1·00
		First Day Cover	....		1·00
		Presentation Pack.	....	1·40	
		Set of 4 Gutter Pairs.	......	2·10	

Plate Nos.: All values 1A, 1B, 1C, 1D (each ×4)

Sheets: 50 (2 panes 5×5)

Imprint: Right-hand corner, bottom margin and left-hand corner, top margin

Quantities sold: 3½p 931,610; 4½p 1,025,044; 8p 450,418; 10p 425,305

Withdrawn: 17.9.75

43 Churchill and Bugler Dunne at Colenso, 1899

44 Churchill and Government Buildings, Douglas

45 Churchill and Manx A.A. Gun Crew

46 Churchill as Freeman of Douglas

Birth Centenary of Sir Winston Churchill

(Des G. Kneale. Photo Courvoisier)

1974 (22 NOV). *Granite paper. Perf* 11½ (C)

54	**43**	3½p multicoloured	....	10	10
55	**44**	4½p multicoloured	....	10	10
56	**45**	8p multicoloured	....	25	35
57	**46**	20p multicoloured	....	75	55
54/7		Set of 4	....	1·10	1·00
		First Day Cover	....		1·40
		Presentation Pack.	....	1·40	
MS58		121×91 mm. Nos. 54/7	....	1·10	1·00
		First Day Cover	....		1·75

No. **MS**58 is inscribed '30th NOV. 1974'.

Sheets: 25 (5×5)

Quantities sold: 3½p 916,748; 4½p 853,537; 8p 424,691; 20p 429,586; miniature sheet 362,089

Withdrawn: 21.11.75

47 Cabin School and Names of Pioneers

48 Terminal Tower Building, John Gill and Robert Carran

49 Robert and Margaret Clague, and Clague House Museum

50 *William T. Graves* and Thomas Quayle

Manx Pioneers in Cleveland, Ohio

(Des J. Nicholson. Photo Courvoisier)

1975 (14 MAR). *Granite paper. Perf* 11½ (C)

59	**47**	4½p multicoloured	....	10	10
60	**48**	5½p multicoloured	....	15	10
61	**49**	8p multicoloured	....	35	40
62	**50**	10p multicoloured	....	50	50
59/62		Set of 4	....	1·00	1·00
		First Day Cover	....		1·10
		Presentation Pack...........		1·40	

Sheets: 50 (5×10)

Quantities sold: 4½p 473,352; 5½p 999,802; 8p 433,352; 10p 447,945

Withdrawn: 13.3.76 (5½p sold out 12.75)

51 Tom Sheard, 1923

52 Walter Handley, 1925

53 Geoff Duke, 1955

54 Peter Williams, 1973

Tourist Trophy Motor Cycle Races (2nd issue)

(Des J. Nicholson. Litho John Waddington)

1975 (28 MAY). *Perf* 13½ (C)

63	**51**	5½p multicoloured	....	10	15
64	**52**	7p multicoloured	....	20	20
65	**53**	10p multicoloured	....	40	30
66	**54**	12p multicoloured	....	40	45
63/6		Set of 4	....	1·00	1·00
		First Day Cover	....		1·75
		Presentation Pack...........		1·40	
		Set of 4 Gutter Pairs........		2·10	

Plate Nos.: 5½p, 7p 1B, 1D (each ×5); 10p 1A, 1B, 1C (each ×5); 12p 1A, 1C (each ×5)

Sheets: 50 (2 panes 5×5)

Imprint: Right-hand corner, bottom margin

Quantities sold: 5½p 633,250; 7p 520,285; 10p 399,710; 12p 440,208

Withdrawn: 27.5.76

55 Goldie and the Nunnery, Douglas

56 Goldie and Map of Africa

57 Goldie and Royal Geographical Society Emblem

58 River Scene on the Niger

50th Death Anniversary of Sir George Goldie

(Des G. Kneale. Photo Courvoisier)

1975 (9 SEPT). *Granite paper. Perf* 11½ (C)

67	**55**	5½p multicoloured	....	10	15
68	**56**	7p multicoloured	....	20	20
69	**57**	10p multicoloured	....	40	30·
70	**58**	12p multicoloured	....	40	45
67/70		Set of 4	....	1·00	1·00
		First Day Cover	....		1·25
		Presentation Pack...........		1·40	

Sheets: 50 (10×5) 7p, 10p; (5×10) others

Quantities sold: 5½p 488,317; 7p 426,849; 10p 373,771; 12p 439,843

Withdrawn: 8.9.76

59 Title Page of Manx Bible

60 Rev. Philip Moore and Ballaugh Old Church

61 Bishop Hildesley and Bishops Court

62 John Kelly saving Bible Manuscript

Christmas and Bicentenary of Manx Bible

(Des J. Nicholson. Litho Questa)

1975 (29 OCT). *Perf* 14 (C)

71	**59**	5½p multicoloured	15	15
72	**60**	7p multicoloured	20	20
73	**61**	11p multicoloured	35	35
74	**62**	13p multicoloured	40	40
71/4		Set of 4	1·00	1·00
		First Day Cover		1·10
		Presentation Pack	1·25	
		Set of 4 Gutter Pairs	2·00	

Plate Nos. 13p 1C, 1D (each ×4); others 1A, 1B (each ×4)

Sheets: 50 (2 panes 5×5)

Quantities sold: 5½p 738,774; 7p 607,377; 11p 405,126; 13p 402,463

63 William Christian listening to Patrick Henry

64 Conveying the Fincastle Resolutions

65 Patrick Henry and William Christian

66 Christian as an Indian Fighter

Bicentenary of American Revolution and Col. William Christian Commemoration

(Des and litho John Waddington)

1976 (12 MAR). *Perf* 13½ (C)

75	**63**	5½p multicoloured	15	15
76	**64**	7p multicoloured	20	20

77	**65**	13p multicoloured	35	35
		a. Black *(face value and inscr)* printed double		
78	**66**	20p multicoloured	50	50
75/8		Set of 4	1·10	1·10
		First Day Cover		1·10
		Presentation Pack	1·50	
		Set of 4 Gutter Pairs	2·25	
MS79		150×90 mm. Nos. 75/8. *Perf* 14 (C)	1·50	1·60
		First Day Cover		2·75
		Presentation Pack	2·25	

Plate Nos.: 5½p, 20p 1A, 1C (each ×4); others 1B, 1D (each ×4)

Sheets: 50 (2 panes 5×5)

Quantities sold: 5½p 487,310; 7p 524,144; 13p 558,348; 20p 424,728; miniature sheet 209,367

Withdrawn: 11.3.77

67 First Horse Tram, 1876

68 'Toast-rack' Tram, 1890

69 Horse-bus, 1895

70 Royal Tram, 1972

Douglas Horse Trams Centenary

(Des J. Nicholson. Photo Courvoisier)

1976 (26 MAY). *Granite paper. Perf* 11½ (C)

80	**67**	5½p multicoloured	10	15
81	**68**	7p multicoloured	15	15

82	**69**	11p multicoloured	. . . .	45	35
83	**70**	13p multicoloured	. . . .	50	45
80/3		Set of 4	. . . .	1·10	1·00
		First Day Cover	. . . .		1·10
		Presentation Pack	. . . .	1·40	

Sheets 25 (5×5)

Quantities sold: 5½p 627,083; 7p 480,417; 11p 391,871; 13p 389,604

Withdrawn: 25.5.77

ISLE OF MAN

ISLE OF MAN

ISLE OF MAN

71 Barroose
Beaker

72 Souvenir
Teapot

73 Laxey Jug

ISLE OF MAN 10ᵖ

ISLE OF MAN 10ᵖ

74 Cronk Aust Food
Vessel

75 Sansbury Bowl

ISLE OF MAN 10ᵖ

76 Knox Urn

Europa. Ceramic Art

(Des J. Nicholson. Photo Courvoisier)

1976 (28 JULY). *Granite paper. Perf* 11½ (C)

84	**71**	5p multicoloured	. . . .	25	20
		a. Strip of 3. Nos. 84/6	. . . .	70	60
85	**72**	5p multicoloured	. . . .	25	20
86	**73**	5p multicoloured	. . . .	25	20
87	**74**	10p multicoloured	. . . .	40	35
		a. Strip of 3. Nos. 87/9	. . . .	1·25	1·10
88	**75**	10p multicoloured	. . . .	40	35
89	**76**	10p multicoloured	. . . .	40	35
84/9		Set of 6	. . . .	1·75	1·50
		First Day Cover	. . . .		3·00
		Presentation Pack	. . . .	2·00	

Sheets: 9 (3×3) containing the three designs of each value horizontally and vertically *se-tenant*

Quantities sold: 5p 256,400 of each design; 10p 262,900 of each design

Sold out: 20.11.76 (5p); 12.76 (10p)

77 Diocesan Banner

78 Onchan Banner

79 Castletown Banner

80 Ramsey Banner

Christmas and Centenary of Mothers' Union

(Des G. Kneale. Litho Questa)

1976 (14 OCT). *Perf* 14½ (C)

90	**77**	6p multicoloured	. . . .	15	15
91	**78**	7p multicoloured	. . . .	15	15
92	**79**	11p multicoloured	. . . .	40	35
93	**80**	13p multicoloured	. . . .	40	45
90/3		Set of 4	. . . .	1·00	1·00
		First Day Cover	. . . .		1·00
		Presentation Pack	. . . .	1·25	

Plate Nos.: 6p 1B (×5); 11p 1A (×5); others 1C (×5)

Sheets: 50 (10×5)

Imprint: Right-hand corner, bottom margin and left-hand corner, top margin

Quantities sold: 6p 905,752; 7p 890,762; 11p 397,807; 13p 390,057

Withdrawn: 13.10.77

81 Queen Elizabeth II

82 Queen Elizabeth and
Prince Philip

83 Queen Elizabeth II

Silver Jubilee

(Des A. Larkins. Litho and recess De La Rue)

1977 (1 MAR). *Perf* 14×13 (7*p*) *or* 13×14 (*others*), *both comb*
94	**81**	6p multicoloured	20	20
95	**82**	7p multicoloured	20	20
96	**83**	25p multicoloured	80	70
94/6		*Set of 3*	1·10	1·00
		First Day Cover		1·00
		Presentation Pack	1·25	
		Set of 3 Gutter Pairs	2·25	

Plate Nos.: 6p, 7p 1A (×5)–2A, 1B (×5)–2B, 1C (×5)–2C, 1D (×5)–2D; 25p 1B, 1D (each ×6)

Sheets: 50 (2 panes 5×5)

Imprint: Right-hand corner, bottom margin

Quantities sold: 6p 942,356; 7p 911,191; 25p 651,101

Withdrawn: 28.2.78

84 Carrick Bay from 'Tom-the-Dipper'

85 View from Ramsey

Europa. Landscapes

(Des J. Nicholson. Litho Questa)

1977 (26 MAY). *Perf* 13½×14 (C)
97	**84**	6p multicoloured	20	20
98	**85**	10p multicoloured	30	30
97/8		*Set of 2*	50	50
		First Day Cover		1·00
		Presentation Pack	1·00	
		Set of 2 Gutter Pairs	1·00	

Plate Nos.: 6p, 1A, 1B, 1C, 1D, 2A, 2B, 2C, 2D (each ×4); 10p 1A, 1B, 1C, 1D (each ×5), 2A–1A–1A–2A–1A, 2B–1B–1B–2B–1B, 2C–1C–1C–2C–1C, 2D–1D–1D–2D–1D

Sheets: 40 (2 panes 4×5)

Imprint: Right-hand corner, bottom margin and left-hand corner, top margin

Quantities sold: 6p 778,685; 10p 843,525

Withdrawn: 25.5.78

86 F. A. Applebee, 1912

87 St. John Ambulance Brigade at Governor's Bridge, *c.* 1938

88 Scouts working Scoreboard

89 John Williams, 1976

Linked Anniversaries

(Des J. Nicholson. Litho John Waddington)

1977 (26 MAY). *Perf* 13½ (C)
99	**86**	6p multicoloured	15	15
100	**87**	7p multicoloured	15	20
101	**88**	11p multicoloured	40	40
102	**89**	13p multicoloured	40	40
99/102		*Set of 4*	1·00	1·00
		First Day Cover		1·00
		Presentation Pack	1·25	
		Set of 4 Gutter Pairs	2·00	

The events commemorated are: 70th anniversary of Manx TT; 70th anniversary of Boy Scouts; centenary of St. John Ambulance Brigade

Plate Nos.: 11p 1A, 1C (each ×4); others 1B, 1D (each ×4)

Sheets: 50 (2 panes 5×5)

Imprint: Right-hand corner, bottom margin

Quantities sold: 6p 525,703; 7p 875,303; 11p 431,053; 13p 440,403

Withdrawn: 25.5.78

90 Old Summer House, Mount Morrison, Peel

91 Wesley preaching in Castletown Square

92 Wesley preaching outside Bradden Church

93 New Methodist Church, Douglas

Bicentenary of the First Visit of John Wesley

(Des and photo Courvoisier)

1977 (19 OCT). *Granite paper. Perf* 11½ (C)

103	**90**	6p multicoloured	. . . .	15	15
104	**91**	7p multicoloured	. . . .	20	20
105	**92**	11p multicoloured	. . . .	35	35
106	**93**	13p multicoloured	. . . .	40	40
103/6		*Set of 4*	. . . .	1·00	1·00
		First Day Cover			1·00
		Presentation Pack		1·25	

Sheets: 50 (5×10)

Quantities sold: 6p 661,755; 7p 976,155; 11p 373,805; 13p 366,905

Withdrawn: 18.10.78

94 H.M.S. *Ben-My-Chree* and Short Type 184 Seaplane, 1915

95 H.M.S. *Vindex* and Bristol Scout C, 1915

96 Boulton Paul Defiant over Douglas Bay, 1941

97 Sepecat Jaguar over Ramsey, 1977

R.A.F. Diamond Jubilee

(Des A. Theobald. Litho John Waddington)

1978 (28 Feb). *Perf* 13½×14

107	**94**	6p multicoloured	. . . .	15	15
108	**95**	7p multicoloured	. . . .	20	20
109	**96**	11p multicoloured	. . . .	35	35
110	**97**	13p multicoloured	. . . .	40	40
107/10		*Set of 4*	. . . .	1·10	1·00
		First Day Cover			1·25
		Presentation Pack		1·50	
		Set of 4 Gutter Pairs		2·25	

Plate Nos.: All values 1A, 1C (each ×4)

Sheets: 50 (2 panes 5×5)

Quantities sold: 6p 690,536; 7p 875,811; 11p 416,082; 13p 422,797

Withdrawn: 27.2.79

98 Watch Tower, Langness

99 Jurby Church

100 Government Buildings

101 Tynwald Hill

102 Milner's Tower

103 Laxey Wheel

104 Castle Rushen

105 St. Ninian's Church

106 Tower of Refuge

107 St. German's Cathedral

108 Point of Ayre Lighthouse

109 Corrin's Tower

110 Douglas Head Lighthouse

111 Fuchsia

112 Manx Cat

113 Chough

114 Viking Warrior

114*a* Queen Elizabeth II

(Des G. Kneale (£2), J. Nicholson (others). Litho Questa (½p to 16p), photo Courvoisier (20p to £2))

1978 (28 FEB)–**81**.

A. *Perf* 14 (C). B. *Perf* 14½ (C) (*both ptg* (*a*))

			A.		B.	
111	**98**	½p multicoloured	10	10	20	10
112	**99**	1p multicoloured	10	10	20	10
113	**100**	6p multicoloured	30	30		†
114	**101**	7p multicoloured	35	35	8·00	6·50
115	**102**	8p multicoloured	25	25	35	35
116	**103**	9p multicoloured	35	35	35	35
117	**104**	10p multicoloured	40	40	35	35
118	**105**	11p multicoloured	40	40	40	40
119	**106**	12p multicoloured	50	50	50	40
120	**107**	13p multicoloured	60	60	40	40
121	**108**	14p multicoloured	45	45	40	40
122	**109**	15p multicoloured	60	60	40	40
123	**110**	16p multicoloured	80	80	25·00	21·00

C. *Granite paper. Perf* 11½ (C)

124	**111**	20p multicoloured (*b*)	40	40
125	**112**	25p multicoloured (*b*)	50	50
126	**113**	50p multicoloured (*b*)	1·00	1·00
127	**114**	£1 multicoloured (*b*)	2·00	2·00
128	**114***a*	£2 multicoloured (*c*)	4·25	4·25
111/28		Set of 18 (*cheapest*)	11·50	11·50
		First Day Covers* (5)		12·50
		Presentation Packs (4)	15·00	

*The most common versions of the three low and medium value first day covers prepared by the Philatelic Bureau were franked with Nos. 111B, 112A/15A, 116B, 117A/18A, 119B, 120A, 121B, 122A and 123B. Some examples can be found with the ½p as No. 111A, the 11p as No. 118B or the 13p as No. 120B. First day covers prepared by dealers or collectors on the island were franked with Nos. 111A/18A, 119B/20B, 121A, 122B and 123A.

Printings: (*a*) 28.2.78; (*b*) 18.10.78; (*c*) 29.9.81

Although both perforations of Nos. 111/23 were printed at the same time, some did not appear in use until some time after 28 February, 1978. Earliest dates for these are as follows: 1p (112B) 8.79, 7p (114B) 8.78, 8p (115B) 6.80, 10p (117B) 8.79, 12p (119A) 9.80.

Plate Nos.: ½, 6, 8, 9, 10, 11, 12, 13, 14, 15, 16p 1A, 1B, 1C, 1D (each ×4); 1p 1A, 1B, 1C, 1D (each ×4) (No. 112A), 1A–1A–2A–1A, 1B–1B–2B–1B, 1C–1C–2C–1C, 1D–1D–2D–1D (Nos. 112A/B); 7p 1A, 1B, 1C, 1D (each ×4) (No. 114A); 2A, 2B, 2C, 2D (each ×4) (No. 114B); £2 A1–1–1–1, B1–1–1–1, others none

Sheets: 25 (5 x 5) (£2); 50 (1, 7, 10, 12, 13, 14, 15, 16p 5×10; others 10×5)

Imprint: ½p to 16p left-hand corner, top margin and right-hand corner, bottom margin; 20p to £1 none; £2 central bottom margin

Withdrawn: 30.6.83 1p to 16p; 31.12.83 20p to £1; 31.12.85 ½p; 30.6.90 £2

115 Queen Elizabeth in Coronation Regalia

25th Anniversary of Coronation

(Des G. Kneale. Litho Questa)

1978 (24 MAY). *Perf* 14½×14 (C)

132	**115**	25p multicoloured	. . . .	75	75
		First Day Cover	. . . .		1·00
		Presentation Pack	. . . .	1·25	
		Gutter Pair	. . . .	1·50	

Plate Nos.: 1A, 1B (each ×6)

Sheets: 50 (2 panes 5×5)

Imprint: Left-hand corner, top margin and right-hand corner, bottom margin

Quantity sold: 575,996

Withdrawn: 23.5.79

116 Wheel-headed Cross-slab

117 Celtic Wheelcross

118 Keeil Chiggyrt Stone

119 Olaf Liotulfson Cross

120 Odd's and Thorleif's Crosses

121 Thor Cross

Europa. Sculpture

(Des J. Nicholson. Photo Courvoisier)

1978 (24 MAY). *Granite paper. Perf* 11½ (C)

133	**116**	6p multicoloured	. . . .	20	15
		a. Strip of 3. Nos. 133/5	. . . .	60	50
134	**117**	6p multicoloured	. . . .	20	15
135	**118**	6p multicoloured	. . . .	20	15
136	**119**	11p multicoloured	. . . .	35	30
		a. Strip of 3. Nos. 136/8	. . . .	1·10	90
137	**120**	11p multicoloured	. . . .	35	30
138	**121**	11p multicoloured	. . . .	35	30
133/8		Set of 6	. . . .	1·50	1·25
		First Day Cover	. . . .		1·25
		Presentation Pack	. . . .	1·60	

Sheets: 9 (3×3) The three designs of each value were printed together, *se-tenant*, in horizontal and vertical strips throughout

Quantities sold: 6p 3,821,152; 11p 3,788,667

Withdrawn: 23.5.79

122 J. K. Ward and Ward Library, Peel

123 Swimmer, Cyclist and Walker

124 American Bald Eagle, Manx Arms and Maple Leaf

125 Lumber Camp at Three Rivers, Quebec

Anniversaries and Events. Events described on stamps

(Des John Waddington (7p), G. Kneale (11p), J. Nicholson (others). Litho John Waddington)

1978 (10 JUNE). *Invisible gum. Perf* 13½ (C)

139	**122**	6p multicoloured	. . . .	15	15
140	**123**	7p multicoloured	. . . .	20	20
141	**124**	11p multicoloured	. . . .	35	35
142	**125**	13p multicoloured	. . . .	40	40
139/42		Set of 4	. . . .	1·00	1·00
		First Day Covers (3)	. . . . . .		1·50
		Presentation Packs (2)	. . . .	1·40	
		Set of 4 Gutter Pairs	. . . . . .	2·25	

Plate Nos.: 6p 1A, 1B, 1C, 1D (each ×4); others 1B, 1D (each ×4)

Sheets: 50 (2 panes 5×5)

Imprint: Central, bottom margin

Quantities sold: 6p 629,041; 7p 873,067; 11p 393,907; 13p 383,048

Withdrawn: 9.6.79

126 Hunt the Wren

Christmas

(Des J. Nicholson. Litho John Waddington)

1978 (18 OCT). *Perf* 13 (C)

143	**126**	5p multicoloured	50	50
		First Day Cover		1·00
		Presentation Pack	1·00	
		Gutter Pair	1·00	

Plate Nos.: 1B, 1D (each ×4)

Sheets: 50 (2 panes 5×5)

Imprint: Central, bottom margin

Quantity sold: 1,000,000

Sold out: By 4.79 (stamp) or 8.79 (presentation pack)

127 P. M. C. Kermode (founder) and *Nassa kermodei*

128 Peregrine Falcon

129 Fulmar

130 *Epitriptus cowini* (fly)

Centenary of Natural History and Antiquarian Society

(Des J. Nicholson. Litho Questa)

1979 (27 FEB). *Perf* 14 (C)

144	**127**	6p multicoloured	15	15
145	**128**	7p multicoloured	20	20
146	**129**	11p multicoloured	35	35
147	**130**	13p multicoloured	40	40
144/7		Set of 4	1·00	1·00
		First Day Cover		1·00
		Presentation Pack	1·50	
		Set of 4 Gutter Pairs	2·10	

Plate Nos.: 6p 1A, 1B, 1C, 1D (each ×4); 13p 1A, 1B (each ×4); others 1C, 1D (each ×4)

Sheets: 50 (2 panes 5×5)

Imprint: Left-hand corner, top margin and right-hand corner, bottom margin

Quantities sold: 6p 642,126; 7p 790,515; 11p 411,863; 13p 390,454

Withdrawn: 26.2.80

131 Postman, 1859

132 Postman, 1979

Europa. Communications

(Des A. Theobald. Litho Questa)

1979 (16 MAY). *Perf* 14½ (C)

148	**131**	6p multicoloured	25	25
149	**132**	11p multicoloured	50	50
148/9		Set of 2	75	75
		First Day Cover		1·00
		Presentation Pack	1·00	

Plate Nos.: 6p 1A, 1B (each ×6); 11p 1A, 1B (each ×5)

Sheets: 20 (4×5)

Imprint: Right-hand corner, bottom margin

Quantities sold: 6p 1,301,039; 11p 1,290,318

Sold out: By 10.79 (stamps)

Withdrawn: 15.5.80 (presentation pack)

133 Viking Longship Emblem

134 'Three Legs of Man' Emblem

135 Viking Raid at Garwick

136 10th-century Meeting of Tynwald

137 Tynwald Hill and St. John's Church

138 Procession to Tynwald Hill

Two types of 3p:

Type I. Wrongly inscribed 'INSULAREM'. '1979' imprint date.

Type II. Inscription corrected to 'INSULARUM'. '1980' imprint date.

Millennium of Tynwald

(Des J. Nicholson. Litho Harrison (3, 4p), John Waddington (others))

1979 (16 MAY)–**80.** (a) Perf 14½×14 (C)

150	**133**	3p multicoloured (Type I) (a) ..		15	15
		a. Booklet pane. Nos. 150×4, 151×2 (4p stamps at top)) ..		80	
		ab. Do. (4p stamps in centre)		1·00	
		b. Type II (b)		10	10
		ba. Booklet pane. Nos. 150b×4, 151×2 (4p stamps at bottom)		75	

151	**134**	4p multicoloured (ab)		15	15
		(b) Perf 13 (C)			
152	**135**	6p multicoloured (a)		15	15
153	**136**	7p multicoloured (a)		20	20
154	**137**	11p multicoloured (a)		30	30
155	**138**	13p multicoloured (a)		45	35
150/5		Set of 6		1·25	1·10
		First Day Cover			1·25
		Presentation Pack		1·60	
		Set of 6 Gutter Pairs		2·50	

See also Nos. 188/9

Printings: (a) 16.5.79; (b) 29.9.80. Inscribed '1980'

Plate Nos.: 3, 4p 1A (×6); 13p 1G (×4); others 1E (×4)

Sheets: 3, 4p 80 (10 panes 2×3, 5 panes 2×2); others 40 (2 panes 4×5). The 3 and 4p values were printed together, *se-tenant*, each pane of 6 containing four 3p and two 4p, the 4p being in either positions 1 and 2 or 3 and 4. The panes of 4 contain the 4p value only. For details of No. 150ba see after No. 189

Imprint: 3, 4p right-hand corner, bottom margin; others central, bottom margin

Quantities sold: 6p 381,334; 7p 465,473; 11p 341,204; 13p 241,162

Withdrawn: 15.5.80 6p to 13p; 25.3.87 3p, 4p

139 Queen and Court on Tynwald Hill

140 Queen and Procession from St. John's Church to Tynwald Hill

Royal Visit

(Des G. Kneale. Litho Questa)

1979 (5 JULY). Perf 14½ (C)

156	**139**	7p multicoloured		35	35
157	**140**	13p multicoloured		50	50
156/7		Set of 2		85	85
		First Day Cover			1·00
		Presentation Pack		1·00	
		Set of 2 Gutter Pairs		1·60	

Plate Nos.: 7p 1A, 1B (each ×4); 13p 1C, 1D (each ×4)

Sheets: 50 (2 panes 5×5)

Imprint: Right-hand corner, bottom margin

Quantities sold: 7p 641,930; 13p 436,516

Withdrawn: 4.7.80

141 Odin's Raven

Voyage of Odin's Raven

(Des J. Nicholson. Litho Questa)

1979 (19 OCT). *Perf* 14×14½ (C)

158	**141**	15p multicoloured	. . . .	70	70
		First Day Cover	. . . .		1·00
		Presentation Pack	. . . .	1·00	
		Gutter Pair	. . . .	1·40	

See also No. **MS**180.

Plate Nos.: 1A, 1B, 1C, 1D (each ×4)
Sheets: 50 (2 panes 5×5)
Imprint: Right-hand corner, bottom margin
Quantity sold: 412,631
Withdrawn: 18.10.80

142 John Quilliam seized by Press Gang

143 Steering H.M.S. *Victory*, Battle of Trafalgar

144 Captain John Quilliam and H.M.S. *Spencer*

145 Captain John Quilliam (member of the House of Keys)

150th Death Anniversary of Captain John Quilliam

(Des A. Theobald. Litho Questa)

1979 (19 OCT). *Perf* 14 (C)

159	**142**	6p multicoloured	. . . .	15	15
160	**143**	8p multicoloured	. . . .	20	20
161	**144**	13p multicoloured	. . . .	35	35
162	**145**	15p multicoloured	. . . .	40	40
159/62		Set of 4	. . . .	1·00	1·00
		First Day Cover	. . . .		1·50
		Presentation Pack	. . . .	1·60	
		Set of 4 Gutter Pairs	. . . . . .	2·00	

Plate Nos.: 6p 1C, 1D (each ×4); others 1A, 1B (each ×4)
Sheets: 50 (2 panes 5×5)
Imprint: Right-hand corner, bottom margin
Quantities sold: 6p 608,876; 8p 858,665; 13p 360,821; 15p 360,400
Withdrawn: 18.10.80

146 Young Girl with Teddybear and Cat

147 Father Christmas with Young Children

Christmas and International Year of the Child

(Des Mrs. E. Moore. Litho John Waddington)

1979 (19 OCT). *Perf* 13 (C)

163	**146**	5p multicoloured	. . . .	25	25
164	**147**	7p multicoloured	. . . .	35	35
163/4		Set of 2	. . . .	60	60
		First Day Cover	. . . .		1·00
		Presentation Pack	. . . .	1·00	
		Set of 2 Gutter Pairs	. . . . . .	1·25	

Plate Nos. Both values 1A, 1B, 1C, 1D (each ×4)
Sheets: 50 (2 panes 5×5)
Imprint: Central, left-hand margin
Quantities sold: 5p 1,036,495; 7p 1,087,734
Withdrawn: 18.10.80

148 Conglomerate Arch, Langness

149 Braaid Circle

150 Cashtal-yn-Ard

151 Volcanic Rocks at Scarlett

152 Sugar-loaf Rock

150th Anniversary of Royal Geographical Society

(Des J. Nicholson. Litho Questa)

1980 (5 FEB). *Perf* 14½ (C)

165	**148**	7p multicoloured	. . . .	20	20
166	**149**	8p multicoloured	. . . .	20	20
167	**150**	12p multicoloured	. . . .	25	25
168	**151**	13p multicoloured	. . . .	35	35
169	**152**	15p multicoloured	. . . .	40	40
165/9		Set of 5	. . . .	1·25	1·25
		First Day Cover	. . . .		1·60
		Presentation Pack	. . . .	1·60	
		Set of 5 Gutter Pairs	. . . . . .	2·50	

Plate Nos.: 12p 1A, 1B, 1C, 1D (each ×4); 15p 1C, 1D (each ×4); others 1A, 1B (each ×4)

Sheets: 50 (2 panes 5×5)

Imprint: Right-hand corner, bottom margin

Quantities sold: 7p 842,859; 8p 837,710; 12p 361,362; 13p 360,261; 15p 360,310

Withdrawn: 4.2.81

153 *Mona's Isle I*

154 *Douglas I*

155 H.M.S. *Mona's Queen II* sinking U-boat

156 H.M.S. *King Orry III* at Surrender of German Fleet

157 *Ben-My-Chree IV*

158 *Lady of Mann II*

150th Anniversary of Isle of Man Steam Packet Company

(Des J. Nicholson. Photo Courvoisier)

1980 (6 MAY). *Granite paper. Perf* 11½ (C)

170	**153**	7p multicoloured	. . . .	20	20
171	**154**	8p multicoloured	. . . .	20	20
172	**155**	11½p multicoloured	. . . .	30	30
173	**156**	12p multicoloured	. . . .	30	30
174	**157**	13p multicoloured	. . . .	40	35
175	**158**	15p multicoloured	. . . .	50	40
170/5		Set of 6	. . . .	1·75	1·60
		First Day Cover	. . . .		1·75
		Presentation Pack	. . . . . .	1·90	
		Set of 6 Gutter Pairs	. . . .	3·50	
MS176		180×125 mm. Nos. 170/5	1·75	1·75
		First Day Cover	. . . .		2·75

No. **MS176** was issued to commemorate the 'London 1980' International Stamp Exhibition.

Cylinder Nos.: All values A1–1–1–1, B1–1–1–1, C1–1–1–1, D1–1–1–1

Sheets: 40 (2 panes 5×4)

Imprint: Central, bottom margin

Quantities sold: 7p 512,449; 8p 624,090; 11½p 381,466; 12p 367,943; 13p 368,138; 15p 376,596; miniature sheet 300,678

Withdrawn: 5.5.81

159 Stained Glass Window, T. E. Brown Room, Manx Museum

160 Clifton College, Bristol

Europa. Personalities. Thomas Edward Brown (poet and scholar) Commemoration

(Des G. Kneale. Photo Courvoisier)

1980 (6 MAY). *Granite paper. Perf* 11½ (C)

177	**159**	7p multicoloured	. . . .	20	20
178	**160**	13½p multicoloured	. . . .	40	40
177/8		Set of 2	. . . .	60	60
		First Day Cover	. . . .		1·00
		Presentation Pack	. . . . . .	1·10	
		Set of 2 Gutter Pairs	. . . .	1·25	

Cylinder Nos.: Both values A1–1–1–1–1, B1–1–1–1–1, C1–1–1–1–1,
D1–1–1–1–1

Sheets: 20 (2 panes 2×5)

Imprint: Bottom margin at right-hand corner of left-hand pane

Quantities sold: 7p 1,726,009; 13½p 1,708,590

Withdrawn: 5.5.81

161 King Olav V and *Norge*
(Norwegian royal yacht)

Visit of King Olav V of Norway, August 1979

(Des J. Nicholson. Litho Questa)

1980 (13 JUNE). *Perf* 14×14½ (C)

179	**161**	12p multicoloured	50	50
		First Day Cover		1·00
		Presentation Pack	1·00	
		Gutter Pair		1·00
MS180		125×157 mm. Nos. 158 and 179	1·00	1·00
		First Day Cover		1·50

No. **MS**180 also commemorates the "NORWEX 80" stamp exhibition, Oslo.

Plate Nos.: 1C, 1D (each ×4)

Sheets: 40 (2 panes 5×4)

Imprint: Right-hand corner, bottom margin

Quantities sold: 12p 449,267; miniature sheet 401,424

Withdrawn: 12.6.81

162 Winter Wren and View
of Calf of Man

163 European Robin and
View of Port Erin
Marine Biological
Station

Christmas and Wildlife Conservation Year

(Des J. Nicholson. Litho John Waddington)

1980 (29 SEPT). *Perf* 13½×14 (C)

181	**162**	6p multicoloured	20	20
182	**163**	8p multicoloured	30	30
181/2		Set of 2	50	50
		First Day Cover		1·00
		Presentation Pack	1·00	
		Set of 2 Gutter Pairs	1·00	

Plate Nos.: 6p 1B, 1D (each ×4); 8p 1A, 1C (each ×4)

Sheets: 40 (2 panes 4×5)

Imprint: Right-hand corner, bottom margin

Quantities sold: 6p 967,976; 8p 942,323

Withdrawn: 28.9.81

164 William Kermode and
Brig *Robert Quayle*,
1819

165 'Mona Vale', Van
Diemen's Land, 1834

166 Ross Bridge, Tasmania

167 'Mona Vale', Tasmania
(completed 1868)

168 Robert Q. Kermode and
Parliament Buildings,
Tasmania

Kermode Family in Tasmania Commemoration

(Des A. Theobald. Litho Questa)

1980 (29 SEPT). *Perf* 14½ (C)

183	**164**	7p multicoloured	20	20
184	**165**	9p multicoloured	25	25
185	**166**	13½p multicoloured	40	35
186	**167**	15p multicoloured	45	40
187	**168**	17½p multicoloured	50	45
183/7		Set of 5	1·60	1·50
		First Day Cover		1·50
		Presentation Pack	2·00	
		Set of 5 Gutter Pairs	3·25	

Plate Nos.: All values 1C, 1D (each ×4)

Sheets: 40 (2 panes 5×4)

Imprint: Right-hand corner, bottom margin

Quantities sold: 7p 416,487; 9p 498,880; 13½p 318,353; 15p 314,837; 17½p 315,107

Withdrawn: 28.9.81

169 Peregrine Falcon

170 Loaghtyn Ram

Booklet stamps

(Des J. Nicholson. Litho Harrison)

1980 (29 SEPT). *Perf* 14½×14 (C)

188	**169**	1p multicoloured	40	40
		a. Booklet pane. Nos. 151, 188 and 189, each ×2	75	
189	**170**	5p multicoloured	40	40
188/9		Set of 2	80	80
		First Day Cover (Nos. 150b ×2, 151×2, 188 and 189) . .		1·10
		Presentation Pack (Nos. 150b ×2, 151×2, 188 and 189) . .	1·25	

In addition to Booklets SB11/12 Nos. 188/9 also come from special booklet sheets of 60. These sheets contain No. 150ba×5 and No. 188a×5.

Plate Nos.: 1A (×7)

Withdrawn: 25.3.87

171 Luggers passing Red Pier, Douglas

172 Peel Lugger *Wanderer* rescuing survivors from the *Lusitania*

173 Nickeys leaving Port St. Mary Harbour

174 Nobby entering Ramsey Harbour

175 Nickeys *Sunbeam* and *Zebra* at Port Erin

Centenary of Royal National Mission to Deep Sea Fishermen

(Des J. Nicholson. Litho Questa)

1981 (24 FEB). *Perf* 14 (C)

190	**171**	8p multicoloured	. . . .	25	25
191	**172**	9p multicoloured	. . . .	30	30
192	**173**	18p multicoloured	. . . .	45	45
193	**174**	20p multicoloured	. . . .	50	50
194	**175**	22p multicoloured	. . . .	50	50
190/4		Set of 5	. . . .	1·75	1·75
		First Day Cover .	. . . .		2·00
		Presentation Pack .	. . . .	2·00	
		Set of 5 Gutter Pairs .	. . . . .	3·50	

Plate Nos.: 8p 1E, 1F (each ×4); 9p 1G, 1H (each ×4); 22p 1A, 1B (each ×4); others 1C, 1D (each ×4)

Sheets: 40 (2 panes 5×4)

Imprint: Right-hand corner, bottom margin

Quantities sold: 8p 566,522; 9p 583,358; 18p 334,765; 20p 315,511; 22p 324,607

Withdrawn: 23.2.82

176 'Crosh Cuirn' Superstition

177 'Bollan Cross' Superstition

Europa. Folklore

(Des J. Nicholson. Litho Questa)

1981 (22 MAY). *Perf* 14½ (C)

195	**176**	8p multicoloured	. . . .	25	25
196	**177**	18p multicoloured	. . . .	75	75
195/6		Set of 2	. . . .	1·00	1·00
		First Day Cover .	. . . .		1·00
		Presentation Pack .	. . . .	1·25	
		Set of 2 Gutter Pairs .	. . . . .	2·00	

Plate Nos.: 1A, 1B (each ×4)

Sheets: 24 (2 panes 3×4)

Imprint: Right-hand corner, bottom margin

Quantities sold: 8p 1,261,267; 18p 1,243,459

Withdrawn: 21.5.82

178 Lt. Mark Wilks (Royal Manx Fencibles) and Peel Castle

179 Ensign Mark Wilks and Fort St. George, Madras

180 Governor Mark Wilks and Napoleon, St. Helena

181 Col. Mark Wilks (Speaker of the House of Keys) and Estate, Kirby

150th Death Anniversary of Colonel Mark Wilks

(Des A. Theobald. Litho Questa)

1981 (22 MAY). *Perf* 14 (C)

197	**178**	8p multicoloured	. . . .	25	25
198	**179**	20p multicoloured	. . . .	50	50
199	**180**	22p multicoloured	. . . .	70	55
200	**181**	25p multicoloured	. . . .	80	80
197/200		Set of 4	. . . .	2·00	1·90
		First Day Cover	. . . .		2·00
		Presentation Pack	. . . .	2·50	
		Set of 4 Gutter Pairs	. . . . . .	4·00	

Plate Nos.: 8, 20p 1A, 1B (each ×5); others 1A, 1B (each ×4)

Sheets: 40 (2 panes 5×4)

Imprint: 22p none; others right-hand corner, bottom margin

Quantities sold: 8p 371,280; 20p 278,840; 22p 294,480; 25p 272,640

Withdrawn: 21.5.82

182 Miss Emmeline Goulden (Mrs. Pankhurst) and Mrs. Sophia Jane Goulden

Centenary of Manx Women's Suffrage

(Des A. Theobald. Litho Questa)

1981 (22 MAY). *Perf* 14 (C)

201	**182**	9p black, olive-grey and stone	. .	50	50
		First Day Cover	. . . .		1·00
		Presentation Pack	. . . .	1·00	
		Gutter Pair	. . . .	1·00	

Plate Nos.: 1C, 1D (each ×3)

Sheets: 40 (2 panes 5×4)

Imprint: Right-hand corner, bottom margin

Quantity sold: 659,760

Withdrawn: 21.5.82

183 Prince Charles and Lady Diana Spencer

Royal Wedding

(Des. G Kneale. Litho Harrison)

1981 (29 JULY). *Perf* 14 (C)

202	**183**	9p black, bright blue & pale blue	50	50
203		25p black, bright blue and pink	. .	1·50	1·50
202/3		Set of 2	. . . .	2·00	2·00
		First Day Cover	. . . .		3·50
		Presentation Pack	. . . .	3·00	
		Set of 2 Gutter Pairs	. . . . . .	4·00	
MS204		130×183 mm. Nos. 202/3×2	. . . .	4·50	4·50
		First Day Cover	. . . .		5·00

Plate Nos.: 9p 1C, 1D (each ×3); 25p 1A, 1B (each ×3)

Sheets: 50 (2 panes 5×5)

Imprint: Central, bottom margin

Quantities sold: 9p 668,864; 25p 474,364; miniature sheet 327,094

Withdrawn: 28.7.82

184 Douglas War Memorial, Poppies and Inscription

185 Major Robert Cain (war hero)

186 Festival of
Remembrance,
Royal Albert Hall

187 T.S.S. *Tynwald* at
Dunkirk, May, 1940

60th Anniversary of The Royal British Legion

(Des A. Theobald. Photo Courvoisier)

1981 (29 SEPT). *Granite paper. Perf* 11½ (C)

205	**184**	8p multicoloured	25	25
206	**185**	10p multicoloured	30	35
207	**186**	18p multicoloured	65	65
208	**187**	20p multicoloured	75	75
205/8		Set of 4	1·75	1·75
		First Day Cover		1·90
		Presentation Pack	2·00	
		Set of 4 Gutter Pairs	3·50	

Cylinder Nos.: 8p A1–1–1–1, B1–1–1–1; others A1–1–1–1–1,
B1–1–1–1–1

Sheets: 40 (2 panes 4×5)

Imprint: Central, bottom margin

Quantities sold: 8p 314,794; 10p 799,326; 18p 284,059; 20p 261,194

Withdrawn: 28.9.82

188 Nativity Scene
(stained glass
window, St. George's
Church)

189 Children from Special
School performing Nativity
Play

Christmas

(Des John Waddington (7p), G. Kneale (9p). Litho John
Waddington)

1981 (29 SEPT). *Perf* 14 (C)

209	**188**	7p multicoloured	25	25
210	**189**	9p multicoloured	35	35
209/10		Set of 2	60	60
		First Day Cover		1·00
		Presentation Pack	1·00	
		Set of 2 Gutter Pairs	1·25	

The 7p value also commemorates the bicentenary of St.
George's Church, Douglas and the 9p the International Year
for Disabled Persons.

Plate Nos.: 7p 1A, 1B (each ×6); 9p 1A, 1B, 1C, 1D (each ×6)

Sheets: 40 (2 panes 2×10)

Imprint: Right-hand corner, bottom margin

Quantities sold: 7p 855,407; 9p 862,892

Withdrawn: 28.9.82

190 Joseph and William
Cunningham (founders
of Manx Boy Scout
Movement) and
Cunningham House
Headquarters

191 Baden-Powell visiting Isle
of Man, 1911

192 Baden-Powell and
Scout Emblem

193 Scouts and
Baden-Powell's Last
Message

194 Scout Salute,
Handshake, Emblem
and Globe

110

75th Anniversary of Boy Scout Movement and 125th Birth Anniversary of Lord Baden-Powell

(Des G. Kneale. Litho Questa)

1982 (23 FEB). *Perf* 14×14½ (19½p) *or* 13½×14 (*others*), *all comb*

211	**190**	9p multicoloured	30	30
212	**191**	10p multicoloured	30	30
213	**192**	19½p multicoloured	60	60
214	**193**	24p multicoloured	70	70
215	**194**	29p multicoloured	90	90
211/15		*Set of 5*	2·50	2·50
		First Day Cover		2·75
		Presentation Pack	3·00	
		Set of 5 Gutter Pairs	5·00	

Plate Nos.: 9p 1A, 1B (each ×4); 29p 1A, 1B (each ×5); others 1C, 1D (each ×4)

Sheets: 40 (2 panes 5×4)

Imprint: Right-hand corner, bottom margin

Quantities sold: 9p 748,353; 10p 868,401; 19½p 364,487; 24p 368,346; 29p 370,466

Withdrawn: 22.2.83

195 *The Principals and Duties of Christianity* (first book printed in Manx, 1707), and Bishop T. Wilson

196 Landing at Derbyhaven (visit of Thomas, 2nd Earl of Derby, 1507)

Europa. Historic Events

(Des A. Theobald. Photo Courvoisier)

1982 (1 JUNE). *Granite paper. Perf* 12×12½ (C)

216	**195**	9p multicoloured	25	25
217	**196**	19½p multicoloured	50	50
216/17		*Set of 2*	75	75
		First Day Cover		1·00
		Presentation Pack	1·00	
		Set of 2 Gutter Pairs	1·50	

Cylinder Nos.: Both values A1–1–1–1–1, B1–1–1–1–1

Sheets: 24 (2 panes 3×4)

Imprint: Right-hand corner, bottom margin

Quantities sold: 9p 1,120,457; 19½p 1,129,315

Withdrawn: 31.5.83

197 Charlie Collier (first TT race (single cylinder) winner) and Tourist Trophy Race, 1907

198 Freddie Dixon (Sidecar and Junior TT winner) and Junior TT race, 1927

199 Jimmie Simpson (TT winner and first to lap at 60, 70 and 80 mph) and Senior TT, 1932

200 Mike Hailwood (winner of fourteen TTs) and Senior TT, 1961

201 Jock Taylor (Sidecar TT winner, 1978, 1980 and 1981) and Sidecar TT (with Benga Johansson), 1980

75th Anniversary of Tourist Trophy Motorcycle Races

(Des J. Nicholson. Litho Questa)

1982 (1 JUNE). *Perf* 14 (C)

218	**197**	9p multicoloured	20	20
219	**198**	10p multicoloured	25	25
220	**199**	24p multicoloured	70	70
221	**200**	26p multicoloured	75	75
222	**201**	29p multicoloured	90	90
218/22		*Set of 5*	2·50	2·50
		First Day Cover		3·00
		Presentation Pack	3·00	
		Stamp Cards (set of 5)	1·25	4·50
		Set of 5 Gutter Pairs	5·00	

Plate Nos.: All values 1B, 1C, 1D (each ×4)

Sheets: 40 (2 panes 5×4)

Imprint: Right-hand corner, bottom margin

Quantities sold: 9p 837,930; 10p 866,223; 24p 351,406; 26p 361,063; 29p 355,690

Withdrawn: 11.6.83

ISLE OF MAN 12p   **202** *Mona I*

ISLE OF MAN 19½p   **203** *Manx Maid II*

150th Anniversary of Isle of Man Steam Packet Company Mail Contract

(Des J. Nicholson. Litho Questa)

1982 (5 OCT). *Perf* 13½ (C)

223	**202**	12p multicoloured	50	50
224	**203**	19½p multicoloured	75	75
223/4		Set of 2	1·25	1·25
		First Day Cover		1·75
		Presentation Pack	1·60	
		Set of 2 Gutter Pairs	2·50	

Plate Nos.: Both values 1A (×4)
Sheets: 40 (2 panes 5×4)
Imprint: Right-hand bottom margin
Quantities sold: 12p 701,044; 19½p 291,100
Withdrawn: 4.10.83

204 The Three Wise Men

205 Snow Scene and Robin

Christmas

(Des and litho John Waddington)

1982 (5 OCT). *Perf* 13 (C)

225	**204**	8p multicoloured	50	50
226	**205**	11p multicoloured	50	50
225/6		Set of 2	1·00	1·00
		First Day Cover		1·25
		Presentation Pack	1·40	
		Set of 2 Gutter Pairs	2·00	

Plate Nos. 8p 1A, 1C (each ×4), 11p 1B, 1D (each ×4)
Sheets: 40 (8p 2 panes 5×4), (11p 2 panes 4×5)
Imprint: Right-hand corner, bottom margin (8p); Top right-hand margin (11p)
Quantities sold: 8p 740,651; 11p 787,552
Withdrawn: 4.10.83

206 Princess Diana with Prince William

21st Birthday of the Princess of Wales and Birth of Prince William

(Des G. Kneale. Litho Questa)

1982 (12 OCT). *Sheet* 100×83 *mm. Perf* 14½×14 (C)

MS227	**206**	50p multicoloured	3·00	3·00
		First Day Cover		4·50
		Presentation Pack	3·25	

Quantity sold: 218,759
Withdrawn: 11.10.83

207 Opening of Salvation Army Citadel, and T. H. Cannell, J.P.

208 Early Meeting-place, and Gen. William Booth

209 Salvation Army Band

210 Treating Lepers, and Lt.-Col. Thomas Bridson

217 Grey Herons

218 Herring-gulls

Centenary of Salvation Army in Isle of Man

(Des A. Theobald. Photo Courvoisier)

1983 (15 FEB). *Granite paper. Perf* 11½ (C)

228	**207**	10p multicoloured	30	30
229	**208**	12p multicoloured	40	40
230	**209**	19½p multicoloured	60	60
231	**210**	26p multicoloured	90	90
228/31		Set of 4	2·00	2·00
		First Day Cover		3·00
		Presentation Pack	2·50	
		Set of 4 Gutter Pairs	4·00	

Cylinder Nos.: All values B1–1–1–1–1

Sheets: 40 (2 panes 4×5)

Imprint: Central, bottom margin

Quantities sold: 10p 467,665; 12p 567,863; 19½p 267,929; 26p 288,069

Withdrawn: 14.2.84

219 Razorbills

220 Great Black-backed Gulls

221 Common Shelducks

222 Oystercatchers

223 Arctic Terns

224 Common Guillemots

211 Atlantic Puffins

212 Northern Gannets

225 Redshanks

226 Mute Swans

213 Lesser Black-backed Gulls

214 Common Cormorants

215 Kittiwakes

216 Shags

227 'Queen Elizabeth II' (Ricardo Macarron)

Sea Birds and Queen's Portrait (£5)

(Des Colleen Corlett (£5), J. Nicholson (others). Litho Questa)

1983 (15 FEB)–**85.** *Perf* 14 (20p to £1), 14×13½ (£5) *or* 14½ (*others*), *all comb*

232	**211**	1p multicoloured (a)	....	30	30
233	**212**	2p multicoloured (a)	....	30	30
234	**213**	5p multicoloured (a)	....	60	40
235	**214**	8p multicoloured (a)	....	60	40
236	**215**	10p multicoloured (a)	....	60	35
237	**216**	11p multicoloured (a)	....	60	35
238	**217**	12p multicoloured (a)	....	70	40
239	**218**	13p multicoloured (a)	....	70	40
240	**219**	14p multicoloured (a)	....	70	40
241	**220**	15p multicoloured (a)	....	80	50
242	**221**	16p multicoloured (a)	....	80	50
243	**222**	18p multicoloured (a)	....	80	60
244	**223**	20p multicoloured (b)	....	90	1·00
245	**224**	25p multicoloured (b)	....	1·00	1·00
246	**225**	50p multicoloured (b)	....	1·75	1·75
247	**226**	£1 multicoloured (b)	....	3·25	3·00
248	**227**	£5 multicoloured (c)	....	10·00	10·00
232/48		Set of 17	....	21·00	19·00
		First Day Covers (4)	......		26·00
		Presentation Packs (4)	....	22·00	

Printings: (a) 15.2.83; (b) 14.9.83; (c) 31.1.85

Plate Nos. 1p to £1 1A, 1B, 1C, 1D (each x 4); £5 1A, 1B (each ×4)

Sheets: 10 (5×2) £5; 50 (5×10) others

Imprint: £5 Right-hand margin; others right-hand corner, bottom margin

Withdrawn: 30.6.88 1p to 18p; 31.12.88 20p to £1; 4.7.94 £5

228 Design Drawings by Robert Casement for the Great Laxey Wheel

229 Robert Casement and the Great Laxey Wheel

Europa. The Great Laxey Wheel

(Des J. Nicholson. Litho Questa)

1983 (18 MAY). *Perf* 14 (C)

249	**228**	10p black, azure and buff	....	40	35
250	**229**	20½p multicoloured	....	60	70
249/50		Set of 2	....	1·00	1·00
		First Day Cover			1·75
		Presentation Pack	......	1·75	
		Set of 2 Gutter Pairs	....	2·00	

Plate Nos.: 10p 1A, 1B (each ×3); 20½p 1A, 1B (each ×4)

Sheets: 12 (2 panes 2×3)

Imprint: Right-hand corner, bottom margin

Quantities sold: 10p 653,743; 20½p 686,084

Withdrawn 17.5.84

230 Nick Keig (international yachtsman) and Trimaran *Three Legs of Man III*

231 King William's College, Castletown

232 Sir William Bragg (winner of Nobel Prize for Physics) and Spectrometer

233 General Sir George White V.C. and Action at Charasiah

150th Anniversary of King William's College

(Des J. Nicholson (10p, 31p), Colleen Corlett (12p, 28p). Photo Courvoisier)

1983 (18 MAY). *Granite paper. Perf* 11½ (C)

251	**230**	10p multicoloured	....	20	20
252	**231**	12p multicoloured	....	30	30
253	**232**	28p multicoloured	....	80	80
254	**233**	31p multicoloured	....	1·00	1·00
251/4		Set of 4	....	2·00	2·00
		First Day Cover	....		3·00
		Presentation Pack	....	2·50	
		Set of 4 Gutter Pairs	......	4·25	

Cylinder Nos.: 10p C1–1–1–1, D1–1–1–1; 12p C1–1–1–1, D1–1–1–1; 28p A1–1–1–1, B1–1–1–1; 31p A1–1–1–1, B1–1–1–1–1

Sheets: 40 (2 panes 5×4)

Imprint: Central bottom margin
Quantities sold: 10p 552,573; 12p 693,004; 28p 263,814; 31p 242,393
Withdrawn: 17.5.84

234 New Post Office Headquarters, Douglas

235 Landing of the Vikings on Man, AD 938

World Communications Year and 10th Anniversary of Isle of Man Post Office Authority.

(Des Colleen Corlett (10p), J. Nicholson (15p). Litho Questa)

1983 (5 JULY). *Perf* 14½ (C)

255	**234**	10p multicoloured	. . . .	40	40
256	**235**	15p multicoloured	. . . .	60	60
255/6		*Set of* 2	. . . .	1·00	1·00
		First Day Cover			1·60
		Presentation Pack		1·60	
		Stamp Cards (set of 2)		60	1·25
		Set of 2 *Gutter Pairs*		2·00	

Plate Nos.: Both values 1A, 1B, 1C, 1D (each ×5)
Sheets: 40 (2 panes 4×5)
Imprint: Central, right-hand margin
Quantities sold: 10p 269,843; 15p 222,013
Withdrawn: 4.7.84

236 Shepherds

Christmas 1983 / ISLE OF MAN 12p

237 Three Kings

Christmas

(Des Colleen Corlett. Litho John Waddington)

1983 (14 SEPT). *Perf* 13 (C)

257	**236**	9p multicoloured	. . . .	50	50
258	**237**	12p multicoloured	. . . .	50	50
257/8		*Set of* 2	. . . .	1·00	1·00
		First Day Cover			1·50
		Presentation Pack		1·25	
		Set of 2 *Gutter Pairs*		2·00	

Plate Nos.: Both values 1A, 1B, 1C, 1D (each ×5)
Sheets: 40 (2 panes 5×4)
Imprint: Right-hand corner, bottom margin
Quantities sold: 9p 642,763; 12p 656,060
Withdrawn: 13.9.84

238 *Manx King* (full-rigged ship)

239 *Hope* (barque)

240 *Rio Grande* (brig)

241 *Lady Elizabeth* (barque)

242 *Sumatra* (barque)

243 Wreck of *Lady Elizabeth* as shown on Falkland Islands Stamp

The Karran Fleet

(Des J. Nicholson (10p to 31p); Colleen Corlett, J. Nicholson and J. Smith (miniature sheet). Litho Questa)

1984 (14 FEB). *Perf* 14 (C)

259	**238**	10p multicoloured	. . . .	40	40
260	**239**	13p multicoloured	. . . .	55	55
261	**240**	20½p multicoloured	. . . .	85	85
262	**241**	28p multicoloured	. . . .	1·00	1·00
263	**242**	31p multicoloured	. . . .	1·10	1·10
259/63		*Set of* 5	. . . .	3·50	3·50
		First Day Cover			4·00
		Presentation Pack		4·00	
		Set of 5 *Gutter Pairs*		7·00	

MS264		103×94 mm. 28p Type **241**; 31p			
		Type **243** (*sold at* 60p)	3·00	3·00
		First Day Cover			4·00
		Presentation Pack		3·50	

No. **MS**264 was issued to commemorate links between the Isle of Man and the Falkland Islands.

Plate Nos.: All values 1A, 1B (each ×4)

Sheets: 40 (2 panes 5×4)

Imprint: Right-hand corner, bottom margin

Quantities sold: 10p 389,278; 13p 417,637; 20½p 253,949; 28p 238,292; 31p 236,196; miniature sheet 137,031

Withdrawn: 13.2.85

244 C.E.P.T. 25th Anniversary Logo

Europa

(Des J. Larrivière, adapted Colleen Corlett. Photo Courvoisier)

1984 (27 APR). *Granite paper. Perf 12×11½ (C)*

265	**244**	10p dull orange, deep reddish brown and pale orange....	35	35
266		20½p lt blue, dp blue & pale blue	70	70
		Set of 2	1·00	1·00
		First Day Cover		2·00
		Presentation Pack	1·60	

Cylinder Nos.: 10p B1–1–1; 20½p A1–1–1

Sheets: 20 (4×5)

Imprint: Central, right-hand margin

Quantities sold: 10p 705,410; 20½p 715,479

Withdrawn: 26.4.85

245 Railway Air Services De Havilland D.H.84 Dragon Mk 2

246 West Coast Air Services De Havilland D.H.86A Dragon Express *Ronaldsway*

247 B.E.A. Douglas DC-3

248 B.E.A. Vickers Viscount 800

249 Telair Britten Norman Islander

50th Anniversary of First Official Airmail to the Isle of Man and 40th Anniversary of International Civil Aviation Organization

(Des A. Theobald. Litho Questa)

1984 (27 APR). *Perf* 14 (C)

267	**245**	11p multicoloured	45	45
268	**246**	13p multicoloured	55	55
269	**247**	26p multicoloured	95	95
270	**248**	28p multicoloured	1·00	1·00
271	**249**	31p multicoloured	1·25	1·25
267/71		*Set of 5*	3·75	3·75
		First Day Cover		4·50
		Presentation Pack	4·00	
		Set of 5 Gutter Pairs	7·50	

Plate Nos. All values 1C, 1D (each ×4)

Sheets: 40 (2 panes 5×4)

Imprint: Right-hand corner, bottom margin

Quantities sold: 11p 399,155; 13p 440,623; 26p 234,165; 28p 173,841; 31p 171,890

Withdrawn: 26.4.85

Year Pack 1983

1984. *Comprises Nos.* 228/47, 249/58

	Year Pack	20·00

Withdrawn: 31.3.85

250 Window from Glencrutchey House, Douglas

251 Window from Lonan Old Church

Christmas. Stained-glass Windows

(Des D. Swinton. Litho John Waddington)

1984 (21 SEPT). *Perf* 14 (C)

272	**250**	10p multicoloured	50	50
273	**251**	13p multicoloured	50	50
272/3		*Set of 2*	1·00	1·00
		First Day Cover		1·40
		Presentation Pack	1·40	
		Set of 2 Gutter Pairs	2·00	

Plate Nos.: Both values 1A, 1C (each ×6)

Sheets: 40 (2 panes 4×5)

Imprint: Top right-hand margin

Quantities sold: 10p 652,870; 13p 668,084

Withdrawn: 20.9.85

252 William Cain's Birthplace, Ballasalla

253 The *Anna* leaving Liverpool, 1852

254 Early Australian Railway

255 William Cain as Mayor of Melbourne, and Town Hall

256 Royal Exhibition Buildings, Melbourne

William Cain (civic leader, Victoria) Commemoration

(Des J. Nicholson. Litho Questa)

1984 (21 SEPT). *Perf* 14½×14 (C)

274	**252**	11p multicoloured	....	35	35
275	**253**	22p multicoloured	....	75	75
276	**254**	28p multicoloured	....	1·00	1·00
277	**255**	30p multicoloured	....	1·10	1·10
278	**256**	33p multicoloured	....	1·25	1·25
274/8		*Set of* 5	....	4·00	4·00
		First Day Cover	....		4·25
		Presentation Pack	....	4·50	
		Set of 5 *Gutter Pairs*	......	8·00	

Plate Nos.: All values 1B (×4)

Sheets: 40 (2 panes 5×4)

Imprint: Right-hand corner, bottom margin

Quantities sold: 11p 393,219; 22p 280,598; 28p 223,515; 30p 220,913; 33p 213,933

Withdrawn: 20.9.85

257 Queen Elizabeth II and Commonwealth Parliamentary Association Badge

258 Queen Elizabeth II and Manx Emblem

Links with the Commonwealth. 30th Commonwealth Parliamentary Association Conference

(Des and litho John Waddington)

1984 (21 SEPT). *Perf* 14 (C)

279	**257**	14p multicoloured	....	50	50
280	**258**	33p multicoloured	....	1·10	1·10
279/80		*Set of* 2	....	1·60	1·60
		First Day Cover	....		2·25
		Presentation Pack	....	2·00	
		Set of 2 *Gutter Pairs*	......	3·25	

Plate Nos.: Both values 1A, 1C (each ×7)

Sheets: 40 (2 panes 5×4)

Imprint: Right-hand corner, bottom margin

Quantities sold: 14p 373,204; 33p 231,073

Withdrawn: 20.9.85

Year Pack 1984

1985 (1 JAN). *Comprises Nos.* 259/80

		Year Pack	....	19·00

Withdrawn: 31.12.85

259 Cunningham House Headquarters, and Mrs. Willie Cunningham and Mrs. Joseph Cunningham (former Commissioners)

260 Princess Margaret, Isle of Man Standard and Guides

261 Lady Olave Baden-Powell opening Guide Headquarters, 1955

262 Guide Uniforms from 1910 to 1985

263 Guide Handclasp, Salute and Early Badge

75th Anniversary of Girl Guide Movement

(Des Colleen Corlett. Photo Courvoisier)

1985 (31 JAN). *Granite paper. Perf* 11½ (C)

281	**259**	11p multicoloured	45	45
282	**260**	14p multicoloured	75	75
283	**261**	29p multicoloured	1·10	1·10
284	**262**	31p multicoloured	1·40	1·40
285	**263**	34p multicoloured	1·60	1·60
281/5		Set of 5	4·75	4·75
		First Day Cover		5·50
		Presentation Pack	5·00	
		Set of 5 Gutter Pairs	9·50	

Cylinder Nos.: 11p, 34p A1–1–1–1–1, B1–1–1–1–1; others A1–1–1–1, B1–1–1–1

Sheets: 40 (2 panes 4×5)

Imprint: Central bottom margin of each pane

Withdrawn: 30.1.86

264 Score of Manx National Anthem

265 William H. Gill (lyricist)

266 Score of Hymn 'Crofton'

267 Dr. John Clague (composer)

Europa. European Music Year

(Des D. Swinton. Photo Courvoisier)

1985 (24 APR). *Granite paper. Perf* 11½ (C)

286	**264**	12p black, orange-brn & chestnut	50	45
		a. Horiz pair. Nos. 286/7	1·00	90
287	**265**	12p black, orange-brn & chestnut	50	45
288	**266**	22p black, brt new blue & new bl	1·00	95
		a. Horiz pair. Nos. 288/9	2·10	1·90
289	**267**	22p black, brt new blue & new bl	1·00	95
286/9		Set of 4	2·75	2·50
		First Day Cover		3·50
		Presentation Pack	3·00	

Cylinder Nos.: Both values A1–1–1, B1–1–1

Sheets: 20 (4×5). The two designs for each value printed together, *se-tenant*, in horizontal pairs throughout the sheets

Imprint: Central, bottom margin

Withdrawn: 23.4.86

268 Charles Rolls in 20 h.p. Rolls-Royce (1906 Tourist Trophy Race)

269 W. Bentley in 3 litre Bentley (1922 Tourist Trophy Race)

270 F. Gerrard in E.R.A. (1950 British Empire Trophy Race)

271 Brian Lewis in Alfa Romeo (1934 Mannin Moar Race)

272 Jaguar 'XJ-SC' ('Roads Open' Car, 1984 Motor-cycle T.T. Races)

273 Tony Pond and Mike Nicholson in Vauxhall 'Chevette' (1981 Rothmans International Rally)

Century of Motoring

(Des A. Theobald. Litho Questa)

1985 (25 MAY). *Perf* 14 (C)

290	**268**	12p multicoloured	. . . .	40	40
		a. *Horiz pair. Nos.* 290/1	. . . .	85	85
291	**269**	12p multicoloured	. . . .	40	40
292	**270**	14p multicoloured	. . . .	55	55
		a. *Horiz pair. Nos.* 292/3	. . . .	1·10	1·10
293	**271**	14p multicoloured	. . . .	55	55
294	**272**	31p multicoloured	. . . .	1·40	1·25
		a. *Horiz pair. Nos.* 294/5	. . . .	2·75	2·50
295	**273**	31p multicoloured	. . . .	1·40	1·25
290/5		*Set of* 6	. . . .	4·25	4·00
		First Day Cover			4·75
		Presentation Pack			
		Stamp Cards (set of 6)	. . . .	2·25	6·00
		Set of 3 *Gutter Blocks of* 4		8·50	

Plate Nos.: All values 1A, 1B (each ×6)

Sheets: 40 (2 panes 4×5). The two designs for each value printed together, *se-tenant*, in horizontal pairs throughout the sheets

Imprint: Right-hand corner, bottom margin of each pane

Withdrawn: 24.5.86

274 Queen Alexandra and Victorian Sergeant with Wife

275 Queen Mary and Royal Air Force Family

276 Earl Mountbatten and Royal Navy Family

277 Prince Michael of Kent and Royal Marine with Parents, 1982

Centenary of the Soldiers', Sailors' and Airmen's Families Association

(Des Colleen Corlett. Litho Questa)

1985 (4 SEPT). *Perf* 14 (C)

296	**274**	12p multicoloured	. . . .	40	40
297	**275**	15p multicoloured	. . . .	55	55
298	**276**	29p multicoloured	. . . .	1·10	1·10
299	**277**	34p multicoloured	. . . .	1·25	1·25
296/9		*Set of* 4	. . . .	3·00	3·00
		First Day Cover			4·50
		Presentation Pack		4·00	
		Set of 4 *Gutter Pairs*		6·00	

Plate Nos. 12p, 34p 1A, 1B, 1C, 1D, 1E, 1F, 1G, 1H (each ×6); others 1A, 1B, 1C, 1D, 1E, 1F, 1G, 1H (each ×5)

Sheets: 40 (2 panes 5×4)

Imprint: Right-hand corner, bottom margin of each pane.

Withdrawn: 3.9.86

278 Kirk Maughold (Birthplace)

279 Lieut.-Gen. Sir Mark Cubbon

280 Memorial Statue, Bangalore, India

Birth Bicentenary of Lieut.-Gen. Sir Mark Cubbon (Indian administrator)

(Des A. Theobald. Litho Questa)

1985 (2 OCT). *Perf* 14 (C)

300	**278**	12p multicoloured	. . . .	45	45
301	**279**	22p multicoloured	. . . .	1·10	1·10
302	**280**	45p multicoloured	. . . .	1·90	1·90
300/2		*Set of* 3	. . . .	3·00	3·00
		First Day Cover			4·50
		Presentation Pack		3·75	
		Set of 3 *Gutter Pairs*		6·00	

Plate Nos.: All values 1A, 1B, 1C, 1D (each ×4)

Sheets: 40 (2 panes 5×4) 12p or (2 panes 4×5) others

Imprint: Right-hand corner, bottom margin of each pane

Withdrawn: 1.10.86

281 St. Peter's Church, Onchan

282 Royal Chapel of St. John, Tynwald

283 Bride Parish Church

Christmas. Manx Churches

(Des A. Theobald. Litho John Waddington)

1985 (2 OCT). *Perf* 13×13½ (C)

303	**281**	11p multicoloured	45	45
304	**282**	14p multicoloured	55	55
305	**283**	31p multicoloured	1·25	1·25
303/5		*Set of 3*	2·00	2·00
		First Day Cover		3·75
		Presentation Pack	3·00	
		Set of 3 Gutter Pairs	4·00	

Plate Nos.: All values 1A, 1B, 1C, 1D (each ×4)

Sheets: 40 (2 panes 5×4)

Imprint: Right-hand corner, bottom margin of each pane

Withdrawn: 1.10.86

Post Office Yearbook

1985 (9 DEC). *Comprises Nos. 248 and 281/305 in slipcase*

Yearbook	38·00

Withdrawn: 9.92

Year Pack 1985

1986 (1 JAN). *Comprises Nos. 281/305 with or without No. 248*

Year Pack with No. 248	30·00
Year Pack without No. 248	20·00

Withdrawn: 30.12.86

284 Swimming

285 Race Walking

286 Rifle-shooting

287 Cycling

Commonwealth Games, Edinburgh

(Des C. Abbott. Litho Questa)

1986 (5 FEB). *Perf* 14½ (C)

306	**284**	12p multicoloured	40	40
307	**285**	15p multicoloured	50	50
308	**286**	31p multicoloured	1·50	1·50
309	**287**	34p multicoloured	1·50	1·50
306/9		*Set of 4*	3·50	3·50
		First Day Cover		4·50
		Presentation Pack	4·00	
		Set of 4 Gutter Pairs	7·00	

No. 309 also commemorates the 50th anniversary of Manx International Cycling Week.

Plate Nos.: All values 1A, 1B, 1C, 1D (each ×5)

Sheets: 40 (2 panes 5×4)

Imprint: Right-hand corner, bottom margin of each pane

Withdrawn: 4.2.87

288 Viking Necklace and Peel Castle

289 Meayll Circle, Rushen

290 Skeleton of Great Deer and Manx Museum

291 Viking Longship Model

292 Open Air Museum, Cregneash

Centenary of Manx Museum

(Des J. Nicholson. Litho Questa)

297 Manx Stoat, Eary Chuslin

298 *Stenobothus stigmaticus* (grasshopper), St. Michael's Isle

1986 (5 FEB). *Perf* 14 (C)

310	**288**	12p multicoloured	. . . .	35	35
311	**289**	15p multicoloured	. . . .	45	45
312	**290**	22p multicoloured	. . . .	85	85
313	**291**	26p multicoloured	. . . .	1·00	1·00
314	**292**	29p multicoloured	. . . .	1·25	1·25
310/14		*Set of 5*	. . . .	3·50	3·50
		First Day Cover			5·00
		Presentation Pack	4·00	
		Set of 5 Gutter Pairs	7·00	

Plate Nos.: All values 1A, 1B, 1C, 1D (each ×6)

Sheets: 40 (2 panes 5×4) 12p, 15p, 29p; (2 panes 4×5) others

Imprint: Right-hand corner, bottom margin (12p, 15p, 29p) or bottom left-hand margin (others)

Withdrawn: 4.2.87

293 Viking Longship

294 Celtic Cross Logo

Manx Heritage Year. Booklet stamps

(Des Colleen Corlett. Litho Harrison)

1986 (10 APR). *Perf* 14½×14 (C)

315	**293**	2p multicoloured	20	20
		a. Booklet pane. Nos. 315×2 and 316×4	2·50	
316	**294**	10p black, apple green and brownish grey	55	55
		a. Booklet pane. No. 316×3 and 3 stamp size labels	2·50	
315/16		*Set of 2*	75	75
		First Day Cover (Nos. 315×1 and 316×2)		1·40
		Presentation Pack (Nos. 315×1 and 316×2)	1·40	

In addition to Booklets SB14/15 Nos. 315/16 also come from special booklet sheets of 60 containing five each of Nos. 315*a* and 316*a*.

Plate Nos. 1A (×7)

Withdrawn: 25.3.87

295 *Usnea articulata* (lichen) and *Neotinea intacta* (orchid), The Ayres

296 Hen Harrier, Calf of Man

Europa. Nature and Environment Protection

(Des J. Nicholson and Nancy Corkish. Photo Courvoisier)

1986 (10 APR). *Granite paper. Perf* 11½ (C)

317	**295**	12p multicoloured	. . . .	60	60
		a. Horiz pair. Nos. 317/18	. . . .	1·25	1·25
318	**296**	12p multicoloured	. . . .	60	60
319	**297**	22p multicoloured	. . . .	95	95
		a. Horiz pair. Nos. 319/20	. . . .	1·90	1·90
320	**298**	22p multicoloured	. . . .	95	95
317/20		*Set of 4*	. . . .	2·75	2·75
		First Day Cover			4·00
		Presentation Pack	3·50	

Cylinder Nos.: Both values A1–1–1–1–1

Sheets: 20 (4×5). The two designs for each value printed together, *se-tenant*, in horizontal pairs throughout the sheets

Imprint: Central, right-hand margin

Withdrawn: 9.4.87

299 Ellanbane (home of Myles Standish)

300 *Mayflower* crossing the Atlantic, 1620

301 Pilgrim Fathers landing at Plymouth, 1620

302 Captain Myles Standish

'Ameripex '86' International Stamp Exhibition, Chicago. Captain Myles Standish of the Mayflower

(Des C. Abbott. Litho Cartor)

1986 (22 MAY). *Perf* 13½ (C)

321	**299**	12p multicoloured	. . . .	35	35
322	**300**	15p multicoloured	. . . .	55	55
323	**301**	31p multicoloured	. . . .	1·40	1·40
324	**302**	34p multicoloured	. . . .	1·60	1·60
321/4		*Set of 4*	. . . .	3·50	3·50
		First Day Cover			4·50
		Presentation Pack	4·25	
MS325		100×75 mm. Nos. 323/4. Perf 12½ . .	2·75	2·75
		First Day Cover			3·75
		Presentation Pack	3·50	

No. **MS**325 also commemorates the 75th anniversary of the World Manx Association.

Plate Nos.: All values 1A, 1B, 1C, 1D (each ×5)

Sheets: 20 (5×4)

Imprint: Right-hand corner, bottom margin

Withdrawn: 21.5.87

303 Prince Andrew in Naval Uniform and Miss Sarah Ferguson

304 Engagement Photograph

Royal Wedding

(Des Colleen Corlett. Litho B.D.T.)

1986 (23 JULY). *Perf* 15×14 (C)

326	**303**	15p multicoloured	. . . .	75	75
327	**304**	40p multicoloured	. . . .	1·50	1·50
326/7		*Set of 2*	. . . .	2·25	2·25
		First Day Cover			3·50
		Presentation Pack	3·00	

Plate Nos.: Both values 1A, 1B (each ×5)

Sheets: 20 (4×5)

Imprint: Right-hand corner, bottom margin

Withdrawn: 22.7.87

305 Prince Philip

306 Queen Elizabeth II

307 Queen Elizabeth II and Prince Philip

Royal Birthdays

(Des Colleen Corlett. Photo Courvoisier)

1986 (28 AUG). *Granite paper. Perf* 11½ (C)

328	**305**	15p multicoloured	. . . .	80	80
		a. Horiz pair. Nos. 328/9	. . . .	1·60	1·60
329	**306**	15p multicoloured	. . . .	80	80
330	**307**	34p multicoloured	. . . .	1·75	1·75
328/30		*Set of 3*	. . . .	3·00	3·00
		First Day Cover			4·00
		Presentation Pack	4·00	
		Souvenir Folder (complete sheets)	16·00	

Nos. 328/30 also commemorate Stockholmia '86 and 350th anniversary of Swedish Post Office.

Cylinder Nos.: 15p A1–1–1–1–1, B1–1–1–1–1, C1–1–1–1–1, D1–1–1–1–1; 34p A1–1–1–1–1, B1–1–1–1–1, C1–1–1–1–1, D1–1–1–1–1

Sheets: 15p 12 (4×3). The two designs printed together, *se-tenant*, in horizontal pairs throughout the sheets; 34p 6 (2×3)

Imprint: Central, bottom margin

Withdrawn: 27.8.87

308 Robins on Globe and 'Peace and Goodwill' in Braille

309 Hands releasing Peace Dove

310 Clasped Hands and 'Peace' in Sign Language

Christmas and International Peace Year

(Des Colleen Corlett. Litho Questa)

1986 (25 SEPT). *Perf* 14 (C)

331	**308**	11p multicoloured	....	50	50
332	**309**	14p multicoloured	....	55	55
333	**310**	31p multicoloured	....	1·25	1·25
331/3		Set of 3	....	2·00	2·00
		First Day Cover	....		3·00
		Presentation Pack	....	2·50	
		Set of 3 Gutter Pairs	......	4·00	

No. 331 also commemorates the 50th anniversary of Manx Blind Welfare Society.

Plate Nos.: All values 1A, 1B, 1C, 1D (each ×5)

Sheets: 40 (2 panes 4×5)

Imprint: Right-hand corner, bottom margin of each pane

Withdrawn: 24.9.87

Year Pack 1986

1986 (25 SEPT). *Comprises Nos.* 306/33

	Year Pack	24·00

Withdrawn: 31.12.87

Post Office Yearbook

1986 (DEC). *Comprises Nos.* 306/14, 315a, 316a, 317/27, 328/30 *in complete sheets, and* 331/3 *in slipcase*

	Yearbook	42·00

Sold out 9.90

311 North Quay

312 Old Fishmarket

313 The Breakwater

314 Jubilee Clock

315 Loch Promenade

316 Beach

Victorian Douglas

(Des A. Theobald. Litho Questa)

1987 (21 JAN–26 MAR). *Perf* 14×14½ (C)

334	**311**	2p multicoloured (a)	....	10	10
		a. Booklet pane. Nos. 334×2, 335×2 and 336×4 (2p stamps at top) (b)		3·25	
		ab. Ditto, but 2p stamps at bottom (b).		3·25	
		b. Booklet pane. Nos. 334/7, each ×2 (b)		3·00	
335	**312**	3p multicoloured (a)	....	10	10
336	**313**	10p multicoloured (a)	....	35	35
337	**314**	15p multicoloured (a)	....	50	50
338	**315**	31p multicoloured (a)	....	1·50	1·50
339	**316**	34p multicoloured (a)	....	1·75	1·75
334/9		Set of 6	....	3·75	3·75
		First Day Cover (Nos. 334/9)			4·50
		First Day Covers (2) (se-tenant strips)			7·00
		Presentation Pack (Nos. 334/9)		4·25	
		Set of 6 Gutter Pairs		7·50	

Printings: (a) 21.1.87; (b) 26.3.87

Plate Nos.: All values 1A, 1B, 1C, 1D (each ×4)

Sheets: 40 (2 panes 5×4). In addition to booklets SB16/17 Nos. 334/7 also come from special booklet sheets of 48 containing 6 each of Nos. 334a/b

Imprint: Right-hand corner, bottom margin of each pane

Withdrawn: 20.1.88 sheets; 15.3.88 booklets

317 'The Old Fishmarket and Harbour, Douglas'

318 'Red Sails at Douglas'

319 'The Double Corner, Peel'

320 'Peel Harbour'

Paintings by John Miller Nicholson

(Des A. Theobald. Litho Cartor)

1987 (18 FEB). *Perf* 13½ (C)

340	**317**	12p multicoloured	....	35	35
341	**318**	26p multicoloured	....	90	90

342	**319**	29p multicoloured	. . . .	1·40	1·40
343	**320**	34p multicoloured	. . . .	1·60	1·60
340/3		Set of 4	. . . .	3·75	3·75
		First Day Cover	. . . .		4·50
		Presentation Pack	. . . .	4·50	
		Set of 4 Gutter Pairs	. . . . . .	7·50	

Plate Nos.: All values 1A, 1B, 1C, 1D (each ×5)

Sheets: 40 (2 panes 5×4)

Imprint: Right-hand corner, bottom margin of each pane

Withdrawn: 17.2.88

321 Sea Terminal, Douglas

322 Tower of Refuge, Douglas

323 Gaiety Theatre, Douglas

324 Villa Marina, Douglas

Europa. Architecture

(Des R. Maddox, Litho B.D.T.)

1987 (29 APR). *Perf* 13½ (C)

344	**321**	12p multicoloured	. . . .	60	60
		a. Horiz pair. Nos. 344/5	. . . .	1·25	1·25
345	**322**	12p multicoloured	. . . .	60	60
346	**323**	22p multicoloured	. . . .	1·10	1·10
		a. Horiz pair. Nos. 346/7	. . . .	2·10	2·10
347	**324**	22p multicoloured	. . . .	1·10	1·10
344/7		Set of 4	. . . .	3·00	3·00
		First Day Cover	. . . .		4·25
		Presentation Pack	. . . .	4·00	

Plate Nos.: Both values 1A, 1B (each ×5)

Sheets: 10 (2×5). The two designs for each value printed together, *se-tenant*, in horizontal pairs throughout the sheets

Imprint: Central, right-hand margin

Withdrawn: 28.4.88

325 Supercharged BMW 50cc, 1939

326 Manx 'Kneeler' Norton 350cc, 1953

327 MV Agusta 500cc 4, 1956

328 Guzzi 500cc V8, 1957

329 Honda 250cc 6, 1967

80th Anniversary of Tourist Trophy Motor-cycle Races

(Des B. Dix. Litho Cartor)

1987 (27 MAY). *Perf* 13½×13 (C)

348	**325**	12p multicoloured	. . . .	40	40
349	**326**	15p multicoloured	. . . .	60	60
350	**327**	29p multicoloured	. . . .	1·00	1·00
351	**328**	31p multicoloured	. . . .	1·10	1·10
352	**329**	34p multicoloured	. . . .	1·40	1·40
348/52		Set of 5	. . . .	4·00	4·00
		First Day Cover	. . . .		5·25
		Presentation Pack	. . . .	4·50	
		Stamp Cards (Set of 5)	. . . .	2·25	5·50
		Set of 5 Gutter Pairs	. . . . . .	8·00	
MS353		150×140 mm. Nos. 348/52. Perf 14×13½ (C)		4·75	4·75
		Souvenir Folder	. . . .	6·00	

Nos. 348/53 also commemorate the centenary of the St. John Ambulance Brigade and the miniature sheet also carries the logo of 'Capex '87' International Stamp Exhibition, Toronto on its margin.

Plate Nos.: 12p, 15p, 29p, 31p, 34p 1A, 1B, 1C, 1D (each ×4); miniature sheet 1A (×4)

Sheets: 40 (2 panes 5×4)

Imprint: Right-hand corner, bottom margin of each pane (sheets) or bottom, right-hand margin (miniature sheet)

Withdrawn: 11.6.88

330 Fuchsia and Wild Roses

331 Field Scabious and Ragwort

332 Wood Anemone and Celandine

333 Violets and Primroses

Wild Flowers

(Des Nancy Corkish. Litho Enschedé)

1987 (9 SEPT). *Perf* 14½ × 13 (C)

354	**330**	16p multicoloured	. . . .	60	60
355	**331**	29p multicoloured	. . . .	1·10	1·10
356	**332**	31p multicoloured	. . . .	1·25	1·25
357	**333**	34p multicoloured	. . . .	1·50	1·50
354/7		*Set of* 4	. . . .	4·00	4·00
		First Day Cover			4·75
		Presentation Pack		4·25	

Plate Nos. All values 1A, 1B (each ×4)

Sheets: 20 (5×4)

Imprint: Right-hand corner, bottom margin

Withdrawn: 8.9.88

334 Stirring the Christmas Pudding

335 Bringing Home the Christmas Tree

336 Decorating the Christmas Tree

Christmas. Victorian Scenes

(Des Colleen Corlett. Litho Questa)

1987 (16 OCT). *Perf* 14 (C)

358	**334**	12p multicoloured	. . . .	50	50
359	**335**	15p multicoloured	. . . .	75	75
360	**336**	31p multicoloured	. . . .	1·25	1·25
358/60		*Set of 3*	. . . .	2·25	2·25
		First Day Cover			3·50
		Presentation Pack		3·00	
		Set of 3 Gutter Pairs		4·50	

Plate Nos.: All values 1A, 1B, 1C, 1D (each ×4)

Sheets: 40 (2 panes 4×5)

Imprint: Right-hand corner, bottom margin of each pane

Withdrawn: 15.10.88

Year Pack 1987

1987 (16 OCT). *Comprises Nos.* 334/52 *and* 354/60

Year Pack . . . . 22·00

Withdrawn: 31.12.88

Post Office Yearbook

1987 (DEC). *Comprises Nos. 334/43, 344/7 in complete sheets, and* **MS**353/60 *in slipcase*

Yearbook . . . . 35·00

Sold out: 5.91

337 Russell Brookes in Vauxhall Opel (Manx Rally winner, 1985)

338 Ari Vatanen in Ford 'Escort' (Manx Rally winner, 1976)

339 Terry Smith in Repco 'March 761' (Hill Climb winner, 1980)

340 Nigel Mansell in Williams/ Honda (British Grand Prix winner, 1986 & 1987)

Motor Sport

(Des C. Abbott. Litho Enschedé)

1988 (10 FEB). *Perf* 13½×14½ (C)

361	**337**	13p multicoloured	. . . .	75	70
362	**338**	26p multicoloured	. . . .	1·25	1·10
363	**339**	31p multicoloured	. . . .	1·40	1·25
364	**340**	34p multicoloured	. . . .	1·60	1·40
361/4		*Set of* 4	. . . .	4·50	4·00
		First Day Cover			4·50
		Presentation Pack		4·75	

Plate Nos.: All values 1A, 1B (each ×4)

Sheets: 10 (2×5)

Imprint: Central, right-hand margin

Withdrawn: 9.2.89

348 Laxey Mine Railway Lewin Locomotive *Ant*

349 Port Erin Breakwater Tramway Locomotive *Henry B. Loch*

341 Horse Tram Terminus, Douglas Bay Tramway

342 Snaefell Mountain Railway

350 Ramsey Harbour Tramway

351 Locomotive No. 7, *Tynwald*, on Foxdale Line

343 Marine Drive Tramway

343*a* Douglas Cable Tramway

351*a* T.P.O. Special leaving Douglas, 3 July 1991

352 Baldwin Reservoir Tramway Steam Locomotive *Injebreck*

344 Douglas Head Incline Railway

345 Manx Electric Railway Tram at Maughold Head

353 I.M.R. No. 13, *Kissack*, near St. Johns

353*a* Manx Northern Railway No. 4, *Caledonia*, at Gob-y-Deigan

346 Douglas Cable Tramway

347 Manx Northern Railway, No. 4, *Caledonia*, at Gob-y-Deigan

353*b* Double-decker Horse Tram, Douglas

354 I.M.R. No. 12, *Hutchinson*, leaving Douglas

355 Groudle Glen Railway Locomotive *Polar Bear*

356 I.M.R. No. 11, *Maitland*, pulling Royal Train, 1963

356a Queen Elizabeth II taking Salute at Trooping the Colour

Manx Railways and Tramways, and Queen's Portrait (£2)

(Des Colleen Corlett (£2), A. Theobald (others). Litho B.D.T. (1p to 19p, 21p, 23p), Questa (20p, 25p to £2))

1988 (10 FEB)–**92.** *Perf* 13 (1p to 19p, 21p, 23p), 14½×15 (20p, 25p to £1) *or* 14½ (£2), *all comb*

365	**341**	1p multicoloured (a)	10	10
366	**342**	2p multicoloured (a)	10	10
367	**343**	3p multicoloured (a)	10	10
		a. Booklet pane. Nos. 367×2, 370 and 373×2 (b)	2·50	
		b. Booklet pane. Nos. 367×2, 371×2 and 374 (d)	2·25	
367c	**343a**	4p multicoloured (g)	10	10
		ca. Booklet pane. Nos. 367c×3, 374 and 377a	2·50	
		cb. Booklet pane. Nos. 367c×3, 374×4 and 377a	3·75	
368	**344**	5p multicoloured (a)	10	10
369	**345**	10p multicoloured (a)	20	25
370	**346**	13p multicoloured (a)	40	30
		a. Booklet pane. Nos. 370×4 and 373×6 (b)	5·00	
371	**347**	14p multicoloured (a)	30	35
		a. Booklet pane. Nos. 371×4 and 374×6 (d)	4·00	
372	**348**	15p multicoloured (af)	30	35
		a. Booklet pane. Nos. 372 and 376×2 (e)	2·25	
		b. Booklet pane. Nos. 372×4 and 376×6 (e)	5·00	
373	**349**	16p multicoloured (a)	40	35
374	**350**	17p multicoloured (ag)	40	40
375	**351**	18p multicoloured (a)	50	40
375a	**351a**	18p multicoloured (h)	50	40
		ab. Booklet pane. Nos. 375a×3 and 377b×2	2·50	
		ac. Booklet pane. Nos. 375a×6 and 377b×4	4·75	
376	**352**	19p multicoloured (af)	50	45
377	**353**	20p multicoloured (c)	50	45
377a	**353a**	21p multicoloured (g)	50	45
377b	**353b**	23p multicoloured (h)	50	50
378	**354**	25p multicoloured (c)	60	55
379	**355**	50p multicoloured (ci)	1·50	1·10
380	**356**	£1 multicoloured (ci)	3·00	2·10
380a	**356a**	£2 multicoloured (e)	5·00	4·25
365/80a		Set of 21	14·00	11·50
		First Day Covers (6)		19·00
		First Day Covers (se-tenant strips) (5)		14·50
		Presentation Packs (4) (ex 4p, 18p (No. 375a), 21p, 23p)	16·00	
		Stamp Cards (1p to £1 ex 4p, 18p (No. 375a), 21p, 23p) ..	8·00	22·00
		Souvenir Folder (1p to £1 ex 4p, 18p (No. 375a), 21p, 23p)	8·00	

Printings: (a) 10.2.88; (b) 16.3.88; (c) 21.9.88; (d) 16.10.89. Inscribed '1989'; (e) 14.2.90. Inscribed '1990'; (f) 1.3.90. Inscribed '1990'; (g) 9.1.91. Inscribed '1991'; (h) 8.1.92. Inscribed '1992'; (i) 16.11.92. Inscribed '1992'

Plate Nos.: 20p, 25p, 50p, £1 1A, 1B (each ×4); £2 1A, 1B (each ×5); others 1A, 1B, 1C, 1D (each ×4)

Sheets: 25 (5×5) (£2) or 50 (5×10) (others). In addition to Booklets Nos. SB18/19 and SB21/4 Nos. 367 and 370/4 also come from special booklet sheets of 50 containing either ten examples of the strips of five or five examples of the strips of ten. No. 372a, a strip of three, was taken from the top or bottom of the strip of ten, No. 372b. The 4p value was only issued in Booklets Nos. SB26/7 and special booklet sheets of 50 containing five vertical strips of No. 367cb, from which No. 367ca could also be obtained, and five extra examples of both Nos. 367c and 377a. In addition to Booklets Nos. SB29/30 No. 375ac was also issued in special booklet sheets of 50 from which No. 375ab could also be obtained.

Imprints: Left-hand margin (£2) or right-hand corner, bottom margin (others).

Withdrawn: 31.12.93 1p to £1; 11.1.94 £2

357 Laying Isle of Man–U.K. Submarine Cable

358 *Flex Service 3* (cable ship)

ISLE OF MAN 22P

359 Earth Station, Braddan

22P ISLE OF MAN

360 'INTELSAT 5' Satellite

Europa. Transport and Communications

(Des C. Abbott. Litho Cartor)

1988 (14 APR). *Perf* 14×13½ (C)

381	**357**	13p multicoloured	. . . .	50	50
		a. *Horiz pair. Nos.* 381/2	. . . .	1·00	1·00
382	**358**	13p multicoloured	. . . .	50	50
383	**359**	22p multicoloured	. . . .	90	90
		a. *Horiz pair. Nos.* 383/4	. . . .	1·75	1·75
384	**360**	22p multicoloured	. . . .	90	90
381/4		*Set of* 4	. . . .	2·50	2·50
		First Day Cover			3·25
		Presentation Pack	3·25	

Plate Nos.: Both values 1A, 1B, 1C, 1D (each ×4)

Sheets: 16 (4×4). The two designs of each value printed together, *se-tenant*, in horizontal pairs throughout the sheets

Imprint: Central, right-hand margin

Withdrawn: 13.4.89

361 *Euterpe* (full-rigged ship) off Ramsey, 1863

362 *Vixen* (topsail schooner) leaving Peel for Australia, 1853

363 *Ramsey* (full-rigged ship) off Brisbane, 1870

364 *Star of India* (formerly *Euterpe*) (barque) off San Diego, 1976

Manx Sailing Ships

(Des J. Nicholson. Litho Questa)

1988 (11 MAY). *Perf* 14 (C)

385	**361**	16p multicoloured	. . . .	50	50
386	**362**	29p multicoloured	. . . .	1·00	1·00
387	**363**	31p multicoloured	. . . .	1·25	1·25
388	**364**	34p multicoloured	. . . .	1·40	1·40
385/8		*Set of* 4	. . . .	3·75	3·75
		First Day Cover			4·75
		Presentation Pack	4·50	
MS389		110×85 mm. Nos. 385 and 388. . . .	2·50	2·50
		First Day Cover			3·50
		Presentation Pack	3·00	

Nos. 386/7 also commemorate the Bicentenary of Australian Settlement

Plate Nos.: All values 1A, 1B (each ×5)

Sheets: 15 (3×5)

Imprint: Bottom, left-hand margin

Withdrawn: 10.5.89

365 'Magellanica' 366 'Pink Cloud' 367 'Leonora'

368 'Satellite' 369 'Preston Guild' 370 'Thalia'

50th Anniversary of British Fuchsia Society

(Des Colleen Corlett. Litho Enschedé)

1988 (21 SEPT). *Perf* 13½×14 (C)

390	**365**	13p multicoloured	. . . .	50	50
391	**366**	16p multicoloured	. . . .	60	60
392	**367**	22p multicoloured	. . . .	80	70
393	**368**	29p multicoloured	. . . .	1·00	1·00
394	**369**	31p multicoloured	. . . .	1·25	1·25
395	**370**	34p multicoloured	. . . .	1·40	1·40
390/5		*Set of* 6	. . . .	5·00	5·00
		First Day Cover			6·00
		Presentation Pack	5·75	

Plate Nos.: All values 1A, 1B (each ×5)

Sheets: 20 (4×5)

Imprint: Right-hand margin

Withdrawn: 20.9.89

371 Long-eared Owl

372 European Robin

373 Grey Partridge

376 Tortoiseshell and White Cat

377 Tortoiseshell Cat

Christmas. Manx Birds

(Des Audrey North. Litho Questa)

1988 (12 OCT). *Perf* 14 (C)

396	**371**	12p multicoloured	. . . .	55	55
397	**372**	15p multicoloured	. . . .	85	85
398	**373**	31p multicoloured	. . . .	1·40	1·40
396/8		Set of 3	. . . .	2·50	2·50
		First Day Cover			3·50
		Presentation Pack	3·25	
		Set of 3 Gutter Pairs	5·00	

Plate Nos.: All values 1A, 1B, 1C, 1D (each ×5)

Sheets: 40 (2 panes 5×4)

Imprint: Right-hand corner, bottom margin of each pane

Withdrawn: 11.10.89

Year Pack 1988

1988 (1 NOV). *Comprises Nos.* 361/7, 368/75, 376/7, 378/80 and 381/98

Year Pack . . . . 32·00

Withdrawn: 31.12.89

Post Office Yearbook

1988 (1 DEC). *Comprises Nos.* 361/7, 368/75, 376/7, 378/80 and 381/98 *in slipcase*

Yearbook . . . . 38·00

Sold out: By 9.93

374 Ginger Cat

375 Black and White Cat

Manx Cats

(Des P. Layton. Litho Questa)

1989 (8 FEB). *Perf* 14 (C)

399	**374**	16p multicoloured	. . . .	50	50
400	**375**	27p multicoloured	. . . .	1·00	1·00
401	**376**	30p multicoloured	. . . .	1·40	1·40
402	**377**	40p multicoloured	. . . .	1·60	1·60
399/402		Set of 4	. . . .	4·00	4·00
		First Day Cover			5·50
		Presentation Pack	4·75	
		Stamp Cards (set of 4)	2·00	6·00
		Set of 4 Gutter Pairs	8·00	

Plate Nos.: 16p, 27p 1C, 1D, 1G, 1H (each ×4); 30p, 40p 1A, 1B, 1E, 1F (each ×4)

Sheets: 40 (2 panes 5×4)

Imprint: Right-hand corner, bottom margin of each pane

Withdrawn: 7.2.90

378 Tudric Pewter Clock, *c.* 1903

379 'Celtic Cross' Watercolour

380 Silver Cup and Cover, 1902–03

381 Gold and Silver Brooches from Liberty's Cymric Range

382 Silver Jewel Box, 1900

125th Birth Anniversary of Archibald Knox (artist and designer)

(Des Colleen Corlett. Litho Cartor)

1989 (8 FEB). *Perf* 13 (C)

403	**378**	13p multicoloured	....	35	35
404	**379**	16p multicoloured	....	45	45
405	**380**	23p multicoloured	....	75	75
406	**381**	32p multicoloured	....	1·40	1·40
407	**382**	35p multicoloured	....	1·50	1·50
403/7		*Set of* 5	....	4·00	4·00
		First Day Cover	....		5·25
		Presentation Pack	....	4·75	
		Set of 5 *Gutter Pairs*	......	8·00	

Plate Nos.: All values 1A, 1B, 1C, 1D (each ×5)

Sheets: 40 (2 panes 4×5) 13p, 16p, 23p; (2 panes 5×4) others

Imprint: Bottom, left-hand margin of each pane (13p, 16p, 23p) or right-hand corner, bottom margin of each pane

Withdrawn: 7.2.90

383 William Bligh and Old Church, Onchan

384 Bligh and Loyal Crew cast Adrift

385 Pitcairn Islands 1989 Bicentenary 90 c. Stamp

386 Norfolk Island 1989 39 c. *Bounty* Stamp

387 Midshipman Peter Heywood and Tahiti

388 H.M.S. *Bounty* anchored off Pitcairn

389 Fletcher Christian and Pitcairn Island

Bicentenary of the Mutiny on the Bounty

(Des C. Abbott. Litho B.D.T.)

1989 (28 APR). *Perf* 14 (C)

408	**383**	13p multicoloured	....	25	30
		a. Booklet pane. Nos. 408/10 and 412/14		3·00	
		b. Booklet pane. Nos. 408/9 and 411/14		3·00	
409	**384**	16p multicoloured	....	30	35
410	**385**	23p multicoloured	....	1·10	1·10
		a. Booklet pane. Nos. 410/11, each ×3		3·00	
411	**386**	27p multicoloured	....	1·10	1·10
412	**387**	30p multicoloured	....	70	70
413	**388**	32p multicoloured	....	75	75
414	**389**	35p multicoloured	....	80	80
408/14		*Set of* 7	....	4·50	4·50
		First Day Cover (*ex Nos.* 410/11)	....		5·00
		Presentation Pack (*ex Nos.* 410/11)	....	4·75	
MS415		110×85 mm. Nos. 410/11 and 414		5·00	4·75
		First Day Cover	....		4·75

Plate Nos.: 13p, 16p, 30p, 32p, 35p 1A, 1B (each ×4)

Sheets: 20 (4×5) 13p, 16p, 30p, 32p, 35p. The 23p and 27p values were only issued in £5.30 booklets and in the miniature sheet. Booklet panes Nos. 408a/b and 410a each contain two vertical rows of three stamps, separated by a central gutter

Imprint: 13p, 16p, 30p, 32p, 35p Central, left-hand margin

Withdrawn: 27.4.90 13, 16, 30, 32, 35p

390 Skipping and Hopscotch

391 Wheelbarrow, Leapfrog and Piggyback

392 Building Model House and Blowing Bubbles

393 Girl with Doll and Doll's House

Europa. Children's Games

(Des Colleen Corlett. Litho Enschedé)

1989 (17 MAY). *Perf* 13½ (C)

416	**390**	13p multicoloured	....	60	60
		a. Horiz pair. Nos. 416/17	....	1·25	1·25
417	**391**	13p multicoloured	....	60	60

418	**392**	23p multicoloured		95	95
		a. *Horiz pair. Nos.* 418/19		1·90	1·90
419	**393**	23p multicoloured		95	95
416/19		*Set of 4*		2·75	2·75
		First Day Cover			4·00
		Presentation Pack		3·50	

Plate Nos.: Both values 1A, 1B (each ×4)

Sheets: 20 (4×5). The two designs for each value printed together, *se-tenant*, in horizontal pairs throughout the sheets

Imprint: Central, right-hand margin

Withdrawn: 16.5.90

394 Atlantic Puffin

395 Black Guillemot

396 Common Cormorant

397 Kittiwake

Sea Birds

(Des W. Oliver. Litho Questa)

1989 (20 SEPT). *Perf* 14 (C)

420	**394**	13p multicoloured		80	80
		a. *Strip of 4. Nos.* 420/3		3·00	
		ab. *Black ptd double*			
421	**395**	13p multicoloured		80	80
422	**396**	13p multicoloured		80	80
423	**397**	13p multicoloured		80	80
420/3		*Set of 4*		3·00	3·00
		First Day Cover			3·50
		Presentation Pack		3·50	

In addition to a double image of the black printing on the design some examples of No. 420*ab* also show three additional impressions of the imprint at the foot of each stamp.

Examples of Nos. 420/3 sold at 'World Stamp Expo '89', held at Washington D.C. between 17 November and 3 December 1989, carried a commemorative inscription on the bottom sheet margin.

Plate Nos.: 1A, 1B, 1C, 1D (each ×4)

Sheets: 16 (4×4). The four designs were printed together, *se-tenant*, in horizontal and vertical strips throughout the sheet which exists with or without perforations across the side margins

Imprint: Central, right-hand margin

Withdrawn: 19.9.90

398 Red Cross Cadets learning Resuscitation

399 Anniversary Logo

400 Signing Geneva Convention, 1864

401 Red Cross Ambulance

402 Henri Dunant (founder)

125th Anniversary of International Red Cross and Centenary of Noble's Hospital, Isle of Man

(Des A. Theobald. Litho Questa)

1989 (16 OCT). *Perf* 14 (C)

424	**398**	14p multicoloured		40	40
425	**399**	17p grey and orange-vermilion ..		65	65
426	**400**	23p multicoloured		90	90
427	**401**	30p multicoloured		1·25	1·25
428	**402**	35p multicoloured		1·50	1·50
424/8		*Set of 5*		4·25	4·25
		First Day Cover			5·00
		Presentation Pack		5·00	
		Set of 5 Gutter Pairs		8·50	

Plate Nos.: 14p, 30p 1A, 1B, 1C, 1D (each ×5); 17p 1A, 1B, 1C, 1D (each ×2); 23p, 35p 1A, 1B, 1C, 1D (each ×4)

Sheets: 40 (2 panes 5×4)

Imprint: Right-hand corner, bottom margin of each pane

Withdrawn: 15.10.90

131

403 Mother with Baby, Jane Crookall Maternity Home

404 Mother with Child

405 Madonna and Child

406 Baptism, St. Ninian's Church

Christmas. 50th Anniversary of Jane Crookall Maternity Home and 75th Anniversary of St. Ninian's Church, Douglas

(Des Colleen Corlett. Litho Questa)

1989 (16 OCT). *Perf* 14½ (C)

429	**403**	13p multicoloured	. . . .	45	45
430	**404**	16p multicoloured	. . . .	55	55
431	**405**	34p multicoloured	. . . .	1·10	1·10
432	**406**	37p multicoloured	. . . .	1·25	1·25
429/32		*Set of 4*	. . . .	3·00	3·00
		First Day Cover	. . . .		4·00
		Presentation Pack	. . . .	3·75	
		Set of 4 Gutter Pairs	. . . . . .	6·00	

Plate Nos.: 13p, 34p 1A, 1B, 1C, 1D (each ×5); 16p, 37p 1A, 1B, 1C, 1D (each ×4)

Sheets: 40 (2 panes 4×5)

Imprint: Right-hand corner, bottom margin of each pane

Withdrawn: 15.10.90

Year Pack 1989

1989 (16 OCT). *Comprises Nos.* 399/409 *and* 412/32
  Year Pack . . . . 28·00

Withdrawn 31.12.90

Post Office Yearbook

1989 (NOV). *Comprises Nos.* 399/409, 412/19, 420/3 *in complete sheet, and* 424/32 *in slipcase*
  Yearbook . . . . 40·00

Sold out: By 9.93

407 'The Isle of Man Express going up a Gradient'

408 'A way we have in the Isle of Man'

409 'Douglas – waiting for the Male Boat'

410 'The Last Toast Rack Home, Douglas Parade'

411 'The Last Isle of Man Boat'

Isle of Man Edwardian Postcards

(Des D. Swinton. Litho B.D.T.)

1990 (14 FEB). *Perf* 14 (C)

433	**407**	15p multicoloured	. . . .	30	30
434	**408**	19p multicoloured	. . . .	55	55
435	**409**	32p multicoloured	. . . .	1·00	1·00
436	**410**	34p multicoloured	. . . .	1·40	1·40
437	**411**	37p multicoloured	. . . .	1·50	1·50
433/7		*Set of 5*	. . . .	4·25	4·25
		First Day Cover	. . . .		5·00
		Presentation Pack	. . . .	4·50	
		Stamp Cards (*set of 5*)	. . . .	2·50	6·00
		Set of 5 Gutter Pairs	. . . . . .	8·50	

Plate Nos.: All values 1A, 1B, 1C, 1D (each ×4)

Sheets: 40 (2 panes 5×4)

Imprint: Right-hand corner, bottom margin of each pane

Withdrawn: 13.2.91

412 Modern Postman

413 Ramsey Post Office, 1990

414 Postman, 1890

415 Douglas Post Office, 1890

Europa. Post Office Buildings

(Des A. Kellett. Litho Cartor)

1990 (18 APR). *Perf* 13½ (C)

438	**412**	15p multicoloured	....	55	55
		a. Horiz pair. Nos. 438/9	....	1·10	1·10
439	**413**	15p multicoloured	....	55	55
440	**414**	24p multicoloured	....	95	95
		a. Horiz pair. Nos. 440/1	....	1·90	1·90
441	**415**	24p multicoloured	....	95	95
438/41		Set of 4	....	2·75	2·75
		First Day Cover	....		3·00
		Presentation Pack	....	3·25	

Plate Nos.: Both values 1A, 1B (each ×4)

Sheets: 20 (4×5). The two designs for each value printed together, *se-tenant*, in horizontal pairs throughout the sheets.

Withdrawn 17.4.91

416 Penny Black

417 Wyon Medal, 1837

418 Wyon's Stamp Essay

419 Perkins Bacon Engine-turned Essay, 1839

420 Twopence Blue, 1840

421 Marginal Block of Four Penny Blacks

150th Anniversary of the Penny Black

(Des Colleen Corlett. Eng Inge Madle (No. **MS**447). Recess and litho (No. **MS**447) or litho (others) Enschedé)

1990 (3 MAY). *Perf* 14×13½ (C)

442	**416**	1p black, buff and gold	......	10	10
		a. Sheetlet. Horiz strip of 5.			
		Nos. 442/6	....	4·50	
		b. Sheetlet. No. 442×25	....	2·50	
		c. Booklet pane. No. 442×8			
		with margins all round	....	50	
443	**417**	19p gold, black and buff	......	65	65
		a. Booklet pane. Nos. 443/6×2			
		with margins all round	....	6·50	
444	**418**	32p multicoloured	....	1·25	1·25
445	**419**	34p multicoloured	....	1·25	1·25
446	**420**	37p multicoloured	....	1·40	1·40
442/6		Set of 5	....	4·00	4·00
		First Day Cover	....		4·75
		Presentation Pack	....	4·50	
MS447	100×71 mm. **421** £1 black, gold				
and buff	....			3·75	3·75
		First Day Cover	....		4·50
		Presentation Pack	....	4·25	

Sheetlet No. 442*a* was reissued on 24 August 1990 overprinted 'From STAMP WORLD LONDON '90 to NEW ZEALAND 1990' for sale at the New Zealand exhibition.

The Penny Black stamps shown on Nos. 442*b/c* each have different corner letters at foot. The sheetlet of 25 was issued in conjunction with a special postal concession which allowed hand-addressed personal mail for the island to be posted for 1p between 10 am and 12 noon on 6 May 1990.

No. **MS**447 also commemorates 'Stamp World London '90' International Stamp Exhibition, London.

Plate Nos.: No. 442*b*, 1A, 1B (each ×3)

Sheets: 5 (5×1) containing Nos. 442/6 *se-tenant*, or 25 (5×5) No. 442 only

Imprint: No. 442*a*. Bottom margin, right-hand corner. No. 442*b*. Central, bottom margin

Withdrawn: 2.5.91

422 Queen Elizabeth the Queen Mother

90th Birthday of Queen Elizabeth the Queen Mother

(Des Colleen Corlett. Litho B.D.T.)

1990 (4 AUG). *Perf* 13×13½ (C)

448	**422**	90p multicoloured	3·00	3·00
		First Day Cover		4·00
		Presentation Pack	3·75	

Plate Nos.: 1A, 1B (each ×5)

Sheets: 20 (5×4) containing ten stamps and ten *se-tenant* inscribed labels

Imprint: Central, right-hand margin

Withdrawn: 3.8.91

423 Hawker Hurricane Mk I, Bristol Type 142 Blenheim Mk I and Home Defence

424 Supermarine Spitfire, Westland Lysander Mk I and Vickers Walrus with Launch

425 Rearming Hawker Hurricane Mk I Fighters

426 Ops Room and Scramble

427 Civil Defence Personnel

428 Anti-aircraft Battery

50th Anniversary of the Battle of Britain

(Des A. Theobald. Litho Questa)

1990 (5 SEPT). *Perf* 14 (C)

449	**423**	15p multicoloured	40	40
		a. *Horiz pair. Nos.* 449/50	80	80
450	**424**	15p multicoloured	40	40
451	**425**	24p multicoloured	90	90
		a. *Horiz pair. Nos.* 451/2	1·75	1·75
452	**426**	24p multicoloured	90	90
453	**427**	29p multicoloured	95	95
		a. *Horiz pair. Nos.* 453/4	1·90	1·90
454	**428**	29p multicoloured	95	95
449/54		*Set of 6*	4·00	4·00
		First Day Cover		6·00
		Presentation Pack	5·00	
		Souvenir Folder (*complete sheets*)	17·00	

Plate Nos.: All values 1A, 1B (each ×4)

Sheets: 8 (2×4). The two designs of each value were printed together, *se-tenant*, in horizontal pairs throughout the sheet, each showing composite panel at foot of Dover cliffs (15p), Weald landscape (24p) or London skyline (29p)

Withdrawn: 4.9.91

429 Churchill with Freedom of Douglas Casket

430 Churchill and London Blitz

431 Churchill and Searchlights over Westminster

432 Churchill with Hawker Hurricane Mk I Fighters

25th Death Anniversary of Sir Winston Churchill

(Des C. Abbott. Litho Cartor)

1990 (5 SEPT). *Perf* 13½ (C)

455	**429**	19p multicoloured	60	60
456	**430**	32p multicoloured	1·10	1·10
457	**431**	34p multicoloured	1·40	1·40
458	**432**	37p multicoloured	1·40	1·40
455/8		*Set of 4*	4·25	4·25
		First Day Cover		5·25
		Presentation Pack	5·00	
		Set of 4 Gutter Pairs	8·50	

Plate Nos.: All values 1A, 1B, 1C, 1D (each ×5)

Sheets: 40 (2 panes 5×4)

Imprint: Right-hand corner, bottom margin of each pane

Withdrawn: 4.9.91

433 Boy on Toboggan and Girl posting Letter

434 Girl on Toboggan and Skaters

435 Boy with Snowman

436 Children throwing Snowballs

Christmas

(Des C. Abbott. Litho B.D.T.)

1990 (10 OCT). *Perf* 13×13½ (C)

459	**433**	14p multicoloured	40	40
460	**434**	18p multicoloured	60	60
461	**435**	34p multicoloured	1·25	1·25
462	**436**	37p multicoloured	1·40	1·40
459/62		Set of 4	3·50	3·50
		First Day Cover		4·00
		Presentation Pack	4·00	
		Set of 4 Gutter Pairs	7·00	
MS463		123×55 mm. As Nos. 459/62 but face values in black	3·50	3·50
		a. Blue (inscriptions) omitted	£600	
		First Day Cover		4·00
		Presentation Pack	4·00	

Plate Nos.: 18p 1A, 1B, 1C, 1D (each ×5); others 1A, 1B, 1C, 1D (each ×6)

Sheets: 40 (2 panes 4×5)

Imprint: Right-hand corner, bottom margin of each pane

Withdrawn: 9.10.91

Year Pack 1990

1990 (10 OCT). *Comprises Nos.* 380a and 433/63

Year Pack . . . . 38·00

Withdrawn: 31.12.91

Post Office Yearbook

1990 (DEC). *Comprises Nos.* 380a, 433/41, 442a/b, **MS**447 and 448/63 *in slipcase*

Yearbook . . . . 42·00

Sold out: By 9.93

437 Henry Bloom Noble and Orphans (Marshall Wane)

438 Douglas (Frederick Frith)

439 Studio Portrait of Three Children (Hilda Newby)

440 Cashtal yn Ard (Christopher Killip)

441 Peel Castle (Colleen Corlett)

Manx Photography

(Des Colleen Corlett. Litho Walsall)

1991 (9 JAN). *Perf* 14 (C)

464	**437**	17p blackish brn, pale brownish grey and black	45	45
465	**438**	21p deep brown and ochre	60	60
466	**439**	26p blackish brown, stone and brownish black	90	90
467	**440**	31p agate, pale grey-brown & blk	1·25	1·25
468	**441**	40p multicoloured	1·50	1·50
464/8		Set of 5	4·25	4·25
		First Day Cover		5·00
		Presentation Pack	5·00	

Plate Nos: 21p 1A–1A, 1B–1B, 40p 1A, 1B (each ×4); others 1A, 1B (each ×3)

Sheets: 20 (4×5)

Imprint: Central, right-hand margin

Withdrawn 8.1.92

442 Lifeboat *Sir William Hillary*, Douglas

443 *Osman Gabriel*, Port Erin

444 *Ann and James Ritchie*, Ramsey

445 *The Gough Ritchie*, Port St. Mary

446 *John Batstone*, Peel

447 'Intelsat' Communications Satellite

448 'Ariane' Rocket Launch and Fishing Boats in Douglas Harbour

449 Weather Satelite and Space Station

450 Ronaldsway Airport, Manx Radio Transmitter and Space Shuttle Launch

Manx Lifeboats

(Des A. Peck. Litho Questa)

1991 (13 FEB). *Perf* 14 (C)

469	**442**	17p multicoloured	45	45
470	**443**	21p multicoloured	60	60
		a. Black ptg double		
471	**444**	26p multicoloured	90	90
472	**445**	31p multicoloured	1·25	1·25
473	**446**	37p multicoloured	1·50	1·50
469/73		Set of 5	4·25	4·25
		First Day Cover		5·00
		Presentation Pack	5·00	
		Set of 5 Gutter Pairs	8·50	

No. 469 is inscribed "HILARY" and No. 471 "JAMES & ANN RITCHIE", both in error.

Plate Nos.: All values 1A, 1B, 1C, 1D (each ×4)

Sheets: 40 (2 panes 5×4)

Imprint: Right-hand corner, bottom margin of each pane

Withdrawn: 12.2.92

Europa. Europe in Space

(Des D. Miller. Litho B.D.T.)

1991 (24 APR). *Perf* 14 (C)

474	**447**	17p multicoloured	70	70
		a. Vert pair. Nos. 474/5	1·40	1·40
475	**448**	17p multicoloured	70	70
476	**449**	26p multicoloured	1·00	1·00
		a. Vert pair. Nos. 476/7	2·00	2·00
477	**450**	26p multicoloured	1·00	1·00
474/7		Set of 4	3·00	3·00
		First Day Cover		3·75
		Presentation Pack	3·25	

Plate Nos: Both values 1A,1B (each ×4)

Sheets: 20 (5×4). The two designs for each value printed together, *se-tenant*, in vertical pairs throughout the sheets, each pair forming a composite design

Imprint: Central, right-hand margin

Withdrawn: 23.4.92

451 Oliver Godfrey with Indian 500cc at Start, 1911

452 Freddie Dixon on Douglas 'Banking' Sidecar, 1923

453 Bill Ivy on Yamaha
   125cc, 1968

454 Giacomo Agostini on
   MV Agusta 500cc,
   1972

455 Joey Dunlop on RVF Honda
   750cc, 1985

80th Anniversary of Tourist Trophy Mountain Course

(Des A. Theobald. Litho Enschedé)

1991 (30 MAY). *Perf* 14½×13 (C)

478	**451**	17p multicoloured	....	40	40
479	**452**	21p multicoloured	....	60	60
480	**453**	26p multicoloured	....	85	85
481	**454**	31p multicoloured	....	1·25	1·25
482	**455**	37p multicoloured	....	1·40	1·40
478/82		*Set of 5*	....	4·00	4·00
		First Day Cover			5·25
		Presentation Pack		4·75	
		Stamp Cards (set of 5)		2·25	5·00
		Set of 5 Gutter Pairs		8·00	
MS483	149×144 mm. Nos. 478/82		......	4·25	4·25
		First Day Cover			6·00
		Souvenir Folder		4·75	

No. **MS**483 was reissued on 16 November 1991 overprinted for the Phila Nippon exhibition, Japan.

Plate Nos: All values 1A, 1B, 1C, 1D (each ×4)

Sheets: 40 (2 panes 5×4)

Imprint: Right-hand corner, bottom margin of each pane

Withdrawn: 29.5.92

Ninth Conference of Commonwealth Postal Administrations, Douglas

(Des Colleen Corlett. Litho B.D.T.)

1991 (1 JULY). *Perf* 13 (C)

MS484	119×77 mm. Nos. 367*c* and 377*a*, each ×2	....	1·50	1·50
		First Day Cover		3·00
		Presentation Pack	3·00	

Withdrawn: 30.6.92

LAXEY HAND-CART

456 Laxey Hand-cart,
   1920

DOUGLAS HORSE DRAWN STEAMER

457 Horse-drawn Steamer,
   Douglas, 1909

MERRYWEATHER HATFIELD PUMP

458 Merryweather
   'Hatfield' Pump,
   1936

DENNIS F8 PUMPING APPLIANCE

459 Dennis 'F8' Pumping
   Appliance, Peel, 1953

VOLVO TURNTABLE LADDER

460 Volvo Turntable Ladder,
   Douglas, 1989

Fire Engines

(Des C. Abbott. Litho Questa)

1991 (18 SEPT). *Perf* 14½ (C)

485	**456**	17p multicoloured	....	40	40
486	**457**	21p multicoloured	....	60	60
487	**458**	30p multicoloured	....	85	85
488	**459**	33p multicoloured	....	1·25	1·25
489	**460**	37p multicoloured	....	1·40	1·40
485/9		*Set of 5*	....	4·00	4·00
		First Day Cover			6·00
		Presentation Pack		4·75	
		Set of 5 Gutter Pairs		8·00	

Plate Nos: All values 1A, 1B, 1C, 1D (each ×5)

Sheets: 40 (2 panes 4×5)

Imprint: Central, gutter margin

Withdrawn: 17.9.92

461 Mute Swans, Douglas
   Harbour

462 Black Swans, Curraghs
   Wildlife Park

463 Whooper Swans, Bishop's Dub, Ballaugh

464 Whistling ('Bewick's') Swans, Eairy Dam, Foxdale

465 Coscoroba Swans, Curraghs Wildlife Park

466 Whooper ('Trumpeter') Swans, Curraghs Wildlife Park

Swans

(Des Colleen Corlett. Litho Cartor)

1991 (18 SEPT). *Perf* 13 (C)

490	**461**	17p multicoloured	. . . .	55	55
		a. Horiz pair. Nos. 490/1	. . . .	1·10	1·10
491	**462**	17p multicoloured	. . . .	55	55
492	**463**	26p multicoloured	. . . .	1·10	1·10
		a. Horiz pair. Nos. 492/3	. . . .	2·25	2·25
493	**464**	26p multicoloured	. . . .	1·10	1·10
494	**465**	37p multicoloured	. . . .	1·40	1·40
		a. Horiz pair. Nos. 494/5	. . . .	2·75	2·75
		ab. Black ptg double	. . . .		
495	**466**	37p multicoloured	. . . .	1·40	1·40
490/5		Set of 6	. . . .	5·50	5·50
		First Day Cover			6·00
		Presentation Pack		6·00	

Plate Nos: All values 1A, 1B (each ×4)

Sheets: 20 (4×5). The two designs of each value were printed together, *se-tenant*, in horizontal pairs throughout the sheet, with the backgrounds forming composite designs

Imprint: Central, bottom margin

Withdrawn: 17.9.92

467 The Three Kings

468 Mary With Manger

469 Shepherds with Sheep

470 Choir of Angels

Christmas. Paper Sculptures

(Des D. Swinton. Litho Walsall)

1991 (14 OCT). (*a*) *Sheet stamps. Perf* 14×14½ (C)

496	**467**	16p multicoloured	. . . .	50	40
497	**468**	20p multicoloured	. . . .	65	70
498	**469**	26p multicoloured	. . . .	80	85
499	**470**	37p multicoloured	. . . .	1·10	1·10
496/9		Set of 4	. . . .	2·75	2·75
		First Day Cover			4·00
		Presentation Pack		3·50	

Plate Nos: All values 1A, 1B, 1C, 1D (each ×4)

Sheets: 40 (2 panes 4×5)

Imprint: Central, gutter margin

Withdrawn: 13.10.92

(*b*) *Booklet stamps. Self-adhesive. Stamps die-cut*

500	**467**	16p multicoloured	. . . .	75	75
		a. Booklet pane. Nos. 500×8 and 501×4	. . . .	10·00	
501	**468**	20p multicoloured	. . . .	1·00	1·00

Year Pack 1991

1991 (14 OCT). *Comprises Nos.* 367c, 377a, 464/82 *and* **MS**484/99

Year Pack . . . . 35·00

Withdrawn: 31.12.92

Post Office Yearbook

1991 (14 OCT). *Comprises Nos.* 367c, 377a, 464/82 *and* **MS**484/99

Yearbook . . . . 40·00

Withdrawn: 30.11.94

471 North African and Italian Campaigns, 1942–43

472 D-Day, 1944

473 Arnhem, 1944

474 Rhine Crossing, 1945

475 Operations in Near, Middle and Far East, 1945–68

476 Liberation of Falkland Islands, 1982

50th Anniversary of Parachute Regiment

(Des A. Theobald. Litho Questa)

1992 (6 FEB). *Perf* 14 (C)

502	**471**	23p multicoloured	. . . .	60	60
		a. *Horiz pair. Nos.* 502/3	. . . .	1·25	1·25
503	**472**	23p multicoloured	. . . .	60	60
504	**473**	28p multicoloured	. . . .	70	70
		a. *Horiz pair. Nos.* 504/5	. . . .	1·40	1·40
505	**474**	28p multicoloured	. . . .	70	70
506	**475**	39p multicoloured	. . . .	1·00	1·00
		a. *Horiz pair. Nos.* 506/7	. . . .	2·00	2·00
507	**476**	39p multicoloured	. . . .	1·00	1·00
502/7		*Set of* 6	. . . .	4·00	4·00
		First Day Cover	. . . .		5·50
		Presentation Pack	. . . .	5·00	
		Souvenir Folder (*complete sheets*)	. . . .	18·00	

Plate Nos: All values 1A, 1B (each ×5)

Sheets: 8 (2×4). The two designs of each value were printed together, *se-tenant*, in horizontal pairs throughout the sheet

Imprint: Top, left-hand margin

Withdrawn: 5.2.93

477 Queen Elizabeth II at Coronation, 1953

478 Queen visiting Isle of Man, 1979

479 Queen in Evening Dress

480 Queen visiting Isle of Man, 1989

481 Queen arriving for Film Premiere, 1990

40th Anniversary of Accession

(Des D. Miller. Litho B.D.T.)

1992 (6 FEB). *Perf* 14 (C)

508	**477**	18p multicoloured	. . . .	50	50
509	**478**	23p multicoloured	. . . .	60	60
510	**479**	28p multicoloured	. . . .	70	70
511	**480**	33p multicoloured	. . . .	1·10	1·10
512	**481**	39p multicoloured	. . . .	1·25	1·25
508/12		*Set of* 5	. . . .	3·75	3·75
		First Day Cover	. . . .		5·50
		Presentation Pack	. . . .	4·75	

Plate Nos: All values 1A, 1B (each ×5)

Sheets: 20 (5×4)

Imprint: Central, bottom margin

Withdrawn: 5.2.93

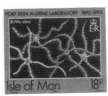

482 Brittle-stars

483 Phytoplankton

484 Herring

485 Great Scallop

139

486 Dahlia Anemone and Delesseria

Centenary of Port Erin Marine Laboratory

(Des Jennifer Toombs. Litho Questa)

1992 (16 APR). Perf 14×14½ (C)

513	**482**	18p multicoloured	....	50	50
514	**483**	23p multicoloured	....	60	60
515	**484**	28p multicoloured	....	70	70
516	**485**	33p multicoloured	....	1·10	1·10
517	**486**	39p multicoloured	....	1·25	1·25
513/17		Set of 5	....	3·75	3·75
		First Day Cover	....		5·00
		Presentation Pack	....	4·75	
		Set of 5 Gutter Pairs	......	7·50	

Plate Nos: All values 1A, 1B, 1C, 1D (each ×4)

Sheets: 40 (2 panes 5×4)

Imprint: Top right-hand side, gutter margin

Withdrawn: 15.4.93

487 The Pilgrim Fathers embarking at Delfshaven

488 Speedwell leaving Delfshaven

489 'Mayflower and Speedwell at Dartmouth' **490** (L. Wilcox)

Europa. 500th Anniversary of Discovery of America by Columbus

(Des C. Abbott. Litho Enschedé)

1992 (16 APR). Perf 14×13½ (C)

518	**487**	18p multicoloured	....	60	60
		a. Horiz. pair. Nos. 518/19	....	1·25	1·25
519	**488**	18p multicoloured	....	60	60
520	**489**	28p multicoloured	....	1·00	1·00
		a. Horiz. pair. Nos. 520/1	....	2·00	2·00

521	**490**	28p multicoloured	....	1·00	1·00
518/21		Set of 4	....	2·75	2·75
		First Day Cover	....		3·75
		Presentation Pack	....	3·75	

Plate Nos: Both values 1A, 1B (each ×5)

Sheets: 20 (4×5). The two designs of each value were printed together, se-tenant, in horizontal pairs throughout the sheet, each pair forming a composite design

Imprint: Central, bottom margin

Withdrawn: 15.4.93

491 Central Pacific Locomotive Jupiter, 1869

492 Union Pacific Locomotive No. 119, 1869

493 Union Pacific Locomotive No. 844, 1992

494 Union Pacific Locomotive No. 3985, 1992

495 Golden Spike Ceremony, 10 May 1869 (Illustration reduced. Actual size 105×73 mm)

Construction of Union Pacific Railroad, 1866–69

(Des A. Peck. Litho Enschedé)

1992 (22 MAY). Perf 13½×14 (C)

522	**491**	33p multicoloured	....	95	95
		a. Horiz. pair. Nos. 522/3 plus label	....	1·90	1·90
		b. Booklet pane. Nos. 522/5×2 and **MS**526	....	9·25	
523	**492**	33p multicoloured	....	95	95

524	**493**	39p multicoloured	1·10	1·10
		a. Horiz pair. Nos. 524/5 plus		
		label	2·25	2·25
525	**494**	39p multicoloured	1·10	1·10
522/5		Set of 4	3·75	3·75
		First Day Cover		5·00
		Presentation Pack	4·75	
		Souvenir Folder (sheets of		
		10)	18·00	
		Stamp Cards (set of 4)	2·25	5·25
MS526	105×73 mm. **495**	£1.50, mult	5·25	5·25
		First Day Cover		5·50
		Presentation Pack	5·50	
		Stamp Card	40	

Booklet pane No. 522b contains two blocks of four of Nos. 522/5 with No. **MS**526 between them. Miniature sheets from the booklet show a white margin and line of roulettes at left and right. In the blocks of four each horizontal pair is separated by a half stamp-size label.

Plate Nos: Both values 1A, 1B (each ×4)

Sheets: 10 (2×5). The two designs for each value were printed together in horizontal pairs separated by a half stamp-size label showing Union Pacific emblem or portraits of Dan and Jack Casement (railroad contractors)

Imprint: Central, right-hand margin

Withdrawn: 21.5.93

496 King Orry V in Douglas Harbour

497 Castletown

498 Port St. Mary

499 Ramsey

Manx Harbours

(Des Colleen Corlett. Litho Walsall)

1992 (18 SEPT). Perf 14½×14 (C)

527	**496**	18p multicoloured	50	50
528	**497**	23p multicoloured	60	60

529	**498**	37p multicoloured	1·25	1·25
530	**499**	40p multicoloured	1·25	1·25
527/30		Set of 4	3·25	3·25
		First Day Cover		4·50
		Presentation Pack	3·50	

Plate Nos: All values 1A, 1B (each ×4)

Sheets: 10 (2×5)

Imprint: Right-hand corner, bottom margin

Withdrawn: 17.9.93

500 King Orry V (ex Saint Eloi) in 1972 and 1992 (illustration reduced. Actual size 111×68 mm)

"Genova '92" International Thematic Stamp Exhibition

(Des Colleen Corlett, Litho Walsall)

1992 (18 SEPT). Sheet 111×68 mm. Perf 14½×14 (C)

MS531	**500**	18p, £1 multicoloured	3·50	3·50
		First Day Cover		4·50
		Presentation Pack	3·75	

Withdrawn: 17.9.93

501 Window, St. German's Cathedral, Peel

502 Reredos, St. Matthew the Apostle, Douglas

503 Window, St. George's, Douglas

504 Reredos, St. Mary of the Isle Catholic Church, Douglas

505 Window, Trinity Methodist Church, Douglas

Christmas, Manx Churches

(Des Colleen Corlett, Litho Questa)

1992 (13 OCT). *Perf* 14½ (C)

532	**501**	17p multicoloured	50	50
533	**502**	22p multicoloured	70	70
534	**503**	28p multicoloured	85	85
535	**504**	37p multicoloured	1·00	1·00
536	**505**	40p multicoloured	1·10	1·10
		a. Gold ptg double		
532/6		Set of 5	3·75	3·75
		First Day Cover		5·50
		Presentation Pack	4·00	
		Set of 5 Gutter Pairs	7·50	

Plate Nos.: 17p, 22p 1A, 1B, 1C, 1D (each ×5); others 1A, 1B (each ×5)

Sheets: 40 (2 panes 4×5)

Imprint: Right-hand corner, bottom margin of each pane

Withdrawn: 12.10.93

Year Pack 1992

1992 (13 OCT). *Comprises Nos.* 502/36

Year Pack .... 35·00

Withdrawn: 31.12.93

Post Office Yearbook

1992 (13 OCT). *Comprises Nos.* 375a, 377b, 502/36 *and* D25

Yearbook .... 45·00

Withdrawn: 30.11.94

506 Mansell on Lap of Honour, British Grand Prix, 1992

507 Mansell in French Grand Prix, 1992

Nigel Mansell's Victory in Formula 1 World Motor Racing Championship

(Des A. Theobald. Litho Walsall)

1992 (8 NOV). *Perf* 13½ (C)

537	**506**	20p multicoloured	50	50
538	**507**	24p multicoloured	75	75
537/8		Set of 2	1·25	1·25
		First Day Cover		1·90
		Presentation Pack	2·00	

Plate Nos. Both values 1A, 1B (each ×4)

Sheets: 50 (5×10)

Imprint : Bottom margin

Withdrawn: 7.11.93.

508 H.M.S. *Amazon* (frigate)

509 *Fingal* (lighthouse tender)

510 *Sir Winston Churchill* (cadet schooner)

511 *Dar Mlodziezy* (full-rigged cadet ship)

512 *Tynwald I* (paddle-steamer)

513 *Ben Veg* (freighter)

514 *Waverley* (paddle-steamer)

515 Royal Yacht *Britannia*

516 *Francis Drake* (ketch)

517 *Royal Viking Sky* (liner)

518 *Lord Nelson* (cadet barque)

519 *Europa* (liner)

520 *Snaefell V* (ferry) leaving Ardrossan

520a *Seacat* (catamaran ferry)

521 *Lady of Mann I* (ferry) off Ramsey

522 *Mona's Queen II* (paddle ferry) leaving Fleetwood

523 *Queen Elizabeth 2* (liner) and *Mona's Queen V* (ferry) off Liverpool

523a Manx Red Ensign

523b Queen Elizabeth II (hologram)

Ships

(Des A. Theobald (1p to 27p), J. Nicholson (30p, 40p, 50p, £1), Colleen Corlett (£2, £5). Litho Questa (£2), Walsall (£5) (hologram by Applied Holographics), Enschedé (others))

1993 (4 JAN)–**97.** *Perf* 14½ (£2), 14½×14 (£5) *or* 13½×13 (*others*), *all comb*

539	**508**	1p multicoloured (a)	. . . .	10	10
540	**509**	2p multicoloured (a)	. . . .	10	10
541	**510**	4p multicoloured (a)	. . . .	10	10
		a. Booklet pane. Nos. 541, 544 and 548 each ×2 (g)	. . . . .	2·00	
542	**511**	5p multicoloured (a)	. . . .	10	10
543	**512**	20p multicoloured (ae)	. . . . . .	40	45
		a. Booklet pane. Nos. 543×2 and 547×3	. . . .	2·50	
		b. Booklet pane. Nos. 543×4 and 547×6	. . . .	4·75	
544	**513**	21p multicoloured (ag)	. . . .	40	45
545	**514**	22p multicoloured (a)	. . . .	45	50
546	**515**	23p multicoloured (a)	. . . .	45	50
547	**516**	24p multicoloured (ae)	. . . .	50	55
548	**517**	25p multicoloured (ag)	. . . .	50	55
549	**518**	26p multicoloured (a)	. . . .	55	60
550	**519**	27p multicoloured (a)	. . . .	55	60
551	**520**	30p multicoloured (b)	. . . .	60	65
552	**520**a	35p multicoloured (f)	. . . .	70	75
553	**521**	40p multicoloured (b)	. . . .	80	85
554	**522**	50p multicoloured (b)	. . . .	1·00	1·10
555	**523**	£1 multicoloured (bg)	. . . .	2·00	2·10
556	**523**a	£2 multicoloured (c)	. . . .	4·00	4·25
557	**523**b	£5 multicoloured (d)	. . . .	10·00	10·50
539/57		Set of 19	. . . .	23·00	24·00
		First Day Covers (6)	. . . . .		28·00
		Presentation Packs (6)	. . . .	27·00	
		Stamp Cards (Nos. 539/51, 553/5)	. . . .	4·75	13·50
		Souvenir Folder (Nos. 539/51, 553/5)	. . . .	10·00	

For 4p, 20p and 24p in similar designs, but smaller, see Nos. 687/93.

Printings: (a) 4.1.93. Inscribed '1993'; (b) 15.9.93. Inscribed '1993'; (c) 12.1.94. Inscribed '1994'; (d) 5.7.94. Inscribed '1994'; (e) 8.2.95. Inscribed '1995'; (f) 11.1.1996. Inscribed '1996'; (g) 14.5.97. Inscribed '1997'

Plate Nos: £2, £5 1A, 1B (each ×4): others 1A, 1B, 1C, 1D (each ×4)

Sheets: 25 (5×5) (£2), 10 (5×2) (£5) or 50 (5×10) (others). In addition to stamp booklets Nos. 543a/b also come from a special booklet sheet of 50 (5×10) which provides either 10 examples of No. 543a or 5 of 543b. No. 541a comes from a special booklet sheet of 30 (5×6)

Imprint: Central, bottom margin (£2, £5) or right-hand corner, bottom margin (others)

524 No. 1 Motor Car and No. 13 Trailer at Groudle Glen Hotel

525 No. 9 Tunnel Car and No. 19 Trailer at Douglas Bay Hotel

526 No. 19 Motor Car and No. 59 Royal Trailer Special at Douglas Bay

527 No. 33 Motor Car, No. 45 Trailer and No. 13 Van at Derby Castle

Centenary of Manx Electric Railway

(Des A. Theobald. Litho B.D.T.)

1993 (3 FEB). *Perf* 14 (C)

559	**524**	20p multicoloured	50	50
		a. Booklet pane. Nos. 559/62 . .	2·50	
560	**525**	24p multicoloured	65	65
561	**526**	28p multicoloured	70	70
562	**527**	39p multicoloured	1·00	1·00
559/62		*Set of 4*	2·50	2·50
		First Day Cover		3·50
		Presentation Pack	3·50	

Booklet pane No. 559*a* exists in four versions, which differ in the order of the stamps within the block of four and in the information printed on the pane margin.

Plate Nos: All values 1A, 1B (each ×4)
Sheets: 10 (2×5)
Imprint: Central, left-hand margin
Withdrawn: 2.2.94

528 'Sir Hall Caine' (statue)

529 'The Brass Bedstead' (painting)

530 Abstract Bronze Sculpture

531 'Polar Bear Skeleton' (drawing)

Europa. Contemporary Art by Bryan Kneale

(Des Colleen Corlett. Litho B.D.T.)

1993 (14 APR). *Perf* 14 (C)

563	**528**	20p multicoloured	55	55
		a. Horiz pair. Nos. 563/4	1·10	1·10
564	**529**	20p multicoloured	55	55

565	**530**	28p multicoloured	90	90
		a. Horiz pair. Nos. 565/6	1·75	1·75
566	**531**	28p multicoloured	90	90
563/6		*Set of 4*	2·50	2·50
		First Day Cover		3·25
		Presentation Pack	3·25	

Plate Nos.: Both values 1A, 1B, 1C (each ×4)
Sheets: 20 (4×5). The two designs for each value printed together, *se-tenant*, in horizontal pairs throughout the sheets
Imprint: Central, right-hand margin
Withdrawn: 13.4.94

532 Graham Oates and Bill Marshall (1933 International Six Day Trial) on Ariel Square Four

533 Sergeant Geoff Duke (1947 Royal Signals Display Team) on Triumph 3T Twin

534 Denis Parkinson (1953 Senior Manx Grand Prix) on Manx Norton

535 Richard Swallow (1991 Junior Classic MGP) on Aermacchi

536 Steve Colley (1992 Scottish Six Day Trial) on Beta Zero

Manx Motor Cycling Events

(Des C. Abbott. Litho Walsall)

1993 (3 JUNE). *Perf* 13½×14 (C)

567	**532**	20p multicoloured	45	45
568	**533**	24p multicoloured	60	60
569	**534**	28p multicoloured	80	80
570	**535**	33p multicoloured	1·10	1·10

571	**536**	39p multicoloured	....	1·25	1·25
567/71		Set of 5	....	3·75	3·75
		First Day Cover	....		4·50
		Presentation Pack	....	4·25	
		Stamp Cards (set of 5)	....	1·75	5·50
MS572		165×120 mm. Nos. 567/71	......	4·00	4·00
		Souvenir Folder	....	4·75	

Plate Nos: All values 1A. 1B. 1C. 1D (each ×4)

Sheets: 20 (4×5)

Imprint: Right-hand corner, bottom margin

Withdrawn: 2.6.94

ISLE OF MAN

ISLE OF MAN

537 *Inachis io* (Peacock)

538 *Argynnis aglaja* (Dark Green Fritillary)

ISLE OF MAN

ISLE OF MAN

539 *Cynthia cardui* (Painted Lady)

540 *Celastrina argiolus* (Holly Blue)

ISLE OF MAN

541 *Vanessa atalanta* (Red Admiral)

Butterflies

(Des Colleen Corlett. Litho Questa)

1993 (15 SEPT). *Perf* 14½ (C)

573	**537**	24p multicoloured	....	75	75
		a. Horiz strip of 5. Nos. 573/7 ..		3·25	
574	**538**	24p multicoloured	....	75	75
575	**539**	24p multicoloured	....	75	75
576	**540**	24p multicoloured	....	75	75
577	**541**	24p multicoloured	....	75	75
573/7		Set of 5	....	3·25	3·25
		First Day Cover			4·00
		Presentation Pack	....	3·50	

Examples of Nos. 573/7 sold at "PhilaKorea '94" and "Singpex '94" come with commemorative cachets on the bottom margin

Plate Nos: 1A, 1B (each ×4)

Sheets: 20 (5×4). The five designs printes together, *se-tenant*, in horizontal strips throughout the sheet

Imprint: Right-hand corner, bottom margin

Withdrawn: 14.9.94

ISLE OF MAN 19ʳ

ISLE OF MAN 23ʳ

542 Children decorating Christmas Tree

543 Girl with Snowman

ISLE OF MAN 28ʳ

ISLE OF MAN 39ʳ

544 Boy opening Presents

545 Girl with Teddy Bear

ISLE OF MAN 40ʳ   **546** Children with Toboggan

Christmas

(Des Christine Haworth. Litho Questa)

1993 (12 OCT). *Perf* 14 (C)

578	**542**	19p multicoloured	....	55	55
579	**543**	23p multicoloured	....	65	65
580	**544**	28p multicoloured	....	80	80
581	**545**	39p multicoloured	....	1·10	1·10
582	**546**	40p multicoloured	....	1·10	1·10
578/82		Set of 5	....	3·75	3·75
		First Day Cover	....		4·00
		Presentation Pack	....	4·00	
		Set of 5 *Gutter Pairs*	......	7·50	

Plate Nos.: All values 1A, 1B, 1C, 1D (each ×4)

Sheets: 40 (2 panes 4×5)

Imprint: Bottom, right-hand margin of each pane

Withdrawn: 11.10.94

Year Pack 1993

1993 (12 OCT). *Comprises Nos. 539/51, 553/5, 559/71 and 573/82*

Year Pack . . . . 25·00

Withdrawn: 31.12.94

Post Office Yearbook

1993 (12 OCT). *Comprises Nos. 539/51, 553/5, 559/71 and 573/82*

Yearbook . . . . 35·00

Sold out: 8.95

547 White-throated Robin   **548** Black-eared Wheatear

549 Goldcrest   **550** Northern Oriole

551 Common Kingfisher   **552** Hoopoe

553 Magpie
(*illustration reduced. Actual size 100×71 mm*)

Calf of Man Bird Observatory

(Des Colleen Corlett. Litho B.D.T.)

1994 (18 FEB). *Perf 13½×13 (No. MS589) or 14 (others), both comb*

583	**547**	20p multicoloured	. . . .	60	60
		a. Pair. Nos. 583/4	. . . .	1·25	1·25
584	**548**	20p multicoloured	. . . .	60	60
585	**549**	24p multicoloured	. . . .	90	90
		a. Pair. Nos. 585/6	. . . .	1·75	1·75
586	**550**	24p multicoloured	. . . .	90	90
587	**551**	30p multicoloured	. . . .	1·00	1·00
		a. Pair. Nos. 587/8	. . . .	2·00	2·00
588	**552**	30p multicoloured	. . . .	1·00	1·00
583/8		Set of 6	. . . .	4·25	4·25
		First Day Cover	. . . .		4·50
		Presentation Pack	. . . .	4·50	
		Souvenir Folder (complete sheets)	. . . .	20·00	
MS589	100×71 mm.	**553** £1 multicoloured		3·00	3·00
		First Day Cover	. . . .		3·25
		Presentation Pack	. . . .	3·25	

No. **MS**589 also commemorates the "Hong Kong '94" philatelic exhibition.

Plate Nos.: All values 1A, 1B (each ×4)

Sheets: 10 (2×5). The two designs for each value printed together, *se-tenant*, in horizontal and vertical pairs throughout the sheets.

Imprint: Central, right-hand margin

Withdrawn: 17.2.95

554 Gaiety Theatre, Douglas   **555** Sports

556 Artist at Work and   **557** T.T. Races and British
Yachts racing   Aerospace Hawk T.1s
                                  of Red Arrows

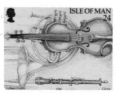

558 Musical Instruments   **559** Laxey Wheel and Manx
                                      Cat

560 Tower of Refuge, Douglas, with Bucket and Spade

561 Cyclist

566 Edward Forbes and Signature

567 *Solaster moretonis* (fossil starfish)

562 Tynwald Day and Classic Car

563 Santa Mince Pie Train, Groudle Glen

568 *Adamsia carciniopados* (anemone) on Hermit Crab

569 *Solaster endeca* (starfish)

Booklet Stamps. Manx Tourism Centenary

(Des Colleen Corlett. Litho Cartor)

1994 (18 FEB). *Perf* 13½ (C)

590	**554**	24p multicoloured	. . . .	60	60
		a. Booklet pane. Nos. 590/9			
		with margins all round	. . . .	5·50	
591	**555**	24p multicoloured	. . . .	60	60
592	**556**	24p multicoloured	. . . .	60	60
593	**557**	24p multicoloured	. . . .	60	60
594	**558**	24p multicoloured	. . . .	60	60
595	**559**	24p multicoloured	. . . .	60	60
596	**560**	24p multicoloured	. . . .	60	60
597	**561**	24p multicoloured	. . . .	60	60
598	**562**	24p multicoloured	. . . .	60	60
599	**563**	24p multicoloured	. . . .	60	60
590/9		Set of 10	. . . .	5·50	5·50
		First Day of Cover	. . . .		6·00
		Presentation Pack	. . . .	6·00	
		Stamp Cards (set of 3)	. . . .	1·25	

Nos. 590/9 were only issued in £2.40 stamp booklets.

Withdrawn: 17.2.95

Europa. Discoveries of Edward Forbes (marine biologist)

(Des Jennifer Toombs. Litho Enschedé)

1994 (5 MAY). *Perf* 13×14½ (C)

600	**564**	20p multicoloured	. . . .	50	50
		a. Horiz strip of 3. Nos. 600/2		1·50	
601	**565**	20p multicoloured	. . . .	50	50
602	**566**	20p multicoloured	. . . .	50	50
603	**567**	30p multicoloured	. . . .	90	90
		a. Horiz strip of 3. Nos. 603/5		2·75	
604	**568**	30p multicoloured	. . . .	90	90
605	**569**	30p multicoloured	. . . .	90	90
600/5		Set of 6	. . . .	3·75	3·75
		First Day Cover	. . . .		4·25
		Presentation Pack	. . . .	4·00	

Plate Nos: Both values 1A, 1B (each ×4)

Sheets: 15 (3×5). The three designs for each value printed together, *se-tenant*, in horizontal strips of 3 throughout the sheets

Imprint: Central, bottom margin

Withdrawn: 4.5.95

570 Maj.-Gen. Bedell Smith and Naval Landing Force including *Ben-My-Chree IV* (ferry)

571 Admiral Ramsay and Naval Ships including *Victoria* and *Lady of Mann* (ferries)

564 *Eubranchus tricolor* (sea slug)

565 *Loligo forbesii* (Common Squid)

147

572 Gen. Montgomery and British Landings

573 Lt.-Gen. Dempsey and 2nd Army Landings

574 Air Chief Marshal Leigh-Mallory, U.S. Paratroops and Aircraft

575 Air Chief Marshal Tedder, British Paratroops and Aircraft

576 Lt.-Gen. Bradley and U.S. 1st Army Landings

577 Gen. Eisenhower and American Landings

50th Anniversary of D-Day

(Des A. Theobald. Litho Questa)

1994 (6 JUNE). *Perf* 14 (C)

606	**570**	4p multicoloured	. . . .	15	15
		a. Horiz pair. Nos. 606/7	. . . .	30	30
607	**571**	4p multicoloured	. . . .	15	15
608	**572**	20p multicoloured	. . . .	70	70
		a. Horiz pair. Nos. 608/9	. . . .	1·40	1·40
609	**573**	20p multicoloured	. . . .	70	70
610	**574**	30p multicoloured	. . . .	80	80
		a. Horiz pair. Nos. 610/11	. . . .	1·50	1·50
611	**575**	30p multicoloured	. . . .	80	80
612	**576**	41p multicoloured	. . . .	1·00	1·00
		a. Horiz pair. Nos. 612/13	. . . .	2·00	2·00
613	**577**	41p multicoloured	. . . .	1·00	1·00
606/13		Set of 8	. . . .	4·75	4·75
		First Day Cover			5·00
		Presentation Pack		6·00	
		Souvenir Folder (complete sheets)		24·00	

Plate Nos.: All values 1A, 1B (each ×5)

Sheets: 8 (2×4). The two designs for each value printed together, *se-tenant*, in horizontal pairs throughout the sheets

Imprint: Central, left-hand margin

Withdrawn: 5.6.95

578 Postman Pat, Jess and Ffinlo at Sea Terminal, Douglas

579 Laxey Wheel

580 Cregneash

581 Manx Electric Railway Trains

582 Peel Harbour

583 Douglas Promenade

584 Postman Pat, Jess, Policeman and Children at Zebra Crossing
(*illustration reduced. Actual size* 110×85 *mm*)

Postman Pat visits the Isle of Man

(Des Colleen Corlett. Litho B.D.T.)

1994 (14 SEPT). *Perf* 13 (*No.* **MS**620) *or* 15×14 (*others*), *both comb*

614	**578**	1p multicoloured	10	10
		a. Booklet pane of 2 with margins all round	20	
615	**579**	20p multicoloured	60	60
		a. Booklet pane of 2 with margins all round	1·00	
616	**580**	24p multicoloured	70	70
		a. Booklet pane of 2 with margins all round	1·25	
617	**581**	30p multicoloured	80	80
		a. Booklet pane of 2 with margins all round	1·50	
618	**582**	36p multicoloured	90	90
		a. Booklet pane of 2 with margins all round	1·75	
619	**583**	41p multicoloured	1·10	1·10
		a. Booklet pane of 2 with margins all round	2·00	
614/19		Set of 6	3·75	3·75
		First Day Cover.		4·00
		Presentation Pack	4·00	
		Stamp Cards (set of 6)	1·75	6·00
MS620	110×85 mm. **584** £1 multicoloured		2·50	2·50
		First Day Cover.		3·00
		Presentation Pack	3·00	

Examples of No. **MS**620 from stamp booklets show a line of roulettes at left.

Plate Nos.: All values 1A, 1B (each ×4)

Sheets: 10 (2×5)

Imprint: Right-hand corner, bottom margin

Withdrawn: 13.9.95

585 Cycling

586 Downhill Skiing

587 Swimming

588 Hurdling

589 Centenary Logo

Centenary of International Olympic Committee

(Des D. Miller. Litho Walsall)

1994 (11 OCT). *Perf* 14×14½ (C)

621	**585**	10p multicoloured	30	30
622	**586**	20p multicoloured	55	55
623	**587**	24p multicoloured	70	70
624	**588**	35p multicoloured	95	95
625	**589**	48p multicoloured	1·40	1·40
621/5		Set of 5	3·50	3·50
		First Day Cover.		3·75
		Presentation Pack	3·75	

Plate Nos: 10p 1A (×4); 20p 1B (×4); 24p 1C (×4); 35p 1D (×4); 48p 1E (×4)

Sheets: 20 (5×4)

Imprint: Central, left-hand margin

Withdrawn: 10.10.95

590 Santa Train to Santon

591 Father Christmas and Postman Pat on Mini Tractor, Douglas

592 Father Christmas and Majorettes in Sleigh, Port St. Mary

Christmas. Father Christmas in the Isle of Man

(Des Colleen Corlett. Litho Cartor)

1994 (11 OCT). *Perf* 13½×14 (23p) *or* 14×13½ (*others*), *all comb*

626	**590**	19p multicoloured	50	50
627	**591**	23p multicoloured	70	70
628	**592**	60p multicoloured	1·60	1·60
626/8		Set of 3	2·50	2·50
		First Day Cover.		3·00
		Presentation Pack	3·00	
		Set of 3 Gutter Pairs	5·00	

Plate Nos.: All values 1A, 1B, 1C, 1D (each ×4)

Sheets: 40 (2 panes 5×4)

Imprint: Central, side margins of each pane

Withdrawn: 10.10.95

Year Pack 1994

1994 (11 OCT). *Comprises Nos. 556 and 583/628, with or without No. 557*

Year Pack with No. 557	42·00
Year Pack without No. 557 . .	38·00

Withdrawn: 31.12.95

Post Office Yearbook

1994 (NOV). *Comprises Nos. 556/7 and 583/628*

Yearbook . . . . 50·00

Sold out: 3.96

593 Foden Steam Wagon, Highway Board Depot, Douglas

594 Clayton and Shuttleworth and Fowler engines pulling Dead Whale

595 Wallis and Steevens at Ramsey Harbour

596 Marshall Engine with Threshing Machine, Ballarhenny

597 Marshall Convertible Steam Roller

Steam Traction Engines

(Des A. Peck. Litho Enschedé)

1995 (8 FEB). *Perf* 13½×13 (C)

629	**593**	20p multicoloured	. . . .	60	60
630	**594**	24p multicoloured	. . . .	70	70
631	**595**	30p multicoloured	. . . .	85	85
632	**596**	35p multicoloured	. . . .	95	95
633	**597**	41p multicoloured	. . . .	1·10	1·10
629/33		Set of 5	. . . .	3·75	3·75
		First Day Cover			4·00
		Presentation Pack	4·00	

Plate Nos.: 35p 1A, 1B, 1C, 1D (each ×4): others 1A, 1B (each ×4)

Sheets: 20 (4×5)

Withdrawn: 7.2.96

598 Car No. 2 and First Train, 1895

599 Car No. 4 in Green Livery and Car No. 3 in Laxey Valley

600 Car No. 6 and Car No. 5 in 1971

601 Goods Car No. 7 and *Caledonia* Steam Locomotive pulling Construction Train

1895·CENTENARY SNAEFELL MOUNTAIN RAILWAY·1995

602 Passenger Car and Argus Char-a-banc at Bungalow Hotel (*illustration reduced. Actual size* 110×87 *mm*)

Centenary of Snaefell Mountain Railway

(Des A. Theobald. Litho B.D.T.)

1995 (8 FEB). *Perf* 14 (C)

634	**598**	20p multicoloured	60	60
		a. Booklet pane. Nos. 634/7 with margins all round	3·00	
635	**599**	24p multicoloured	70	70
636	**600**	35p multicoloured	95	95
637	**601**	42p multicoloured	1·10	1·10
634/7		Set of 4	3·00	3·00
		First Day Cover		3·25
		Presentation Pack	3·25	
MS638	110×87 mm.	**602** £1 multicoloured	2·50	2·50
		a. Booklet pane. As No. **MS**638 with additional margins all round showing further inscriptions at right and left	2·50	
		First Day Cover		2·75
		Presentation Pack	2·75	

Booklet pane No. 634*a* exists in three versions which differ in the order of the stamps within the block of four.

Examples of No. **MS**638 from booklet No. SB39 show a white margin, description of the design and line of roulettes at left and an additional inscription, '1895. CENTENARY SNAEFELL MOUNTAIN RAILWAY. 1995', vertically in the margin at right.

Plate Nos.: All values 1A, 1B (each ×4)

Sheets: 10 (2×5)

Imprint: Central, left-hand margin

Withdrawn: 7.2.96

603 Peace Doves forming Wave and Tower of Refuge, Douglas Bay

604 Peace Dove breaking Barbed Wire

Europa. Peace and Freedom

(Des Colleen Corlett and M. Magleby (20p), Colleen Corlett (30p). Litho Enschedé)

1995 (28 APR). *Perf* 14×13½ (C)

639	**603**	20p multicoloured	50	50
640	**604**	30p multicoloured	75	75
639/40		Set of 2	1·25	1·25
		First Day Cover		1·75
		Presentation Pack	1·75	

Plate Nos.: Both values 1A, 1B (each ×5)

Sheets: 10 (5×2)

Imprint: Central, bottom margin

Withdrawn: 27.4.96

605 Spitfire, Tank and Medals

606 Typhoon, Anti-aircraft Gun and Medals

607 Lancaster, Escort Carrier and Medals

608 U.S. Navy Aircraft, Jungle Patrol and Medals

151

609 Celebrations in Parliament Square

610 V.E. Day Bonfire

615 Richard Seaman in Delage, 1936

616 Prince Bira in ERA R2B 'Romulus', 1937

611 Street Party

612 King George V1 and Queen Elizabeth on Isle of Man in July, 1945

617 Kenelm Guinness in Sunbeam 1, 1914

618 Freddie Dixon in Riley, 1934

50th Anniversary of End of Second World War

(Des A. Theobald. Litho B.D.T.)

1995 (8 MAY). *Perf* 14 (C)

641	**605**	10p multicoloured	. . . .	30	30
		a. *Horiz pair. Nos.* 641/2	. . . .	60	60
642	**606**	10p multicoloured	. . . .	30	30
643	**607**	20p multicoloured	. . . .	55	55
		a. *Horiz pair. Nos.* 643/4	. . . .	1·10	1·10
644	**608**	20p multicoloured	. . . .	55	55
645	**609**	24p multicoloured	. . . .	70	70
		a. *Horiz pair. Nos.* 645/6	. . . .	1·40	1·40
646	**610**	24p multicoloured	. . . .	70	70
647	**611**	40p multicoloured	. . . .	1·10	1·10
		a. *Horiz pair. Nos.* 647/8	. . . .	2·25	2·25
648	**612**	40p multicoloured	. . . .	1·10	1·10
641/8		*Set of 8*	. . . .	4·75	4·75
		First Day Cover	. . . .		5·25
		Presentation Pack	. . . .	5·00	
		Souvenir Folder (*complete sheets*)	. . . .	19·00	

Plate Nos.: All values 1A, 1B, 1C (each ×4)

Sheets: 8 (2×4). The two designs for each value printed together, *se-tenant*, in horizontal pairs throughout the sheets

Imprint: Central, left-hand margin

Withdrawn: 7.5.96

613 Reg Parnell in Maserati '4 CLT', 1951

614 Stirling Moss in Frazer Nash, 1951

619 John Napier in Arrol Johnston, 1905 (*illustration reduced. Actual size 103×73 mm*)

90th Anniversary of Motor Racing on Isle of Man

(Des N. Sykes. Litho Questa)

1995 (8 MAY). *Perf* 14 (C)

649	**613**	20p multicoloured	. . . .	60	60
650	**614**	24p multicoloured	. . . .	75	75
651	**615**	30p multicoloured	. . . .	85	85
652	**616**	36p multicoloured	. . . .	1·00	1·00
653	**617**	41p multicoloured	. . . .	1·10	1·10
654	**618**	42p multicoloured	. . . .	1·10	1·10
649/54		*Set of 6*	. . . .	4·75	4·75
		First Day Cover	. . . .		5·25
		Presentation Pack	. . . .	5·00	
MS655		103×73 mm. **619** £1 multicoloured		2·50	2·50
		First Day Cover	. . . .		2·75
		Presentation Pack	. . . .	2·75	

Plate Nos.: All values 1A, 1B (each ×5)

Sheets: 20 (5×4)

Imprint: Right-hand corner, bottom margin

Withdrawn: 7.5.96

620 Thomas the Tank Engine and Bertie Bus being Unloaded

621 Mail Train

622 Bertie and Engines at Ballasalla

623 Viking the Diesel Engine, Port Erin

624 Thomas and Railcar at Snaefell Summit

625 Engines racing past Laxey Wheel

50th Anniversary of Thomas the Tank Engine Stories by Revd. Awdry. 'Thomas the Tank Engine's Dream'

(Des O. Bell. Litho B.D.T.)

1995 (15 AUG). *Perf* 14 (C)

656	**620**	20p multicoloured		60	60
		a. *Booklet pane. Nos. 656/7 with margins all round*		1·25	
		b. *Booklet pane. Nos. 656 and 661 with margins all round.* .		1·75	
657	**621**	24p multicoloured		75	75
		a. *Booklet pane. Nos. 657/8 with margins all round*		1·50	
658	**622**	30p multicoloured		85	85
		a. *Booklet pane. Nos. 658/9 with margins all round*		1·75	
659	**623**	36p multicoloured		1·00	1·00
		a. *Booklet pane. Nos. 659/60 with margins all round*		2·00	
660	**624**	41p multicoloured		1·10	1·10
		a. *Booklet pane. Nos. 660/1 with margins all round*		2·25	

661	**625**	45p multicoloured		1·25	1·25
656/61		*Set of* 6		5·00	5·00
		First Day Cover			5·25
		Presentation Pack		5·25	
		Stamp Cards (*set of* 6)		1·75	6·50

Plate Nos.: All values 1A, 1B (each ×4)

Sheets: 10 (2×5)

Imprint: Central, bottom margin

Withdrawn: 14.8.96

626 *Amanita muscaria*

627 *Boletus edulis*

628 *Coprinus disseminatus*

629 *Pleurotus ostreatus*

630 *Geastrum triplex*

631 Shaggy Ink Cap and Bee Orchid
(*illustration reduced. Actual size* 100×71 mm)

Fungi

(Des Colleen Corlett. Litho Enschedé)

1995 (1 SEPT). *Perf* 13½ (C)

662	**626**	20p multicoloured	. . . .	50	50
663	**627**	24p multicoloured	. . . .	65	65
664	**628**	30p multicoloured	. . . .	85	85
665	**629**	35p multicoloured	. . . .	95	95
666	**630**	45p multicoloured	. . . .	1·25	1·25
662/6		Set of 5	. . . .	3·75	3·75
		First Day Cover	. . . .		4·00
		Presentation Pack	. . . .	4·00	
MS667		100×71 mm. **631** £1 multicoloured		2·50	2·50
		First Day Cover	. . . .		2·75
		Presentation Pack	. . . .	2·75	

No. **MS**667 is inscribed "Singapore World Stamp Exhibition 1st–10th September 1995" on the sheet margin.

Plate Nos.: All values 1A, 1B, 1C (each ×4)

Sheets: 20 (4×5)

Imprint: Right-hand corner, bottom margin

Withdrawn: 31.8.96

632 St. Catherine's Church, Port Erin

633 Robin on Holly Branch

634 St. Peter's Church and Wild Flowers

635 Hedgehog hibernating under Farm Machinery

Christmas

(Des Colleen Corlett. Litho B.D.T.)

1995 (10 OCT). *Perf* 14 (C)

668	**632**	19p multicoloured	. . . .	50	50
669	**633**	23p multicoloured	. . . .	60	60
670	**634**	42p multicoloured	. . . .	1·10	1·10
671	**635**	50p multicoloured	. . . .	1·40	1·40
668/71		Set of 4	. . . .	3·25	3·25
		First Day Cover	. . . .		3·50
		Presentation Pack	. . . .	3·50	
		Set of 4 Gutter Pairs	. . . . . .	6·50	

Plate Nos: All values 1A, 1B, 1C (each ×4)

Sheets: 40 (2 panes 5×4)

Imprint: Right-hand corner, bottom margin

Withdrawn: 9.10.96

Year Pack 1995

1995 (10 OCT). *Comprises Nos.* 629/71

	Year Pack	38·00

Withdrawn: 31.12.96

Post Office Yearbook

1995 (OCT). *Comprises Nos.* 629/38, 639/40 *in sheets of* 10 *and* 641/71

	Yearbook	42·00

Sold out: By 5.97

636 Langness Lighthouse

637 Point of Ayre Lighthouse

638 Chicken Rock Lighthouse

639 Calf of Man Lighthouse

640 Douglas Head Lighthouse

641 Maughold Head Lighthouse

Lighthouses

(Des D. Swinton. Litho Questa)

1996 (24 JAN). *Perf* 14 (C)

672	**636**	20p multicoloured	55	55
		a. *Booklet pane. No.* 672×4 *with margins all round*	1·60	
673	**637**	24p multicoloured	65	65
		a. *Booklet pane. No.* 673×4 *with margins all round*	2·00	
674	**638**	30p multicoloured	85	85
		a. *Booklet pane. Nos.* 674 *and* 676, *each* ×2, *with margins all round*	2·75	
675	**639**	36p multicoloured	1·00	1·00
		a. *Booklet pane. Nos.* 675 *and* 677, *each* ×2, *with margins all round*	3·25	
676	**640**	41p multicoloured	1·10	1·10
677	**641**	42p multicoloured	1·10	1·10
672/7		Set of 6	4·75	4·75
		First Day Cover		5·00
		Presentation Pack	5·00	
		Set of 6 Gutter Pairs	9·50	

Plate Nos.: All values 1A, 1B (each ×5)

Sheets: 40 (2 panes 4×5) 20p, 30p, 41p; (2 panes 5×4) others

Imprint: Central, left-hand margin (20p, 30p, 41p) or central, bottom margin (others)

Withdrawn: 22.1.97

642 White Manx Cat and Celtic Interlaced Ribbons

643 Cat and Union Jack Ribbons

644 Cat on Rug in German Colours, Mouse and Brandenburg Gate

645 Cat, U.S.A. Flag and Statue of Liberty

646 Cat, Map of Australia and Kangaroo

647 Cat and Kittens
(*illustration reduced. Actual size* 100×71 *mm*)

Manx Cats

(Des Nancy Corkish. Litho B.D.T.)

1996 (14 MAR). *Perf* 13½×13 (*No.* **MS**683) *or* 14 (*others*), *both comb*

678	**642**	20p multicoloured	60	60
679	**643**	24p multicoloured	75	75
680	**644**	36p multicoloured	1·00	1·00
681	**645**	42p multicoloured	1·10	1·10
682	**646**	48p multicoloured	1·25	1·25
678/82		Set of 5	4·25	4·25
		First Day Cover		4·50
		Presentation Pack	4·50	
		Stamp Cards (set of 5)	1·50	5·75
MS683		100×71 mm. **647** £1.50, mult	3·50	3·50
		First Day Cover		3·75
		Presentation Pack	3·75	

For No. **MS**683 with 'CAPEX '96' logo see No. **MS**712.

Plate Nos.: All values 1A, 1B (each ×4)

Sheets: 10 (2×5)

Imprint: Central, left-hand margin

Withdrawn: 13.3.97

648 Douglas Borough Arms

Centenary of Douglas Borough

(Des Colleen Corlett. Litho B.D.T.)

1996 (14 MAR). *Self-adhesive. Die-cut perf* 9×10

684	**648**	(20p) multicoloured	40	45
		First Day Cover		1·25
		Presentation Pack	1·10	

No. 684 was printed in sheets of 40, each stamp surrounded by white backing paper divided by roulettes. The actual stamps are separated from the backing paper by die-cut perforations. It was initially sold for 20p. and was only valid for postage within the Isle of Man.

Plate Nos: 1A, 1B (each ×4)

Sheets: 40 (8×5)

Imprint: Right-hand corner, bottom margin

651 *Sir Winston Churchill* (cadet schooner)

653 *Tynwald I* (paddle-steamer), 1846

657 *Francis Drake* (ketch)

Ships

(Des A. Theobald. Litho Walsall)

1996 (21 APR). *As Nos.* 541, 543 *and* 547, *but smaller as* T **651/7**. *Perf* 14 (C)

687	**651**	4p multicoloured	10	10
		a. *Booklet pane. Nos.* 687, 689 and 693, *each* ×2	1·90	
689	**653**	20p multicoloured	40	45
693	**657**	24p multicoloured	50	55
687/93		*Set of 3*	1·00	1·10
		First Day Cover		1·75
		Presentation Pack	1·75	

The 20p and 24p show the positions of the face value and Queen's head reversed

Plate Nos.: All values 1A, 1B (each ×4)

Sheets: 100 (10×10)

Imprint: Right-hand corner, bottom margin

665 Princess Anne (President, Save the Children Fund) and Children

666 Queen Elizabeth II and People of the Commonwealth

Europa. Famous Women

(Des D. Miller. Litho B.D.T.)

1996 (21 APR). *Perf* 14 (C)

701	**665**	24p multicoloured	60	60
702	**666**	30p multicoloured	80	80
701/2		*Set of 2*	1·40	1·40
		First Day Cover		1·75
		Presentation Pack	1·75	

The background designs of Nos. 701/2 continue onto the vertical sheet margins.

Plate Nos: Both values 1A, 1B (each ×4)

Sheets: 10 (2×5)

Withdrawn: 20.4.97

667 Alec Bennett

668 Stanley Woods

669 Artie Bell

670 Joey and Robert Dunlop

671 R.A.F. Red Arrows Display Team
(*illustration reduced. Actual size* 100×70 *mm*)

Tourist Trophy Motorcycle Races. Irish Winners

(Des J. Dunne. Litho Questa)

1996 (30 MAY). *Perf* 14 (C)

703	**667**	20p multicoloured	. . . .	65	65
704	**668**	24p multicoloured	. . . .	70	70
705	**669**	45p multicoloured	. . . .	1·25	1·25
706	**670**	60p multicoloured	. . . .	1·50	1·50
703/6		*Set of* 4	. . . .	3·75	3·75
		First Day Cover			4·00
		Presentation Pack		4·00	
		Souvenir Folder		12·00	
		Set of 4 *Gutter Pairs*		8·00	
MS707	100×70 mm.	**671** £1 multicoloured		2·50	2·50
		First Day Cover			2·75
		Presentation Pack		2·75	

The souvenir folder contains Nos. 703/7, together with the stamps and miniature sheet in similar designs issued by Ireland.

Plate Nos.: 20p 1A, 1B (each ×4); 24p 1A (×4); 45p 1C (×4); 60p 1D (×4)

Sheets: 40 (2 panes 2×10)

Imprint: Right-hand corner, bottom margin

Withdrawn: 29.5.97

672 National Poppy Appeal Trophy

673 Manx War Memorial, Braddan

674 Poppy Appeal Collection Box

675 Royal British Legion Badge

75th Anniversary of Royal British Legion

(Des C. Abbott. Litho B.D.T.)

1996 (8 JUNE). *Perf* 14 (C)

708	**672**	20p multicoloured	. . . .	60	60
709	**673**	24p multicoloured	. . . .	65	65
710	**674**	42p multicoloured	. . . .	1·10	1·10
711	**675**	75p multicoloured	. . . .	2·10	2·10
708/11		*Set of* 4	. . . .	4·00	4·00
		First Day Cover			4·25
		Presentation Pack		4·25	

Plate Nos.: 75p 1A, 1B, 1C (each ×4): others 1A (×4)

Sheets: 40 (8×5)

Imprint: Right-hand corner, bottom margin

Withdrawn: 7.6.97

'CAPEX '96' International Stamp Exhibition, Toronto

1996 (8 JUNE). *No. No.* **MS**683 *additionally inscribed with* 'CAPEX '96' *exhibition logo on sheet margin.*

MS712	100×71 mm.	**647** £1.50, mult	3·50	3·50
		First Day Cover		3·75

Withdrawn: 31.7.97

676 U.N.I.C.E.F. Projects in Mexico

677 Projects in Sri Lanka

678 Projects in Colombia

679 Projects in Zambia

680 Projects in Afghanistan

681 Projects in Vietnam

50th Anniv of U.N.I.C.E.F.

(Des C. Abbott. Litho Enschedé)

1996 (18 SEPT). *Perf* 13½×14 (C)

713	**676**	24p multicoloured	. . . .	50	55
		a. Horiz pair. Nos. 713/14		1·00	1·10
714	**677**	24p multicoloured	. . . .	50	55
715	**678**	30p multicoloured	. . . .	60	65
		a. Horiz pair. Nos. 715/16		1·25	1·25
716	**679**	30p multicoloured	. . . .	60	65
717	**680**	42p multicoloured	. . . .	85	90
		a. Horiz pair. Nos. 717/18		1·75	1·75
718	**681**	42p multicoloured	. . . .	85	90
713/18		*Set of* 6	. . . .	3·50	4·25
		First Day Cover			4·50
		Presentation Pack		4·00	

Plate Nos.: All values 1A, 1B (each ×4)

Sheets: 40 (10×4). The two designs for each value printed together, *se-tenant*, in horizontal pairs throughout the sheets.

Imprint: Right-hand corner, bottom margin

Withdrawn: 17.9.97

682 Labrador

683 Border Collie

684 Dalmatian

685 Mongrel

686 English Setter

687 Alsatian

688 Dogs at Work
(*illustration reduced. Actual size* 100×71 *mm*)

Dogs

(Des Colleen Corlett. Litho Questa)

1996 (18 SEPT). *Perf* 13½×14 (*No.* **MS**725) *or* 14½ (*others*), both comb

719	**682**	20p multicoloured	45	45
		a. *Booklet pane. No.* 719×4 with margins all round	1·60	
720	**683**	24p multicoloured	55	55
		a. *Booklet pane. No.* 720×4 with margins all round	2·00	
721	**684**	31p multicoloured	65	65
		a. *Booklet pane. Nos.* 721/4 with margins all round	3·50	
722	**685**	38p multicoloured	80	80
723	**686**	43p multicoloured	90	90
724	**687**	63p multicoloured	1·40	1·40
719/24		*Set of* 6	4·75	4·75
		First Day Cover		5·25
		Presentation Pack	5·00	
MS725		100×71 mm. **688** £1.20, mult	2·75	2·75
		a. *Booklet pane. As No.* **MS**725, *but with additional white margins all round separated by roulette*	2·75	
		First Day Cover		3·25
		Presentation Pack	3·25	

Plate Nos: All values 1A (×4)

Sheets: 10 (2×5)

Imprint: Left-hand corner, bottom margin

Withdrawn: 17.9.97

689 'Snowman and Pine Trees' (David Bennett)

690 'Three-legged Father Christmas' (Louis White)

691 'Family around Christmas Tree' (Robyn Whelan)

692 'Father Christmas in Sleigh' (Claire Bradley)

158

Christmas. Children's Paintings

(Adapted Colleen Corlett. Litho Walsall)

1996 (2 NOV). *Perf* 14×14½ (C)

726	**689**	19p multicoloured	. . . .	40	45
727	**690**	23p multicoloured	. . . .	45	50
728	**691**	50p multicoloured	. . . .	1·00	1·10
729	**692**	75p multicoloured	. . . .	1·50	1·60
726/9		Set of 4	. . . .	3·25	3·50
		First Day Cover	. . . .		4·00
		Presentation Pack	. . . .	4·00	

Plate Nos: All values 1A, 1B (each ×4)

Sheets: 40 (5×8)

Imprint: Right-hand corner. bottom margin

Withdrawn: 1.11.97

Year Pack 1996

1996 (NOV). *Comprises Nos.* 552 *and* 672/729

Year Pack . . . . 39·00

Post Office Yearbook

1996 (NOV). *Comprises Nos.* 552 *and* 672/729

Yearbook . . . . 42·00

693 Primroses and Cashtyl ny Ard

694 Lochtan Sheep and Lambs

695 Daffodils, Duck and Ducklings

696 Dabchick with Young and Frog on Lily Pad

Spring in Man

(Des Colleen Corlett. Litho B.D.T.)

1997 (12 FEB). *Perf* 14 (C)

730	**693**	20p multicoloured	. . . .	40	45
731	**694**	24p multicoloured	. . . .	50	55
732	**695**	43p multicoloured	. . . .	85	90
733	**696**	63p multicoloured	. . . .	1·25	1·40
730/3		Set of 4	. . . .	3·00	3·25
		First Day Cover	. . . .		3·75
		Presentation Pack	. . . .	3·75	
		Set of 4 Gutter Pairs	. . . . . .	6·25	

Plate Nos.: All values 1A, 1B (each ×4)

Sheets: 40 (2 panes 5×4)

Imprint: Right-hand corner, bottom margin

697 Barn Owl

698 Short-eared Owl

699 Long-eared Owl

700 Little Owl

701 Snowy Owl

702 Tawny Owl

703a Long-eared Owl
(*illustration reduced. Actual size* 100×71 mm)

Owls

(Des J. Paul. Litho B.D.T.)

1997 (12 FEB). *Perf* 13 (*No.* **MS**740) *or* 14 (*others*), *both comb*

734	**697**	20p multicoloured	40	45
		a. Booklet pane. No. 734×4		
		with margins all round	1·60	
735	**698**	24p multicoloured	50	55
		a. Booklet pane. No. 735×4		
		with margins all round	2·00	
736	**699**	31p multicoloured	60	65
		a. Booklet pane. Nos. 736/9		
		with margins all round	3·50	
737	**700**	36p multicoloured	75	80
738	**701**	43p multicoloured	85	90
739	**702**	56p multicoloured	1·10	1·25
734/9		Set of 6	4·00	4·50
		First Day Cover		5·00
		Presentation Pack	5·00	
		Stamp Cards (set of 6)	1·75	6·75
MS740		100×71 mm. **703**a £1.20, mult . .	2·40	2·50
		a. Booklet pane. As No.		
		MS740 but with additional		
		white margins all round and		
		with line of roulettes at left. .	2·40	
		First Day Cover		3·25
		Presentation Pack	3·00	

No. **MS**740 includes the 'HONG KONG '97' International Stamp Exhibition Logo on the sheet margin.

Plate Nos.: All values 1A, 1B (each ×4)

Sheets: 10 (5×2)

Imprint: Bottom, right-hand margin

704 Moddey Dhoo, Peel Castle

705 Fairies in Tree and Cottage

706 Fairies at Fairy Bridge

707 Giant Finn MacCooil and Calf of Man

708 The Buggane of St. Trinian's

709 Fynoderee and Farm

Europa. Tales and Legends

(Des Colleen Corlett. Litho Enschedé)

1997 (24 APR). *Perf* 13½×14 (C)

741	**704**	21p multicoloured	40	45
742	**705**	25p multicoloured	50	55
743	**706**	31p multicoloured	60	65
744	**707**	36p multicoloured	70	75
745	**708**	37p multicoloured	75	80
746	**709**	43p multicoloured	85	90
741/6		Set of 6	3·75	4·00
		First Day Cover		4·50
		Presentation Pack	4·50	

Plate Nos.: All values 1A, 1B, 1C, 1D (each ×4)

Sheets: 10 (2×5)

710 Sopwith Tabloid

711 Grumman Tiger (winner of 1996 Schneider Trophy)

712 BAe ATP (15th anniv of Manx Airlines)

713 BAe 146-200 (15th anniv of Manx Airlines)

714 Boeing 757 200 (largest aircraft to land on Isle of Man)

715 Earman Biplane (1st Manx flight, 1911)

716 Spitfire

717 Hawker Hurricane

Manx Aircraft

(Des R. Carter. Litho Questa)

1997 (24 APR). *Perf* 14 (C)

747	**710**	21p multicoloured	40	45
		a. Horiz pair. Nos. 747/8	80	90
748	**711**	21p multicoloured	40	45
749	**712**	25p multicoloured	50	55
		a. Horiz pair. Nos. 749/50	1·00	1·10
750	**713**	25p multicoloured	50	55
751	**714**	31p multicoloured	60	65
		a. Horiz pair. Nos. 751/2	1·10	1·25
752	**715**	31p multicoloured	60	65
753	**716**	36p multicoloured	70	75
		a. Horiz pair. Nos. 753/4	1·40	1·50
754	**717**	36p multicoloured	70	75
747/54		Set of 8	4·25	4·75
		First Day Cover		5·25
		Presentation Pack	5·25	
		Souvenir Folder (complete sheets)	18·00	

Plate Nos.: All values 1A (×4)

Sheets: 8 (2×4) the two designs for each value printed together, *se-tenant*, in horizontal pairs throughout the sheets, the backgrounds forming composite designs

718 14th Hole, Ramsey Golf Club

719 15th Hole, King Edward Bay Golf and Country Club

720 17th Hole, Rowany Golf Club

721 8th Hole, Castletown Golf Links

722*a* Golf Ball
(*illustration reduced. Actual size* 100×71 *mm*)

Golf

(Des D. Swinton. Litho Questa)

1997 (29 MAY). *Perf* 14 (C)

755	**718**	21p multicoloured	40	45
		a. Booklet pane. No. 755×3 with margins all round	1·25	
756	**719**	25p multicoloured	50	55
		a. Booklet pane. No. 756×3 with margins all round	1·50	
757	**720**	43p multicoloured	85	90
		a. Booklet pane. Nos. 757/8 each ×2 with margins all round	3·75	
758	**721**	50p multicoloured	1·00	1·10
755/8		Set of 4	2·75	3·00
		First Day Cover		3·50
		Presentation Pack	3·50	
		Set of 4 Gutter Pairs	5·75	
MS759		100×71 mm. **722***a* £1.30, mult ..	2·50	2·75
		a. Booklet pane. As No. **MS**759, but with additional white margins all round	2·50	
		First Day Cover		3·25
		Presentation Pack	3·25	

No. **MS**759 includes the 'PACIFIC 97' International Stamp Exhibition logo on the sheet margin.

Plate Nos.: All values 1A, 1B (each ×4)

Sheets: 40 (2 panes 5×4)

Imprint: Right-hand corner, bottom margin of each pane

723*a* Royal Yacht *Britannia*
(*illustration reduced. Actual size* 130×90 *mm*)

Return of Hong Kong to China

(Litho Walsall)

1997 (1 JULY). *Sheet* 130×90 *mm containing stamp as No.* 546 *with changed imprint date. Wmk Mult Crown CA Diagonal. Perf* 13×13½ (C)
MS760 **723***a* 23p multicoloured 45 50

724 Steve Colley   **725** Steve Saunders

726 Sammy Miller   **727** Don Smith

F.I.M. 'Trial des Nations' Motorcycle Team Trials

(Des R. Organ. Litho Cartor)

1997 (23 SEPT). *Perf* 13½ (C)
761	**724**	21p multicoloured	. . . .	40	45
762	**725**	25p multicoloured	. . . .	50	55
763	**726**	37p multicoloured	. . . .	75	80
764	**727**	44p multicoloured	. . . .	90	95
761/4		Set of 4	. . . .	2·50	2·75
		First Day Cover	. . . .		3·25
		Presentation Pack	. . . .	3·25	
		Set of 4 Gutter Pairs	. . . . . .	5·25	

Plate Nos.: All values 1A, 1B (each ×4)
Sheets: 40 (2 panes 5×4) 21p, 44p; (2 panes 4×5) 25p, 37p
Imprint: Central, gutter margin

728 Angel and Shepherd   **729** Angel and King

730 The Nativity

Christmas

(Des Jennifer Toombs. Litho B.D.T.)

1997 (3 NOV). *Perf* 14 (C)
765	**728**	20p multicoloured	. . . .	40	45
766	**729**	24p multicoloured	. . . .	50	55
767	**730**	63p multicoloured	. . . .	1·25	1·40
765/7		Set of 3	. . . .	2·00	2·40
		First Day Cover	. . . .		3·00
		Presentation Pack	. . . .	3·00	

Plate Nos.: 20p, 24p 1A (×5); 63p 1A, 1B (each ×5)
Sheets:
Imprint:

731 Engagement of Princess Elizabeth and Lieut. Philip Mountbatten, 1947   **732** Wedding Photograph, 1947

733 At Ascot, 1952

734 Golden Wedding Photograph, 1997

735a Queen Elizabeth and Prince Philip at Peel, 1989

Golden Wedding of Queen Elizabeth and Prince Philip

(Des Colleen Corlett. Litho and die-stamped Questa)

1997 (3 NOV). *Perf* 14 (*No.* **MS**772) *or* 14×14½, *both comb*

768	**731**	50p sepia and gold	. . . .	1·00	1·10
		a. Strip of 4. Nos. 768/71	. . . .	4·00	
769	**732**	50p multicoloured	. . . .	1·00	1·10
770	**733**	50p multicoloured	. . . .	1·00	1·10
771	**734**	50p multicoloured	. . . .	1·00	1·10
768/71		Set of 4	. . . .	4·00	4·50
		First Day Cover	. . . .		4·75
		Presentation Pack	. . . .		4·75
		Souvenir Folder (complete			
		sheet and **MS**772)	. . . . .	19·00	
MS772	100×72 mm. **735**a £1 multicoloured			2·00	2·10
		First Day Cover	. . . .		2·75

Plate Nos.: 1A (×5)

Sheets: 16 (4×4). Nos. 768/71 were printed together, *se-tenant*, as horizontal or vertical strips of 4 throughout the sheets

Imprint: Right-hand corner, bottom margin

Year Pack 1997

1997 (3 NOV). *Comprises Nos. 730/72*

Year Pack . . . . 37·00

Post Office Yearbook

1997 (3 NOV). *Comprises Nos. 730/72*

Yearbook . . . . 42·00

SOUVENIR POSTAL STATIONERY POSTCARDS

The following postcards were issued by the Isle of Man Postal Authority in connection with various philatelic exhibitions and, with the exception of Nos. PC8, PC11, and PC15/16 show imprinted stamp designs.

'San Marino 82'

1982 (1 SEPT). *Card showing imprinted stamp design as No. 217. Sold at 30p*

PC1 19½p multicoloured . . . . 1·00 1·00

Withdrawn: 30.4.84

'Tembal 83', Basel

1983 (21 MAY). *Card showing imprinted stamp design as No. 250. Sold at 30p*

PC2 20½p multicoloured . . . . 1·10 1·40

Withdrawn: 20.5.84

'Espana 84', Madrid

1984 (27 APR). *Card showing imprinted stamp design as No. 266. Sold at 30p*

PC3 20½p multicoloured . . . . 1·10 1·40

Withdrawn: 26.4.85

'Ausipex 84', Melbourne

1984 (21 SEPT). *Card showing imprinted stamp design as No. 278. Sold at 40p*

PC4 33p multicoloured . . . . 1·75 2·25

Withdrawn: 20.9.85

'Italia 85', Rome

1985 (25 OCT). *Card showing imprinted stamp designs as Nos. 292/3. Sold at 40p*

PC5 14p+14p multicoloured . . . . 1·25 2·50

Withdrawn: 24.10.86

'Ameripex 86', Chicago

1986 (22 MAY). *Card showing imprinted stamp design as No. 302. Sold at 40p*

PC6 34p multicoloured . . . . 2·25 2·50

Withdrawn: 21.5.87

'Stockholmia 86', Stockholm

1986 (28 AUG). *Card showing imprinted stamp designs as Nos. 305/6. Sold at 40p*

PC7 15p+15p multicoloured . . . . 1·00 1·25

Withdrawn: 27.8.87

'Hafnia 87', Copenhagen

1987 (16 OCT). *Card with Nos. 358/9 affixed. Sold at 50p*

PC8 12p+15p multicoloured . . . . 1·25 1·50

Withdrawn: 15.10.88

'Finlandia 88', Helsinki

1988 (1 JUNE). *Card showing imprinted stamp designs as Nos.* 371 *and* 375. *Sold at* 50p
PC9   14p+18p multicoloured . . . .   1·00   1·00

Withdrawn: 31.5.89

'Sydpex 88', Sydney

1988 (30 JULY). *Card showing imprinted stamp designs as Nos.* 386/7. *Sold at* 60p
PC10   29p+31p multicoloured . . . .   1·25   1·40

Withdrawn: 29.7.89

'Filacept 88', The Hague

1988 (18 OCT). *Card with Nos.* 383/4 *affixed. Sold at* 50p
PC11   22p+22p multicoloured . . . .   1·00   1·10

Withdrawn: 17.10.89

'Belgica 90', Brussels

1990 (2 JUNE). *Card showing imprinted stamp designs as Nos.* 442 *and* 446. *Sold at* 50p
PC12   1p+37p multicoloured . . . .   1·00   1·10

Withdrawn: 2.93

'Essen 94'. Centenary of Picture Postcards

1994 (5 MAY). *Cards showing imprinted stamp design as No.* 338. *Sold at* 80p *the pair*
PC13   31p multicoloured (Douglas) . . . .   1·00   1·10
PC14   31p multicoloured (Ramsey) . . . .   1·00   1·10

Withdrawn: 4.5.95

'Jakarta 95'

1995 (19 AUG). *Sold at* 15p
PC15   Komodo Dragon   50   75

'Beijing 95'

1995 (16 SEPT). *Sold at* 15p
PC16   Great Wall of China   50   75

MANX POSTAL MUSEUM POSTCARDS

1987 (23 MAR). *Sold at* 10p
PM1   Reopening of Regent Street Post Office, Douglas   30   1·00

Sold out: By 2.90

1989 (28 APR). *Sold at* 15p
PM2   Bicentenary of the Mutiny on the *Bounty*   30   1·50

Sold out: By 1.93

1990 (10 APR). *Sold at* 18p
PM3   'CUNARD 150' Exhibition, Liverpool. Sinking of *Lusitania* (as No. 191)   35   1·50

Sold out: By 2.94

POSTAGE DUE STAMPS

D **1**   D **2**   D **3** Badge of
                                            Post Office
                                            Authority

(Des and litho Questa)

1973 (5 JULY). *Perf* 14×13½ (C)

D1	D **1**	½p red, black & bistre-yellow (*ab*)	1·75	1·50
D2		1p red, black and cinnamon (*ab*) . .	65	65
D3		2p red, black & lt apple-green (*ab*)	15	20
		a. *Positive offset of red ptg on back*	25	25
D4		3p red, black and grey (*ab*)	25	25
D5		4p red, black & carmine-rose (*ab*)	25	35
D6		5p red, black and cobalt (*ab*)	40	40
D7		10p red, black & light lavender (*ab*)	50	50
D8		20p red, black & pale turq-grn (*ab*)	90	90
D1/8		Set of 8	4·50	4·25
		Presentation Pack (ptg b)	6·00	

Printings: (*a*) 5.7.73; (*b*) 1.9.73. Examples of printing (*b*) are known used from mid-August onwards.

Prices quoted above are for printing (*b*), which can be identified by the letter "A" added after "1973" at the foot of the stamp. Collectors should beware of spurious examples with the "A" removed. Price for set of 8 from printing (*a*) £30 *unused or used*

Plate Nos: All values 1A, 1B (each ×3)

Sheets: 100 (10×10)

Imprint: Right-hand corner, bottom margin, and left-hand corner, top margin

Sold-out: Printing (*a*) between 13.8.73 and 10.9.73. Printing (*b*) ½p by 12.74; 1p by 2.75; 2p and 3p by 5.75; others by 31.12.75

(Des and litho Questa)

1975 (8 JAN). *Perf* 14×13½ (C)

D9	D **2**	½p black, red & greenish yellow	10	10
D10		1p black, red and flesh	10	10
D11		4p black, red and rose-lilac	10	10
D12		7p black, red & lt greenish blue	20	20
D13		9p black, red and brownish grey	25	25
D14		10p black, red and bright mauve	30	30
D15		50p black, red and orange-yellow	1·10	1·10
D16		£1 black, red & turquoise-green	2·00	2·00
D9/16		Set of 8	3·75	3·75
		First Day Cover		5·00
		Presentation Pack	4·25	

Plate Nos.: All values 1A, 1B (each ×3)

Sheets: 100 (10×10)

Imprint: Left-hand corner, bottom margin

Withdrawn: 31.12.82 (1p to £1): 31.12.85 ½p

(Litho B.D.T.)

1982 (5 OCT). *Centres multicoloured; background colour given. Perf* 14½×14 (C)

D17	D **3**	1p turquoise-green	....	10	10
D18		2p mauve	....	10	10
D19		5p greenish blue	....	10	10
D20		10p reddish lilac	....	20	25
D21		20p grey	....	40	45
D22		50p buff	....	1·00	1·10
D23		£1 salmon	....	2·00	2·10
D24		£2 bright blue	....	4·00	4·25
D17/24		*Set of* 8	....	7·75	8·25
		First Day Cover.	....		11·00
		Presentation Pack.	....	8·25	

Plate Nos: All values 1A (×5)

Sheets: 50 (10×5)

Imprint: Right-hand corner, bottom margin

D **4**

(Des Colleen Corlett, Litho B.D.T.)

1992 (18 SEPT). *Perf* 13×13½ (C)

D25	D **4**	£5 multicoloured	....	10·00	10·50
		First Day Cover.	....		11·00
		Presentation Pack.	....	11·00	

Plate Nos: 1A, 1B (each ×4)

Sheets: 50 (10×5)

Imprint: Right-hand corner, bottom margin

STAMP BOOKLETS

PRICES. Prices are given for complete booklets. All booklets to No. SB7 are stitched.

B **1** Derbyhaven

1973 (5 JULY–17 OCT). *Coloured covers as Type* B **1**, *printed in black*

Type B **1**. *Yellow cover*
SB1   10p booklet containing 2×2½p (No. 16), 2×2p (No. 15) and 2×1p (No. 12) (*ab*) .... 14·00

Ballaugh Church, Green cover
SB2   25p booklet containing 10×2½p (No. 16) (*ab*)   3·25

Peel Castle. Stone cover
SB3   30p booklet containing 10×3p (No. 17) (*a*) .. 24·00
SB3*a*   As SB3 but cover in buff (*b*).............. 24·00

Quayside, Douglas. Lavender-grey cover
SB4   50p booklet containing 8×2½p (No. 16) and 10×3p (No. 17) (*a*) .... 11·00
SB4*a*   As SB4 but grey-green cover (*b*) .... 9·00

Nos. SB1/4 were made up from ordinary sheets, the stamps being in vertical pairs with stitching through the side margins. Stamps from both sides of the sheets were used, so that panes come either upright or inverted.

Printings: (a) 5.7.73: (b) 17.10.73

STAMP SACHETS. These are cardboard covers, with stamps loose inside, contained in clear plastic sachets. Details of these sachets are given, but they are not priced, being outside the scope of this catalogue.

B **2**

1973 (5 JULY–1 NOV). *Stamp Sachets. Covers as Type* B **2**
    10p sachet containing 5×1p (No. 12) and 3×2½p (No. 16)
    10p sachet containing 2×1p (No. 12) and 3×3p (No. 17) (1 Nov)

B **3** Old Laxey Bridge
(*illustration reduced. Actual size* 89×51 *mm*)

1974 (1 APR). *Coloured covers as Type* B **3**, *printed in black*

Type B **3**. *Buff cover*
SB5 30p booklet containing 8×½p (No. 12), 4×3p
     (No. 17) and 4×3½p (No. 18) . . . .   2·00

Monk's Bridge, Ballasalla, Green cover
SB6 40p booklet containing 4×½p (No. 12), 8×3p
     (No. 17) and 4×3½p (No. 18) . . . .   2·00

St. Michael's Chapel, Langness, Red cover
SB7 50p booklet containing 12×3p (No. 17) and
     4×3½p (No. 18) . . . .   2·00

Nos. SB5/7 contain panes of four, and were produced in the same way as Nos. SB1/4.

1974 (29 JULY). *Stamp Sachets. Cover designs as Nos.* SB5/7, *but inscriptions redrawn, Contents unchanged*
30p sachet Pink cover
40p sachet Green cover
50p sachet Yellow cover

1975 (25 APR–16 JUNE). *Stamp Sachets. Blue cover showing Post Office badge*
20p sachet containing 3×2p (No. 15) and 4×3½p (No. 18) attached to cover by the selvedge
20p sachet containing 1×½p (No. 12), 2×1½p (No. 14) and 3×5½p (No. 22), loose or attached to selvedge (28 May)
20p sachet containing 4×½p (No. 12), 2×1½p (No. 14) and 3×5p (No. 21), loose or attached to selvedge (16 June)

1976 (20 SEPT)–**79**. *Stamp Sachet. Blue cover similar to Type* B **3**, *showing Castle Rushen and Castletown Harbour*
20p sachet containing 2×1p (No. 13) and 3×6p (No. 23)
20p sachet containing 2×1p (No. 13) and 3×6p (No. 139) (3.79)

B **4** Viking Longship
(*illustration reduced. Actual size* 81×49 *mm*)

Millenium of Tynwald

1979 (16 MAY). *Folded card covers as Type* B **4**
SB8 20p booklet containing 4×3p and 2×4p (No. 150*ab*) (blue cover) . . . .   1·25
SB9 40p booklet containing 8×3p and 4×4p (No. 150*a*×2) (pink cover) . . . .   1·40
SB10 60p booklet containing 12×3p and 6×4p (No. 150*a*×3) (yellow cover) . . . .   2·00

Examples of Nos. SB8/9 are known containing the wrong pane.

Withdrawn: 28.9.80

1980 (29 SEPT). *Folded card covers as Type* B **4**
SB11 40p booklet containing 2×1p, 4×3p, 4×4p and
     2×5p (Nos. 150*ba* and 188*a*) (pink cover   1·25
     showing Manx Loaghtyn Ram) . . . .
SB12 80p booklet containing 4×1p, 8×3p, 8×4p and
     4×5p (Nos. 150*ba* and 188*a* each ×2) (green   2·50
     cover showing Peregrine Falcon) . . . .

Withdrawn: 9.4.86

1985 (12 JUNE). *Booklet No.* SB11 *with cover surcharged* 50p' *and an additional loose* 10p *stamp inside*
SB13 50p booklet containing Nos. 150*ba*, 188*a* and
     one 10p (No. 236) . . . .   6·75

Withdrawn: 9.4.86

B **5** Celtic Cross Logo
(*illustration reduced. Actual size* 80×48 *mm*)

Manx Heritage Year

1986 (10 APR). *Folded card covers as Type* B **5**
SB14 50p booklet containing 2×1p, 2×4p, 2×5p and
                                          4·00
     3×10p (Nos. 188*a* and 316*a*) (olive-green
     cover)
SB15 £1.14 booklet containing 2×1p, 2×2p, 4×3p,
     4×4p, 2×5p and 7×10p (Nos. 150*ba*, 188*a*,
     315*a* and 316*a*) (greenish blue cover) . . . . . .   7·50

Withdrawn: 25.3.87

B **6** Loch Promenade
(*illustration reduced. Actual size 82×48 mm*)

Victorian Douglas

1987 (26 MAR). *Folded card covers as Type* B **6**
SB16   50p booklet containing either No. 334*a* or
            334*ab* (orange-brown and deep yellow-green
            cover Type B **6**) . . . .   3·25
SB17   £1.10 booklet containing either Nos. 334*a*, or
            334*ab*, and 334*b* (orange-brown and bright
            scarlet cover showing The Breakwater) . . . .   6·25

Withdrawn: 15.3.88

B **7** Baldwin Reservoir Tramway Steam Locomotive *Injebreck*
(*illustration reduced. Actual size 82×48 mm*)

Manx Railways and Tramways

1988 (16 MAR). *Folded multicoloured card covers as Type* B **7**
SB18   50p booklet containing No. 367*a* (cover Type
            B **7**) . . . .   2·50
SB19   £1.99 booklet containing Nos. 367*a* and 370*a*
            (cover showing Manx Electric Railway train at
            Maughold Head) . . . .   7·50

Withdrawn: 15.10.89

B **8** 'Mutineers casting Bligh adrift' (Robert Dodd)
(*illustration reduced. Actual size 155×100 mm*)

Bicentenary of The Mutiny on the Bounty

1989 (28 APR). *Multicoloured cover as Type* B **8**. *Booklet
contains text and illustrations on interleaving pages.
Stitched*
SB20   £5.30 booklet containing Nos. 408*a*/*b*, 410*a*
            and **MS**415 . . . .   12·00

Examples of No. **MS**415 from the booklet have wider
margins than the normal miniature sheets.

Withdrawn: 2.92

Manx Railways and Tramways

1989 (16 OCT). *Folded multicoloured covers as Type* B **7**
SB21   50p booklet containing No. 367*b* (cover
            showing Port Erin Breakwater Tramway
            Locomotive *Henry B. Loch*) . . . .   2·25
SB22   £2.09 booklet containing Nos. 367*b* and 371*a*
            (cover showing Douglas Cable Tramway) . . . .   6·25

Withdrawn: 13.2.90

Manx Railways and Tramways

1990 (14 FEB). *Folded multicoloured covers as Type* B **7**
SB23   50p booklet containing No. 372*a* (cover
            showing Marine Drive Tramway) . . . .   2·25
SB24   £1.74 booklet containing No. 372*b* (cover
            showing Ramsey Harbour Tramway) . . . . . .   5·00

Withdrawn: 8.1.91

B **9** Penny Black
(*illustration reduced. Actual size 125×75 mm*)

150th Anniversary of the Penny Black and 'Stamp World London 90' International Stamp Exhibition, London

1990 (3 MAY). *Black and ochre cover as Type B* **9**. *Booklet contains text and illustrations on interleaving pages. Stapled.*

SB25 £3.50 booklet containing Nos. 442c, 443a and **MS**447 . . . . 7·75

Withdrawn: 23.9.93

Manx Railways and Tramways

1991 (9 JAN). *Folded multicoloured covers as Type B* **7**.

SB26 50p booklet containing No. 367ca (cover, 80×48 mm, showing Groudle Glen Railway steam locomotive *Polar Bear*) . . . . 2·50

SB27 £1 booklet containing No. 367cb (cover, 56×43 mm, showing I.M.R. No. 11 *Maitland* pulling Royal Train, 1963). . . . . 3·75

Withdrawn: 7.1.92

B **10** Three Kings
(*illustration reduced. Actual size* 150×105 mm)

Christmas

1991 (14 OCT). *Deep violet cover as Type B* **10**. *Stitched*
SB28 £4.16 booklet containing No. 500a×2 . . . . . . 20·00

Withdrawn: 23.9.93

Manx Railways and Tramways

1992 (8 JAN). *Folded multicoloured covers as Type B* **7**, *but* 56×43 mm
SB29 £1 booklet containing No. 375ab (cover showing double-decker horse tram, Douglas) 2·50
SB30 £2 booklet containing No. 375ac (cover showing T.P.O. Special) . . . . 4·75

Withdrawn: 3.1.93

B **11** Union Pacific No. 119, 1869
(*illustration reduced. Actual size* 119×74 mm)

Construction of Union Pacific Railroad

1992 (22 MAY). *Multicoloured cover as Type B* **11**. *Pane attached by selvedge*
SB31 £4.38 booklet containing pane No. 522b . . . . 9·25

Withdrawn: 27.4.94

B **12** *Francis Drake*
(ketch)

Ships

1993 (4 JAN). *Multicoloured covers as Type B* **12**. *Panes attached by selvedge*
SB32 £1.10 booklet containing pane No. 543a (cover Type B **12** . . . . 2·50
SB33 £2.20 booklet containing pane No. 543b (cover showing *Tynwald I*) . . . . 4·75

Withdrawn: 20.4.96

B **13** No. 9 Tunnel Car and Crew
(*illustration reduced. Actual size* 160×98 mm)

Centenary of Manx Electric Railway

1993 (3 FEB). *Multicoloured cover as Type B* **13**. *Stitched*
SB34 £4.44 booklet containing pane No. 559a×4   9·50

Withdrawn: 27.4.94

B **14** (*illustration reduced.
Actual size* 62×95 *mm*)

Christmas

1993 (12 OCT). *Folded multicoloured covers as Type B* **14**.
Panes attached by selvedge
SB35 £1.90 booklet containing No. 578×10 (cover
Type B **14**) . . . .   4·25
SB36 £2.30 booklet containing No. 579×10 (cover
showing No. 579) . . . .   5·00

Withdrawn: 10.10.95

B **15** (*illustration reduced. Actual size* 134×85 *mm*)

Manx Tourism Centenary

1994 (18 FEB). *Multicoloured cover as Type B* **15**. *Pane
attached by selvedge*
SB37 £2.40 booklet containing pane No. 590a and
pane of 12 (3×4) greetings labels . . . .   5·50

Sold out: By 9.95

B **16** Postman Pat, Jess, Ferry and Aircraft
(*illustration reduced. Actual size* 152×85 *mm*)

Postman Pat visits the Isle of Man

1994 (14 SEPT). *Multicoloured cover as Type B* **16** *cut out to
show stamps from first pane. Booklet contains text and
illustrations on labels attached to panes. Stitched*
SB38 £4.04 booklet containing Nos. 614a/19a,
MS620 and pane of 8 character labels . . . . . .   10·00

Withdrawn: By 2.97

B **17** Car and Passengers at Snaefell Summit
(*illustration reduced. Actual size* 162×97 *mm*)

Centenary of Snaefell Mountain Railway

1995 (8 FEB). *Black, scarlet and grey cover as Type B* **17**.
*Booklet contains text and illustrations on labels attached to
panes. Stitched*
SB39 £4.63 booklet containing No. 634a×3 and
MS638a . . . .   9·00

Withdrawn: By 2.97

B **18** Thomas the Tank Engine
(*illustration reduced. Actual size* 151×80 *mm*)

50th Anniversary of Thomas the Tank Engine Stories by Revd. Awdry. "Thomas the Tank Engine's Dream"

1995 (15 AUG). *Multicoloured cover as Type B* **18** *cut out to show stamps from first pane. Stitched*
SB40   £3.92 booklet containing Nos. 656a/b, 657a, 658a, 659a and 660a . . . .   8·00

Withdrawn: By 2.97

B **19** Aerial view of Langness Lighthouse
    (*illustration reduced. Actual size 130×82 mm*)

Lighthouses

1996 (24 JAN). *Multicoloured cover as Type B* **19**. *Booklet contains text and illustrations on interleaving pages. Stitched*
SB41   £4.74 booklet containing Nos. 672a/5a. . . . . .   9·50
Withdrawn: By 5.97

Ships

1996 (21 APR). *Multicoloured cover as Type B* **12**. *Pane attached by selvedge*
SB42   96p booklet containing pane No. 687a (cover showing *Sir Winston Churchill*) . . . .   1·90
Sold out: 5.97

B **20** (*illustration reduced. Actual size 118×81 mm*)
Dogs

1996 (18 SEPT). *Multicoloured cover as Type B* **20**. *Booklet contains text and illustrations on interleaving pages. Stitched*
SB43   £4.71 booklet containing Nos. 719a, 720a, 721a and **MS**725a . . . .   9·50
Withdrawn: 17.9.97

B **21** Tawny Owl
    (*illustration reduced. Actual size 152×80 mm*)

Owls

1997 (12 FEB). *Multicoloured cover as Type B* **21**. *Booklet contains text and illustrations on interleaving pages. Stitched.*
SB44   £4.62, booklet containing Nos. 734a/40a . . . .   9·25

Ships

1997 (14 MAY). *Multicoloured cover as Type B* **12**. *Pane attached by selvedge.*
SB45   £1 booklet containing pane No. 541a (cover showing Royal Yacht *Britannia*) . . . .   2·00
    a. With extra loose 4p stamp and optd inside front cover . . . .   2·00
    No. SB45a was issued from booklet machines until 1 July 1997 when the postal rates were revised.

Withdrawn: 31.12.97 No. SB45a.

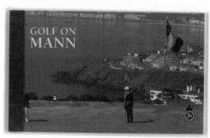

B **22** King Edward Bay Golf and Country Club
    (*illustration reduced. Actual size 160×96 mm*)

Golf

1997 (29 MAY). *Multicoloured cover as Type B* **22**. *Booklet contains text and illustrations on panes and interleaving pages. Stitched.*
SB46   £4.54, booklet containing Nos. 755a/57a and **MS**759a . . . .   9·00

JERSEY

THE GERMAN OCCUPATION 1940–1945

Soon after the commencement of the occupation of Jersey by German forces on 1 July, 1940 orders were given by the German Commandant to the Island's Postmaster for stocks of the currently available stamps to be forwarded to the Jersey printers, J. T. Bigwood, for overprinting with a swastika and 'JERSEY 1940'. All values of the 1937–8 definitives from ½d to 10s, excluding the 1d, were so overprinted as were the 1940 Postal Centenary stamps, excluding the 1d, but whilst this was in progress the Bailiff of Jersey protested to the German Commandant who referred the matter to Berlin and was ordered to destroy the stocks. Four complete sets to 1s, and a few singles, however, are known to exist. At the same time Bigwoods prepared a local 1d stamp incorporating the arms of Jersey and the words 'ETATS DE JERSEY'. These were printed in imperforate sheets of thirty (10×3) and are known with and without a swastika and '1940' overprint. These also were destroyed with the exception of two sheets of each which have been cut up for collectors and a damaged sheet with the overprint which is complete. There is also a complete sheet of the unoverprinted stamp in the National Postal Museum.

Jersey eventually issued locally printed ½d and 1d stamps, the 1d on 1 April, 1941 and the ½d on 29 January, 1942. No distinct shades exist though both values come on newsprint paper and, in addition, the 1d is known on chalk-surfaced paper.

In June 1943 a pictorial set of six stamps from ½d to 3d was issued, the designer being the well-known Jersey artist Edmund Blampied. Two values, the 1d and 2½d, are known on newsprint paper.

Both these and the earlier issues remained on sale untill 13 April, 1946 after which date they could no longer be used.

1

2

The Swastika Overprints

1940. *Prepared for use but not issued. Stamps of Great Britain overprinted by J. T. Bigwood, States' Printers*

(a) On 1937–9 definitive issue

Cat. No.	Type No.		Unused
SW1	1	½d green	£1500
SW2		1½d red-brown	£1500
SW3		2d orange	£1500
SW4		2½d ultramarine	£1500
SW5		3d violet	£1500

SW6	1	4d grey-green	£1500
SW7		5d brown	£1500
SW8		6d purple	£1500
SW9		7d emerald-green	£1500
SW10		8d bright carmine	£1500
SW11		9d deep olive-green	£1500
SW12		10d turquise-blue	£1500
SW13		1s bistre-brown	£1500

(b) On 1940 Stamp Centenary issue

SW14	2	½d green	£1500
SW15		1½d red-brown	£1500
SW16		2d orange	£1500
SW17		2½d ultramarine	£1500
SW18		3d violet	£1500

3

4

(Des R. W. Cutland. Typo J. T. Bigwood)

1940. *Prepared for use but not issued. No wmk. Imperforate*

SW19	3	1d scarlet	£1500
SW20	4	1d scarlet	£1500

5 Arms of Jersey

Stamps issued during the German Occupation

(Des Major N. V. L. Rybot. Typo *Jersey Evening Post*, St. Helier)

1941–43. *White paper. No wmk. Perf* 11 (L)

1	**5**	½d bright green (29.1.42)	3·75	3·00
		a. Imperf between (vertical pair)	£700	
		b. Imperf between (horizontal pair)	£600	
		c. Imperf (pair)	£200	
		d. On greyish paper (1.43)	5·00	5·75
2		1d scarlet (1.4.41)	4·00	3·00
		a. Imperf between (vertical pair)	£700	
		b. Imperf between (horizontal pair)	£600	
		c. Imperf (pair)	£225	
		d. On chalk-surfaced paper	40·00	38·00
		e. On greyish paper (1.43)	5·00	5·75
1		First Day Cover (plain)		7·00
2		First Day Cover (plain)		7·00

Sheets: 60 (6×10)

Imprint: ½d 'EVENING POST', JERSEY, JANUARY, 1942
1d 'EVENING POST', JERSEY, 17/3/41

Quantities printed: ½d 703,500; 1d 1,030,620

Withdrawn and invalidated: 13.4.46

6 Old Jersey Farm

7 Portelet Bay

8 Corbière Lighthouse

9 Elizabeth Castle

10 Mont Orgueil Castle

11 Gathering Vraic (seaweed)

Pictorial Issue

(Des E. Blampied. Eng H. Cortot. Typo French Govt Printing Works, Paris)

1943 (1 JUNE)–**44**. No wmk. Perf 13½ (C)

3	**6**	½d green	7·00	5·50
		a. Rough, grey paper (6.10.43)	8·50	8·50
4	**7**	1d scarlet	1·50	75
		a. On newsprint (28.2.44)	2·50	2·00
5	**8**	1½d brown (8.6.43)	3·00	3·00
6	**9**	2d orange-yellow (8.6.43)	4·00	3·00
7	**10**	2½d blue (29.6.43)	2·00	1·75
		a. On newsprint (25.2.44)	1·00	1·50
		ba. Thin paper (design shows through on reverse)	£200	
8	**11**	3d violet (29.6.43)	1·00	2·75
3/8		Set of 6	15·00	16·00
		First Day Covers (3)		70·00

Printings: The sheets of the various printings were dated in the sheet corners as follows:

½d 1st Printing 1/5/43
2nd Printing 3/5/43
3rd Printing 6/10/43
1d 1st Printing 7/5/43
2nd Printing 8/5/43
3rd Printing 7/10/43
4th Printing 28/2/44
1½d 1st Printing 17/5/43
2nd Printing 18/5/43
2d 1st Printing 20/5/43
2nd Printing 21/5/43
2½d 1st Printing 31/5/43
2nd Printing 25/2/44
3d 1st Printing 4/6/43
2nd Printing 5/6/43

Sheets: 60 (2 panes 3×10)

Imprint: None

Quantities printed: ½d (No. 3) 360,000; ½d (No. 3a) 120,000; 1d (No. 4) 960,000; 1d (No. 4a) 240,000; 1½d 360,000; 2d 360,000; 2½d (No. 7) 360,000; 2½d (Nos. 7a/b) 360,000; 3d 360,000

Withdrawn and invalidated: 13.4.46

REGIONAL ISSUES

Although specifically issued for regional use, these issues were initially valid for use throughout Great Britain. However, they ceased to be valid in Jersey and Guernsey from 1 October, 1969 when these islands each established their own independent postal administration and introduced their own stamps.

DATES OF ISSUE. Conflicting dates of issue have been announced for some of the regional issues, partly explained by the stamps being released on different dates by the Philatelic Bureau in Edinburgh or the Philatelic Counter in London and in the regions. We have adopted the practice of giving the earliest known dates, since once released the stamps could have been used anywhere in the U.K.

INVALIDATION. The regional issues of Jersey were invalidated for use in Jersey and Guernsey on 1 November, 1969 (although Guernsey granted a further extension for British and regional stamps till the end of March 1970). The stamps continued to be valid for use in the rest of the United Kingdom until 29 February, 1972. Those still current remained on sale at philatelic sales counters until 30 September, 1970.

11a Multiple Crowns

12

13

(Des E. Blampied (Type **12**), W. Gardner (Type **13**). Portrait by Dorothy Wilding Ltd. Photo Harrison)

1958–67. *Wmk Type* **11**a. *Perf* 15×14 (C)

9	**12**	2½d carmine-red (8.6.64)	....	35	60
		a. *Imperf three sides* (*pair*)	....	£2000	
10	**13**	3d deep lilac (18.8.58)	....	35	30
		p. *One centre phosphor band* (9.6.67)	....	20	20
11		4d ultramarine (7.2.66)	....	25	30
		p. *Two phosphor bands* (5.9.67)	....	20	25
9/11		*Set of 3*	....	60	1·00
9		*First Day Cover*	....		22·00
10		*First Day Cover*	....		17·00
11		*First Day Cover*	....		7·50

Cylinder Nos.: 2½d 1; 3d (ord) 1, 2; 3d (phos) 2; 4d (ord) 1; 4d (phos) 1

Sheets: 240 (12×20)

Quantities sold (ordinary only): 2½d 4,770,000; 3d 35,169,720; 4d 6,623,040

Withdrawn: 31.8.66 2½d

Sold out: 10.67 3d (ordinary); 11.67 4d (ordinary); 10.68 3d and 4d (phosphor)

1968–69. *No wmk. Chalk-surfaced paper. One centre phosphor band* (4d *values*) *or two phosphor bands* (5d). *Perf* 15×14 (C)

12	**13**	4d olive-sepia (4.9.68)	....	20	25
13		4d bright vermilion (26.2.69)	....	20	35
14		5d Royal blue (4.9.68)	....	20	50
12/14		*Set of 3*		50	1·00
12, 14		*First Day Cover*	....		2·00

Cylinder Nos.: 4d (olive-sepia) 1; 4d (bright vermilion) 1; 5d 1

Withdrawn: 30.9.69 (locally), 30.9.70 (British Philatelic Counters) 4d olive-sepia, 4d bright vermilion and 5d

INDEPENDENT POSTAL ADMINISTRATION

Jersey established their own independent postal administration on 1 October, 1969 and introduced their own stamps.

NO WATERMARK. All the following issues are on unwatermarked paper.

16 Portelet Bay

17 La Corbière Lighthouse

18 Mont Orgueil Castle by Night

19 Arms and Royal Mace

20 Jersey Cow

21 Chart of the English Channel

22 Mont Orgueil Castle by Day

23 Queen Elizabeth II (after Cecil Beaton)

14 Elizabeth Castle

15 La Hougue Bie (Prehistoric Tomb)

24 Jersey Airport

25 Legislative Chamber

26 The Royal Court

27 Queen Elizabeth II
(after Cecil Beaton)

(Des V. Whiteley. Photo Harrison (½d to 1s 9d), Courvoisier (others))

1969 (1 OCT)–**70**. *Granite paper (2s 6d to £1). Multicoloured; frame colours given. Perf 14 (½d to 1s. 9d) or 12 (others), all comb*

15	**14**	½d ochre (*a*)	10	70
		a. Thick paper (a)	1·00	1·25
16	**15**	1d brown (*abc*)	15	20
		a. Booklet stamp with blank margins* (a)	75	
		b. Thick paper (a)	50	60
17	**16**	2d claret (*a*)	10	15
		a. Thinner paper (bc)	25	25
18	**17**	3d ultramarine (*a*)	20	15
		a. Thinner paper (d)	40	40
		b. Orange omitted	£110	
19	**18**	4d yellow-olive (*a*)	15	10
		a. Booklet stamp with blank margins* (a)	40	
		b. Thinner paper (c)	40	50
20	**19**	5d bistre (*a*)	15	10
		a. Thinner paper (c)	40	40
21	**20**	6d yellow-brown (*ab*)	25	30
		a. Thinner paper (e)	8·00	8·00
22	**21**	9d orange-brown (*a*)	40	75
		a. Thinner paper (d)	2·50	2·75
23	**22**	1s reddish lilac (*a*)	75	75
		a. Thinner paper (c)	1·75	2·00
24	**21**	1s 6d myrtle-green (*a*)	1·25	1·25
		a. Thinner paper (d)	2·75	3·00
25	**23**	1s 9d pale myrtle-green (*a*)	1·25	1·25
		a. Thinner paper (c)	11·00	10·00
26	**24**	2s 6d black and pale mauve (*a*) . .	2·00	1·75
27	**25**	5s black and pale blue (*a*)	11·00	7·00
28	**26**	10s black and pale slate-blue (*a*) . .	26·00	17·00
		a. Error. Green border†	£4500	
29	**27**	£1 pale bistre (*af*)††	2·00	1·50
15/29		*Set of 15*	40·00	27·00
		First Day Cover		28·00
15/29		*Presentation Packs (3)*	48·00	

*Nos. 16a and 19a are on medium paper. No. 16b on thick paper comes from 7s and 10s booklets.

†During the final printing of the 10s a sheet was printed in the colours of the 50p, No. 56, ie. green border instead of slate.

††Printing (*f*) is the decimal issue which can be positively distinguished by the inscriptions in the left sheet margin which read 'Sheet value £25' at bottom and 'Value per row £5' at top instead of 'Sheet value £25 0s. 0d.' and 'Value per row £5 0s. 0d.' respectively. It exists with more blue in the Queen's dress and less red in the drapery but this printing also includes intermediate shades close to printing (*a*).

The thinner paper varieties result from a deliberate change as the thicker paper did not adhere well; it may be further distinguished by the gum which is white instead of creamy.

There are a number of shades in this issue which are in part due to the variation in the paper.

There was no postal need for the ½d value as the ½d coin had been withdrawn prior to its issue in anticipation of decimalisation.

Printings: (*a*) 1.10.69; (*b*) 18.2.70; (*c*) 15.4.70; (*d*) 5.5.70; (*e*) 27.5.70; (*f*) 3.73

Cylinder Nos.: ½d, 1d, 2d, 4d, 1s 1A (×5); 3d 1A (×7): 5d, 6d, 9d, 1s 6d, 1s 9d 1A (×6): 2s 6d to £1 None

Sheets: 60 (6×10) ½d to 1s 6d; (10×6) 1s 9d; 25 (5×5) 2s 6d to £1

Quantities sold: ½d 999,439; 1d 1,050,124; 2d 726,837; 3d 635,019; 4d 7,148,849; 5d 4,886,016; 6d 550,766; 9d 954,649; 1s 577,086; 1s 6d 419,872; 1s 9d 306,674; 2s 6d 244,894; 5s 206,629; 10s 179,981; £1 271,194

Withdrawn: 14.2.72 (except ½d, sold out 10.69, and £1 withdrawn 31.8.77)

Invalidated: 14.2.72 (except £1)

28 First Day Cover

Inauguration of Post Office

(Des R. Sellar. Photo Harrison)

1969 (1 OCT). *Multicoloured; background colours given. Perf 14 (C)*

30	**28**	4d magenta	25	20
31		5d new blue	30	30
32		1s 6d red-brown	1·25	1·60
33		1s 9d bright emerald	1·25	1·60
30/3		*Set of 4*	2·75	3·25
		First Day Cover		5·00
		Presentation Pack.	3·50	

Cylinder Nos.: All values 1A (×4)

Sheets: 60 (6×10)

Quantities sold: 4d 1,483,686; 5d 742,820; 1s 6d 272,155; 1s 9d 238,856

Withdrawn: 1.10.70

Invalidated: 14.2.72

29 'Lord Coutanche'
(Sir James Gunn)

30 'Sir Winston
Churchill'
(Van Praag)

33 'A Tribute to Enid
Blyton'

34 'Rags to Riches'

35 'Gourmet's Delight'

31 'Liberation' (Edmund
Blampied)

36 'We're the Greatest'

'Battle of Flowers' Parade

(Des Jennifer Toombs. Photo Courvoiser)

32 S.S. *Vega* (unknown
artist)

1970 (28 JULY). *Granite paper. Perf* 11½ (C)

38	**33**	4d multicoloured	. . . .	25	25
39	**34**	5d multicoloured	. . . .	40	40
40	**35**	1s 6d multicoloured	. . . .	7·00	2·50
41	**36**	1s 9d multicoloured	. . . .	7·25	2·50
38/41		Set of 4	. . . .	13·00	5·00
		First Day Cover	. . . .		5·00
		Presentation Pack	. . . .	15·00	

Sheets: 50 (5×10)

Quantities sold: 4d 1,905,109; 5d 1,498,301; 1s 6d 262,072; 1s 9d
231,077

Withdrawn: 27.7.71

Invalidated: 14.2.72

25th Anniversary of Liberation

(Des Rosalind Dease from paintings. Photo Courvoisier)

1970 (9 MAY). *Granite paper. Perf* 11½ (C)

34	**29**	4d multicoloured	. . . .	25	25
35	**30**	5d multicoloured	. . . .	25	25
36	**31**	1s 6d multicoloured	. . . .	1·75	1·75
37	**32**	1s 9d multicoloured	. . . .	1·75	1·75
34/7		Set of 4	. . . .	3·50	3·50
		First Day Cover	. . . .		4·50
		Presentation Pack	. . . .	3·75	

A special Presentation Pack in gold, red and blue-green on
olive was given to Jersey schoolchildren (*Price* £15). The
normal Presentation Pack is printed in gold and blue-green

Sheets: 50 (10×5) 4d, 5d; (5×10) 1s 6d, 1s 9d

Quantities sold: 4d 1,617,751; 5d 1,296,678; 1s 6d 334,468; 1s 9d
319,893

Withdrawn: 9.5.71

Invalidated: 14.2.72

37 Martello Tower,
Archirondel

Decimal Currency

(Des V. Whiteley. Photo Harrison (½ to 9p), Courvoisier (others))

1970–74. Designs as Type **47** etc., but with values inscribed in decimal currency and new design (6p). Chalk-surfaced paper (4½p, 5½p, 8p), granite paper (10p, 20p, 50p)

42	**14**	½p multicoloured (bgk)	10	10
		a. Booklet stamp with blank margins (b)	40	
43	**17**	1p multicoloured (bn).	10	10
		a. Orange omitted		
44	**20**	1½p multicoloured (b)	10	10
45	**18**	2p multicoloured (b)	10	10
		a. Booklet stamp with blank margins	1·25	
46	**19**	2½p multicoloured (bk).	10	10
		a. Booklet stamp with blank margins (b)	40	
		ab. Gold (Mace) omitted.	£350	
		ac. Gold (Mace) ptg double	£275	
47	**15**	3p multicoloured (bch)	10	10
		a. Booklet stamp with blank margins (e)	50	
48	**16**	3½p multicoloured (bh).	15	15
		a. Booklet stamp with blank margins (h)	50	
49	**21**	4p multicoloured (bfimo)	15	15
49a	**19**	4½p multicoloured (j)	20	20
		ab. Uncoated paper	£350	
50	**22**	5p multicoloured (blmo).	10	15
50a	**20**	5½p multicoloured (j)	40	25
51	**37**	6p multicoloured (b)	25	30
52	**21**	7½p multicoloured (b)	30	40
52a	**18**	8p multicoloured (j)	25	25
53	**23**	9p multicoloured (b)	50	30
54	**24**	10p multicoloured (adh)	50	55
55	**25**	20p multicoloured (adh)	75	75
56	**26**	50p multicoloured (al)	1·75	1·75
42/56		Set of 18	5·00	5·00
		First Day Cover (3)		10·00
42/56, 29		Presentation Packs (4)	7·00	

Gum: From 1974 printings appeared with dextrin added to the PVA gum giving a bluish-green tinge and mottled appearance. These are on the ½, 2½, 3 and 3½p. The 4½ and 5½p only come with dextrin, and the 10, 20 and 50p only with gum arabic.

The Presentation Packs for this series exist in two different sizes, 4¼ in × 5½ in of the initial supply and 8½ in × 4½ in for replacement stock.

Printings: (a) 1.10.70; (b) 15.2.71; (c) 1.8.72; (d) 15.11.72; (e) 1.12.72; (f) 1.10.73; (g) 3.12.73; (h) 1.7.74; (i) 12.8.74; (j) 31.10.74; (k) 1.11.74; (l) 28.1.75; (m) 1.4.75; (n) 21.4.75; (o) 30.10.75

Plate Nos.: ½p, 2p, 3½p, 6p, 8p 1A (×5); 1p 1A (×7), 2A–1A (×6) (n); 1½p, 2½p, 4½p, 5½p, 7½p, 9p 1A (×6); 3p 1A (×5), 1A (×4)–2A (h); 4p 1A (×6), 2A–1A (×5) (mo); 5p 1A (×5), 2A–1A (×4) (mo); 10p to 50p None

Sheets: 50 (5×10) ½p to 8p; (10×5) 9p; 25 (5×5) 10p to 50p

Quantities sold: ½p 2,247,128; 1p 1,654,860; 1½p 817,871; 2p 2,305,239; 2½p 5,096,912; 3p 4,780,836; 3½p 2,069,095; 4p 3,908,727; 4½p 349,157; 5p 3,593,226; 5½p 333,125; 6p 1,072,224; 7½p 538,810; 8p 329,361; 9p 458,977; 10p 862,524; 20p 765,524; 50p 490,675

Withdrawn: 31.1.77 (½p to 9p); 31.8.77 (others)

38 White Eared-Pheasant

39 Thick-billed Parrot

40 Western Black and White Colobus Monkey

41 Ring-tailed Lemur

Wildlife Preservation Trust (First Series)

(Des Jennifer Toombs. Photo Courvoisier)

1971 (12 MAR). Granite paper. Perf 11½ (C)

57	**38**	2p multicoloured	75	25
58	**39**	2½p multicoloured	75	25
59	**40**	7½p multicoloured	7·75	3·75
60	**41**	9p multicoloured	8·00	3·75
57/60		Set of 4	15·50	7·25
		First Day Cover		8·50
		Presentation Pack.	17·50	

See also Nos. 73/6, 217/21, 324/9, 447/51 and 818/23.

Sheets: 50 (5×10) 2p, 9p; (10×5) others

Quantities sold: 2p 1,025,544; 2½p 1,363,427; 7½p 233,147; 9p 220,710

Withdrawn: 11.3.72

42 Royal British Legion Badge

43 Poppy Emblem and Field

44 Jack Counter VC, and Victoria Cross

45 Crossed Tricolour and Union Jack

50th Anniversary of Royal British Legion

(Des G. Drummond, Litho Questa)

1971 (15 JUNE). *Perf* 14 (C)

61	**42**	2p multicoloured	50	50
62	**43**	2½p multicoloured	50	50
63	**44**	7½p multicoloured	2·40	2·40
64	**45**	9p multicoloured	2·40	2·40
61/4		Set of 4	5·00	5·00
		First Day Cover		5·00
		Presentation Pack	5·50	

Plate Nos.: 2p, 2½p 1A, 1B (each ×4); others 1A, 1B (each ×5)

Sheets: 50 (5×10)

Imprint: Right-hand corner, bottom margin

Quantities sold: 2p 1,381,873: 2½p 1,529,866; 7½p 239,477; 9p 226,407

Withdrawn: 14.6.72

46 'Tante Elizabeth' (E. Blampied)

47 'English Fleet in the Channel' (P. Monamy)

48 'The Boyhood of Raleigh' (Millais)

49 'The Blind Beggar' (W. W. Ouless)

Paintings

(Des and photo Courvoisier)

1971 (5 OCT). *Granite paper. Perf* 11½ (C)

65	**46**	2p multicoloured	15	15
66	**47**	2½p multicoloured	20	20
67	**48**	7½p multicoloured	2·75	2·50
68	**49**	9p multicoloured	2·75	2·75
65/8		Set of 4	5·25	5·00
		First Day Cover		5·00
		Presentation Pack	6·75	

See also Nos. 115/18 and 213/16.

Sheets: 50 (5×10) 2p, 9p; (10×5) others

Quantities sold: 2p 1,243,198; 2½p 1,490,595; 7½p 264,532; 9p 251,770

Withdrawn: 4.10.72

50 Jersey Fern

51 Jersey Thrift

52 Jersey Orchid

53 Jersey Viper's Bugloss

Wild Flowers of Jersey

(Des G. Drummond. Photo Courvoisier)

1972 (18 JAN). *Granite paper. Perf* 11½ (C)

69	**50**	3p multicoloured	25	15
70	**51**	5p multicoloured	60	45
71	**52**	7½p multicoloured	2·25	2·25
72	**53**	9p multicoloured	2·50	2·25
69/72		Set of 4	5·00	4·50
		First Day Cover		5·00
		Presentation Pack	6·50	

Sheets: 50 (5×10)

Quantities sold: 3p 1,124,878; 5p 332,764; 7½p 202,404; 9p 196,998

Withdrawn: 17.1.73

54 Cheetah

55 Rothschild's Mynah

56 Spectacled Bear

57 Tuatara

Wildlife Preservation Trust (Second Series)

(Des Jennifer Toombs. Photo Courvoisier)

1972 (17 MAR). *Granite paper. Perf* 11½ (C)

73	**54**	2½p multicoloured	....	65	20
74	**55**	3p multicoloured	....	40	35
75	**56**	7½p multicoloured	....	1·40	1·50
76	**57**	9p multicoloured	....	1·75	1·75
73/6		Set of 4	....	3·75	3·25
		First Day Cover	....		4·75
		Presentation Pack	....	5·00	

Sheets: 50 (10×5) 3p; (5×10) others

Quantities sold: 2½p 1,223,916; 3p 1,631,752; 7½p 279,935; 9p 235,968

Withdrawn: 16.3.73

58 Artillery Shako

59 Shako (2nd North Regt)

60 Shako (5th South-West Regt)

61 Helmet (3rd Jersey Light Infantry)

Royal Jersey Militia

(Des and photo Courvoisier)

1972 (27 JUNE). *Granite paper. Perf* 11½ (C)

77	**58**	2½p multicoloured	....	15	15
78	**59**	3p multicoloured	....	20	20
79	**60**	7½p multicoloured	....	70	50
80	**61**	9p multicoloured	....	90	60
77/80		Set of 4	....	1·75	1·25
		First Day Cover	....		3·00
		Presentation Pack	....	3·00	

Sheets: 50 (10×5)

Quantities sold: 2½p 1,240,393; 3p 1,857,224; 7½p 300,554; 9p 271,832

Withdrawn: 26.6.73

62 Princess Anne

63 Queen Elizabeth and Prince Philip

64 Prince Charles

65 The Royal Family

Royal Silver Wedding

(Des G. Drummond from photographs by D. Groves. Photo Courvoisier)

1972 (1 NOV). *Granite paper. Perf* 11½ (C)

81	**62**	2½p multicoloured	10	10
82	**63**	3p multicoloured	10	10
83	**64**	7½p multicoloured	40	40
84	**65**	20p multicoloured	60	50
81/4		Set of 4	1·10	1·00
		First Day Cover		2·00
		Presentation Pack	1·50	

Sheets: 25 (5×5)

Quantities sold: 2½p 1,743,240; 3p 1,638,566; 7½p 424,029; 20p 418,824

Sold out: by 23.1.73 (7½p, 20p); 16.5.73 (3p)

Withdrawn: 31.10.73 (2½p)

66 Silver Wine Cup and Christening Cup

67 Gold Torque

68 Royal Seal of Charles II

69 Armorican Bronze Coins

Centenary of La Société Jersiaise

(Des G. Drummond. Photo Courvoisier)

1973 (23 JAN). *Granite paper. Perf* 11½ (C)

85	**66**	2½p violet-blue, new blue and black	10	10
86	**67**	3p bright cerise, orange-yellow and black	10	10
87	**68**	7½p multicoloured	40	40
88	**69**	9p multicoloured	50	50
85/8		Set of 4	1·00	1·00
		First Day Cover		1·25
		Presentation Pack	1·25	

Sheets: 50 (10×5) 3p, 7½p; (5×10) others

Quantities sold: 2½p 2,008,923; 3p 2,437,421; 7½p 363,543; 9p 327,917

Sold out: by 31.10.73 (7½p)

Withdrawn: 22.1.74 (2½p, 3p, 9p)

70 Balloon *L'Armee de La Loire* and Letter, Paris, 1870

71 Astra Seaplane, 1912

72 Supermarine Sea Eagle

73 De Havilland D.H.86 Dragon Express *Giffard Bay*

Jersey Aviation History

(Des and photo Courvoisier)

1973 (16 MAY). *Granite paper. Perf* 11½ (C)

89	**70**	3p multicoloured	10	10
90	**71**	5p multicoloured	15	15
91	**72**	7½p multicoloured	50	40
92	**73**	9p multicoloured	65	50
89/92		Set of 4	1·25	1·00
		First Day Cover		1·50
		Presentation Pack	1·50	

Sheets: 50 (5×10)

Quantities sold: 3p 3,085,497; 5p 641,583; 7½p 368,069; 9p 356,379

Sold out: by 31.10.73 (7½p)

Withdrawn: 15.5.74 (3p, 5p, 9p)

74 *North Western*

75 *Calvados*

76 *Carteret*

77 *Caesarea*

179

Centenary of Jersey Eastern Railway

(Des G. Drummond. Photo Courvoisier)

1973 (6 AUG). *Granite paper. Perf* 11½ (C)

93	**74**	2½p multicoloured	....	10	10
94	**75**	3p multicoloured	....	10	10
95	**76**	7½p multicoloured	....	50	40
96	**77**	9p multicoloured	....	65	50
93/6		Set of 4	....	1·25	1·00
		First Day Cover	....		2·00
		Presentation Pack	....	1·50	

Sheets: 50 (5×10)

Quantities sold: 2½p 1,591,063; 3p 3,051,097; 7½p 396,919; 9p 365,310

Sold out: by 31.10.73 (7½p)

Withdrawn: 5.8.74 (2½p, 3p, 9p)

78 Princess Anne and Captain Mark Phillips

Royal Wedding

(Des and photo Courvoisier)

1973 (14 NOV). *Granite paper. Perf* 11½ (C)

97	**78**	3p multicoloured	....	10	10
98		20p multicoloured	....	90	90
97/8		Set of 2	....	1·00	1·00
		First Day Cover	....		1·00
		Presentation Pack	....	1·00	

Sheets: 25 (5×5)

Quantities sold: 3p 1,988,407; 20p 522,793

Withdrawn: 30.11.74

79 Spider Crab

80 Conger Eel

81 Lobster

82 Tuberculate Ormer

Marine Life

(Des Jennifer Toombs. Photo Courvoisier)

1973 (15 NOV). *Granite paper. Perf* 11½ (C)

99	**79**	2½p multicoloured	....	10	10
100	**80**	3p multicoloured	....	10	10
101	**81**	7½p multicoloured	....	45	35
102	**82**	20p multicoloured	....	70	55
99/102		Set of 4	....	1·25	1·00
		First Day Cover	....		1·00
		Presentation Pack	....	1·50	

Sheets: 50 (5×10)

Quantities sold: 2½p 1,596,526; 3p 1,243,541; 7½p 501,541; 20p 517,440

Sold out: by 28.2.74 (7½p)

Withdrawn: 30.11.74 (2½p, 3p, 20p)

83 Freesias

84 Anemones

85 Carnations and Gladioli

86 Daffodils and Iris

Spring Flowers

(Des G. Drummond. Photo Courvoisier)

1974 (13 FEB). *Granite paper. Perf* 11½ (C)

103	**83**	3p multicoloured	....	10	10
104	**84**	5½p multicoloured	....	20	10
105	**85**	8p multicoloured	....	50	40
106	**86**	10p multicoloured	....	60	50
103/6		Set of 4	....	1·25	1·00
		First Day Cover	....		1·50
		Presentation Pack	....	1·50	

Sheets: 50 (10×5)

Quantities sold: 3p 1,239,968; 5½p 590,376; 8p 475,665; 10p 507,542

Withdrawn: 28.2.75

87 First U.K. Pillar-box and Contemporary Cover

88 Jersey Postmen, 1862 and 1969

89 Modern Pillar-box and Cover

90 Mail Transport, 1874 and 1974

Centenary of Universal Postal Union

(Des G. Drummond. Photo Courvoisier)

1974 (7 JUNE). *Granite paper. Perf* 11½ (C)

107	**87**	2½p multicoloured	. . . .	10	10
108	**88**	3p multicoloured	. . . .	10	10
109	**89**	5½p multicoloured	. . . .	35	30
110	**90**	20p multicoloured	. . . .	85	60
107/10		Set of 4	. . . .	1·25	1·00
		First Day Cover	. . . .		1·00
		Presentation Pack	. . . .	1·50	

Sheets: 50 (5×10)

Quantities sold: 2½p 461,174; 3p 1,380,018; 5½p 421,674; 20p 386,348

Withdrawn: 30.6.75

91 John Wesley

92 Sir William Hillary

93 Canon Wace

94 Sir Winston Churchill

Anniversaries. Events described on stamps

(Des, recess and litho De La Rue)

1974 (31 JULY). *Perf* 13×14 (C)

111	**91**	3p agate and light cinnamon	. .	10	10
112	**92**	3½p blackish violet & light azure		10	10
113	**93**	8p blue-black and pale rose-lilac		30	35
114	**94**	20p black and pale buff	. . . . . .	70	65
		a. Pale buff (background) omitted	. . . .		
111/14		Set of 4	. . . .	1·00	1·00
		First Day Cover	. . . .		1·00
		Presentation Pack	. . . .	1·25	

Plate Nos.: 3p and 20p 1A–1A, 1B–1B; 3½p and 8p 1A–1A, 1B–1B, 2A–1A, 2B–1B

Sheets: 50 (10×5)

Imprint: Right-hand corner, bottom margin

Quantities sold: 3p 908,852; 3½p 2,355,391; 8p 338,397; 20p 409,291

Withdrawn: 31.7.75

95 *Catherine* and *Mary* (royal yachts)

96 French Two-decker

97 Dutch Vessel

98 Battle of Cap La Hague, 1692

Marine Paintings by Peter Monamy

(Des and photo Courvoisier)

1974 (22 NOV). *Granite paper. Perf* 11½ (C)

115	**95**	3½p multicoloured	....	10	10
116	**96**	5½p multicoloured	....	20	15
117	**97**	8p multicoloured	....	30	30
118	**98**	25p multicoloured	....	80	60
115/18		Set of 4	....	1·25	1·00
		First Day Cover	....		1·50
		Presentation Pack	....	1·50	

Sheets: 50 (10×5) 8p; (5×10) others
Quantities sold: 3½p 1,670,994; 5½p 448,137; 8p 416,296; 25p 415,991
Withdrawn: 30.11.75

99 Potato Digger

100 Cider Crusher

101 Six-Horse Plough

102 Hay Cart

Nineteenth-Century Farming

(Des G. Drummond. Photo Courvoisier)

1975 (25 FEB). *Granite paper. Perf* 11½ (C)

119	**99**	3p multicoloured	....	10	10
120	**100**	3½p multicoloured	....	10	15
121	**101**	8p multicoloured	....	35	35
122	**102**	10p multicoloured	....	55	50
119/22		Set of 4	....	1·00	1·00
		First Day Cover	....		1·00
		Presentation Pack	....	1·25	

Sheets: 50 (5×10)
Quantities sold: 3p 588,185; 3½p 1,025,295; 8p 432,432; 10p 457,196
Withdrawn: 28.2.76

103 H.M. Queen Elizabeth, the Queen Mother (photograph by Cecil Beaton)

Royal Visit

(Des and photo Courvoisier)

1975 (30 MAY). *Granite paper. Perf* 11½ (C)

123	**103**	20p multicoloured	....	75	75
		First Day Cover	....		1·50
		Presentation Pack	....	1·25	

Cylinder Nos.: A1–1–1–1–1, B1–1–1–1–1
Sheets: 25 (5×5)
Quantity sold: 572,675
Withdrawn: 31.5.76

104 Nautilus Shell

105 Parasol

106 Deckchair

107 Sandcastle with flags of Jersey and the U.K.

Jersey Tourism

(Des A. Games. Photo Courvoisier)

1975 (6 JUNE). *Designs based on holiday posters. Granite paper. Perf* 11½ (C)

124	**104**	5p multicoloured	....	10	10
125	**105**	8p multicoloured	....	15	15
126	**106**	10p multicoloured	....	35	35
127	**107**	12p multicoloured	....	50	50
124/7		Set of 4	....	1·00	1·00
		First Day Cover	....		1·00
		Presentation Pack	....	1·25	
MS128		147×69 mm. Nos. 124/7	....	1·00	1·10
		First Day Cover	....		1·25

Cylinder Nos.: All values A1–1–1–1–1, B1–1–1–1–1
Sheets: 50 (10×5)
Quantities sold: 5p 1,377,519; 8p 368,521; 10p 467,278; 12p 389,574; miniature sheet 298,689
Withdrawn: 30.6.76

108 Common Tern

109 British Storm Petrel

110 Brent Geese

111 Shag

Sea Birds

(Des Jennifer Toombs. Photo Courvoisier)

1975 (28 JULY). *Granite paper. Perf* 11½ (C)

129	**108**	4p multicoloured	....	15	15
130	**109**	5p multicoloured	....	15	15
131	**110**	8p multicoloured	....	40	35
132	**111**	25p multicoloured	....	70	45
129/32		Set of 4	....	1·25	1·00
		First Day Cover	....		1·50
		Presentation Pack	....	1·75	

Sheets: 50 (10×5)

Quantities sold: 4p 872,260; 5p 2,871,390; 8p 384,550; 25p 362,160

Withdrawn: 31.7.76

112 Armstrong Whitworth Siskin IIIA

113 Supermarine Southampton 1 Flying Boat

114 Supermarine Spitfire Mk I

115 Folland Fo.141 Gnat T 1

50th Anniversary of Royal Air Forces Association, Jersey Branch

(Des A. Theobald. Photo Courvoisier)

1975 (30 OCT). *Granite paper. Perf* 11½ (C)

133	**112**	4p multicoloured	....	10	10
134	**113**	5p multicoloured	....	15	15
135	**114**	10p multicoloured	....	40	30
136	**115**	25p multicoloured	....	75	60
133/6		Set of 4	....	1·25	1·00
		First Day Cover	....		1·50
		Presentation Pack	....	1·75	

Cylinder Nos.: All values A1–1–1–1–1, B1–1–1–1–1

Sheets: 50 (5×10)

Quantities sold: 4p 1,496,640; 5p 1,805,624; 10p 581,627; 25p 407,423

Withdrawn: 30.10.76

116 Map of Jersey Parishes

117 Zoological Park

118 St. Mary's Church

119 Seymour Tower

120 La Corbière Lighthouse

121 St. Saviour's Church

122 Elizabeth Castle

123 Gorey Harbour

183

124 Jersey Airport

125 Grosnez Castle

126 Bonne Nuit Harbour

127 Le Hocq Tower

128 Morel Farm

129 Parish Arms and Island Scene

130 Flag and Map

131 Postal H.Q. and Badge

132 Parliament, Royal Court and Arms

133 Lieutenant-Governor's Flag and Government House

134 Queen Elizabeth II (photograph by Alex Wilson)

Parish Arms and Views

(Des Courvoisier (£2), G. Drummond (others). Litho Questa (½p to 15p). Photo Courvoisier (others))

1976–80. Granite paper (20p to £2). Perf 14½ (½p to 15p) or 12 (others), all comb

137	**116**	½p multicoloured (af)		10	10
138	**117**	1p multicoloured (af)		10	10
		a. Booklet pane of 4 (No. 138×2 plus 2 se-tenant labels) (b)		1·00	
		b. Booklet pane. No. 138×4 (begh)		1·00	
139	**118**	5p multicoloured (ad)		15	15
		a. Booklet pane of 4 (b)		50	
140	**119**	6p multicoloured (ad)		15	15
		a. Booklet pane of 4 (eg)		60	
141	**120**	7p multicoloured (ad)		20	20
		a. Booklet pane of 4 (bh)		60	
142	**121**	8p multicoloured (ad)		20	20
		a. Booklet pane of 4 (eg)		80	
143	**122**	9p multicoloured (a)		25	25
		a. Booklet pane of 4 (h)		1·00	
144	**123**	10p multicoloured (af)		25	25
145	**124**	11p multicoloured (a)		30	25
146	**125**	12p multicoloured (a)		30	30
147	**126**	13p multicoloured (a)		35	35
148	**127**	14p multicoloured (a)		35	40
149	**128**	15p multicoloured (a)		40	45
150	**129**	20p multicoloured (c)		50	50
151	**130**	30p multicoloured (c)		75	75
152	**131**	40p multicoloured (c)		1·00	1·00
153	**132**	50p multicoloured (c)		1·25	1·00
154	**133**	£1 multicoloured (c)		2·50	2·25
155	**134**	£2 multicoloured (d)		4·50	4·25
137/55		Set of 19		12·00	11·50
		First Day Covers (4)			12·00
		Presentation Packs (4)	13·00		

Printings: (a) 29.1.76; (b) 5.4.76; (c) 20.8.76; (d) 16.11.77; (e) 28.2.78; (f) 31.8.78; (g) 1.10.79; (h) 6.5.80

Plate or cylinder Nos.: ½p to 9p, 13p, 14p 1A, 1B, 1C, 1D (each ×4); 10p 1A, 1B, 1C, 1D (each ×4), 1B–1B–1B–2B, 2A–1A–1A–2A, 2B–1B–1B–2B, 2C–1C–1C–2C, 2D–1D–1D–2D; 11p 1A, 1B, 1C, 1D (each ×5); 12p 1A, 1B, 1C, 1D (each ×4), 1A–1A–2A–2A, 1B–1B–2B–2B, 1C–1C–2C–2C, 1D–1D–2D–2D; 15p 1A, 1B, 1C, 1D (each ×4), 1A–2A–1A–1A, 1B–2B–1B–1B, 1C–2C–1C–1C, 1D–2D–1D–1D, 1A–2A–2A–1A, 1B–2B–1B–1B, 1C–2C–2C–1C, 1D–2D–2D–1D, 1A–3A–2A–1A, 1B–3B–2B–1B, 1C–3C–2C–1C, 1D–3D–2D–1D; 20p A1–1–1–1, B1–1–1–1, C1–1–1–1,

D1–1–1–1–1; 30p, £1 A1–1–1–1–1, B1–1–1–1–1; 40p, 50p
A1–1–1–1, B1–1–1–1; £2 A1–1–1–1–1–1,
B1–1–1–1–1–1–1, C1–1–1–1–1–1–1, D1–1–1–1–1–1–1

Sheets: 50 (5×10) ½p to 15p; 25 (5×5) others

Imprint: Right-hand corner, bottom margin (½p to 15p); central, bottom
margin (others)

Withdrawn: 27.2.82 ½p to 9p (sheets); 20.4.82 1p, 5p to 9p (booklets);
31.7.82 10p to 15p; 28.2.83 20p to £1; 31.3.92 £2

135 Sir Walter Ralegh and
Map of Virginia

136 Sir George Carteret
and Map of New
Jersey

37 Philippe D'Auvergne
and Long Island
Landing

138 John Copley and
Sketch

'Links with America'

(Des M. Orbell. Photo Courvoisier)

1976 (29 MAY). *Granite paper. Perf* 11½ (C)

160	**135**	5p multicoloured	. . . .	10	10
161	**136**	7p multicoloured	. . . .	15	15
162	**137**	11p multicoloured	. . . .	40	35
163	**138**	13p multicoloured	. . . .	45	50
160/3		Set of 4	. . . .	1·00	1·00
		First Day Cover			1·25
		Presentation Pack		1·25	

Cylinder Nos.: 5p, 11p A1–1–1–1–1, B1–1–1–1–1; others A1–1–1–1,
B1–1–1–1

Sheets: 25 (5×5)

Quantities sold: 5p 980,029; 7p 1,352,629; 11p 582,706; 13p 435,561

Withdrawn: 31.5.77

139 Dr. Grandin and Map
of China

140 Sampan on the Yangtze

141 Overland Trek

142 Dr. Grandin at work

Birth Centenary of Dr. Lilian Grandin (medical missionary)

(Des Jennifer Toombs. Photo Courvoisier)

1976 (25 NOV). *Granite paper. Perf* 11½ (C)

164	**139**	5p multicoloured	. . . .	10	10
165	**140**	7p lt yellow, yellow-brown & blk		15	15
166	**141**	11p multicoloured	. . . .	50	35
167	**142**	13p multicoloured	. . . .	50	50
164/7		Set of 4	. . . .	1·10	1·00
		First Day Cover			1·00
		Presentation Pack		1·25	

Cylinder Nos.: 7p A1–1–1, B1–1–1; 13p A1–1–1–1–1, B1–1–1–1–1;
others A1–1–1–1, B1–1–1–1

Sheets: 50 (5×10)

Quantities sold: 5p 757,843; 7p 1,043,198; 11p 384,436; 13p 354,096

Withdrawn: 30.11.77

143 Coronation, 1953
(photograph by
Cecil Beaton)

144 Visit to Jersey, 1957

145 Queen Elizabeth II (photograph by Peter Grugeon)

Silver Jubilee

(Des G. Drummond. Photo Courvoisier)

1977 (7 FEB). *Granite paper. Perf* 11½ (C)

168	**143**	5p multicoloured	....	25	15
169	**144**	7p multicoloured	....	30	20
170	**145**	25p multicoloured	....	90	80
168/70		*Set of 3*	....	1·25	1·00
		First Day Cover	....		1·00
		Presentation Pack	....	1·50	

Cylinder Nos.: All values A1–1–1–1–1, B1–1–1–1–1

Sheets: 25 (5×5)

Imprint: Central, bottom margin

Quantities sold: 5p 1,220,986; 7p 1,212,639; 25p 681,241

Withdrawn: 28.2.78

146 Coins of 1871 and 1877

147 One-twelfth shilling, 1949

148 Silver Crown, 1966

149 £2 Piece, 1972

Centenary of Currency Reform

(Des D. Henley. Litho Questa)

1977 (25 MAR). *Perf* 14 (C)

171	**146**	5p multicoloured	....	10	10
172	**147**	7p multicoloured	....	15	15
173	**148**	11p multicoloured	....	40	35
174	**149**	13p multicoloured	....	45	50
171/4		*Set of 4*	....	1·00	1·00
		First Day Cover	....		1·00
		Presentation Pack	....	1·25	

Plate Nos.: 7p 1A, 1B (each ×5), 1A–2A–1A (×3), 1B–2B–1B (×3); others 1A, 1B (each ×5)

Sheets: 50 (5 ×10)

Imprint: Right-hand corner, bottom margin

Quantities sold: 5p 1,029,661; 7p 923,950; 11p 383,834; 13p 368,249

Withdrawn: 31.3.78

150 Sir William Weston and *Santa Anna*, 1530

151 Sir William Drogo and Ambulance, 1877

152 Duke of Connaught and Ambulance, 1917

153 Duke of Gloucester and Stretcher-team, 1977

St. John Ambulance Centenary

(Des A. Theobald. Litho Questa)

1977 (24 JUNE). *Perf* 14×13½ (C)

175	**150**	5p multicoloured	....	10	10
176	**151**	7p multicoloured	....	15	15
177	**152**	11p multicoloured	....	40	35
178	**153**	13p multicoloured	....	45	50
175/8		*Set of 4*	....	1·00	1·00
		First Day Cover	....		1·25
		Presentation Pack	....	1·25	

Plate Nos.: 5p 1A, 1B, 1C (each ×5); 7p, 11p 1A, 1B, 1C (each ×6); 13p 1A, 1B, 1C (each ×5), 1B–2B–1B–1B–1B

Sheets: 40 (8×5)

Imprint: Bottom corner, right-hand margin

Quantities sold: 5p 849,532; 7p 1,089,526; 11p 421,039; 13p 370,887

Withdrawn: 30.6.78

158 Harry Vardon Statuette and Map of Royal Jersey Course

159 Harry Vardon's Grip and Swing

154 Arrival of Queen Victoria, 1846

155 Victoria College, 1852

160 Harry Vardon's Putt

161 Golf Trophies and Book by Harry Vardon

Centenary of Royal Jersey Golf Club

(Des Jennifer Toombs. Litho Questa)

1978 (28 FEB). *Perf* 14 (C)

183	**158**	6p multicoloured	. . . .	15	15
184	**159**	8p multicoloured	. . . .	20	20
185	**160**	11p multicoloured	. . . .	50	35
186	**161**	13p multicoloured	. . . .	50	40
183/6		*Set of 4*	. . . .	1·25	1·00
		First Day Cover	. . . .		1·50
		Presentation Pack	. . . .	1·50	

Plate Nos.: 6p 1A, 1B (each ×5); 8p, 11p 1A, 1B (each ×4); 13p 1A, 1B (each ×4), 2A–1A–1A–1A, 2B–1B–1B–1B

Sheets: 50 (5×10)

Imprint: Right-hand corner, bottom margin

Quantities sold: 6p 837,427; 8p 851,904; 11p 466,343; 13p 368,648

Withdrawn: 28.2.79

156 Sir Galahad Statue, 1924

157 College Hall

125th Anniversary of Victoria College

(Des R. Granger Barrett. Litho Questa)

1977 (29 SEPT). *Perf* 14½ (C)

179	**154**	7p multicoloured	. . . .	20	20
180	**155**	10½p multicoloured	. . . .	25	20
		a. Black ptg double	. . . .		
181	**156**	11p multicoloured	. . . .	30	35
182	**157**	13p multicoloured	. . . .	35	35
179/82		*Set of 4*	. . . .	1·00	1·00
		First Day Cover	. . . .		1·25
		Presentation Pack	. . . . . .	1·25	

Plate Nos.: 7p 1A, 1B (each ×6), 1A–1A–2A–1A–1A–1A, 1B–1B–2B–1B–1B–1B; 13p 1A, 1B (each ×6); others 1A, 1B (each ×5)

Sheets: 50 (5×10) 7 and 10½p, (10×5) others

Imprint: Right-hand corner, bottom margin

Quantities sold: 7p 1,496,997; 10½p 906,669; 11p 528,293; 13p 371,251

Withdrawn: 30.9.78

162 Mont Orgueil Castle

163 St. Aubin's Fort

164 Elizabeth Castle

Europa. Fortifications

(Des from paintings by Thomas Philips. Photo Courvoisier)

1978 (1 MAY). *Granite paper. Perf* 11½ (C)

187	**162**	6p multicoloured	. . . .	20	20
188	**163**	8p multicoloured	. . . .	40	40
189	**164**	10½p multicoloured	. . . .	50	50
187/9		Set of 3	. . . .	1·00	1·00
		First Day Cover	. . . .		1·00
		Presentation Pack	. . . . . .	1·00	

Cylinder Nos.: All values A1–1–1–1–1, B1–1–1–1–1, C1–1–1–1–1, D1–1–1–1–1

Sheets: 20 (5×4)

Imprint: Central, bottom margin

Quantities sold: 6p 2,602,412; 8p 2,592,722; 10½p 2,564,535

Withdrawn: 31.5.79

165 'Gaspé Basin' (P. J. Ouless)

166 Map of Gaspé Peninsula

167 *Century* (brigantine)

168 Early Map of Jersey

169 St. Aubin's Bay, Town and Harbour

Links with Canada

(Des R. Granger Barrett. Litho Questa)

1978 (9 JUNE). *Perf* 14½ (C)

190	**165**	6p multicoloured	. . . .	15	15
191	**166**	8p multicoloured	. . . .	20	20
192	**167**	10½p multicoloured	. . . .	25	25
193	**168**	11p multicoloured	. . . .	40	30
194	**169**	13p multicoloured	. . . .	45	35
190/4		Set of 5	. . . .	1·25	1·10
		First Day Cover	. . . .		1·40
		Presentation Pack	. . . . . .	1·40	

Plate Nos.: 6p 1A, 1B, 1C, 1D (each ×5); others 1A, 1B, 1C, 1D (each ×6)

Sheets: 50 (5 ×10)

Imprint: Right-hand corner, bottom margin

Quantities sold: 6p 1,047,825; 8p 1,095,489; 10½p 999,002; 11p 443,932; 13p 367,472

Withdrawn: 30.6.79

170 Queen Elizabeth and Prince Philip

171 Hallmarks of 1953 and 1977

25th Anniversary of Coronation

(Des and photo Courvoisier)

1978 (26 JUNE). *Granite paper. Perf* 11½ (C)

195	**170**	8p silver, black and cerise	. . . .	30	30
196	**171**	25p silver, black and new blue	. .	70	70
195/6		Set of 2	. . . .	1·00	1·00
		First Day Cover	. . . .		1·00
		Presentation Pack	. . . .	1·25	

Cylinder Nos.: Both values A1–1–1, B1–1–1

Sheets: 50 (10×5)

Quantities sold: 8p 1,060,259; 25p 459,558

Withdrawn: 30.6.79

172 Mail Cutter, 1778–1827

173 *Flamer*, 1831–37

174 *Diana*, 1877–90

175 *Ibex*, 1891–1925

176 *Caesarea*, 1960–75

Bicentenary of England–Jersey Government Mail Packet Service

(Des Jersey P.O. Litho Harrison)

1978 (18 OCT). *Perf* 14½×14 (C)

197	**172**	6p black, yellow-brown and greenish yellow	15	15
198	**173**	8p black, dull yellowish green and pale yellow-green	20	20
199	**174**	10½p black, ultramarine & cobalt	40	30
200	**175**	11p blk, purple & pale rose-lilac	45	35
201	**176**	13p black, Venetian red and pink	50	45
197/201		*Set of 5*	1·50	1·25
		First Day Cover		1·60
		Presentation Pack	1·75	

Plate Nos.: All values 1A, 1B (each ×3)

Sheets: 50 (5 ×10)

Imprint: Right-hand corner, bottom margin

Quantities sold: 6p 1,157,597; 8p 1,149,500; 10½p 528,170; 11p 468,589; 13p 371,210

Withdrawn: 31.10.79

177 Jersey Calf

178 'Ansom Designette' (calf presented to the Queen, 27 June, 1978)

9th World Jersey Cattle Bureau Conference

(Des Jersey P.O. and Questa. Litho Questa)

1979 (1 MAR). *Perf* 13½ (C)

202	**177**	6p multicoloured	20	20
		a. Gold ptg double	£400	
203	**178**	25p multicoloured	80	80
		a. Gold ptg double	£400	
202/3		*Set of 2*	1·00	1·00
		First Day Cover		1·00
		Presentation Pack	1·25	

Plate Nos.: Both values 1A, 1B, 1C, 1D, 1E, 1F (each ×8)

Sheets: 20 (4×5)

Imprint: Right-hand corner, bottom margin

Withdrawn: 29.2.80

179 Jersey Pillar Box, c 1860

180 Clearing a Modern Jersey Post Box

181 Telephone Switchboard, c 1900

182 Modern S.P.C. Telephone System

Europa. Communications

(Des Jennifer Toombs. Litho Questa)

1979 (1 MAR). *Thin paper.* A. *Perf* 14 (C) B. *Perf* 14½ (C)

			A		B	
204	**179**	8p multicoloured	25	25	†	
		a. Horiz pair. Nos. 204/5	50	50	†	
		b. Thick paper ..	—	—	25	25
		ba. Horiz pair. Nos. 204b/5b	—	—	50	50
205	**180**	8p multicoloured	25	25	†	
		b. Thick paper ..	—	—	25	25
206	**181**	10½p multicoloured	30	30	30	30
		a. Horiz pair. Nos. 206/7	60	65	60	65
		b. Thick paper ..	75	—	†	
		ba. Horiz pair. Nos. 206b/7b	1·60	—	†	
207	**182**	10½p multicoloured	30	30	30	30
		b. Thick paper ..	75	—	†	
		c. Greenish blue omitted.	†		£400	—
204/7		*Set of 4*	1·00	1·00	1·00	1·00
		First Day Cover (*Nos.* 204A/5A, 206B/7B)				1·25
		First Day Cover (*Nos.* 204A/5A, 206A/7A)				
		Presentation Pack (*either perforation*)			1·40	

Although both perforations were supplied to Jersey at the same time the 8p perforated 14½ is not known used before early April.

Plate Nos.: Both values 1A, 1B, 1C, 1D, 1E, 1F, 1G, 1H (each ×8)

Sheets: 20 (4×5) the two designs of each value were printed together, *se-tenant*, in horizontal pairs throughout

Imprint: Central, bottom margin

Quantities sold: 8p 5,149,852; 10½p 3,047,039

Withdrawn: 29.2.80

183 Percival Mew Gull
Golden City

184 De Havilland D.H.C.1
Chipmunk

185 Druine D.31 Turbulent

186 De Havilland D.H.82A
Tiger Moth

187 North American AT-6 Harvard

25th Anniversary of International Air Rally

(Des A. Theobald. Photo Courvoisier)

1979 (24 APR). *Granite paper. Perf* 11½ (C)

208	**183**	6p multicoloured	15	15
209	**184**	8p multicoloured	20	20
210	**185**	10½p multicoloured	40	20
211	**186**	11p multicoloured	45	25
212	**187**	13p multicoloured	50	30
208/12		*Set of* 5	1·50	1·00
		First Day Cover		1·60
		Presentation Pack	1·75	

Cylinder Nos.: 13p A1–1–1–1–1, B1–1–1–1–1, C1–1–1–1–1, D1–1–1–1–1; others A1–1–1–1, B1–1–1–1, C1–1–1–1, D1–1–1–1

Sheets: 20 (5×4)

Imprint: Central, bottom margin

Quantities sold: 6p 1,327,279; 8p 1,338,234; 10½p 433,127; 11p 457,566; 13p 426,528

Withdrawn: 30.4.80

188 'My First Sermon'

189 'Orphans'

190 'The Princes in the Tower'

191 'Christ in the House of His Parents'

International Year of the Child and 150th Birth Anniversary of Millais

(Des Jersey P.O. and Courvoisier. Photo Courvoisier)

1979 (13 AUG). *Granite paper. Perf* 12×12½ (25p) or 12×11½ (*others*), *all comb*

213	**188**	8p multicoloured	25	15
214	**189**	10½p multicoloured	30	25
215	**190**	11p multicoloured	30	25
216	**191**	25p multicoloured	55	45
213/16		*Set of 4*	1·25	1·00
		First Day Cover		1·60
		Presentation Pack	1·60	

Cylinder Nos.: 25p A1–1–1–1–1, B1–1–1–1–1; others A1–1–1–1–1, B1–1–1–1–1, C1–1–1–1–1, D1–1–1–1–1

Sheets: 20 (4×5) 25p or (5×4) others

Quantities sold: 8p 1,187,969; 10½p 953,826; 11p 508,316; 25p 463,234

Withdrawn: 30.8.80

192 Pink Pigeon

193 Orang-utan

194 Waldrapp Ibis

199 Plan of Elizabeth
Castle

200 Map of Jersey showing
Fortresses

195 Lowland Gorilla

196 Rodriguez Flying Fox

Fortresses. Drawings by Thomas Phillips

(Litho Enschedè)

1980 (5 FEB). *Perf* 13×13½ (25p) *or* 13½×13 (*others*), *all comb*

222	**197**	8p multicoloured	30	25
223	**198**	11½p multicoloured	35	30
224	**199**	13p multicoloured	55	45
225	**200**	25p multicoloured	80	70
222/5		Set of 4	1·75	1·50
		First Day Cover		1·60
		Presentation Pack	2·00	

Sheets: 20 (4×5)

Imprint: Right-hand corner, bottom margin

Quantities sold: 8p 665,647; 11½p 363,246; 13p 415,790; 25p 379,743

Withdrawn: 28.2.81

Wildlife Preservation Trust (Third Series)

(Des Jennifer Toombs. Photo Courvoisier)

1979 (8 NOV). *Granite paper. Perf* 11½ (C)

217	**192**	6p multicoloured	15	15
218	**193**	8p multicoloured	20	20
219	**194**	11½p multicoloured	50	25
220	**195**	13p multicoloured	55	25
221	**196**	15p multicoloured	60	30
217/21		Set of 5	1·75	1·00
		First Day Cover		2·25
		Presentation Pack	2·00	

Cylinder Nos.: All values A1–1–1–1–1, B1–1–1–1–1, C1–1–1–1–1, D1–1–1–1–1

Sheets: 20 (11½p 4×5 others 5×4)

Imprint: Right-hand corner, bottom margin

Quantities sold: 6p 1,128,144; 8p 1,080,889; 11½p 559,534; 13p 443,140; 15p 433,115

Withdrawn: 30.11.80

201 Sir Walter Ralegh and Paul Ivy **202**
(engineer) discussing Elizabeth
Castle

197 Plan of Mont Orgueil

198 Plan of La Tour de
St. Aubin

203 Sir George Carteret receiving rights **204**
to Smith's Island, Virginia, from
King Charles II

Europa. Personalities. Links with Britain

(Des Jersey Post Office and Questa. Litho Questa)

1980 (6 MAY). *Perf* 14 (C)

226	**201**	9p	multicoloured	20	20
227	**202**	9p	multicoloured	20	20
			a. Horiz pair. Nos. 226/7	50	50
228	**203**	13½p	multicoloured	40	35
229	**204**	13½p	multicoloured	40	35
			a. Horiz pair. Nos. 228/9	80	70
226/9			*Set of* 4	1·25	1·10
			First Day Cover		1·60
			Presentation Pack	1·60	

Plate Nos.: Both values 1A, 1B, 1C, 1D, 1E, 1F (each ×4)

Sheets: 20 (4×5). The two designs of each value were printed together, *se-tenant*, in horizontal pairs throughout, forming composite designs.

Imprint: Central, left-hand margin

Quantities sold: 9p 4,793,980; 13½p 2,638,136

Withdrawn: 31.5.81

205 Planting

206 Digging

207 Weighbridge

Centenary of Jersey Royal Potato

(Des R. Granger Barrett. Litho Questa)

1980 (6 MAY). *Perf* 14 (C)

230	**205**	7p	multicoloured	15	15
231	**206**	15p	multicoloured	35	35
232	**207**	17½p	multicoloured	60	60
230/2			*Set of* 3	1·00	1·00
			First Day Cover		1·40
			Presentation Pack	1·60	

Plate Nos.: All values 1A, 1B, 1C, 1D, 1E, 1F (each ×6)

Sheets: 20 (4×5)

Imprint: Central, left-hand margin

Quantities sold: 7p 1,379,048; 15p 383,956; 17½p 375,082

Withdrawn: 31.5.83

208 Three Lap Event

209 Jersey International Road Race

210 Scrambling

211 Sand Racing (saloon cars)

212 National Hill Climb

60th Anniversary of Jersey Motor-cycle and Light Car Club

(Des A. Theobald. Photo Courvoisier)

1980 (24 JULY). *Granite paper. Perf* 11½ (C)

233	**208**	7p	multicoloured	25	25
234	**209**	9p	multicoloured	25	25
235	**210**	13½p	multicoloured	45	45
236	**211**	15p	multicoloured	50	50
237	**212**	17½p	multicoloured	55	55
233/7			*Set of* 5	1·75	1·75
			First Day Cover		2·00
			Presentation Pack	2·00	

Cylinder Nos.: 7p, 15p A1–1–1–1–1, B1–1–1–1–1, C1–1–1–1–1, D1–1–1–1–1; others A1–1–1–1, B1–1–1–1, C1–1–1–1, D1–1–1–1

Sheets: 20 (5×4)

Imprint: Left-hand corner, bottom margin

Quantities sold: 7p 1,452,280; 9p 1,426,548; 13½p 384,861; 15p 350,608; 17½p 338,658

Withdrawn: 31.7.81

213 *Eye of the Wind*

214 Diving from Inflatable Dinghy

215 Exploration of Papua New Guinea

216 Captain Scott's *Discovery*

217 Using Aerial Walkways, Conservation Project, Sulawesi

218 *Eye of the Wind*, and Goodyear Aerospace Airship *Europa*

Operation Drake and 150th Anniversary of Royal Geographical Society (14p)

(Des G. Drummond. Litho Questa)

1980 (1 OCT). *Perf* 14 (C)

238	**213**	7p multicoloured	20	20
239	**214**	9p multicoloured	25	25
240	**215**	13½p multicoloured	35	35
241	**216**	14p multicoloured	45	35
242	**217**	15p multicoloured	45	35
		a. Black (*face value and inscr*) ptg double		
243	**218**	17½p multicoloured	55	45
		a. Black (*face value and inscr*) ptg double		
238/43		Set of 6	2·00	1·75
		First Day Cover		2·00
		Presentation Pack	2·00	

Plate Nos.: All values 1A, 1B, 1C, 1D, 1E, 1F (each ×6)

Sheets: 20 (5×4)

Imprint: Upper left-hand margin

Quantities sold: 7p 1,631,558; 9p 1,071,684; 13½p 432,201; 14p 357,109; 15p 357,922; 17½p 351,215

Withdrawn: 31.10.81

219   **220**

221   **222**

Bicentenary of Battle of Jersey. Details of painting 'The Death of Major Peirson' by J. S. Copley

(Photo Courvoisier)

1981 (6 JAN). *Granite paper. Perf* 12½×12 (C)

244	**219**	7p multicoloured	25	25
245	**220**	10p multicoloured	30	30
246	**221**	15p multicoloured	60	60
247	**222**	17½p multicoloured	80	80
244/7		Set of 4	1·75	1·75
		First Day Cover		1·75
		Presentation Pack	2·00	
MS248		144×97 mm. Nos. 244/7	2·00	2·00
		First Day Cover		3·00

Stamps from No. **MS**248 are without white margins.

Cylinder Nos.: All values A1–1–1–1–1, B1–1–1–1–1

Sheets: 20 (5×4)

Imprint: Right-hand corner, bottom margin

Quantities sold: 7p 997,416; 10p 1,107,456; 15p 367,971; 17½p 359,794; miniature sheet 469,953

Withdrawn: 31.1.82

223 De Bagot   **224** De Carteret   **225** La Cloche

226 Dumaresq

227 Payn

228 Janvrin

247 Auvergne

248 Remon

229 Poingdestre

230 Pipon

231 Marett

232 Le Breton

233 Le Maistre

234 Bisson

249 Jersey Crest and
Map of Channel

250 'Queen Elizabeth II'
(Norman Hepple)

235 Robin

236 Herault

237 Messervy

238 Fiott

239 Malet

240 Mabon

241 De St.
Martin

242 Hamptonne

243 Badier

244 L'Arbalestier

245 Journeaulx

246 Lempriere

Arms of Jersey Families

(Des Courvoisier (£5). G. Drummond (ohers). Litho Questa
(½p to £1). Photo Courvoisier (£5))

1981 (24 FEB)–**88**. *Granite paper* (£5). *Perf* 15×14 (16*p*, 17*p*,
18*p*, 19*p*, 26*p*, 75*p*), 12½×12 (£5) *or* 14 (*others*), *all comb*

249	**223**	½p black, silver & turq-grn (*a*) . .	20	20
250	**224**	1p multicoloured (*a*)	10	10
		a. Booklet pane of 6 (acf)	20	
		b. Perf 15×14 (o)	25	25
251	**225**	2p multicoloured (*a*)	10	10
		a. Booklet pane of 6 (cf)	70	
		b. Perf 15×14 (io)	20	20
		ba. Booklet pane of 6 (l)	20	
252	**226**	3p multicoloured (*a*)	20	30
		a. Booklet pane of 6 (a)	60	
		b. Perf 15×14 (ik)	10	10
		ba. Booklet pane of 6 (h)	85	
253	**227**	4p black, silver and mauve (*a*) . .	25	15
		a. Perf 15×14 (k)	20	25
		ab. Booklet pane of 6 (mq)	70	
254	**228**	5p multicoloured (*a*)	15	15
		a. Perf 15×14 (k)	35	35
255	**229**	6p multicoloured (*a*)	20	20
		a. Perf 15×14 (k)	50	20
256	**230**	7p multicoloured (*a*)	20	20
		a. Booklet pane of 6 (ac)	90	
257	**231**	8p multicoloured (*a*)	25	25
		a. Booklet pane of 6 (f)	1·50	
258	**232**	9p multicoloured (*ae*)	30	30
		a. Perf 15×14 (h)	35	35
		ab. Booklet pane of 6 (h)	2·25	
		ac. 'Ghost impression' from No.		
		261a*		

259	**233**	10p multicoloured (a)	30	30
		a. Booklet pane of 6 (ac)	1·50	
		b. Perf 15×14 (l)	35	35
		ba. Booklet pane of 6 (l)	1·60	
260	**234**	11p multicoloured (be)	35	35
		a. Booklet pane of 6 (f)	1·75	
		b. Perf 15×14 (m)	40	45
		ba. Booklet pane of 6 (m)	1·75	
261	**235**	12p multicoloured (be)	50	40
		a. Perf 15×14 (hg)	40	25
		ab. Booklet pane of 6 (hq)	1·75	
262	**236**	13p multicoloured (b)	40	40
		a. Perf 15×14 (i)	60	60
263	**237**	14p multicoloured (b)	45	45
		a. Perf 15×14 (i)	50	50
		ab. Booklet pane of 6 (l)	1·75	
264	**238**	15p multicoloured (b)	45	45
		a. Perf 15×14 (mo)	45	45
		ab. Booklet pane of 6 (m)	1·75	
265	**239**	16p multicoloured (jo)	45	45
		a. Booklet pane of 6 (q)	2·25	
266	**240**	17p multicoloured (j)	50	50
266a	**241**	18p multicoloured (p)	75	75
266b	**242**	19p multicoloured (p)	80	80
267	**243**	20p black, silver and lemon (b) . .	60	60
		a. Perf 15×14 (k)	90	90
268	**244**	25p black and dull blue (d)	60	60
268a	**223**	26p black, silver and carmine (p)	60	60
269	**245**	30p multicoloured (d)	90	90
		a. Perf 15×14 (k)	1·10	1·10
270	**246**	40p multicoloured (d)	1·25	1·25
		a. Perf 15×14 (m)	1·25	1·25
271	**247**	50p multicoloured (d)	1·50	1·50
		a. Perf 15×14 (m)	1·60	1·60
272	**248**	75p multicoloured (n)	2·25	1·75
273	**249**	£1 multicoloured (d)	3·25	3·00
274	**250**	£5 multicoloured (g)	11·00	10·50
249/74		*Set of 29*	25·00	23·00
		First Day Covers (7)		27·00
		Presentation Packs (4)	28·00	
		Set of 11 Gutter Pairs (½p to 10p)	4·00	

*Examples of No. 258ac show an impression of the blue (shield) plate from the 12p value. The error was caused by an impression of the 12p plate remaining on the transfer roller.

No. 258a only occurs in the £2.16 stamp booklet issued 27 April 1984, No. 259b from the £3.12 booklet of 1 April 1986, No. 260b from the £3.60 booklet of 6 April 1987 and No. 261a from the £2.16 booklet of 27 April 1984 and the £3.84 booklet of 17 May 1988.

Nos. 252b first occurred in the £2.16 stamp booklet of 27 April 1984, but was subsequently issued in sheets.

Printings: (a) 24.2.81; (b) 28.7.81; (c) 1.12.81; (d) 23.2.82; (e) 11.6.82; (f) 19.4.83; (g) 17.11.83; (h) 27.4.84; (i) 15.11.84; (j) 25.10.85; (k) 4.3.86; (l) 1.4.86; (m) 6.4.87; (n) 23.4.87; (o) 12.1.88; (p) 26.4.88; (q) 17.5.88

Plate and Cylinder Nos.: ½p, 20p 1A, 1B, 1C, 1D, 1E, 1F, 1G, 1H (each ×3); 6p, 11p, 12p, 13p, 14p, 50p, 75p 1A, 1B, 1C, 1D, 1E, 1F, 1G, 1H (each ×5); 10p 1A, 1B, 1C, 1D, 1E, 1F, 1G, 1H (each ×5), 2A–1A (×4), 2B–1B (×4), 2C–1C (×4), 2D–1D (×4), 2E–1E (×4), 2F–1F (×4), 2G–1G (×4), 2H–1H (×4); 25p 1A–1A, 1B–1B, 1C–1C, 1D–1D, 1E–1E, 1F–1F, 1G–1G, 1H–1H; 26p 1A, 1B, 1C, 1D, 1F, 1G, 1H

(each ×3); £1 1A, 1B, 1C, 1D, 1E, 1F, 1G, 1H (each ×6); £5 A1–1–1–1–1, B1–1–1–1–1, C1–1–1–1–1, D1–1–1–1–1; others 1A, 1B, 1C, 1D, 1E, 1G, 1H (each ×4)

Sheets: £1 25 (5×5): £5 10 (5×2) others 50 (10×5)

Imprint: Right-hand corner, bottom margin

Withdrawn: 31.12.85 ½p; 30.4.87 £1; 31.3.90 1p to 10p; 31.1.91 11p to 20p; 31.3.91 25p to 75p; 30.4.97 £5

251 Knight of Hambye slaying Dragon

252 Servant slaying Knight and awaiting Execution

253 St. Brelade celebrating Easter on Island

254 Island revealing itself as Huge Fish

Europa. Folklore

(Des Jennifer Toombs. Litho Questa)

1981 (7 APR). *Perf* 14½ (C)

275	**251**	10p multicoloured	. . . .	25	25
276	**252**	10p multicoloured	. . . .	25	25
		a. Horiz pair. Nos. 275/6		55	55
277	**253**	18p multicoloured	. . . .	50	50
278	**254**	18p multicoloured	. . . .	50	50
		a. Horiz pair. Nos. 277/8		1·10	1·10
275/8		*Set of 4*		1·50	1·40
		First Day Cover			1·60
		Presentation Pack		2·00	

Legends: 10p, Slaying of the Dragon of Lawrence by the Knight of Hambye; 18p, Voyages of St. Brelade.

Plate Nos.: 10p 1A, 1B, 1C, 1D, 1E, 1F, 1G, 1H (each ×6); 18p 1A, 1B, 1C, 1D, 1E, 1F, 1G, 1H (each ×5)

Sheets: 20 (4×5). The two designs of each value were each printed together, *se-tenant*, in horizontal pairs throughout

Imprint: Central, left-hand margin

Quantities sold: 10p 3,459,902; 18p 2,494,444

Withdrawn: 30.4.82

255 Harbour by Gaslight

256 Quay

257 Royal Square

258 Halkett Place

259 Central Market

150th Anniversary of Gas Lighting in Jersey

(Des R. Granger Barrett. Photo Courvoisier)

1981 (22 MAY). *Granite paper. Perf* 11½ (C)

279	**255**	7p multicoloured	. . . .	25	25
280	**256**	10p multicoloured	. . . .	30	30
281	**257**	18p multicoloured	. . . .	45	45
282	**258**	22p multicoloured	. . . .	55	55
283	**259**	25p multicoloured	. . . .	65	65
279/83		*Set of 5*	. . . .	2·00	2·00
		First Day Cover			2·00
		Presentation Pack	2·00	

Cylinder Nos.: All values A1–1–1–1–1, B1–1–1–1–1, C1–1–1–1–1, D1–1–1–1–1

Sheets: 20 (5×4)

Imprint: Left-hand corner, bottom margin

Quantities sold: 7p 1,433,090; 10p 1,416,051; 18p 384,043; 22p 417,191; 25p 333,402

Withdrawn: 31.5.82

260 Prince Charles and Lady Diana Spencer

Royal Wedding

(Des Jersey P.O. and Courvoisier. Photo Courvoisier)

1981 (28 JULY). *Granite paper. Perf* 11½ (C)

284	**260**	10p multicoloured	. . . .	75	75
285		25p multicoloured	. . . .	1·75	1·75
284/5		*Set of 2*	. . . .	2·50	2·50
		First Day Cover			4·00
		Presentation Pack	4·00	

Cylinder Nos.: Both values A1–1–1–1–1, B1–1–1–1–1

Sheets: 20 (5×4)

Imprint: Left-hand corner, bottom margin

Quantities sold: 10p 935,571; 25p 580,597

Withdrawn: 31.7.82

261 Christmas Tree in Royal Square

262 East Window, Parish Church, St. Helier

263 Boxing Day Meet of Jersey Drag Hunt

Christmas

(Des A. Copp. Litho Questa)

1981 (29 SEPT). *Perf* 14½ (C)

286	**261**	7p multicoloured	. . . .	25	25
287	**262**	10p multicoloured	. . . .	40	40
		a. Black (face value, inscr and choir) printed double		
288	**263**	18p multicoloured	. . . .	50	50
286/8		*Set of 3*	. . . .	1·00	1·00
		First Day Cover			1·25
		Presentation Pack	1·60	
		Postcards (Set of 3)	1·00	2·50

Plate Nos.: All values 1A, 1B, 1C, 1D, 1E, 1F, 1G, 1H (each ×5)

Sheets: 20 (4×5)

Imprint: Central, left-hand margin

Quantities sold: 7p 1,437,626; 10p 1,386,934; 18p 422,693

Withdrawn: 30.9.82

264 Jersey, 16,000 B.C.

265 10,000 B.C.

266 7,000 B.C. **267** 4,000 B.C.

Europa. Historic Events

(Des A. Copp. Litho Questa)

1982 (20 APR). *Perf* 14 (C)

289	**264**	11p multicoloured	. . . .	30	30
290	**265**	11p multicoloured	. . . .	30	30
291	**266**	19½p multicoloured	. . . .	70	60
292	**267**	19½p multicoloured	. . . .	70	60
289/92		Set of 4	. . . .	1·75	1·60
		First Day Cover	. . . .		1·75
		Presentation Pack	. . . . . .	2·00	

Plate Nos.: All values 1A, 1B, 1C, 1D, 1E, 1F (each ×6)

Sheets: 20 (Nos. 289, 292, 4×5; others 5×4)

Imprint: Central, left-hand margin

Quantities sold: 11p (both designs) 3,414,424; 19½p (both designs) 2,307,769

Withdrawn: 30.4.83

268 Rollo, Duke of Normandy, William the Conqueror and 'Clameur de Haro'

269 John of England, Philippe Auguste of France and Siege of Rouen

270 Jean Martell (brandy merchant), early Still and view of Cognac

271 Victor Hugo, 'Le Rocher des Proscrits' (rock where he used to meditate) and Marine Terrace

272 Pierre Teilhard de Chardin (philosopher) and 'Maison Saint Louis' (science institute)

273 Père Charles Rey (scientist), anemo-tachymeter and The Observatory, St. Louis

Links with France

(Des R. Granger Barrett. Litho Questa)

1982 (11 JUNE–7 SEPT). *Perf* 14 (C)

293	**268**	8p multicoloured	. . . .	25	25
		a. Horiz pair. Nos. 293/4	. . . .	50	50
		b. Booklet pane. Nos. 293/4 each ×2 (7.9.82)	. . . .	1·00	
294	**269**	8p multicoloured	. . . .	25	25
295	**270**	11p multicoloured	. . . .	35	35
		a. Horiz pair. Nos. 295/6	. . . .	70	70
		b. Booklet pane. Nos. 295/6 each ×2 (7.9.82)	. . . .	1·40	
296	**271**	11p multicoloured	. . . .	35	35
297	**272**	19½p multicoloured	. . . .	60	60
		a. Horiz pair. Nos. 297/8	. . . .	1·25	1·25
		b. Booklet pane. Nos. 297/8 each ×2 (7.9.82)	. . . .	2·50	
		c. Black (face value and inscr) printed double	. . . .		
298	**273**	19½p multicoloured	. . . .	60	60
		c. Black (face value and inscr) printed double	. . . .		
293/8		Set of 6	. . . .	2·25	2·25
		First Day Cover	. . . .		2·25
		Presentation Pack	. . . . . .	2·50	

Each booklet pane has margins all round and text, in English or French, printed on the binding selvedge.

Nos. 297c and 298c come from an example of booklet pane No. 297b.

Plate Nos.: All values 1A, 1B, 1C, 1D (each ×4)

Sheets: 20 (4×5). The two designs of each value were printed together, *se-tenant*, in horizontal pairs throughout

Imprint: Central, left-hand margin

Quantities sold: 8p (sheet stamps) 2,019,854; 11p (both designs) 1,914,536; 19½p (both designs) 828,272

Withdrawn: 30.6.83 (sheets)

274 Sir William Smith and Proclamation of King George V, Jersey, 1910

275 Sir William Smith and Lord Baden-Powell at Boys' Brigade Display, 1903

276 Boys' Brigade Band, Jersey Liberation Parade, 1945

277 Lord and Lady Baden-Powell in St. Helier, 1924

278 Scouts in Summer Camp, Jersey

Youth Organizations

(Des A. Theobald. Photo Courvoisier)

1982 (18 NOV). *Granite paper. Perf* 11½ (C)

299	**274**	8p multicoloured	. . . .	25	25
300	**275**	11p multicoloured	. . . .	30	30
301	**276**	24p multicoloured	. . . .	60	60
302	**277**	26p multicoloured	. . . .	75	75
303	**278**	29p multicoloured	. . . .	90	90
299/303		Set of 5	. . . .	2·50	2·50
		First Day Cover	. . . .		3·25
		Presentation Pack	. . . .	3·00	

Nos. 299/303 were issued on the occasion of the 75th anniversary of the Boy Scout Movement, the 125th birth anniversary of Lord Baden-Powell and the centenary of the Boys Brigade (1983).

Cylinder Nos.: All values A1–1–1–1–1, B1–1–1–1–1, C1–1–1–1–1, D1–1–1–1–1

Sheets: 20 (11p, 26p 5×4; others 4×5)

Imprint: Lower left-hand margin

Quantities sold: 8p 1,006,110; 11p 1,006,206; 24p 242,482; 26p 255,359; 29p 244,746

Withdrawn: 30.11.83

279 H.M.S. *Tamar* with H.M.S. *Dolphin* at Port Egmont

280 H.M.S. *Dolphin* and H.M.S. *Swallow* off Magellan Strait

281 Discovering Pitcairn Island

282 Carteret taking possession of English Cove, New Zealand

283 H.M.S. *Swallow* sinking a Pirate, Macassar Strait

284 H.M.S. *Endymion* leading Convoy from West Indies

Jersey Adventurers (First Series). 250th Birth Anniv of Philippe de Carteret

(Des R. Granger Barrett. Litho Questa)

1983 (15 FEB). *Perf* 14×14½ (C)

304	**279**	8p multicoloured	. . . .	25	25
		a. Black *(face value and inscr)* printed double	. . . .		
305	**280**	11p multicoloured	. . . .	30	30
		a. Black *(face value and inscr)* printed double	. . . .		
306	**281**	19½p multicoloured	. . . .	50	50
307	**282**	24p multicoloured	. . . .	70	70
		a. Black *(face value and inscr)* printed double	. . . .		
308	**283**	26p multicoloured	. . . .	85	75
		a. Black *(face value and inscr)* printed double	. . . .		
309	**284**	29p multicoloured	. . . .	1·00	85
304/9		Set of 6	. . . .	3·25	3·00
		First Day Cover	. . . .		3·75
		Presentation Pack	. . . . . .	3·75	

See also Nos. 417/21 and 573/8.

Plate Nos.: All values 1A, 1B, 1C, 1D, 1E, 1F (each ×6)

Sheets: 20 (4×5)

Imprint: Central, left-hand margin

Quantities sold: 8p 983,227; 11p 979,640; 19½p 377,535; 24p 264,595; 26p 279,424; 29p 254,023

Withdrawn: 29.2.84

285 1969 5s. Legislative Chamber Definitive

286 Royal Mace

287 1969 10s. Royal Court Definitive showing Green Border Error

288 Bailiff's Seal

Europa

(Des G. Drummond. Litho Questa)

1983 (19 APR). *Perf* 14½ (C)

310	**285**	11p multicoloured	. . . .	50	50
		a. Horiz pair. Nos. 310/11	. . . .	1·00	1·00
311	**286**	11p multicoloured	. . . .	50	50
312	**287**	19½p multicoloured	. . . .	75	75
		a. Horiz pair. Nos. 312/13	. . . .	1·50	1·50
313	**288**	19½p multicoloured	. . . .	75	75
310/13		Set of 4	. . . .	2·25	2·25
		First Day Cover	. . . .		2·75
		Presentation Pack	. . . . . .	3·00	

Plate Nos.: Both values 1A, 1B, 1C, 1D, 1E, 1F (each ×6)

Sheets: 20 (4×5). The two designs of each value were printed together, *se-tenant*, in horizontal pairs throughout

Imprint: Central, left-hand margin

Quantities sold: 11p (both designs) 2,973,691; 19½p (both designs) 1,301,579

Withdrawn: 30.4.84

289 Charles Le Geyt and Battle of Minden

290 London to Weymouth Mail Coach

291 P.O. Mail Packet *Chesterfield* attacked by French Privateer

292 Mary Godfray and the Hue Street Post Office

293 Mail Steamer leaving St. Helier Harbour

World Communications Year and 250th Birth Anniversary of Charles Le Geyt (first Jersey postmaster)

(Des A. Copp. Litho Questa)

1983 (21 JUNE). *Perf* 14 (C)

314	**289**	8p multicoloured	. . . .	25	25
315	**290**	11p multicoloured	. . . .	35	35
316	**291**	24p multicoloured	. . . .	75	75
317	**292**	26p multicoloured	. . . .	90	90
318	**293**	29p multicoloured	. . . .	1·10	1·10
314/18		Set of 5	. . . .	3·00	3·00
		First Day Cover	. . . .		3·50
		Presentation Pack	. . . .	3·25	

Plate Nos.: All values 1A, 1B, 1C, 1D (each ×5)

Sheets: 20 (4×5)

Imprint: Central, left-hand margin

Quantities sold: 8p 1,136,008; 11p 961,725; 24p 244,690; 26p 247,654; 29p 230,325

Withdrawn: 30.6.84

294 Assembly Emblem

13th General Assembly of the A.I.P.L.F. (Association Internationale des Parlementaires de Langue Française)

(Des A. Copp. Litho Questa)

1983 (21 JUNE). *Perf* 14½ (C)

319	**294**	19½p multicoloured	. . . .	75	75
		First Day Cover	. . . .		1·75
		Presentation Pack	. . . . . .	1·25	

Plate Nos.: 1A, 1B, 1C, 1D (each ×5)

Sheets: 20 (4×5)

Imprint: Central, left-hand margin

Quantity sold: 312,304

Withdrawn: 30.6.84

295 'Cardinal Newman'

296 'Incident in the French Revolution'

297 'Thomas Hardy'

298 'David with the Head of Goliath'

50th Death Anniversary of Walter Ouless (artist)

(Des and photo Courvoisier)

1983 (20 SEPT). *Granite paper. Perf* 11½ (C)

320	**295**	8p multicoloured	....	25	25
321	**296**	11p multicoloured	....	45	45
322	**297**	20½p multicoloured	....	85	85
323	**298**	31p multicoloured	....	1·25	1·25
320/3		*Set of 4*	....	2·50	2·50
		First Day Cover			3·00
		Presentation Pack	......	3·00	

Cylinder Nos.: All values A1, B1 (each ×5)

Sheets: 20 (4×5) 31p or (5×4) others

Imprint: Central, left-hand margin

Quantities sold: 8p 1,054,200; 11p 1,055,429; 20½p 424,049; 31p 216,128

Withdrawn: 30.9.84

299 Golden Lion Tamarin

300 Snow Leopard

301 Jamaican Boa

302 Round Island Gecko

303 Coscoroba Swan

304 St. Lucia Amazon

Wildlife Preservation Trust (Fourth Series)

(Des W. Oliver. Litho Questa)

1984 (17 JAN). *Perf* 13½×14 (C)

324	**299**	9p multicoloured	....	30	30
325	**300**	12p multicoloured	....	40	40
326	**301**	20½p multicoloured	....	60	60
327	**302**	26p multicoloured	....	95	75
328	**303**	28p multicoloured	....	1·10	90
329	**304**	31p multicoloured	....	1·10	90
324/9		*Set of 6*	....	4·00	3·50
		First Day Cover	....		4·50
		Presentation Pack	......	4·25	

Plate Nos.: 20½p 1B, 1C, 1E, 1F (each ×4); others 1A, 1B, 1C, 1D, 1E, 1F (each ×4)

Sheets: 20 (5×4)

Imprint: Central, left-hand margin

Quantities sold: 9p 1,229,713; 12p 1,365,973; 20½p 266,444; 26p 239,180; 28p 255,205; 31p 221,422

Withdrawn: 31.1.85

305 C.E.P.T. 25th Anniversary Logo

Europa

(Des J. Larrivière. Litho Questa)

1984 (12 MAR). *Perf* 14½×15 (C)

330	**305**	9p cobalt, ultramarine & black		30	30
331		12p light green, green and black		40	40
332		20½p rose-lilac, dp magenta & blk		70	70
330/2		*Set of* 3		1·25	1·25
		First Day Cover			1·75
		Presentation Pack		1·75	

Plate Nos.: All values 1A, 1B, 1C, 1D, 1E, 1F (each ×3)

Sheets: 20 (4×5)

Imprint: Central, left-hand margin

Quantities sold: 9p 1,352,245; 12p 1,388,802; 20½p 742,046

Withdrawn: 31.3.85

306 Map showing Commonwealth

Links with the Commonwealth

(Des A. Copp. Litho Questa)

1984 (12 MAR). *Sheet* 108×74 *mm. Perf* 15×14½ (C)

MS333	**306**	75p multicoloured		2·50	2·50
		First Day Cover			4·00
		Presentation Pack		4·00	

Quantity sold: 215,566

Withdrawn: 31.3.85

307 *Sarah Bloomshoft* at Demie de Pas Light, 1906

308 *Hearts of Oak* and *Maurice Georges*, 1949

309 *Elizabeth Rippon* and *Hanna*, 1949

310 *Elizabeth Rippon* and *Santa Maria*, 1951

311 *Elizabeth Rippon* and *Bacchus*, 1973

312 *Thomas James King* and *Cythara*, 1983

Centenary of the Jersey R.N.L.I. Lifeboat Station

(Des G. Palmer. Litho Questa)

1984 (1 JUNE). *Perf* 14½ (C)

334	**307**	9p multicoloured		40	40
335	**308**	9p multicoloured		40	40
336	**309**	12p multicoloured		50	50
337	**310**	12p multicoloured		50	50
338	**311**	20½p multicoloured		90	75
339	**312**	20½p multicoloured		90	75
334/9		*Set of* 6		3·25	3·00
		First Day Cover			4·50
		Presentation Pack		4·00	
		Postcard (as No. 339)		1·25	3·00

Plate Nos.: All values 1A, 1B, 1C, 1D, 1E, 1F (each ×5)

Sheets: 20 (4×5)

Imprint: Central, left-hand margin

Quantities sold: 9p (No. 334) 485,538; 9p (No. 335) 435, 647; 12p (No. 336) 534, 920; 12p (No. 337) 518,807; 20½p (No. 338) 298, 935; 20½p (No. 339) 290,945

Withdrawn: 30.6.85

313 Bristol Type 170 Freighter Mk 32

314 Airspeed A.S.57 Ambassador 2

315 De Havilland D.H.114 Heron 1B

316 De Havilland D.H.89A Dragon Rapide

40th Anniversary of International Civil Aviation Organization

(Des G. Drummond. Litho Questa)

1984 (24 JULY). *Perf* 14 (C)

340	**313**	9p multicoloured		30	30
341	**314**	12p multicoloured		40	40

342	**315**	26p multicoloured	....	1·00	90
343	**316**	31p multicoloured	....	1·25	1·10
340/3		*Set of 4*	....	2·75	2·50
		First Day Cover	....		4·00
		Presentation Pack	....	4·00	

Plate Nos.: All values 1A, 1B, 1C, 1D (each ×4)

Sheets: 20 (4×5)

Imprint: Central, left-hand margin

Quantities sold: 9p 563,394; 12p 751,072; 26p 262,640; 31p 193,703

Withdrawn: 31.7.85

317 'Robinson Crusoe leaves the Wreck'

318 'Edinburgh Castle'

319 'Maori Village'

320 'Australian Landscape'

321 'Waterhouse's Corner, Adelaide'

322 'Captain Cook at Botany Bay'

Links with Australia. Paintings by John Alexander Gilfillan

(Des R. Granger Barrett. Photo Courvoisier)

1984 (21 SEPT). *Granite paper. Perf* 11½×12 (C)

344	**317**	9p multicoloured	....	30	30
345	**318**	12p multicoloured	....	40	40
346	**319**	20½p multicoloured	....	75	75
347	**320**	26p multicoloured	....	95	95
348	**321**	28p multicoloured	....	1·00	1·00
349	**322**	31p multicoloured	....	1·10	1·10
344/9		*Set of 6*		4·00	4·00
		First Day Cover	....		4·25
		Presentation Pack	......	4·25	
		Postcards (Set of 3 as Nos. 347/9)	....	1·75	5·00

Cylinder Nos.: All values A1, B1 (each ×6)

Sheets: 20 (4×5)

Imprint: Central, left-hand margin

Quantities sold: 9p 541,384; 12p 635,192; 20½p 210,119; 26p 234,836; 28p 188,052; 31p 192,353

Withdrawn: 30.9.85

323 'B.L.C. St. Helier'

324 'Oda Mt Bingham'

Christmas. Jersey Orchids (First Series)

(Photo Courvoisier)

1984 (15 NOV). *Granite paper. Perf* 12×11½ (C)

350	**323**	9p multicoloured	....	50	45
351	**324**	12p multicoloured	....	75	65
350/1		*Set of 2*	....	1·25	1·00
		First Day Cover	....		1·60
		Presentation Pack	....	1·50	

See also Nos. 433/7 and 613/17.

Cylinder Nos.: Both values A1, B1, C1, D1 (each ×6)
Sheets: 20 (4×5)
Imprint: Central, left-hand margin
Quantities sold: 9p 1,197,796; 12p 1,116,097
Withdrawn: 30.11.85

325 'Hebe off Corbière, 1874'

326 'The *Gaspe* engaging the *Diomede*'

327 'The Paddle-steamer *London* entering Naples, 1856'

328 'The *Rambler* entering Cape Town, 1840'

329 'St. Aubin's Bay from Mount Bingham, 1872'

Death Centenary of Philip John Ouless (artist)

(Photo Harrison)

1985 (26 FEB). *Perf* 14×15 (C)

352	**325**	9p multicoloured	....	30	30
353	**326**	12p multicoloured	....	40	40
354	**327**	22p multicoloured	....	80	80
355	**328**	31p multicoloured	....	1·25	1·10
356	**329**	34p multicoloured	....	1·40	1·25
352/6		Set of 5	....	3·75	3·50
		First Day Cover	....		5·00
		Presentation Pack	....	4·25	

Cylinder Nos.: 31p 1B (×5); others 1A, 1B (each ×5)
Sheets: 20 (4×5)
Imprint: Central, left-hand margin
Quantities sold: 9p 463,589; 12p 405,133; 22p 407,598; 31p 193,772; 34p 185,467
Withdrawn: 28.2.86

330 John Ireland (composer) and Faldouet Dolmen

331 Ivy St. Helier (actress) and His Majesty's Theatre, London

332 Claude Debussy (composer) and Elizabeth Castle

Europa. European Music Year

(Des Jennifer Toombs. Litho Questa)

1985 (23 APR). *Perf* 14 (C)

357	**330**	10p multicoloured	....	40	40
358	**331**	13p multicoloured	....	55	55
359	**332**	22p multicoloured	....	1·00	90
357/9		Set of 3	....	1·75	1·60
		First Day Cover	....		2·50
		Presentation Pack	....	2·50	

Plate Nos.: 10p 1A, 1B, 1C, 1D, 1E, 1F (each ×5); 13p 1A, 1C, 1D, 1E, 1F (each ×5); 22p 1A, 1B, 1D, 1E, 1F (each ×5)

Sheets: 20 (4×5)

Imprint: Central, left-hand margin

Quantities sold: 10p 916,040; 13p 766,179; 22p 620,375

Withdrawn: 30.4.86

Plate Nos.: All values 1A, 1B, 1C, 1D, 1E, 1F (each ×4)

Sheets: 20 (5×4)

Imprint: Central, left-hand margin

Quantities sold: 10p 943,351; 13p 944,724; 29p 175,365; 31p 183,551; 34p 175,842

Withdrawn: 30.5.86

333 Girls' Brigade   **334** Girl Guides (75th anniversary)

338 *Duke of Normandy* at Cheapside   **339** Saddletank at First Tower

335 Prince Charles and Jersey Youth Service Activities Base   **336** Sea Cadet Corps

340 *La Moye* at Millbrook   **341** *St Heliers* at St. Aubin

337 Air Training Corps

342 *St Aubyns* at Corbière

International Youth Year

(Des A. Theobald. Litho Questa)

1985 (30 MAY). *Perf* 14½×14 (C)

360	**333**	10p multicoloured	30	30
361	**334**	13p multicoloured	50	50
362	**335**	29p multicoloured	1·00	1·00
363	**336**	31p multicoloured	1·10	1·00
364	**337**	34p multicoloured	1·25	1·10
360/4		*Set of* 5	3·75	3·50
		First Day Cover		4·25
		Presentation Pack	4·00	

Jersey Western Railway

(Des G. Palmer. Photo Courvoisier)

1985 (16 JULY). *Granite paper. Perf* 11½ (C)

365	**338**	10p multicoloured	55	55
366	**339**	13p multicoloured	70	70
367	**340**	22p multicoloured	1·10	1·10
368	**341**	29p multicoloured	1·25	1·25
369	**342**	34p multicoloured	1·40	1·40
365/9		*Set of* 5	4·50	4·50
		First Day Cover		4·75
		Presentation Pack	5·00	

Cylinder Nos.: 10p, 13p A1, B1 (each ×5); others A1 (×5)

Sheets: 20 (4×5)

Imprint: Central, left-hand margin

Quantities sold: 10p 708,912; 13p 706,189; 22p 249,659; 29p 179,849; 34p 179,977

Withdrawn: 31.7.86

343 Memorial Window to Revd. James Hemery (former Dean) and St. Helier Parish Church

344 Judge Francis Jeune, Baron St. Helier, and Houses of Parliament

345 Silverware by Pierre Amiraux

346 Francis Voisin (merchant) and Russian Port

347 Robert Brohier, Schweppes Carbonation Plant and Bottles

348 George Ingouville, V.C., R.N., and Attack on Viborg

300th Anniversary of Huguenot Immigration

(Des R. Granger Barrett. Litho Questa)

1985 (10 SEPT). *Perf* 14 (C)

370	**343**	10p multicoloured	. . . .	30	30
		a. Booklet pane of 4	. . . .	1·25	
371	**344**	10p multicoloured	. . . .	30	30
		a. Booklet pane of 4	. . . .	1·25	
372	**345**	13p multicoloured	. . . .	45	45
		a. Booklet pane of 4	. . . .	1·75	
373	**346**	13p multicoloured	. . . .	45	45
		a. Booklet pane of 4	. . . .	1·75	
		ab. Black (face value and inscr) printed double	. . . .		
374	**347**	22p multicoloured	. . . .	75	75
		a. Booklet pane of 4	. . . .	2·50	
		b. Black (inscr) printed double. .			
375	**348**	22p multicoloured	. . . .	75	75
		a. Booklet pane of 4	. . . .	2·50	
370/5		Set of 6	. . . .	2·75	2·75
		First Day Cover	. . . .		4·00
		Presentation Pack	. . . .	3·75	

Each booklet pane has margins all round and text printed on the binding selvedge.

Plate Nos.: 13p (No. 372) 1A, 1B, 1C, 1D (each ×4); 22p (No. 375) 1A, 1C, 1D (each ×5); others 1A, 1B, 1C, 1D (each ×5)

Sheets: 20 (4×5)

Imprint: Central, left-hand margin

Quantities sold (sheets): 10p (No. 370) 308,085; 10p (No. 371) 310,475; 13p (No. 372) 488,224; 13p (No. 373) 477,764; 22p (No. 374) 259,921; 22p (No. 375) 253,607

Withdrawn: 30.9.86 (sheets)

349 Howard Davis Hall, Victoria College

350 Schooner *Westward*

351 Howard Davis Park, St. Helier

352 Howard Davis Experimental Farm, Trinity

Thomas Davis (philanthropist) Commemoration

(Des A. Copp. Litho Cartor)

1985 (25 OCT). *Perf* 13½ (C)

376	**349**	10p multicoloured	. . . .	40	40
377	**350**	13p multicoloured	. . . .	60	60
378	**351**	31p multicoloured	. . . .	1·10	1·10
379	**352**	34p multicoloured	. . . .	1·25	1·25
376/9		Set of 4	. . . .	3·00	3·00
		First Day Cover	. . . .		4·00
		Presentation Pack	. . . .	4·00	

Plate Nos.: 10p 1A, 1B, 1C, 1D (each ×5); 13p 2A, 2B, 2C, 2D (each ×5); 31p 3A, 3B, 3C, 3D (each ×5); 34p 4A, 4B, 4C, 4D (each ×5)

Sheets: 20 (4×5)

Imprint: Central, left-hand margin

Quantities sold: 10p 939,104; 13p 831,351; 31p 170,020; 34p 156,653

Withdrawn: 31.10.86

357 Aspects of Communications in 1910 and 1986 on TV screens

Appearance of Halley's Comet

(Des Jennifer Toombs. Litho Cartor)

1986 (4 MAR). *Perf* 13½×13 (C)

383	**355**	10p multicoloured	....	40	40
384	**356**	22p multicoloured	....	85	85
385	**357**	31p multicoloured	....	1·25	1·25
383/5		*Set of 3*	....	2·25	2·25
		First Day Cover	....		2·75
		Presentation Pack	....	3·25	

Plate Nos.: All values 1A, 1B, 1C, 1D (each ×5)

Sheets: 20 (4×5)

Imprint: Central, left-hand margin

Quantities sold: 10p 552,062; 22p 245,111; 31p 182,390

Withdrawn: 31.3.87

353 'Amaryllis belladonna' (Pandora Sellars) **354** 'A Jersey Lily' (Lily Langtry) (Sir John Millais)

Jersey Lilies

(Des C. Abbott. Litho Questa)

1986 (28 JAN). *Perf* 15×14½ (C)

380	**353**	13p multicoloured	....	75	75
381	**354**	34p multicoloured	....	1·50	1·50
380/1		*Set of 2*	....	2·25	2·25
		First Day Cover	....		2·75
		Presentation Pack	....	2·75	
MS382		140×96 mm. Nos. 380×4 and 381		4·25	4·25
		First Day Cover	....		4·75
		Presentation Pack	....	4·50	

Plate Nos.: 13p 1A, 1B, 1C, 1D, 1E, 1F, 1G, 1H (each ×6); 34p 1A, 1B, 1C, 1D (each ×5)

Sheets: 20 (4×5); (5×4) 34p

Imprint: Central, left-hand margin

Quantities sold: 13p 444,175; 34p 169,811; miniature sheet 157,575

Withdrawn: 31.1.87

358 Dwarf Pansy **359** Sea Stock

360 Sand Crocus

Europa. Environmental Conservation

(Des Pandora Sellars. Litho Questa)

1986 (21 APR). *Perf* 14½×14 (C)

386	**358**	10p multicoloured	....	35	35
387	**359**	14p multicoloured	....	65	65
388	**360**	22p multicoloured	....	95	95
386/8		*Set of 3*	....	1·75	1·75
		First Day Cover	....		2·50
		Presentation Pack	....	2·50	

355 King Harold, William of Normandy and Halley's Comet, 1066 (Bayeux Tapestry)

356 Lady Carteret, Edmond Halley, Map and Comet

Plate Nos.: 22p 1A, 1B, 1C, 1E, 1F (each ×5); others 1A, 1B, 1C, 1D, 1E, 1F (each ×5)

Sheets: 20 (5×4)

Imprint: Central, left-hand margin

Quantities sold: 10p 892,977; 14p 892,631; 22p 612,513

Withdrawn: 30.4.87

361 Queen Elizabeth II (from photo by Karsh)

60th Birthday of Queen Elizabeth II

(Photo Courvoisier)

1986 (21 APR). *Granite paper. Perf* 14½ (C)

389	**361**	£1 multicoloured	. . . .	3·25	3·25
		First Day Cover			3·75
		Presentation Pack		3·75	

No. 389 was retained in use as part of the current definitive series until replaced by No. 500.

For a £2 value in this design see No. 491*b*.

Cylinder Nos.: A1, B1, C1, D1 (each ×6)

Sheets: 20 (4×5)

Imprint: Central, left-hand margin

Quantity sold: 431,591

Withdrawn: 31.5.90

362 Le Rât Cottage

363 The Elms (Trust Headquarters)

364 Morel Farm

365 Quétivel Mill

366 La Vallette

50th Anniversary of the National Trust for Jersey

(Des A. Copp. Litho Cartor)

1986 (17 JUNE). *Perf* 13½×13 (C)

390	**362**	10p multicoloured	. . . .	30	30
391	**363**	14p multicoloured	. . . .	45	45
392	**364**	22p multicoloured	. . . .	80	80
393	**365**	29p multicoloured	. . . .	90	90
394	**366**	31p multicoloured	. . . .	95	95
390/4		Set of 5	. . . .	3·00	3·00
		First Day Cover			3·75
		Presentation Pack		4·00	

Plate Nos.: All values 1A, 1B, 1C, 1D (each ×5)

Sheets: 20 (4×5)

Imprint: Central, left-hand margin

Quantities sold: 10p 946,735; 14p 919,823; 22p 427,370; 29p 173,763; 31p 178,353

Withdrawn: 30.6.87

367 Prince Andrew and Miss Sarah Ferguson

Royal Wedding

(Des A. Copp. Litho Cartor)

1986 (23 JULY). *Perf* 13½ (C)

395	**367**	14p multicoloured	. . . .	50	50
396		40p multicoloured	. . . .	1·50	1·50
395/6		Set of 2	. . . .	2·00	2·00
		First Day Cover			3·00
		Presentation Pack		3·00	

Plate Nos.: Both values 1A, 1B, 1C, 1D (each ×6)

Sheets: 20 (5×4)

Imprint: Central, left-hand margin

Quantities sold: 14p 991,943; 40p 267,312

Withdrawn: 31.7.87

368 'Gathering Vraic'

369 'Driving Home in the Rain'

370 'The Miller'

371 'The Joy Ride'

372 'Tante Elizabeth'

Birth Centenary of Edmund Blampied (artist)

(Des A. Copp. Litho Questa)

1986 (28 AUG). *Perf* 14 (C)

397	**368**	10p multicoloured	40	40
398	**369**	14p black, brownish grey & lt bl	70	70
399	**370**	29p multicoloured	1·00	1·00
400	**371**	31p black, brownish grey and pale orange	1·25	1·25
401	**372**	34p multicoloured	1·40	1·40
397/401		*Set of 5*	4·25	4·25
		First Day Cover		5·00
		Presentation Pack	5·00	

Plate Nos.: 14p, 31p 1A, 1B, 1C, 1D (each ×3); others 1A, 1B, 1C, 1D (each ×5)

Sheets: 20 (4×5)

Imprint: Central, left-hand margin

Quantities sold: 10p 885,979; 14p 675,290; 29p 163,085; 31p 157,559; 34p 151,128

Withdrawn: 31.8.87

373 Island Map on Jersey Lily, and Dove holding Olive Branch

374 Mistletoe Wreath encircling European Robin and Dove

375 Christmas Cracker releasing Dove

Christmas. International Year of Peace

(Des G. Taylor. Litho Questa)

1986 (4 NOV). *Perf* 14½×14 (C)

402	**373**	10p multicoloured	40	40
403	**374**	14p multicoloured	60	60
404	**375**	34p multicoloured	1·25	1·25
402/4		*Set of 3*	2·00	2·00
		First Day Cover		3·25
		Presentation Pack	3·00	

Plate Nos.: All values 1A, 1B, 1C, 1D, 1E, 1F (each ×6)

Sheets: 20 (5×4)

Imprint: Central, left-hand margin

Quantities sold: 10p 947,614; 14p 940,123; 34p 169,269

Withdrawn: 30.11.87

Post Office Yearbook

1986 (4 NOV). *Comprises Nos.* 380/404

		Yearbook	30·00

Withdrawn: 31.1.88

376 *Westward* under Full Sail

377 T. B. Davis at the Helm

378 *Westward* overhauling *Britannia*

379 *Westward* fitting-out at St. Helier

Racing Schooner Westward

(Des A. Copp. Litho Cartor)

1987 (15 JAN). *Perf* 13½ (C)

405	**376**	10p multicoloured	....	40	40
406	**377**	14p multicoloured	....	60	60
407	**378**	31p multicoloured	....	1·25	1·10
408	**379**	34p multicoloured	....	1·40	1·25
405/8		Set of 4	....	3·25	3·00
		First Day Cover	....		4·50
		Presentation Pack	....	4·50	

Plate Nos.: All values 1A, 1B, 1C, 1D (each ×5)

Sheets: 20 (4×5)

Imprint: Central, left-hand margin

Quantities sold: 10p 519,330; 14p 370,229; 31p 173,046; 34p 158,754

Withdrawn: 31.1.88

380 De Havilland D.H.86 Dragon Express *Belcroute Bay*

381 Boeing 757 and Douglas DC-9-15

382 Britten Norman "long nose" Trislander and Islander

383 Shorts 330 and Vickers Viscount 800

384 B.A.C. One Eleven 500 and Handley Page H.P.R.7 Dart Herald

50th Anniversary of Jersey Airport

(Des G. Palmer. Litho Questa)

1987 (3 MAR). *Perf* 14 (C)

409	**380**	10p multicoloured	....	30	30
410	**381**	14p multicoloured	....	50	50
411	**382**	22p multicoloured	....	70	70
412	**383**	29p multicoloured	....	1·10	1·10
413	**384**	31p multicoloured	....	1·25	1·25
409/13		Set of 5	....	3·50	3·50
		First Day Cover	....		4·50
		Presentation Pack	....	4·50	

Plate Nos.: All values 1A, 1B, 1C, 1D (each ×4)

Sheets: 20 (4×5)

Imprint: Central, left-hand margin

Quantities sold: 10p 313,733; 14p 281,226; 22p 368,486; 29p 155,159; 31p 167,709

Withdrawn: 31.3.88

385 St. Mary and St. Peter's Roman Catholic Church

386 Villa Devereux, St. Brelade

387 Fort Regent Leisure Centre, St. Helier

Europa. Modern Architecture

(Des A. Copp. Litho Questa)

1987 (23 APR). *Perf* 15×14 (C)

414	**385**	11p multicoloured	....	45	45
415	**386**	15p multicoloured	....	65	65
416	**387**	22p multicoloured	....	90	90
414/16		Set of 3	....	1·75	1·75
		First Day Cover	....		3·00
		Presentation Pack	....	3·00	

Plate Nos.: 11p, 15p 1A, 1B, 1C, 1D, 1E, 1F, 1G, 1H, 1I, 1J (each ×6); 22p 1A, 1B, 1C, 1D, 1E, 1F, 1G, 1H (each ×6)

Sheets: 10 (2×5)

Imprint: Central, left-hand margin

Quantities sold: 11p 847,735; 15p 883,825; 22p 467,615

Withdrawn: 30.4.88

388 H.M.S. *Racehorse* and H.M.S. *Carcass* (bomb-ketches) trapped in Arctic

389 H.M.S. *Alarm* on Fire, Rhode Island

390 H.M.S. *Arethusa* wrecked off Ushant

391 H.M.S. *Rattlesnake* stranded on Isle de Trinidad

392 Mont Orgueil Castle and Fishing Boats

Jersey Adventurers (Second Series). Philippe D'Auvergne

(Des R. Granger Barrett. Litho Questa)

1987 (9 JULY). *Perf* 14 (C)

417	**388**	11p multicoloured	40	40
418	**389**	15p multicoloured	50	50
419	**390**	29p multicoloured	90	80
420	**391**	31p multicoloured	1·00	90
421	**392**	34p multicoloured	1·10	1·00
417/21		Set of 5	3·50	3·25
		First Day Cover		4·50
		Presentation Pack	4·25	

See also Nos. 501/6 and 539/44.

Plate Nos.: All values 1A, 1B, 1C, 1D (each ×4)

Sheets: 20 (4×5)

Imprint: Central, left-hand margin

Quantities sold: 11p 694,506; 15p 897,162; 29p 138,711; 31p 144,518; 34p 140,968

Withdrawn: 31.7.88

393 Grant of Lands to Normandy, 911 and 933

394 Edward the Confessor and Duke Robert I of Normandy landing on Jersey, 1030

395 King William's Coronation, 1066, and Fatal Fall, 1087

396 Death of William Rufus, 1100, and Battle of Tinchebrai, 1106

397 Civil War between Matilda and Stephen, 1135–41

398 Henry inherits Normandy, 1151: John asserts Ducal Rights in Jersey, 1213

900th Death Anniversary of William the Conqueror

(Des Jennifer Toombs. Litho Cartor)

1987 (9 SEPT.–16 OCT). *Perf* 13½ (C)

422	**393**	11p multicoloured (a)	40	40
		a. Booklet pane of 4 (b)	2·00	
423	**394**	15p multicoloured (a)	45	45
		a. Booklet pane of 4 (b)	2·25	
424	**395**	22p multicoloured (a)	80	80
		a. Booklet pane of 4 (b)	3·50	

425	**396**	29p multicoloured (*a*)	95	95
		a. *Booklet pane of* 4 (*b*)......	4·50	
426	**397**	31p multicoloured (*a*)	1·10	1·10
		a. *Booklet pane of* 4 (*b*)......	5·00	
427	**398**	34p multicoloured (*a*)	1·25	1·25
		a. *Booklet pane of* 4 (*b*)......	5·50	
422/7		*Set of* 6	4·50	4·50
		First Day Cover		5·50
		Presentation Pack	5·00	

Each booklet pane has margins all round and text printed on the binding selvedge.

Printings: (a) 9.9.87; (b) 16.10.87

Plate Nos.: All values 1A, 1B, 1C, 1D (each ×6)

Imprint: Central, left-hand margin

Quantities sold (sheets): 11p 869,726; 15p 968,815; 22p 217,160; 29p 139,905; 31p 147,527; 34p 143,684

Withdrawn: 30.9.88 (sheets)

399 'Grosnez Castle'

400 'St. Aubin's Bay'

401 'Mont Orgueil Castle'

402 'Town Fort and Harbour, St. Helier'

403 'The Hermitage'

Christmas. Paintings by John Le Capelain

(Photo Courvoisier)

1987 (3 NOV). *Granite paper. Perf* 11½ (C)

428	**399**	11p multicoloured	40	40
429	**400**	15p multicoloured	60	60
430	**401**	22p multicoloured	80	80
431	**402**	31p multicoloured	1·10	1·10
432	**403**	34p multicoloured	1·25	1·25
428/32		*Set of* 5	3·75	3·75
		First Day Cover		4·50
		Presentation Pack	4·75	

Cylinder Nos.: 11p, 15p, 22p A1, B1 (each ×6); 31p, 34p A1 (×6)

Sheets: 20 (5×4)

Imprint: Central, left-hand margin

Quantities sold: 11p 951,916; 15p 874,209; 22p 371,992; 31p 154,824; 34p 145,550

Withdrawn: 30.11.88

Post Office Yearbook

1987 (3 NOV). *Comprises Nos.* 272 *and* 405/32

	Yearbook	....	25·00

Withdrawn: 28.2.89

404 *Cymbidium pontac*

405 *Odontioda* Eric Young

406 *Lycaste auburn* Seaford and Ditchling

407 *Odontoglossum* St. Brelade

408 *Cymbidium mavourneen* Jester

Jersey Orchids (Second Series)

(Litho Questa)

1988 (12 JAN). *Perf* 14 (C)

433	**404**	11p multicoloured	50	50
434	**405**	15p multicoloured	60	60
435	**406**	29p multicoloured	1·00	1·00
436	**407**	31p multicoloured	1·10	1·10
437	**408**	34p multicoloured	1·25	1·25
433/7		*Set of* 5	4·00	4·00
		First Day Cover		5·00
		Presentation Pack	4·50	

Plate Nos.: All values 1A, 1B, 1C, 1D (each ×5)

Sheets: 20 (4×5) 11p, 29p, 34p; (5×4) 15p, 31p

Imprint: Central, left-hand margin

Quantities sold: 11p 558,185; 15p 374,117; 29p 143,613; 31p 162,096; 34p 151,193

Withdrawn: 31.1.89

409 Labrador Retriever

410 Wire-haired Dachshund

411 Pekingese

412 Cavalier King Charles Spaniel

413 Dalmatian

Centenary of Jersey Dog Club

(Des P. Layton. Litho Questa)

1988 (2 MAR). *Perf* 14 (C)

438	**409**	11p multicoloured	50	50
439	**410**	15p multicoloured	75	75
440	**411**	22p multicoloured	1·10	1·10
441	**412**	31p multicoloured	1·10	1·10
442	**413**	34p multicoloured	1·25	1·25
438/42		Set of 5	4·25	4·25
		First Day Cover		5·00
		Presentation Pack	4·75	

Plate Nos.: All values 1A, 1B, 1C, 1D (each ×4)

Sheets: 20 (4×5)

Imprint: Central, left-hand margin

Quantities sold: 11p 371,583; 15p 374,953; 22p 178,132; 31p 154,530; 34p 146,628

Withdrawn: 31.3.89

414 De Havilland D.H.C.7 Dash Seven, London Landmarks and Jersey Control Tower

415 Weather Radar and Jersey Airport Landing System

416 Hydrofoil, St. Malo, and Elizabeth Castle, St. Helier

417 Port Control Tower and Jersey Radio Maritime Communication Centre, La Moye

Europa. Transport and Communications

(Des A. Copp. Litho Cartor)

1988 (26 APR). *Perf* 14×13½ (*horiz*) or 13½×14 (*vert*), both comb

443	**414**	16p multicoloured	50	50
444	**415**	16p multicoloured	50	50
445	**416**	22p multicoloured	90	90
446	**417**	22p multicoloured	90	90
443/6		Set of 4	2·50	2·50
		First Day Cover		3·25
		Presentation Pack	3·00	

Plate Nos.: Nos. 443/4, 446 1A, 1B, 1C, 1D (each ×5); No. 445 1A, 1B, 1C, 1D (each ×6)

Sheets: 20 (4×5) Nos. 443, 445; (5×4) Nos. 444, 446

Imprint: Central, left-hand margin

Quantities sold: 16p (No. 443) 881,324; 16p (No. 444) 865,868; 22p (No. 445) 509,086; 22p (No. 446) 510,104

Withdrawn: 30.4.89

418 Rodriguez Fody **419** Volcano Rabbit

420 White-faced Marmoset **421** Ploughshare Tortoise

422 Mauritius Kestrel

Wildlife Preservation Trust (Fifth Series)

(Des W. Oliver. Litho Cartor)

1988 (6 JULY). *Perf* 13½×14 (*vert*) *or* 14×13½ (*horiz*), *both comb*

447	**418**	12p multicoloured	55	55
448	**419**	16p multicoloured	70	70
449	**420**	29p multicoloured	1·10	1·10
450	**421**	31p multicoloured	1·25	1·25
451	**422**	34p multicoloured	1·40	1·40
447/51		Set of 5	4·50	4·50
		First Day Cover		5·00
		Presentation Pack	5·00	

Plate Nos.: All values 1A, 1B, 1C, 1D (each ×6)

Sheets: 20 (5×4) 12p, 29p, 34p; (4×5) 16p, 31p

Imprint: Central, left-hand margin

Quantities sold: 12p 875,722; 16p 969,800; 29p 146,567; 31p 155,348; 34p 151,723

Withdrawn: 31.7.89

423 Rain Forest Leaf Frog, Costa Rica **424** Archaeological Survey, Peru

425 Climbing Glacier, Chile **426** Red Cross Centre, Solomon Islands

427 Underwater Exploration, Australia **428** *Zebu* (brigantine) returning to St. Helier

Operation Raleigh

(Des V. Ambrus. Photo Courvoisier)

1988 (27 SEPT). *Granite paper. Perf* 12 (C)

452	**423**	12p multicoloured	45	45
453	**424**	16p multicoloured	55	55
454	**425**	22p multicoloured	80	80
455	**426**	29p multicoloured	1·00	1·00
456	**427**	31p multicoloured	1·10	1·10
457	**428**	34p multicoloured	1·25	1·25
452/7		Set of 6	4·50	4·50
		First Day Cover		5·50
		Presentation Pack	5·00	

No. 455 also commemorates the 40th anniversary of the World Health Organization.

Cylinder Nos.: All values A1 (×5)

Sheets: 20 (5×4)

Imprint: Central, left-hand margin

Quantities sold: 12p 706,594; 16p 507,077; 22p 226,791; 29p 127,647; 31p 127,658; 34p 128,055

Withdrawn: 30.9.89

429 St. Clement

430 St. Ouen

431 St. Brelade

432 St. Lawrence

Christmas. Jersey Parish Churches (First Series)

(Des P. Layton. Litho B.D.T.)

1988 (15 NOV). *Perf* 13½ (C)

458	**429**	12p multicoloured	. . . .	35	35
459	**430**	16p multicoloured	. . . .	60	60
460	**431**	31p multicoloured	. . . .	90	90
461	**432**	34p multicoloured	. . . .	95	95
458/61		*Set of 4*	. . . .	2·50	2·50
		First Day Cover			3·50
		Presentation Pack		3·75	
		Postcards (set of 4)		1·75	5·50

See also Nos. 535/8 and 597/600.

Plate Nos.: All values 1A, 1B, 1C, 1D (each ×5)

Sheets: 20 (4×5)

Imprint: Central, left-hand margin

Quantities sold: 12p 964,161; 16p 917,883; 31p 170,477; 34p 159,688

Withdrawn: 30.11.89

Post Office Yearbook

1988 (15 NOV). *Comprises Nos. 266a/b, 268a and 433/61*

	Yearbook	26·00

Withdrawn: 23.10.89

433 Talbot 'Type 4 CT Tourer', 1912

434 De Dion 'Bouton Type 1-D', 1920

435 Austin 7 'Chummy', 1926

436 Ford 'Model T', 1926

437 Bentley 8 Litre, 1930

438 Cadillac '452A-V16 Fleetwood Sports Phaeton', 1931

Vintage Cars (First Series)

(Des A. Copp. Litho Questa)

1989 (31 JAN). *Perf* 14 (C)

462	**433**	12p multicoloured	. . . .	40	40
463	**434**	16p multicoloured	. . . .	60	60
464	**435**	23p multicoloured	. . . .	75	75
		a. Black (inscr etc) printed double			
465	**436**	30p multicoloured	. . . .	90	90
466	**437**	32p multicoloured	. . . .	1·10	1·10
467	**438**	35p multicoloured	. . . .	1·25	1·25
462/7		*Set of 6*	. . . .	4·50	4·50
		First Day Cover			5·50
		Presentation Pack		5·00	

See also Nos. 591/6.

Plate Nos.: 12p, 30p 1A, 1B (each ×4); 16p, 32p 1C, 1D (each ×4); 23p, 35p 1A, 1B, 1C, 1D (each ×4)

Sheets: 20 (4×5)

Imprint: Central, left-hand margin

Quantities sold: 12p 253,257; 16p 230,695; 23p 228,895; 30p 130,974; 32p 144,798; 35p 148,189

Withdrawn: 31.1.90

439 Belcroute Bay

440 High Street, St. Aubin

441 Royal Jersey Golf Course

442 Portelet Bay

443 Les Charrières D'Anneport

444 St. Helier Marina

445 Sand Yacht Racing, St. Ouen's Bay

446 Rozel Harbour

447 St. Aubin's Harbour

448 Jersey Airport

449 Corbière Lighthouse

450 Val de la Mare

451 Elizabeth Castle

452 Greve de Lecq

453 Samarès Manor

454 Bonne Nuit Harbour

455 Grosnez Castle

456 Augrès Manor

457 Central Market

458 St. Brelade's Bay

459 St. Ouen's Manor

460 La Hougue Bie

461 Mont Orgueil Castle

462 Royal Square, St. Helier

463 Queen Elizabeth II (from photo by Karsh)

464 Arms of King George VI

Jersey Scenes

(Des G. Drummond (1p to 75p). Photo Courvoisier (£2), Litho Questa (£4), B.D.T. (others))

1989 (21 MAR)–**95**. *Perf* 11½×12 (£2), 15×14 (£4) *or* 13×13½ (*others*), *all comb*

468	**439**	1p multicoloured (*a*)	10	10
469	**440**	2p multicoloured (*a*)	10	10
470	**441**	4p multicoloured (*a*)	10	10
		a. Booklet pane of 6 with margins all round (*d*)	60	
471	**442**	5p multicoloured (*a*)	10	10
		a. Booklet pane of 6 with margins all round (*f*)	75	
472	**443**	10p multicoloured (*a*)	20	25
473	**444**	13p multicoloured (*a*)	25	30
474	**445**	14p multicoloured (*ae*)	30	35
		a. Booklet pane of 6 with margins all round (*d*)	2·00	
		b. Booklet pane of 8 with margins all round (*i*)	2·75	
475	**446**	15p multicoloured (*ae*)	30	35
		a. Booklet pane of 6 with margins all round (*f*)	2·00	
476	**447**	16p multicoloured (*ah*)	30	35
		a. Booklet pane of 8 with margins all round (*i*)	3·50	
477	**448**	17p multicoloured (*aj*)	35	40
478	**449**	18p multicoloured (*akm*)	35	40
		a. Booklet pane of 6 with margins all round (*d*)	2·50	
479	**450**	19p multicoloured (*ano*)	40	45
480	**451**	20p multicoloured (*ae*)	40	45
		a. Booklet pane of 6 with margins all round (*f*)	3·00	
481	**452**	21p multicoloured (*b*)	40	45
482	**453**	22p multicoloured (*bh*)	45	50
		a. Booklet pane of 8 with margins all round (*i*)	4·25	
483	**454**	23p multicoloured (*bjkmo*)	45	50
484	**455**	24p multicoloured (*b*)	50	55
485	**456**	25p multicoloured (*b*)	50	55
486	**457**	26p multicoloured (*bh*)	50	55
487	**458**	27p multicoloured (*b*)	55	60
488	**459**	30p multicoloured (*c*)	60	65
489	**460**	40p multicoloured (*c*)	80	85
490	**461**	50p multicoloured (*c*)	1·00	1·10
491	**462**	75p multicoloured (*c*)	1·50	1·60
491*b*	**463**	£2 multicoloured (*g*)	4·00	4·25
491*c*	**464**	£4 multicoloured (*l*)	8·00	8·25
468/91*c*		Set of 26	22·00	23·00
		First Day Covers (5)		30·00
		Presentation Packs (5)	22·50	

For £1 value as No. 491*b* see No. 389.

Printings: (*a*) 21.3.89; (*b*) 16.1.90; (*c*) 13.3.90; (*d*) 3.5.90; (*e*) 13.11.90; (*f*) 12.2.91; (*g*) 19.3.91; (*h*) 7.1.92; (*i*) 22.5.92; (*j*) 11.1.93; (*k*) 18.2.94; (*l*) 24.1.95; (*m*) 21.3.95; (*n*) 1.9.95; (*o*) 12.11.96

Cylinder or Plate Nos.: £2 A1, B1, C1, D1 (each ×6); £4 1A (×5); others 1A, 1B, 1C, 1D, 1E, 1F (each ×4)

Sheets: £2 20 (4×5); £4 10 (5×2); others 50 (5×10)

Imprint: Left-hand corner, bottom margin (£4) or central, left-hand margin (others)

465 Agile Frog

466 *Heteropterus morpheus* (butterfly)

467 Barn Owl

468 Green Lizard

Endangered Jersey Fauna

(Des W. Oliver. Litho Cartor)

1989 (25 APR). *Perf* 13½×13 (*Nos. 492 and* 495), 13×13½ (*No.* 493) *or* 13½×14 (*No.* 494), *all comb*

492	**465**	13p multicoloured	1·00	1·00
493	**466**	13p multicoloured	1·00	1·00
494	**467**	17p multicoloured	1·10	1·10
495	**468**	17p multicoloured	1·10	1·10
492/5		Set of 4	3·75	3·75
		First Day Cover..........		4·00
		Presentation Pack........	4·25	

Plate Nos.: All designs 1A, 1B, 1C, 1D (each ×5)

Sheets: 20 (4×5) Nos. 492 and 495; (5×4) Nos. 493/4

Imprint: Central, left-hand margin

Quantities sold: 13p (No. 492) 650,061; 13p (No. 493) 589,329; 17p (No. 494) 552,582; 17p (No. 495) 515,262

Withdrawn: 30.4.90

469 Toddlers' Toys

470 Playground Games

471 Party Games

472 Teenage Sports

Europa. Children's Toys and Games

(Des from clay plaques by Clare Luke. Litho Questa)

1989 (25 APR). *Perf* 14 (C)

496	**469**	17p multicoloured	50	50
497	**470**	17p multicoloured	50	50
498	**471**	23p multicoloured	90	90
499	**472**	23p multicoloured	90	90
496/9		Set of 4	2·50	2·50
		First Day Cover..........		3·00
		Presentation Pack........	3·25	

Plate Nos.: All designs 1A, 1B, 1C, 1D, 1E, 1F (each ×4)

Sheets: 20 (4×5)

Imprint: Central, left-hand margin

Quantities sold: 17p (No. 496) 473,930; 17p (No. 497) 471,124; 23p (No. 498) 424,212; 23p (No. 499) 424,340

Withdrawn: 30.4.90

473 Queen Elizabeth II and Royal Yacht *Britannia* in Elizabeth Harbour

Royal Visit

(Des A. Copp. Litho Questa)

1989 (24 MAY). *Perf* 14½ (C)

500	**473**	£1 multicoloured	3·00	3·00
		First Day Cover..........		4·00
		Presentation Pack........	4·00	

No. 500 was retained in use as part of the current definitive series until replaced by No. 634.

Sheets: 20 (4×5)

Imprint: Central, left-hand margin

Withdrawn: 30.6.94

474 Philippe D'Auvergne presented to Louis XVI, 1786

475 Storming the Bastille, 1789

JERSEY 23

476 Marie de Bouillon and Revolutionaries, 1790

JERSEY 30

477 Auvergne's Headquarters at Mont Orgueil, 1795

JERSEY 32

478 Landing Arms for Chouan Rebels, 1796

JERSEY 35

479 The Last Chouan Revolt, 1799

Bicentenary of the French Revolution. Philippe D'Auvergne

(Des V. Ambrus. Litho Cartor)

1989 (7 JULY). *Perf* 13½ (C)

501	**474**	13p multicoloured	. . . .	45	45
		a. *Booklet pane of 4*		1·25	
502	**475**	17p multicoloured	. . . .	60	60
		a. *Booklet pane of 4*		2·00	
503	**476**	23p multicoloured	. . . .	80	80
		a. *Booklet pane of 4*		2·50	
504	**477**	30p multicoloured	. . . .	1·10	1·10
		a. *Booklet pane of 4*		4·25	
505	**478**	32p multicoloured	. . . .	1·10	1·10
		a. *Booklet pane of 4*		4·25	
506	**479**	35p multicoloured	. . . .	1·25	1·25
		a. *Booklet pane of 4*		4·75	
501/6		*Set of 6*	. . . .	4·75	4·75
		First Day Cover			5·50
		Presentation Pack		5·50	

Each booklet pane has margins all round and text printed on the binding selvedge.
See also Nos. 539/44.

Plate Nos.: All values 1A, 1B, 1C, 1D (each ×4)

Sheets: 20 (5×4)

Imprint: Central, left-hand margin

Quantities sold: 13p 637,422; 17p 840,904; 23p 408,967; 30p 133,642; 32p 148,474; 35p 151,639

Withdrawn: 31.7.90

480 *St. Helier* off Elizabeth Castle

JERSEY 17

481 *Caesarea II* off Corbière Lighthouse

JERSEY 27

482 *Reindeer* in St. Helier Harbour

JERSEY 32

483 *Ibex* racing *Frederica* off Portelet

JERSEY 35

484 *Lynx* off Noirmont

Centenary of Great Western Railway Steamer Service to Channel Islands

(Des G. Palmer. Litho Questa)

1989 (5 SEPT). *Perf* 13½×14 (C)

507	**480**	13p multicoloured	. . . .	40	40
508	**481**	17p multicoloured	. . . .	50	50
509	**482**	27p multicoloured	. . . .	1·00	1·00
510	**483**	32p multicoloured	. . . .	1·25	1·25
511	**484**	35p multicoloured	. . . .	1·40	1·40
507/11		*Set of 5*	. . . .	4·00	4·00
		First Day Cover			4·75
		Presentation Pack		4·50	

Plate Nos.: 13p, 27p 1A, 1B (each ×4); 17p, 32p 1C, 1D (each ×4); 35p 1A, 1B, 1C, 1D (each ×4)

Sheets: 20 (4×5)

Imprint: Central, left-hand margin

Quantities sold: 13p 265,382; 17p 294,992; 27p 135,226; 32p 128,966; 35p 134,800

Withdrawn: 28.9.90

485 Gorey Harbour

486 La Corbière

487 Grève de Lecq

488 Bouley Bay

489 Mont Orgueil

150th Birth Anniversary of Sarah Louisa Kilpack (artist)

(Litho Enschedé)

1989 (24 OCT). *Perf* 13×12½ (C)

512	**485**	13p multicoloured	. . . .	40	40
513	**486**	17p multicoloured	. . . .	50	50
514	**487**	23p multicoloured	. . . .	1·00	1·00
515	**488**	32p multicoloured	. . . .	1·25	1·25
516	**489**	35p multicoloured	. . . .	1·40	1·40
512/16		*Set of 5*	. . . .	4·00	4·00
		First Day Cover	. . . .		4·75
		Presentation Pack	. . . .	4·50	

Plate Nos.: 13p, 17p 1A, 1B, 1C (each ×5); 23p, 32p, 35p 1A, 1B (each ×5)

Sheets: 20 (4×5)

Imprint: Central, left-hand margin

Quantities sold: 13p 649,308; 17p 571,503; 23p 159,487; 32p 138,562; 35p 137,950

Withdrawn: 31.10.90

Post Office Yearbook

1989 (24 OCT). *Comprises Nos. 462/80 and 492/516*

              Yearbook . . . . 29·00

Sold out: 12.11.90

490 Head Post Office, Broad Street, 1969

491 Postal Headquarters, Mont Millais, 1990

492 Hue Street Post Office, 1815

493 Head Post Office, Halkett Place, 1890

Europa. Post Office Buildings

(Des P. Layton. Litho Cartor)

1990 (13 MAR). *Perf* 13½×14 (*vert*) *or* 14×13½ (*horiz*), *both comb*

517	**490**	18p multicoloured	. . . .	50	50
518	**491**	18p multicoloured	. . . .	50	50
519	**492**	24p multicoloured	. . . .	90	90
520	**493**	24p multicoloured	. . . .	90	90
517/20		*Set of 4*	. . . .	2·50	2·50
		First Day Cover	. . . .		3·50
		Presentation Pack	. . . .	4·00	

Plate Nos.: All designs 1A, 1B, 1C, 1D (each ×5)

Sheets: 20 (5×4) 18p; (4×5) 24p

Imprint: Central, left-hand margin

Quantities sold: 18p (No. 517) 596,221; 18p (No. 518) 595,918; 24p (No. 519) 400,441; 24p (No. 520) 406,656

Withdrawn: 31.3.91

494 'Battle of Flowers' Parade

495 Sports

496 Mont Orgueil
Castle and
German Under-
ground Hospital
Museum

497 Salon Culinaire

500 Radio Jersey
Broadcaster

501 Channel Television
Studio Cameraman

Festival of Tourism

(Des A. Copp. Litho Enschedé)

1990 (3 MAY). *Perf* 14×13½ (C)

521	**494**	18p multicoloured	. . . .	60	60
522	**495**	24p multicoloured	. . . .	75	75
523	**496**	29p multicoloured	. . . .	95	95
524	**497**	32p multicoloured	. . . .	1·00	1·00
521/4		*Set of 4*	. . . .	3·00	3·00
		First Day Cover	. . . .		4·00
		Presentation Pack	. . . .	4·00	
MS525		151×100 mm. Nos. 521/4	. . . .	3·00	3·00
		First Day Cover	. . . .		4·25
		Presentation Pack	. . . .	4·00	

Plate Nos.: 18p 1A, 1B, 1C, 1D, 1E (each ×5); 24p 1A, 1B, 1C, 1D
(each ×5); 29p 1A (×5); 32p 1A, 1B (each ×5)

Sheets: 20 (5×4)

Imprint: Central, left-hand margin

Quantities sold: 18p 630,610; 24p 252,670; 29p 168,528; 32p
127,334; miniature sheet 110,177

Withdrawn: 31.5.91

International Literacy Year. Jersey News Media

(Des A. Copp. Litho Cartor)

1990 (26 JUNE). *Perf* 13½ (C)

526	**498**	14p multicoloured	. . . .	55	55
527	**499**	18p multicoloured	. . . .	60	60
528	**500**	34p multicoloured	. . . .	1·10	1·10
529	**501**	37p multicoloured	. . . .	1·10	1·10
526/9		*Set of 4*	. . . .	3·00	3·00
		First Day Cover	. . . .		3·50
		Presentation Pack	. . . .	3·75	

Plate Nos.: All values 1A, 1B, 1C, 1D (each ×4)

Sheets: 20 (4×5)

Imprint: Central, left-hand margin

Quantities sold: 14p 926,906; 18p 795,733; 34p 121,842; 37p
129,468

Withdrawn: 30.6.91

498 Early Printing Press and
Jersey Newspaper
Mastheads

499 Modern Press, and
Offices of *Jersey
Evening Post* in 1890
and 1990

502 British Aerospace
Hawk T.1

503 Supermarine Spitfire

504 Hawker Hurricane Mk I

505 Vickers-Armstrong
Wellington

506 Avro Type 683 Lancaster

50th Anniversary of Battle of Britain

(Des G. Palmer. Litho Questa)

1990 (4 SEPT). *Perf* 14 (C)

530	**502**	14p multicoloured	. . . .	45	45
531	**503**	18p multicoloured	. . . .	50	50
532	**504**	24p multicoloured	. . . .	75	75
533	**505**	34p multicoloured	. . . .	1·40	1·40
534	**506**	37p multicoloured	. . . .	1·40	1·40
530/4		Set of 5	. . . .	4·00	4·00
		First Day Cover	. . . .		4·75
		Presentation Pack	. . . .	4·50	

Plate Nos.: 14p, 34p 1A, 1B (each ×5); 18p, 37p 1C, 1D (each ×5);
24p 1A, 1B, 1C, 1D (each ×5)

Sheets: 20 (4×5)

Imprint: Central, left-hand margin

Quantities sold: 14p 495,815; 18p 519,684; 24p 206,541; 34p
136,330; 37p 134,747

Withdrawn: 30.9.91

507 St. Helier

508 Grouville

509 St. Saviour

510 St. John

Christmas. Jersey Parish Churches (Second Series)

(Des P. Layton. Litho B.D.T.)

1990 (13 NOV). *Perf* 13½ (C)

535	**507**	14p multicoloured	. . . .	40	40
536	**508**	18p multicoloured	. . . .	60	60
537	**509**	34p multicoloured	. . . .	1·10	1·10
538	**510**	37p multicoloured	. . . .	1·25	1·25
535/8		Set of 4	. . . .	3·00	3·00
		First Day Cover	. . . .		3·75
		Presentation Pack	. . . .	3·75	
		Postcards (set of 4)	. . . . . .	2·00	6·00

Plate Nos.: All values 1A, 1B, 1C, 1D (each ×5)

Sheets: 20 (4×5)

Imprint: Central, left-hand margin

Quantities sold: 14p 948,076; 18p 690,282; 34p 141,514; 37p
147,468

Withdrawn: 30.11.91

Post Office Yearbook

1990 (13 NOV). *Comprises Nos.* 481/91 *and* 517/38
Yearbook . . . . 28·00

Withdrawn: 30.11.91

511 Prince's Tower,
La Hougue Bie

512 Auvergne's Arrest in
Paris

513 Auvergne plotting
against Napoleon

514 Execution of George
Cadoudal

515 H.M.S. *Surly* (cutter)
attacking French
Convoy

516 Auvergne's Last Days
in London

175th Death Anniversary of Philippe d'Auvergne

(Des V. Ambrus. Litho Cartor)

1991 (22 JAN). *Perf* 13½ (C)

539	**511**	15p multicoloured	. . . .	50	50
540	**512**	20p multicoloured	. . . .	60	60
541	**513**	26p multicoloured	. . . .	80	80

542	**514**	31p multicoloured	. . . .	1·00	1·00
543	**515**	37p multicoloured	. . . .	1·25	1·25
544	**516**	44p multicoloured	. . . .	1·40	1·40
539/44		Set of 6	. . . .	5·00	5·00
		First Day Cover	. . . .		5·75
		Presentation Pack	. . . .	5·75	

Plate Nos.: All values 1A, 1B, 1C, 1D (each ×4)

Sheets: 20 (4×5)

Imprint: Central, left-hand margin

Quantities sold: 15p 709,403; 20p 454,921; 26p 159,902; 31p 140,379; 37p 341,103; 44p 153,157

Withdrawn: 31.1.92

517 'Landsat 5' and Thematic Mapper Image over Jersey

518 'ERS-1' Earth Resources Remote Sensing Satellite

519 'Meteosat' Weather Satellite

520 'Olympus' Direct Broadcasting Satellite

Europa. Europe in Space

(Des A. Copp. Litho Enschedé)

1991 (19 MAR). Perf 14½×13 (C)

545	**517**	20p multicoloured	. . . .	55	55
546	**518**	20p multicoloured	. . . .	55	55
547	**519**	26p multicoloured	. . . .	85	85
548	**520**	26p multicoloured	. . . .	85	85
545/8		Set of 4	. . . .	2·50	2·50
		First Day Cover	. . . .		3·50
		Presentation Pack	. . . .	3·50	

Plate Nos.: All designs 1A, 1B, 1C (each ×5)

Sheets: 20 (5×4)

Imprint: Central, left-hand margin

Quantities sold: 20p (No. 545) 682,799; 20p (No. 546) 690,871; 26p (No. 547) 442,476; 26p (No. 548) 439,415

Withdrawn: 31.3.92

521 1941 1d. Stamp (50th anniv of first Jersey postage stamp)

522 Steam Train (centenary of Jersey Eastern Railway extension to Gorey Pier)

523 Jersey Cow and Herd Book (125th anniv of Jersey Herd Book)

524 Stone-laying Ceremony (painting by P. Ouless) (150th anniv of Victoria Harbour)

525 Marie Bartlett and Hospital (250th anniversary of Marie Bartlett's hospital bequest)

Anniversaries

(Des A. Copp. Litho Cartor)

1991 (16 MAY). Perf 13½ (C)

549	**521**	15p multicoloured	. . . .	40	40
550	**522**	20p multicoloured	. . . .	60	60
551	**523**	26p multicoloured	. . . .	80	80
552	**524**	31p multicoloured	. . . .	90	90
553	**525**	53p multicoloured	. . . .	1·75	1·75
549/53		Set of 5	. . . .	4·00	4·00
		First Day Cover	. . . .		5·00
		Presentation Pack	. . . .	5·00	

Plate Nos.: All values 1A, 1B, 1C, 1D (each ×4)

Sheets: 20 (5×4)

Imprint: Central, left-hand margin

Quantities sold: 15p 618,479; 20p 608,585; 26p 245,772; 31p 133,604; 53p 135,394

Withdrawn: 30.5.92

526 *Melitaea cinxia*

527 *Euplagia quadripunctaria*

528 *Deilephilia porcellus*

529 *Inachis io*

Butterflies and Moths

(Des W. Oliver. Litho Enschedé)

1991 (9 JULY). *Perf* 13×12½ (C)

554	**526**	15p multicoloured	40	40
555	**527**	20p multicoloured	50	50
556	**528**	37p multicoloured	1·60	1·60
557	**529**	57p multicoloured	2·00	2·00
554/7		Set of 4	4·00	4·00
		First Day Cover		4·75
		Presentation Pack	4·50	

Plate Nos.: All values 1A, 1B, 1C (each ×4)

Sheets: 20 (4×5)

Imprint: Central, left-hand margin

Quantities sold: 15p 489,632; 20p 646,607; 37p 130,494; 57p 142,646

Withdrawn: 31.7.92

530 Drilling for Water, Ethiopia

531 Building Construction, Rwanda

532 Village Polytechnic, Kenya

533 Treating Leprosy, Tanzania

534 Ploughing, Zambia

535 Immunisation Clinic, Lesotho

Overseas Aid

(Des A. Theobald. Litho B.D.T.)

1991 (3 SEPT). *Perf* 13½×14 (C)

558	**530**	15p multicoloured	50	40
559	**531**	20p multicoloured	60	65
560	**532**	26p multicoloured	80	80
561	**533**	31p multicoloured	1·00	1·00
562	**534**	37p multicoloured	1·25	1·25
563	**535**	44p multicoloured	1·40	1·40
558/63		Set of 6	5·00	5·00
		First Day Cover		5·75
		Presentation Pack	5·75	

Plate Nos.: All values 1A, 1B (each ×4)

Sheets: 20 (4×5)

Imprint: Central, left-hand margin

Quantities sold: 15p 517,917; 20p 644,721; 26p 177,179; 31p 115,769; 37p 111,112; 44p 142,024

Withdrawn: 30.9.92

536 'This is the Place for Me'

537 'The Island Come True'

538 'The Never Bird'

539 'The Great White Father'

543 Lapwing

544 Fieldfare

Christmas. Illustrations by Edmund Blampied for J. M. Barrie's 'Peter Pan'

(Litho Questa)

1991 (5 NOV). *Perf* 14 (C)

564	**536**	15p multicoloured	. . . .	40	40
565	**537**	20p multicoloured	. . . .	65	65
566	**538**	37p multicoloured	. . . .	1·25	1·25
567	**539**	53p multicoloured	. . . .	1·60	1·60
564/7		*Set of* 4	. . . .	3·50	3·50
		First Day Cover			4·25
		Presentation Pack		4·50	

Sheets: 20 (5×4)

Imprint: Central, left-hand margin

Quantities sold: 15p 917,860; 20p 693,203; 37p 128,585; 53p 117,877

Withdrawn: 30.11.92

Post Office Yearbook

1991 (5 NOV). *Comprises Nos.* 491*b and* 539/67

Yearbook . . . . 29·00

Sold out: By 9.93

Winter Birds

(Des W. Oliver. Litho Cartor)

1992 (7 JAN). *Perf* 13½×14 (C)

568	**540**	16p multicoloured	. . . .	50	45
569	**541**	22p multicoloured	. . . .	70	60
570	**542**	28p multicoloured	. . . .	80	70
571	**543**	39p multicoloured	. . . .	1·25	1·00
572	**544**	57p multicoloured	. . . .	1·75	1·50
568/72		*Set of* 5	. . . .	4·50	4·25
		First Day Cover			5·50
		Presentation Pack		5·25	

See also Nos. 635/9.

Plate Nos.: All values 1A, 1B, 1C, 1D (each ×4)

Sheets: 20 (5×4)

Imprint: Central, left-hand margin

Quantities sold: 16p 481,678; 22p 462,647; 28p 268,973; 39p 151,671; 57p 132,065

Withdrawn: 30.1.93

545 Shipping at Shanghai, 1860

546 Mesny's Junk running Taiping Blockade, 1862

547 General Mesny outside River Gate, 1874

548 Mesny in Burma, 1877

540 Pied Wagtail

541 Firecrest

542 Common Snipe

549 Mesny and Governor Chang, 1882

550 Mesny in Mandarin's Sedan Chair, 1886

Jersey Adventurers (Third Series). 150th Birth Anniversary of William Mesny

(Des V. Ambrus. Litho Cartor)

1992 (25 FEB). *Perf* 13½ (C)

573	**545**	16p multicoloured	50	50
		a. *Black printed double*		
		b. *Booklet pane of 4*	1·25	
574	**546**	16p multicoloured	50	50
		a. *Booklet pane of 4*	1·25	
575	**547**	22p multicoloured	75	75
		a. *Booklet pane of 4*	1·75	
576	**548**	22p multicoloured	75	75
		a. *Booklet pane of 4*	1·75	
577	**549**	33p multicoloured	1·00	1·00
		a. *Booklet pane of 4*	2·50	
578	**550**	33p multicoloured	1·00	1·00
		a. *Booklet pane of 4*	2·50	
573/8		*Set of 6*	4·00	4·00
		First Day Cover		4·75
		Presentation Pack	4·75	

Each booklet pane has margins all round and text printed on the binding selvedge.

Plate Nos.: All values 1A, 1B, 1C, 1D (each ×4)

Sheets: 20 (4×5)

Imprint: Central, left-hand margin

Quantities sold: 16p (No. 573) 346,732; 16p (No. 574) 336,655; 22p (No. 575) 377,299; 22p (No. 576) 360,220; 33p (No. 577) 129,904; 33p (No. 578) 130,637

Withdrawn: 27.2.93 (sheets)

551 *Tickler* (brigantine)

552 *Hebe* (brig)

553 *Gemini* (barque)

554 *Percy Douglas* (full-rigged ship)

Jersey Shipbuilding

(Des A. Copp. Litho Questa)

1992 (14 APR). *Perf* 14 (C)

579	**551**	16p multicoloured	50	50
580	**552**	22p multicoloured	80	70
581	**553**	50p multicoloured	1·60	1·50
582	**554**	57p multicoloured	1·90	1·75
579/82		*Set of 4*	4·25	4·00
		First Day Cover		4·75
		Presentation Pack	4·75	
MS583	148×98 mm. Nos. 579/82		4·25	4·00
		First Day Cover		4·75
		Presentation Pack	4·75	

Plate Nos.: 16p 1A, 1B, 1C, 1D, 1E, 1F (each ×4); 22p, 57p 1A, 1B, 1C, 1D (each ×4); 50p 1A, 1B (each ×4)

Sheets: 20 (5×4)

Imprint: Central, left-hand margin

Quantities sold: 16p 673,830; 22p 462,972; 50p 138,158; 57p 111,044; miniature sheet 126,594

Withdrawn: 30.4.93

555 John Bertram (ship owner) and Columbus

556 Sir George Carteret (founder of New Jersey)

557 Sir Walter Ralegh (founder of Virginia)

Europa. 500th Anniversary of Discovery of America by Columbus

(Des V. Ambrus. Litho Questa)

1992 (14 APR). *Perf* 14×14½ (C)

584	**555**	22p multicoloured	70	70
585	**556**	28p multicoloured	85	85
586	**557**	39p multicoloured	1·25	1·25
584/6		*Set of 3*	2·50	2·50
		First Day Cover		3·75
		Presentation Pack	3·50	

Plate Nos.: 22p 1A, 1B (each ×5); 28p 1A, 1B, 1C, 1D (each ×5); 39p 1C, 1D (each ×5)

Sheets: 20 (4×5)

Imprint: Central, left-hand margin

Quantities sold: 22p 459,817; 28p 664,537; 39p 298,597

Withdrawn: 30.4.93

558 'Snow Leopards' (Allison Griffiths)

559 'Three Elements' (Nataly Miorin)

560 'Three Men in a Tub' (Amanda Crocker)

561 'Cockatoos' (Michelle Millard)

Batik Designs

(Litho Questa)

1992 (23 JUNE). *Perf* 14½ (C)

587	**558**	16p multicoloured	. . . .	50	50
588	**559**	22p multicoloured	. . . .	70	70
589	**560**	39p multicoloured	. . . .	1·25	1·25
590	**561**	57p multicoloured	. . . .	1·75	1·75
587/90		Set of 4	. . . .	3·75	3·75
		First Day Cover	. . . .		5·00
		Presentation Pack	. . . .	4·75	

Plate Nos.: 16p, 39p 1A, 1B (each ×4); 22p, 57p 1C, 1D (each ×4)

Sheets: 20 (5×4)

Imprint: Central, left-hand margin

Quantities sold: 16p 427,970; 22p 472,443; 39p 112,188; 57p 113,465

Withdrawn: 30.6.93

562 Morris Cowley 'Bullnose', 1925

563 Rolls Royce 20/25, 1932

564 Chenard and Walker T5, 1924

565 Packard 900 series Light Eight, 1932

566 Lanchester 21, 1927

567 Buick 30 Roadster, 1913

Vintage Cars (Second Series)

(Des A. Copp. Litho Enschedé)

1992 (8 SEPT). *Perf* 13×12½ (C)

591	**562**	16p multicoloured	. . . .	35	35
592	**563**	22p multicoloured	. . . .	50	50
593	**564**	28p multicoloured	. . . .	80	80
594	**565**	33p multicoloured	. . . .	90	90
595	**566**	39p multicoloured	. . . .	1·10	1·10
596	**567**	50p multicoloured	. . . .	1·50	1·50
591/6		Set of 6	. . . .	4·50	4·50
		First Day Cover	. . . .		5·75
		Presentation Pack	. . . .	5·75	

Plate Nos.: All values 1A, 1B (each ×4)

Sheets: 20 (4×5)

Imprint: Central, left-hand margin

Quantities sold: 16p 434,984; 22p 426,734; 28p 290,202; 33p 134,477; 39p 124,759; 50p 127,917

Withdrawn: 30.9.93

568 Trinity

569 St. Mary

570 St. Martin   **571** St. Peter

Christmas. Jersey Parish Churches (Third Series)

(Des P. Layton. Litho B.D.T.)

1992 (3 NOV). *Perf* 13½ (C)

597	**568**	16p multicoloured	40	35
598	**569**	22p multicoloured	55	60
599	**570**	39p multicoloured	1·00	1·00
600	**571**	57p multicoloured	1·40	1·40
597/600		*Set of 4*	3·00	3·00
		First Day Cover		4·25
		Presentation Pack	4·25	
		Postcards (set of 4)	2·00	5·25

Plate Nos.: All values 1A, 1B, 1C, 1D (each ×5)

Sheets: 20 (4×5)

Imprint: Central, left-hand margin

Quantities sold: 16p 894,098; 22p 729,413; 39p 93,764; 57p 95,936

Withdrawn: 30.11.93

Post Office Yearbook

1992 (3 NOV). *Comprises Nos.* 568/600

      Yearbook . . . .   32·00

Sold out: By 10.95

 572 Farmhouse

 573 Trinity Church

 574 Daffodils and Cows

 575 Jersey Cows

 576 Sunbathing

 577 Windsurfing

 578 Crab (Queen's head at left)

 579 Crab (Queen's head at right)

 580 'Singin' in the Rain' Float

 581 'Dragon Dance' Float

 582 'Bali, Morning of the World' Float

 583 'Zulu Fantasy' Float

Booklet Stamps

(Des A. Copp. Litho B.D.T.)

1993 (11 JAN). *Perf* 13 (C)

601	**572**	(–) multicoloured	40	45
		a. Booklet pane. Nos. 601/4, each ×2, with margins all round . .	3·25	
602	**573**	(–) multicoloured	40	45
603	**574**	(–) multicoloured	40	45
604	**575**	(–) multicoloured	40	45
605	**576**	(–) multicoloured	50	55
		a. Booklet pane. Nos. 605/8, each ×2, with margins all round . .	4·00	
606	**577**	(–) multicoloured	50	55
607	**578**	(–) multicoloured	50	55
608	**579**	(–) multicoloured	50	55
609	**580**	(–) multicoloured	60	65
		a. Booklet pane. Nos. 609/12, each ×2, with margins all round	5·00	
610	**581**	(–) multicoloured	60	65
611	**582**	(–) multicoloured	60	65
612	**583**	(–) multicoloured	60	65
601/12		*Set of 12*	5·75	6·25
		First Day Cover		6·00
		Presentation Pack.	6·50	

The above do not show face values, but are inscribed 'BAILIWICK POSTAGE PAID' (Nos. 601/4), 'U.K. MINIMUM POSTAGE PAID' (Nos. 605/8) or 'EUROPE POSTAGE PAID' (Nos. 609/12). They were initially sold at 17p, 23p or 28p, but Nos. 601/4 and 609/12 were increased to 18p and 30p on 10 January 1994 and Nos. 601/4 to 19p on 4 July 1995. On 10 March 1997 Nos. 601/4 were increased to 20p, Nos. 605/8 to 24p and Nos. 609/12 to 31p.

 **584** *Phragmipedium* Eric Young 'Jersey'

 **585** *Odontoglossum* Augres 'Trinity'

586 *Miltonia* St.
Helier
'Colomberie'

587 *Phragmipedium pearcei*

588 *Calanthe* Grouville 'Gorey'

Jersey Orchids (Third Series)

(Litho Enschedé)

1993 (26 JAN). *Perf* 14×13 (C)

613	**584**	17p multicoloured	....	50	35
		a. Black printed double	......		
614	**585**	23p multicoloured	....	75	45
		a. Black printed double	......		
615	**586**	28p multicoloured	....	90	65
		a. Black printed double	......		
616	**587**	39p multicoloured	....	1·25	1·25
617	**588**	57p multicoloured	....	1·75	1·75
		a. Black printed double	......		
613/17		Set of 5	....	4·50	4·00
		First Day Cover	....		4·50
		Presentation Pack	....	5·00	

Plate Nos.: 17p, 23p 1A, 1B, 1C (each ×5); 28p, 39p, 57p 1A, 1B (each ×5)

Sheets: 20 (5×4)

Imprint: Central, left-hand margin

Quantities sold: 17p 391,802; 23p 391,444; 28p 188,149; 39p 141,610; 57p 141,463

Withdrawn: 31.1.94

589 Douglas DC-3 Dakota

590 Wight Seaplane

591 Avro Shackleton
A.E.W.2

592 Gloster Meteor Mk III
and De Havilland
D.H.100 Vampire FB.5

593 Hawker Siddeley
Harrier GR.1A

594 Panavia Tornado F
Mk 3

75th Anniversary of Royal Air Force

(Des A. Theobald. Litho Questa)

1993 (1 APR). *Perf* 14 (C)

618	**589**	17p multicoloured	....	50	50
619	**590**	23p multicoloured	....	70	70
620	**591**	28p multicoloured	....	80	80
621	**592**	33p multicoloured	....	90	90
622	**593**	39p multicoloured	....	1·10	1·10
623	**594**	57p multicoloured	....	1·60	1·60
618/23		Set of 6	....	5·00	5·00
		First Day Cover	....		5·25
		Presentation Pack	....	5·50	
MS624	147×98 mm. Nos. 619 and 623....			3·50	3·50
		First Day Cover	....		4·50
		Presentation Pack	....	4·75	

Nos. 618/24 also commemorate the 50th anniversary of the Royal Air Force Association and the 40th anniversary of the first air display on Jersey.

Plate Nos.: 17p, 23p 1A, 1B, 1C, 1D (each ×4); 28p, 33p, 39p, 57p 1A, 1B (each ×4)

Sheets: 20 (5×4)

Imprint: Central, left-hand margin

Quantities sold: 17p 578,871; 23p 581,661; 28p 184,066; 33p 140,430; 39p 144,522; 57p 159,447; miniature sheet 113,236

Withdrawn: 30.4.94

595 'Jersey's Opera House' (Ian Rolls)

596 'The Ham and Tomato Bap' (Jonathan Hubbard)

597 'Vase of Flowers' (Neil MacKenzie)

Europa. Contemporary Art

(Litho Cartor)

1993 (1 APR). *Perf* 13½×14 (C)

625	**595**	23p multicoloured	70	70
626	**596**	28p multicoloured	85	85
627	**597**	39p multicoloured	1·25	1·25
625/7		*Set of 3*	2·50	2·50
		First Day Cover		3·00
		Presentation Pack	3·00	

Plate Nos.: All values 1A, 1B, 1C, 1D (each ×4)

Sheets: 20 (5×4)

Imprint: Central, left-hand margin

Quantities sold: 23p 422,536; 28p 340,206; 39p 230,510

Withdrawn: 30.4.94

598 1943 Occupation ½d Stamp

599 1943 1d Stamp

600 1943 1½d Stamp

601 1943 2d Stamp

602 1943 2½d Stamp

603 1943 3d Stamp

50th Anniversary of Edmund Blampied's Occupation Stamps

(Des G. Drummond. Litho Cartor)

1993 (2 JUNE). *Perf* 13½ (C)

628	**598**	17p myrtle-green, pale grn & blk	40	45
629	**599**	23p vermilion, salmon-pink & blk	55	55
630	**600**	28p chocolate, cinnamon & black	75	75
631	**601**	33p reddish orge, salmon & blk	90	90
632	**602**	39p royal blue, cobalt and black	1·25	1·25
633	**603**	50p bright magenta, pale mauve and black	1·40	1·40
628/33		*Set of 6*	4·75	4·75
		First Day Cover		5·25
		Presentation Pack	5·25	

Plate Nos.: All values 1A, 1B, 1C, 1D (each ×3)

Sheets: 20 (4×5)

Imprint: Central, left-hand margin

Quantities sold: 17p 549,708; 23p 565,711; 28p 174,159; 33p 120,570; 39p 93,502; 50p 99,135

Withdrawn: 30.6.94

604 Queen Elizabeth II (from painting by Marca McGregor)

40th Anniversary of Coronation

(Litho Questa)

1993 (2 JUNE). *Perf* 14½ (C)

634	**604**	£1 multicoloured (*ab*)	. . . .	2·00	2·10
		First Day Cover			3·50
		Presentation Pack			3·50

No. 634 was retained in use as part of the current definitive series.

Printings: (*a*) 2.6.93; (*b*) 1.9.95

Plate Nos.: 1A, 1B, 1C, 1D (each ×4)

Sheets: 20 (5×4)

Imprint: Central, left-hand margin

605 Short-toed Treecreeper

606 Dartford Warbler

607 Common Wheatear

608 Cirl Bunting

609 Jay

Summer Birds

(Des W. Oliver. Litho Cartor)

1993 (7 SEPT). *Perf* 13½×14 (C)

635	**605**	17p multicoloured	. . . .	50	50
636	**606**	23p multicoloured	. . . .	75	75
637	**607**	28p multicoloured	. . . .	85	85
638	**608**	39p multicoloured	. . . .	1·25	1·25
639	**609**	57p multicoloured	. . . .	1·75	1·75
635/9		*Set of 5*	. . . .	4·50	4·50
		First Day Cover			4·50
		Presentation Pack		5·00	

Plate Nos.: All values 1A, 1B, 1C, 1D (each ×4)

Sheets: 20 (5×4)

Imprint: Central, left-hand margin

Quantities sold: 17p 495,975; 23p 496,942; 28p 170,135; 39p 139,630; 57p 138,994

Withdrawn: 30.9.94

610 Two Angels holding 'Hark the Herald Angels Sing' Banner

611 Two Angels playing Harps

612 Two Angels playing Violins

613 Two Angels holding 'Once in Royal David's City' Banner

Christmas. Stained Glass Windows by Henry Bosdet from St. Aubin on the Hill Church

(Des N. MacKenzie. Litho Enschedé)

1993 (2 NOV). *Perf* 14×13 (C)

640	**610**	17p multicoloured	. . . .	45	45
641	**611**	23p multicoloured	. . . .	65	65

642	**612**	39p multicoloured	. . . .	1·25	1·25
643	**613**	57p multicoloured	. . . .	1·90	1·90
640/3		Set of 4	. . . .	3·75	3·75
		First Day Cover	. . . .		4·50
		Presentation Pack	. . . .	4·50	

Plate Nos.: All values 1A, 1B, 1C (each ×4)

Sheets: 20 (5×4)

Imprint: Central, left-hand margin

Quantities sold: 17p 877,806; 23p 744,661; 39p 110,131; 57p 108,703

Withdrawn: 30.11.94

Post Office Yearbook

1993 (2 NOV). *Comprises Nos.* 601/43

| | Yearbook | . . . . | 33·00 |

Sold out: By 9.97

614 *Coprinus comatus*

615 *Amanita muscaria*

616 *Cantharellus cibarius*

617 *Macrolepiota procera*

618 *Clathrus ruber*

Fungi

(Des W. Oliver. Litho Questa)

1994 (11 JAN). *Perf* 14½ (C)

644	**614**	18p multicoloured	. . . .	45	45
645	**615**	23p multicoloured	. . . .	70	70
646	**616**	30p multicoloured	. . . .	90	90
647	**617**	41p multicoloured	. . . .	1·25	1·25
648	**618**	60p multicoloured	. . . .	1·75	1·75
644/8		Set of 5	. . . .	4·50	4·50
		First Day Cover	. . . .		4·75
		Presentation Pack	. . . .	5·00	

Plate Nos.: 18p 1A (×4); 23p 1B (×4); 30p 1C (×4); 41p 1D (×4); 60p 1E (×4)

Sheets: 20 (5×4)

Imprint: Central, left-hand margin

Quantities sold: 18p 735,158; 23p 482,461; 30p 188,095; 41p 184,418; 60p 137,309

Withdrawn: 30.1.95

619a Pekingese (*illustration reduced. Actual size* 110×75 mm)

'Hong Kong '94' International Stamp Exhibition. 'Chinese Year of the Dog'

(Des P. Layton, adapted A. Copp. Litho Questa)

1994 (18 FEB). *Sheet* 110×75 mm. *Perf* 15×14½ (C)

MS649	**619**a	£1 multicoloured	. . . .	3·00	3·00
		First Day Cover	. . . .		3·75
		Presentation Pack	. . . .	3·75	

Quantity sold: 120,029

Withdrawn: 28.2.95

620 Maine Coon

621 British Shorthair

622 Persian

623 Siamese

624 Non-pedigree

627 Chambered Passage, La Hougue Bie

628 Transporting Stones

Europa. Archaeological Discoveries

(Des A. Copp. Litho Enschedé)

1994 (5 APR). *Perf* 13½×14 (C)

655	**625**	23p multicoloured	. . . .	50	50
		a. Horiz pair. Nos. 655/6	. . . .	1·00	1·00
656	**626**	23p multicoloured	. . . .	50	50
657	**627**	30p multicoloured	. . . .	75	75
		a. Horiz pair. Nos. 657/8	. . . .	1·50	1·50
658	**628**	30p multicoloured	. . . .	75	75
655/8		*Set of* 4	. . . .	2·25	2·25
		First Day Cover			3·25
		Presenation Pack	3·25		

Plate Nos.: Both values 1A, 1B (each ×4)

Sheets: 20 (4×5) the two horizontal designs for each value printed together, *se-tenant*, in horizontal pairs throughout the sheets

Imprint: Central, left-hand margin

Quantities sold: 23p (both designs) 744,339; 30p (both designs) 549,722

Withdrawn: 29.4.95

21st Anniversary of Jersey Cat Club

(Des P. Layton. Litho B.D.T)

1994 (5 APR). *Perf* 14 (C)

650	**620**	18p multicoloured	. . . .	45	45
651	**621**	23p multicoloured	. . . .	70	60
652	**622**	35p multicoloured	. . . .	90	80
653	**623**	41p multicoloured	. . . .	1·25	1·10
654	**624**	60p multicoloured	. . . .	1·75	1·75
650/4		*Set of* 5	. . . .	4·50	4·25
		First Day Cover			5·00
		Presentation Pack	5·00		

Plate Nos.: 35p 1A, 1B, 1C, 1D (each ×4); others 1A, 1B (each ×4)

Sheets: 20 (5×4) 18p, 35p, 60p; (4×5) 23p, 41p

Imprint: Central, left-hand margin

Quantities sold: 18p 491,500; 23p 490,820; 35p 221,769; 41p 185,206; 60p 132,276

Withdrawn: 29.4.95

629 Gliders and Towing Aircraft approaching France

630 Landing Craft approaching Beaches

625 Mammoth Hunt, La Cotte de St. Brelade

626 Stone Age Hunters pulling Mammoth into Cave

631 Disembarking from Landing Craft on Gold Beach

632 British Troops on Sword Beach

231

633 Spitfires over Beaches **634** Invasion Map

50th Anniversary of D-Day

(Des A. Theobald. Litho B.D.T.)

1994 (6 JUNE). *Perf* 13½×14 (C)

659	**629**	18p multicoloured	60	50
		a. Booklet pane. Nos. 659/60, each ×3, with margins all round	2·75	
		b. Booklet pane. Nos. 659/64, with margins all round	6·00	
660	**630**	18p multicoloured	60	50
661	**631**	23p multicoloured	80	70
		a. Booklet pane. Nos. 661/2, each ×3, with margins all round	5·50	
662	**632**	23p multicoloured	80	70
663	**633**	30p multicoloured	90	80
		a. Booklet pane. Nos. 663/4, each ×3, with margins all round	6·00	
664	**634**	30p multicoloured	90	80
659/64		Set of 6	4·00	3·50
		First Day Cover	4·50	
		Presentation Pack	4·50	

No. 659*b* was also available as a loose pane from the Philatelic Bureau.

Plate Nos.: All values 1A, 1B (each ×4)

Sheets: 20 (4×5)

Imprint: Central, left-hand margin

Quantities sold: No. 659, 361,667; No. 660, 365,169; No. 661, 377,546; No. 662, 367,033; No. 663, 229,455; No. 664, 226,520

Withdrawn: 30.6.95

635 Sailing **636** Rifle Shooting

637 Hurdling **638** Swimming

639 Hockey

Centenary of International Olympic Committee

(Des A. Theobald. Litho Questa)

1994 (6 JUNE). *Perf* 14 (C)

665	**635**	18p multicoloured	45	45
666	**636**	23p multicoloured	60	60
667	**637**	30p multicoloured	85	85
668	**638**	41p multicoloured	1·10	1·10
669	**639**	60p multicoloured	1·50	1·50
665/9		Set of 5	4·00	4·00
		First Day Cover		4·75
		Presentation Pack	4·75	

Plate Nos.: All values 1A (×4)

Sheets: 20 (5×4)

Imprint: Central, left-hand margin

Quantities sold: 18p 279,163; 23p 276,438; 30p 178,234; 41p 183,875; 60p 133,357

Withdrawn: 30.6.95

640 Strawberry Anemone **641** Hermit Crab and Parasitic Anemone

642 Velvet Swimming Crab **643** Common Jellyfish

Marine Life

(Des W. Oliver. Litho Cartor)

1994 (2 AUG). *Perf* 13½ (C)

670	**640**	18p multicoloured	45	45
671	**641**	23p multicoloured	60	60

672 **642** 41p multicoloured .... 1·25 1·25
673 **643** 60p multicoloured .... 1·60 1·60
670/3   *Set of* 4 .... 3·50 3·50
    First Day Cover .... 4·75
    Presentation Pack .... 4·75

Plate Nos.: All values 1A, 1B, 1C, 1D (each ×4)

Sheets: 20 (4×5)

Imprint: Central, left-hand margin

Quantities sold: 18p 465,890; 23p 453,750; 41p 171,459; 60p 175,656

Withdrawn: 31.8.95

644 Condor 10 Wavepiercer Catamaran

645 Map of Jersey and Pillar Box

646 Vicker's Type 953 Vanguard of B.E.A.

647 Shorts 360 of Aurigny Air Services

648 *Caesarea* (Sealink ferry)

25th Anniversary of Jersey Postal Administration

(Des A. Copp. Litho Questa)

1994 (1 OCT). *Perf* 14 (C)
674 **644** 18p multicoloured 45 45
675 **645** 23p multicoloured 60 60
676 **646** 35p multicoloured 85 75
677 **647** 41p multicoloured .... 1·10 1·00
678 **648** 60p multicoloured .... 1·50 1·40
674/8   *Set of* 5 .... 4·00 3·75
    First Day Cover .... 5·00
    Presentation Pack .... 5·00
MS679 150×100 mm. Nos. 674/8 .... 3·75 3·75
    First Day Cover .... 5·00
    Presentation Pack .... 5·00

Plate Nos.: All values 1A (×5)

Sheets: 20 (5×4)

Imprint: Central, left-hand margin

Quantities sold: 18p 473,837; 23p 472,468; 35p 184,871; 41p 186,653; 60p 182,108; miniature sheet 76,623

Withdrawn: 31.10.95

649 'Away in a Manger'

650 'Hark! the Herald Angels Sing'

651 'While Shepherds watched'

652 'We Three Kings of Orient Are'

Christmas. Carols

(Des A. Copp. Litho Questa)

1994 (8 NOV). *Perf* 14 (C)
680 **649** 18p multicoloured 45 45
681 **650** 23p multicoloured 60 60
682 **651** 41p multicoloured .... 1·25 1·25
683 **652** 60p multicoloured .... 1·60 1·60
680/3   *Set of* 4 .... 3·50 3·50
    First Day Cover .... 4·75
    Presentation Pack .... 4·75

Plate Nos.: All values 1A, 1B (each ×4)

Sheets: 20 (5×4)

Imprint: Central, left-hand margin

Quantities sold: 18p 981,010; 23p 883,715; 41p 174,413; 60p 179,888

Withdrawn: 30.11.95

Post Office Yearbook

1994 (8 NOV). *Comprises Nos.* **MS**248 *and* 644/83
    Yearbook .... 37·00

653 Dog and 'GOOD LUCK'

654 Rose and 'WITH LOVE'

655 Chick and 'CONGRAT-ULATIONS'

656 Bouquet of Flowers and 'THANK YOU'

657 Dove with Letter and 'WITH LOVE'

658 Cat and 'GOOD LUCK'

659 Carnations and 'THANK YOU'

660 Parrot and 'CONGRATU-LATIONS'

661 Pig and 'HAPPY NEW YEAR'

Greetings Stamps

(Des A. Copp. Litho B.D.T.)

1995 (24 JAN). *Perf* 13 (C)

684	**653**	18p multicoloured	35	40
		a. Horiz strip of 4. Nos. 684/7	1·40	
		b. Booklet pane of 9. Nos. 684/92	4·50	
685	**654**	18p multicoloured	35	40
686	**655**	18p multicoloured	35	40
687	**656**	18p multicoloured	35	40
688	**657**	23p multicoloured	45	50
		a. Horiz strip of 4. Nos. 688/91	1·75	
689	**658**	23p multicoloured	45	50
690	**659**	23p multicoloured	45	50
691	**660**	23p multicoloured	45	50
692	**661**	60p multicoloured	1·25	1·40
684/92		*Set of 9*	4·00	4·50
		First Day Cover (Nos. 684/91)		5·25
		First Day Cover (No. 692)		1·90
		Presentation Pack	5·25	

No. 692 commemorates the Chinese New Year of the Pig.

Plate Nos.: All values 1A, 1B, 1C, 1D (each ×4)

Sheets: 60p 10 (5×2); others 20 (4×5) the four designs for each value printed together, *se-tenant*, in horizontal strips of 4 throughout the sheets

Imprint: Central, left-hand margin

Withdrawn: 31.1.96 (sheets)

662 'Captain Rawes'

663 'Brigadoon'

664 'Elsie Jury'

665 'Augusto L'Gouveia Pinto'

666 'Bella Romana'

Camellias

(Des and litho Questa)

1995 (21 MAR). *Perf* 14½ (C)

693	**662**	18p multicoloured	55	50
694	**663**	23p multicoloured	70	70
695	**664**	30p multicoloured	80	80
696	**665**	35p multicoloured	85	85
697	**666**	41p multicoloured	1·00	1·00
693/7		*Set of 5*	3·50	3·50
		First Day Cover		4·00
		Presentation Pack	4·00	

Plate Nos.: All values 1A (×5)

Sheets: 20 (5×4)

Imprint: Central, left-hand margin

Withdrawn: 31.3.96

667 'Liberation' (sculpture, Philip Jackson)

Europa. Peace and Freedom

(Des A. Theobald. Litho Cartor)

1995 (9 MAY). *Perf* 13½ (C)

698	**667**	23p black and dull violet-blue ..	55	55
699		30p black and rose-pink	70	75
698/9		*Set of* 2	1·25	1·25
		First Day Cover		2·00
		Presentation Pack	2·00	

Plate Nos.: Both values 1A, 1B, 1C (each ×4)

Sheets: 10 (5×2)

Imprint: Bottom margin

Withdrawn: 31.5.96

668 Bailiff and Crown Officers in Launch

669 *Vega* (Red Cross supply ship)

670 H.M.S. *Beagle* (destroyer)

671 British Troops in Ordnance Yard, St. Helier

672 King George VI and Queen Elizabeth in Jersey

673 Unloading Supplies from Landing Craft, St. Aubin's

674a Royal Family with Winston Churchill on Buckingham Palace Balcony, V.E. Day (*illustration reduced. Actual size* 110×75 *mm*)

50th Anniversary of Liberation

(Des A. Theobald. Litho B.D.T.)

1995 (9 MAY). *Perf* 15×14 (C)

700	**668**	18p multicoloured	40	40
		a. Booklet pane. Nos. 700/1, each ×3, with margins all round	2·00	
701	**669**	18p multicoloured	40	40
702	**670**	23p multicoloured	60	60
		a. Booklet pane. Nos. 702/3, each ×3, with margins all round	2·75	
703	**671**	23p multicoloured	60	60
704	**672**	60p multicoloured	1·50	1·50
		a. Booklet pane. Nos. 704/5, each ×3, with margins all round	7·50	
705	**673**	60p multicoloured	1·50	1·50
700/5		*Set of* 6	4·50	4·50
		First Day Cover		5·00
		Presentation Pack	5·00	
MS706		110×75 mm. **674a** £1 multicoloured	2·50	2·50
		a. Booklet pane. As No. **MS**706 with additional margins all round showing arms, mace and inscriptions	2·50	
		First Day Cover		3·00
		Presentation Pack	3·00	

Plate Nos.: All values 1A, 1B (each ×4)

Sheets: 20 (4×5)

Imprint: Central, left-hand margin

Withdrawn: 31.5.96 (sheets)

675 Bell Heather

676 Sea Campion

677 Spotted Rock-rose

678 Thrift

679 Sheep's-bit Scabious

680 Field Bind-weed

681 Common Bird's-foot Trefoil

682 Sea-holly

683 Common Centaury

684 Dwarf Pansy

European Nature Conservation Year. Wild Flowers

(Des N. Parlett. Litho B.D.T.)

1995 (4 JULY). *Perf* 13 (C)

707	**675**	19p multicoloured	45	45
		a. Horiz strip of 5. Nos. 707/11	2·25	
708	**676**	19p multicoloured	45	45
709	**677**	19p multicoloured	45	45
710	**678**	19p multicoloured	45	45
711	**679**	19p multicoloured	45	45
712	**680**	23p multicoloured	50	50
		a. Horiz strip of 5. Nos. 712/16	2·50	
713	**681**	23p multicoloured	50	50
714	**682**	23p multicoloured	50	50
715	**683**	23p multicoloured	50	50
716	**684**	23p multicoloured	50	50
707/16		Set of 10	4·75	4·75
		First Day Cover		5·25
		Presentation Pack	5·00	

Plate Nos.: Both values 1A, 1B (each ×4)

Sheets: 20 (5×4) the five designs for each value printed together, *se-tenant*, in horizontal strips of 5 throughout the sheets, the backgrounds forming composite designs

Imprint: Central, left-hand margin

Withdrawn: 31.7.96

685 *Precis almana*

686 *Papilio palinurus*

687 *Catopsilia scylla*

688 *Papilio rumanzovia*

689 *Troides helena*

Butterflies

(Des W. Oliver. Litho Questa)

1995 (1 SEPT). *Perf* 14 (C)

717	**685**	19p multicoloured	45	45
718	**686**	23p multicoloured	60	60
719	**687**	30p multicoloured	75	75
720	**688**	41p multicoloured	1·00	1·00
721	**689**	60p multicoloured	1·60	1·60
717/21		Set of 5	4·00	4·00
		First Day Cover		4·50
		Presentation Pack	4·50	
MS722		150×100 mm. Nos. 720/1	2·50	2·50
		a. 41p value imperforate		
		First Day Cover		3·00
		Presentation Pack	3·00	

No. **MS**722 includes the "Singapore '95" International Stamp Exhibition logo on the sheet margin and shows the two stamp designs without frames.

Plate Nos.: All values 1A (×4)

Sheets: 20 (5×4)

Imprint: Central, left-hand margin

Withdrawn: 30.9.96

690 Peace Doves and
United Nations
Anniversary Emblem

691 Symbolic Wheat and
Anniversary Emblem

50th Anniversary of United Nations

(Des A. Copp. Litho Enschedé)

1995 (24 OCT). *Perf* 13×14½ (C)

723	**690**	19p cobalt and royal blue	45	45
724	**691**	23p turq-green & dp blue-green	50	50
725		41p dp blue-green & turq-green	85	85
726	**690**	60p royal blue and cobalt	1·40	1·40
723/6		*Set of 4*	3·00	3·00
		First Day Cover		3·50
		Presentation Pack	3·50	

Plate Nos.: 19p, 23p 1A, 1B (each ×2); others 1A (×2)
Sheets: 20 (5×4)
Imprint: Central, left-hand margin
Withdrawn: 31.10 96

692 'Puss in Boots'

693 'Cinderella'

694 'Sleeping Beauty'

695 'Aladdin'

Christmas. Pantomimes

(Des V. Ambrus. Litho Cartor)

1995 (24 OCT). *Perf* 13½ (C)

727	**692**	19p multicoloured	. . . .	45	45
728	**693**	23p multicoloured	. . . .	50	50
729	**694**	41p multicoloured	. . . .	85	85
730	**695**	60p multicoloured	. . . .	1·40	1·40
727/30		*Set of 4*	3·25	3·25
		First Day Cover		3·50
		Presentation Pack	3·50	

Plate Nos.: All values 1A, 1B, 1C, 1D (each ×4)
Sheets: 20 (5×4)
Imprint: Central, left-hand margin
Withdrawn: 31.10.96

Post Office Yearbook

1995 (24 OCT). *Comprises Nos.* 491c *and* 684/730
Yearbook . . . . 40·00

696a Rat with Top Hat
(*illustration reduced. Actual size* 110×75 *mm*)

Chinese New Year ('Year of the Rat')

(Des V. Ambrus. Litho Questa)

1996 (19 FEB). *Sheet* 110×75 *mm. Perf* 13½×14 (C)

MS731	**696**a	£1 multicoloured	2·50	2·50
		First Day Cover		2·75
		Presentation Pack	2·75	

Withdrawn: 28.2.97

697 African Child and Map

698 Children and Globe

699 European Child and
Map

700 South American Child
and Map

701 Asian Child and Map

702 South Pacific Child and Map

704 Elizabeth Garrett (first British woman doctor)

705 Emmeline Pankhurst (suffragette)

50th Anniversary of U.N.I.C.E.F.

(Des A. Copp. Litho Questa)

1996 (19 FEB). *Perf* 14½ (C)

732	**697**	19p multicoloured	. . . .	50	50
733	**698**	23p multicoloured	. . . .	60	60
734	**699**	30p multicoloured	. . . .	80	80
735	**700**	35p multicoloured	. . . .	95	95
736	**701**	41p multicoloured	. . . .	1·10	1·10
737	**702**	60p multicoloured	. . . .	1·60	1·60
732/7		*Set of* 6	. . . .	5·00	5·00
		First Day Cover	. . . .		5·25
		Presentation Pack	. . . .	5·00	

Plate Nos.: All values 1A (×4)

Sheets: 20 (4×5)

Imprint: Central, left-hand margin

Withdrawn: 28.2.97

Europa. Famous Women

(Des Jennifer Toombs. Litho B.D.T.)

1996 (25 APR). *Perf* 13½×14 (C)

739	**704**	23p multicoloured	. . . .	60	60
740	**705**	30p multicoloured	. . . .	80	80
739/40		*Set of* 2	. . . .	1·40	1·40
		First Day Cover	. . . .		1·75
		Presentation Pack	. . . . . .	1·75	

Plate Nos.: 23p 1A, 1B, 1C (each ×4); 30p 1A, 1B, 1C, 1D, 1E (each ×4)

Sheets: 10 (5×2)

Imprint: Bottom margin

Withdrawn: 30.4.97

706 Player shooting at Goal

707 Two Players chasing Ball

703 Queen Elizabeth II (from photo by T. O'Neill)

70th Birthday of Queen Elizabeth II

(Litho Questa)

1996 (21 APR). *Perf* 14×15 (C)

738	**703**	£5 multicoloured	. . . .	10·00	10·50
		First Day Cover	. . . .		11·00
		Presentation Pack	. . . .	11·00	

No. 738 will be retained as part of the current definitive series.

Plate Nos.: 1A (×5)

Sheets: 10 (2×5)

Imprint: Central, left-hand margin

708 Player avoiding Tackle

709 Two Players competing for Ball

710 Players heading Ball

European Football Championship, England

(Des A. Theobald. Litho B.D.T.)

1996 (25 APR). *Perf* 13½×14 (C)

741	**706**	19p multicoloured	. . . .	50	50
742	**707**	23p multicoloured	. . . .	70	70
743	**708**	35p multicoloured	. . . .	95	95
744	**709**	41p multicoloured	. . . .	1·10	1·10
745	**710**	60p multicoloured	. . . .	1·75	1·75
741/5		*Set of* 5	. . . .	4·50	4·50
		First Day Cover	. . . .		4·75
		Presentation Pack	. . . .	4·75	

Plate Nos.: 19p, 23p 1A, 1B (each ×4); others 1A (×4)

Sheets: 20 (5×4)

Imprint: Central, left-hand margin

Withdrawn: 30.4.97

711 Rowing

712 Judo

713 Fencing

714 Boxing

715 Basketball

716a Olympic Torch and Stadium
(*illustration reduced. Actual size* 150×100 *mm*)

Sporting Anniversaries

(Des A. Theobald. Litho Questa)

1996 (8 JUNE). *Perf* 13½ (*No.* **MS**751) *or* 14 (*others*), *both comb*

746	**711**	19p multicoloured	. . . .	50	50
747	**712**	23p multicoloured	. . . .	70	70
748	**713**	35p multicoloured	. . . .	95	95
749	**714**	41p multicoloured	. . . .	1·10	1·10
750	**715**	60p multicoloured	. . . .	1·75	1·75
746/50		*Set of* 5	. . . .	4·50	4·50
		First Day Cover	. . . .		4·75
		Presentation Pack	. . . .	4·75	
MS751		150×100 mm. **716***a* £1 mult. . . .		2·50	2·50
		First Day Cover	. . . .		2·75
		Presentation Pack	. . . .	2·75	

Anniversaries:—Nos. 746/8, 750/1, Centenary of Modern Olympic Games; No. 749, 50th anniversary of International Amateur Boxing Association.

No. **MS**751 also includes the "CAPEX '96" International Stamp Exhibition logo.

Plate Nos.: All values 1A (×4)

Sheets: 20 (5×4)

Imprint: Central, left-hand margin

Withdrawn: 30.6.97

717 Bay on North Coast

718 Portelet Bay

719 Greve de Lecq Bay

720 Beauport Beach

721 Plemont Bay

722 St. Brelade's Bay

Tourism. Beaches

(Des A. Copp. Litho B.D.T.)

1996 (8 JUNE). *Perf* 14 (C)

752	**717**	19p multicoloured	....	50	50
		a. Booklet pane. Nos. 752/3, each ×3, with margins all round	....	2·50	
		b. Booklet pane. Nos. 752/7, with margins all round	....	4·25	
753	**718**	23p multicoloured	....	60	60
754	**719**	30p multicoloured	....	80	80
		a. Booklet pane. Nos. 754/5, each ×3, with margins all round	....	4·00	
755	**720**	35p multicoloured	....	95	95
756	**721**	41p multicoloured	....	1·10	1·10
		a. Booklet pane. Nos. 756/7, each ×3, with margins all round	....	6·00	
757	**722**	60p multicoloured	....	1·60	1·60
752/7		Set of 6	....	5·00	5·00
		First Day Cover	....		5·25
		Presentation Pack	....	5·25	
		Postcards (set of 6)	......	2·40	7·50

Plate Nos.: 19p, 23p 1A, 1B (each ×4); others 1A (×4)
Sheets: 20 (5×4)
Imprint: Central, left-hand margin
Withdrawn: 30.6.97 (sheets)

723 Drag Hunt

724 Pony and Trap

725 Training Racehorses on Beach

726 Show-jumping

727 Pony Club Event

728 Shire Mare and Foal

Horses

(Des P. Layton. Litho Enschedé)

1996 (13 SEPT). *Perf* 13½×14 (C)

758	**723**	19p multicoloured	....	40	45
759	**724**	23p multicoloured	....	45	50
760	**725**	30p multicoloured	....	60	65
761	**726**	35p multicoloured	....	70	75
762	**727**	41p multicoloured	....	80	85
763	**728**	60p multicoloured	....	1·25	1·40
758/63		Set of 6	....	3·75	4·25
		First Day Cover	....		5·00
		Presentation Pack	....	5·00	
		Postcards (set of 6)	......	2·40	7·50

Plate Nos.: All values 1A, 1B (each ×4)
Sheets: 20 (4×5)
Imprint: Central, left-hand margin
Withdrawn: 30.9.97

729 The Journey to Bethlehem

730 The Shepherds

731 The Nativity

732 The Three Kings

Christmas

(Des V. Ambrus. Litho Cartor)

1996 (12 NOV). *Perf* 13×13½ (C)

764	**729**	19p multicoloured	....	40	45
765	**730**	23p multicoloured	....	45	50
766	**731**	30p multicoloured	....	60	65
767	**732**	60p multicoloured	....	1·40	1·40
764/7		Set of 4	....	2·50	3·00
		First Day Cover	....		3·50
		Presentation Pack	....	3·50	

Plate Nos.: All values 1A, 1B, 1C (each ×4)
Sheets: 20 (4×5)
Imprint: Central, left-hand margin
Withdrawn: 28.11.97

Post Office Yearbook

1996 (12 NOV). *Comprises Nos.* **MS**731/63
          Yearbook . . . . 35·00

733*a* Jersey Cow wearing Scarf
  (*illustration reduced. Actual size* 110×75 *mm*)

Chinese New Year (*'Year of the Ox'*)

(Des V. Ambrus. Litho Questa)

1997 (7 FEB). *Sheet* 110×74 *mm. Perf* 14×13½ (C)
MS768 **733***a* £1 multicoloured . . . . 2·00   2·10
           First Day Cover. . . . .   2·50
           Presentation Pack . . . . 2·75

'HONG KONG '97' International Stamp Exhibition

1997 (7 FEB). *No.* **MS**768 *optd with exhibition emblem in black and* 'JERSEY AT HONG KONG '97' *in red, both on sheet margin*
MS769 **733***a* £1 multicoloured . . . . 2·00   2·10
           First Day Cover. . . . .   2·50
           Presentation Pack . . . . 2·75

734 Lillie the Cow on the
     Beach

735 Lillie taking
     Photograph

736 Carrying Bucket and
     Spade

737 Eating Meal at Mont
     Orgueil

Tourism. *'Lillie the Cow'*

(Des A. Copp. Litho B.D.T.)

1997 (12 FEB). *Self-adhesive. Perf* 9½ (C)
770	**734**	(23p) multicoloured	. . . .	50	55
771	**735**	(23p) multicoloured	. . . .	50	55
772	**736**	(23p) multicoloured	. . . .	50	55
773	**737**	(23p) multicoloured	. . . .	50	55
770/3		*Set of* 4	. . . .	2·00	2·10
		First Day Cover	. . . .		2·40
		Presentation Pack	. . . . . .	2·75	

Nos. 770/3, which are inscribed 'UK MINIMUM POSTAGE PAID', come, *se-tenant*, in strips of 4 or rolls of 100 with the surplus self-adhesive paper around each stamp removed. Nos. 770/3 were initially sold at 23p each: this was increased to 24p on 10 March 1997.

738 Red-breasted
     Merganser

739 Common Tern

740 Black-headed Gull

741 Dunlin

742 Puffin

743 Oystercatcher

744 Redshank

745 Shag

241

Seabirds and Waders

(Des N. Parlett. Litho Questa)

1997 (12 FEB). *Perf* 14½ (C)

774	**738**	1p multicoloured	....	10	10
775	**739**	10p multicoloured	....	20	25
776	**740**	15p multicoloured	....	30	35
777	**741**	20p multicoloured	....	40	45
778	**742**	24p multicoloured	....	45	50
779	**743**	37p multicoloured	....	75	80
780	**744**	75p multicoloured	....	1·50	1·60
781	**745**	£2 multicoloured	....	4·00	4·25
774/81		Set of 8	....	7·50	8·00
		First Day Cover	....		8·25
		Presentation Pack	....	8·50	
		Postcards (set of 8)	......	3·25	11·00
MS782		136×130 mm. Nos. 774/81	......	7·50	8·00
		Souvenir Folder	....	9·50	

Plate Nos.: 1p, 20p, 24p, £2 1A, 1B, 1C, 1D (each ×4); 10p, 15p, 37p, 75p 1A, 1B (each ×4); MS782 1A (×4)

Sheets: 20 (4×5)

Imprint: Central, left-hand margin

762 De Havilland D.H.95 Flamingo

763 Handley Page H.P.R. Marathon

764 De Havilland D.H.114 Heron

765 Boeing 737-236

766 Britten Norman Trislander

767 BAe 146-200

60th Anniversary of Jersey Airport

(Des A. Theobald. Litho Enschedé)

1997 (10 MAR). *Perf* 13½×14 (C)

801	**762**	20p multicoloured	....	40	45
802	**763**	24p multicoloured	....	50	55
803	**764**	31p multicoloured	....	60	65
804	**765**	37p multicoloured	....	75	80
805	**766**	43p multicoloured	....	85	90
806	**767**	63p multicoloured	....	1·25	1·40
801/6		Set of 6	....	4·25	4·75
		First Day Cover	....		5·00
		Presentation Pack	....	5·00	

Plate Nos.: All values 1A, 1B, 1C (each ×4)

Sheets: 20 (4×5)

Imprint: Central, left-hand margin

768 The Bull of St. Clement

769 The Black Horse of St. Ouen

770 The Black Dog of Bouley Bay

771 Les Fontaines des Mittes

Europa. Tales and Legends

(Des Jennifer Toombs. Litho B.D.T.)

1997 (15 APR). *Perf* 15×14 (C)

807	**768**	20p multicoloured	....	40	45
808	**769**	24p multicoloured	....	50	55
809	**770**	31p multicoloured	....	60	65
810	**771**	63p multicoloured	....	1·25	1·40
807/10		Set of 4	....	2·75	3·00
		First Day Cover	....		3·50
		Presentation Pack	....	3·50	

Nos. 808/9 include the 'EUROPA' emblem.

Plate Nos.: All values 1A, 1B (each ×5)

Sheets: 10 (5×2)

Imprint: Bottom margin

'Pacific '97' International Stamp Exhibition, San Francisco

1997 (29 MAY). *No.* **MS**782 *optd with exhibition emblem on sheet margin.*
MS811 136×130 mm. Nos. 774/81 ...... 7·50 8·00
Souvenir Folder .... 9·50

772 Cycling

773 Archery

774 Windsurfing

775 Gymnastics

776 Volleyball

777 Running

7th Island Games, Jersey

(Des A. Theobald. Litho B.D.T.)

1997 (28 JUNE). *Perf* 13½ (C)
812 **772** 20p multicoloured 40 45
  *a. Booklet pane. Nos. 812/13,
  each × 3, with margins all
  round* .... 2·50
  *b. Booklet pane. Nos. 812/17,
  with margins all round* .... 4·25
813 **773** 24p multicoloured 50 55
814 **774** 31p multicoloured 60 65
  *a. Booklet pane. Nos. 814/15,
  each × 3, with margins all
  round* .... 4·00
815 **775** 37p multicoloured 75 80

816 **776** 43p multicoloured 85 90
  *a. Booklet pane. Nos. 816/17,
  each × 3, with margins all
  round* .... 6·25
817 **777** 63p multicoloured .... 1·25 1·40
812/17   *Set of 6* .... 4·25 4·75
  First Day Cover .... 5·00
  Presentation Pack .... 5·00

Plate Nos.: 20p, 24p 1A, 1B (each ×4); others 1A (×4)
Sheets: 20 (5×4)
Imprint: Central, left-hand margin

778 Mallorcan Midwife Toad

779 Aye-Aye

780 Echo Parakeet

781 Pigmy Hog

782 St. Lucia Whip-tail

783 Madagascar Teal

Wildlife Preservation Trust (Sixth Series)

(Des W. Oliver. Litho Cartor)

1997 (2 SEPT). *Perf* 13 (C)
818 **778** 20p multicoloured 40 45
819 **779** 24p multicoloured 50 55
820 **780** 31p multicoloured 60 65
821 **781** 37p multicoloured 75 80
822 **782** 43p multicoloured 85 90
823 **783** 63p multicoloured .... 1·25 1·40
818/23   *Set of 6* .... 4·25 4·75
  First Day Cover .... 5·00
  Presentation Pack .... 5·00

Plate Nos.: All values 1A, 1B (each ×4)
Sheets: 20 (5×4)
Imprint: Central, left-hand margin

784 Ash

785 Elder

786 Beech

787 Sweet Chestnut

788 Hawthorn

789 Common Oak

Trees

(Des Norah Bryan. Litho Questa)

1997 (2 SEPT). *Perf* 14½ (C)

824	**784**	20p multicoloured	....	40	45
825	**785**	24p multicoloured	....	50	55
826	**786**	31p multicoloured		60	65
827	**787**	37p multicoloured	....	75	80
828	**788**	43p multicoloured		85	90
829	**789**	63p multicoloured	....	1·25	1·40
824/9		Set of 6	....	4·25	4·75
		First Day Cover	....		5·00
		Presentation Pack	....	5·00	

Plate Nos.: 20p, 24p 1A, 1B (each ×4); others 1A (×4)
Sheets: 20 (5×4)
Imprint: Central, left-hand margin

790 Father Christmas and
Reindeer outside
Jersey Airport

791 Father Christmas with
Presents, St. Aubin's
Harbour

792 Father Christmas in
Sleigh, Mont Orgueil
Castle

793 Father Christmas with
Children, Royal Square,
St. Helier

Christmas

(Des Colleen Corlett. Litho B.D.T.)

1997 (11 NOV). *Perf* 14 (C)

830	**790**	20p multicoloured	....	40	45
831	**791**	24p multicoloured	....	50	55
832	**792**	31p multicoloured		60	65
833	**793**	63p multicoloured	....	1·25	1·40
830/3		Set of 4	....	2·75	3·00
		First Day Cover	....		3·50
		Presentation Pack	....	3·50	

Plate Nos.: 20p, 31p 1A, 1B (each ×5); others 1A, 1B (each ×4)
Sheets: 20 (4×5)
Imprint: Central, left-hand margin

794 Wedding Photograph,
1947

795 Queen Elizabeth and
Prince Philip, 1997

796a Full-length Wedding Photograph, 1947
(*illustration reduced. Actual size* 150×100 *mm*)

Golden Wedding of Queen Elizabeth and Prince Philip

(Des G. Drummond. Litho Questa)

1997 (20 NOV). *Perf* 13½ (**MS**836) *or* 14½ (*others*), *both comb*

834	**794**	50p multicoloured	1·00	1·10
		a. Horiz pair. Nos. 834/5	2·00	2·25
835	**795**	50p multicoloured	1·00	1·10
834/5		*Set of* 2	2·00	2·25
		First Day Cover		2·75
		Presentation Pack	2·75	
MS836	150×100 mm.	**796a** £1.50, mult	3·00	3·25
		First Day Cover		3·75

Plate Nos.: 1A, 1B, 1C, 1D (each ×5)

Sheets: 20 (4×5). The two designs were printed together, *se-tenant*, in horizontal pairs throughout the sheets

Imprint: Central, left-hand margin

Year Pack 1997

1997 (20 NOV). *Comprises Nos.* **MS**768, 770/81, 801/10 *and* 812/36

Year Pack . . . . 45·00

Post Office Yearbook

1997 (20 NOV). *Comprises Nos.* **MS**768, 770/81, 801/10 *and* 812/36

Yearbook . . . . 50·00

COMMEMORATIVE POSTAL STATIONERY ENVELOPE

40th Anniversary of Liberation

1985 (7 MAY). *Cover showing imprinted stamp design as No. 36. Sold at 25p*

PS1	13p multicoloured	1·00	1·50

Quantity sold: 79,744

Sold out: 6.85

POSTAGE DUE STAMPS

D **1**   D **2** Map   D **3** Map

(Des F. Guenier. Litho Bradbury, Wilkinson)

1969 (1 OCT). *Perf* 14×13½ (C)

D1	D **1**	1d bluish violet (*ab*)	....	1·50	1·50
D2		2d sepia (*ad*)	....	2·25	2·00
D3		3d magenta (*ad*)	....	3·00	2·75
D4	D **2**	1s bright emerald (*acd*)	.....	9·00	7·50
D5		2s 6d olive-grey (*acd*)	......	21·00	16·00
D6		5s vermilion (*ad*)	....	30·00	27·00
D1/6		Set of 6	....	60·00	50·00
		Set of 6 Gutter Pairs	....	£175	

Sheets: 120 (2 panes 6×10)

Imprint: Central, bottom margin

Printings: (*a*) 1.10.69; (*b*) 16.12.69; (*c*) 18.2.70; (*d*) 6.6.70

Quantities sold: 1d 98,535; 2d 181,601; 3d 155,832; 1s 174,599; 2s 6d 205,962; 5s 200,698

Withdrawn and Invalidated: 14.2.72

Decimal Currency

(Des F. Guenier. Litho Bradbury, Wilkinson)

1971 (15 FEB)–*75*. *Perf* 14×13½ (C)

D7	D **3**	½p black (*a*)		10	10
D8		1p violet-blue (*a*)	....	10	10
D9		2p olive-grey (*a*)	....	10	10
D10		3p reddish purple (*a*)	....	10	10
D11		4p pale red (*a*)	....	10	10
D12		5p bright emerald (*a*)	......	15	15
D13		6p yellow-orange (*b*)	....	15	15
D14		7p bistre-yellow (*b*)	....	15	15
D15		8p light greenish blue (*c*)	..	25	25
D16		10p pale olive-grey (*a*)	......	35	35
D17		11p ochre (*c*)	....	35	40
D18		14p violet (*a*)	....	40	45
D19		25p myrtle-green (*b*)	......	80	90
D20		50p dull purple (*c*)	....	1·40	1·50
D7/20		Set of 14	....	4·00	4·25
		Presentation Pack	....	4·50	

Printings: (*a*) 15.2.71; (*b*) 12.8.74; (*c*) 1.5.75

Plate Nos.: 3p 1*a*, 1*d*; 8, 25p 1*b*, 1*c*, 1*d*; 11p 1*a*, 1*b*, 1*d*; others 1*a*, 1*b*, 1*c*, 1*d*

Sheets: 50 (5×10)

Quantities sold: ½p 313,604; 1p 281,598; 2p 205,263; 3p 183,353; 4p 180,948; 5p 199,771; 6p 161,580; 7p 156,534; 8p 154,904; 10p 198,530; 11p 151,638; 14p 147,075; 25p 158,663; 50p 146,602

Imprint: Central, bottom margin

Withdrawn: 31.1.79

D **4** Arms of St. Clement and Dovecote at Samares

D **5** Arms of St. Lawrence and Handois Reservoir

D **6** Arms of St. John and Sorel Point

D **7** Arms of St. Ouen and Pinnacle Rock

D **8** Arms of St. Peter and Quetivel Mill

D **9** Arms of St. Martin and St. Catherine's Breakwater

D **10** Arms and Harbour of St. Helier

D **11** Arms of St. Saviour and Highlands College

D **12** Arms of St. Brelade and Beauport Bay

D **13** Arms of Grouville and La Hougue Bie

D **14** Arms of St. Mary and Perry Farm

D **15** Arms of Trinity and Bouley Bay

(Des G. Drummond. Litho Questa)

1978 (17 JAN). *Perf* 14 (C)

D21	D **4**	1p blue-green and black	10	10
D22	D **5**	2p orange-yellow and black . .	10	10
D23	D **6**	3p lake-brown and black.	10	10
D24	D **7**	4p orange-vermilion and black. .	10	10
D25	D **8**	5p ultramarine and black	10	10
D26	D **9**	10p brown-olive and black	20	20
D27	D **10**	12p greenish blue and black. . . .	25	25
D28	D **11**	14p red-orange and black	25	30
D29	D **12**	15p bright magenta and black . .	25	30
D30	D **13**	20p yellow-green and black	35	40
D31	D **14**	50p deep brown and black	90	1·10
D32	D **15**	£1 chalky blue and black	2·00	2·25
D21/32		*Set of 12*	4·25	4·75
		Presentation Pack	4·50	

Plate Nos.: All values 1A–1A, 1B–1B, 1C–1C, 1D–1D, 1E–1E, 1F–1F

Sheets: 50 (10×5)

Imprint: Right-hand corner, bottom margin

Withdrawn: 30.9.83

D **16** St. Brelade   D **17** St. Aubin   D **18** Rozel

D **19** Greve de Lecq   D **20** Bouley Bay   D **21** St. Catherine

D **22** Gorey   D **23** Bonne Nuit   D **24** La Rocque

D **25** St. Helier   D **26** Ronez   D **27** La Collette

D **28** Elizabeth Castle   D **29** Upper Harbour Marina

(Des G. Drummond. Litho Questa)

1982 (7 SEPT). *Perf* 14 (C)

D33	D **16**	1p brt turquoise-green & black	10	10
D34	D **17**	2p chrome yellow and black . .	10	10
D35	D **18**	3p lake-brown and black.	10	10
D36	D **19**	4p red and black	10	10
D37	D **20**	5p bright blue and black	10	10
D38	D **21**	6p yellow-olive and black	10	15
D39	D **22**	7p reddish mauve and black . .	15	20
D40	D **23**	8p bright orange-red and black	15	20
D41	D **24**	9p bright green and black	20	25
D42	D **25**	10p turquoise-blue and black . .	20	25
D43	D **26**	20p apple-green and black	40	45
D44	D **27**	30p bright purple and black	60	65
D45	D **28**	40p dull orange and black.	80	85
D46	D **29**	£1 bright reddish violet & black	2·00	2·10
D33/46		*Set of 14*	4·50	5·00
		Presentation Pack	4·75	

Plate Nos.: All values 1A, 1B, 1C, 1D, 1E, 1F, 1G, 1H (each ×2)

Sheets: 50 (10×5)

Imprint: Right-hand corner, bottom margin

STAMP BOOKLETS

PRICES given are for complete booklets. All booklets are stitched unless otherwise stated.

B **1** Map

1969 (1 OCT)–**70**.

2s Booklet. Blue cover as Type B **1**
SB1   Containing 5×4d (No. 19*a*), 4×1d (No. 16*a*), all in panes of one with wide margins .... 2·25

B **2** Arms and Royal Mace

7s Booklet. Yellow cover as Type B **2**
SB2   Containing 12×4d (No. 19), 6×5d (No. 20), 6×1d (No. 16*b*), all in vertical pairs .... 13·00
SB2*a*   Containing 12×4d (No. 19*b*), 6×5d (No. 20*a*), 6×1d (No. 16), all in vertical pairs (5.5.70) .. £110

10s Booklet. Pink cover as Type B **2** *showing Mont Orgueil Castle*
SB3   Containing 14×4d (No. 19), 12×5d (No. 20), 4×1d (No. 16*b*), all in vertical pairs .... 11·00
SB3*a*   Containing 14×4d (No. 19*b*), 12×5d (No. 20*a*), 4×1d (No. 16), all in vertical pairs (5.5.70) .. 35·00

Special printings in sheets of 48 were made for manufacturing the 2s. booklets, but the 7s. and 10s. booklets were made up from ordinary sheets, using vertical pairs with stitching through the side margins. Stamps from both sides of the sheet were utilised so that the panes come inverted.

Decimal Currency

1971 (15 FEB).

10p Booklet. Blue cover as Type B **1** *showing Martello Tower*
SB4   Containing 2×½p (No. 42*a*), 2×2p (No. 45*a*) and 2×2½p (No. 46*a*). Each stamp with wide margin *at bottom* .... 1·00
SB4*a*   Containing 2×½p (No. 42*a*), 2×2p (No. 45*a*) and 2×2½p (No. 46*a*). Each stamp with wide margin *at top* .... 3·25

35p Booklet. Yellow cover as Type B **2** *showing The Royal Court*
SB5   Containing 10×2p (No. 45) and 6×2½p (No. 46)   1·25

50p Booklet. Pink cover as Type B **2** *showing Elizabeth Castle*
SB6   Containing 10×2p (No. 45) and 12×2½p (No. 46) .... 2·50

The panes for Nos. SB4/a were produced in sheets of 48, of which half were *tête-bêche*. In consequence, half the booklets have the blank margin at the bottom (SB4), and the other half at the top (SB4*a*).

Owing to the postal information printed in the booklets being out of date, supplies of Nos. SB4/a dispensed from machines between 10 July and early September 1972 bore an adhesive label on the front with the words 'RATE TO UNITED KINGDOM LETTERS up to 4 ozs. and postcards 3p' in two lines. They were primarily to warn holiday-makers of the new rate and were issued only through the machines. Of these about 52,000 were sold.

Quantities sold: SB4/a 244,544; SB5 20,875; SB6 17,638

1972 (15 MAY).

20p Booklet. Green cover as Type B **2** *showing Jersey Cow*
SB7   Containing 8×2½p (No. 46), all in vertical pairs. .   3·25

30p Booklet. Yellow cover as Type B **2** *showing Portelet Bay*
SB8   Containing 10×3p (No. 47), all in vertical pairs. . 28·00

50p Booklet. Pink cover as Type B **2** *showing La Corbière Lighthouse*
SB9   Containing 8×2½p (No. 46) and 10×3p (No. 47), all in vertical pairs .... 1·50

1972 (1 DEC).

10p Booklet. Orange cover as Type B **1** *showing Legislative Chamber*
SB10   Containing 3×½p (No. 42*a*), 1×2½p (No. 45*a*) and 2×3p (No. 47*a*). Each stamp with wide margin *at bottom* 75
SB10*a* As SB10 but with margin *at top* 75

Quantity sold: 126,877

1973 (1 JUNE).

10p *Booklet. Green cover as Type* B **1** *showing Mont Orgueil by night*
SB11   Contents as No. SB10. Each stamp with wide margin *at bottom*   75
SB11*a*   As SB11 but with margin *at top*   75

Quantity sold: 109,129

1973 (10 SEPT).

20p *Booklet. Green cover as Type* B **2** *showing Jersey Wildlife Preservation Trust species*
SB12   Containing 8×2½p (No. 46) . . . .   4·25

30p *Booklet. Buff cover as Type* B **2** *showing Jersey Wild Flowers*
SB13   Containing 10×3p (No. 47) . . . .   2·50

50p *Booklet. Blue cover as Type* B **2** *showing 'English Fleet in the Channel' by Peter Monamy*
SB14   Containing 8×2½p (No. 46) and 10×3p (No. 47)   1·75

Quantities sold: SB12 8,790; SB13 11,450; SB14 14,145

1974 (7 JAN). *Jersey Wildlife Preservation Trust*

20p *Booklet. Green cover as Type* B **2** *showing Spectacled Bear*
SB15   Containing 8×2½p (No. 46) . . . .   1·75

30p *Booklet. Yellow cover as Type* B **2** *showing White-eared Pheasant*
SB16   Containing 10×3p (No. 47) . . . .   1·75

50p *Booklet. Red cover as Type* B **2** *showing Thick-billed Parrot*
SB17   Containing 8×2½p (No. 46) and 10×3p (No. 47)   1·75

Quantities sold: SB15 14,283; SB16 14,049; SB17 15,976

1974 (1 JULY).

10p *Booklet. Orange cover as Type* B **1** *showing Jersey Airport*
SB18   Containing 1×3p (No. 47*a*) and 2×3½p (No. 48*a*). Each stamp with wide margin *at bottom*   75
SB18*a*   As SB18 but with margin *at top*   75

Quantity sold: 129,235

1974 (1 JULY). *Jersey Wildlife Preservation Trust*

60p *Booklet. Pink cover as Type* B **2** *showing Ring-tailed Lemur*
SB19   Containing 6×3p (No. 47) and 12×3½p (No. 48)   2·00

Quantity sold: 22,274

1974 (1 OCT). *Jersey Wildlife Preservation Trust*

60p *Booklet. Green cover as Type* B **2** *showing Tuatara Lizard*
SB20   Contents as No. SB19 . . . .   2·00

Quantity sold: 20,984

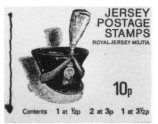

B **3** Artillery Shako

1975 (25 FEB). *Military Headgear*

10p *Booklet. Grey cover as Type* B **3**
SB21   Containing 1×½p (No. 42*a*), 2×3p (No. 47*a*) and 1×3½p (No. 48*a*). Each stamp with wide margin *at bottom*   75
SB21*a*   As SB21 but with margin *at top*   75

20p *Booklet. Rose cover as Type* B **3** *showing Shako, 2nd North Regt*
SB22   Containing 2×3p (No. 47*a*) and 4×3½p (No. 48*a*). Each stamp with wide margin *at bottom* . . . .   1·00
SB22*a*   As SB22 but with margin *at top* . . . .   1·00

Quantities sold: SB21/*a* 37,849; SB22/*a* 38,854

STAMP SACHETS These are booklet covers with the stamps loose inside and contained in clear plastic sachets. They are noted but not priced as such items are outside the scope of this checklist.

B **4** Post Office Crest

1975 (1 APR). 20p *Stamp Sachet. Red cover as Type* B **4**
Containing 2×1p (No. 43), 2×4p (No. 49) and 2×5p (No. 50)

JERSEY POSTAGE STAMPS
AVIATION HISTORY

£1 Contents 8 at 1p 8 at 4p 12 at 5p

B **5** Astra Biplane
(*illustration reduced. Actual size 94×56 mm*)

1975 (21 APR). *Aviation History. Pale blue cover* (SB23) *or yellow cover* (SB24)

50p Booklet as Type B **2** *showing Supermarine Sea Eagle*
SB23   Containing 6×1p (No. 43), 6×4p (No. 49) and
        12×5p (No. 50) . . . .   1·50

£1 Booklet as Type B **5**
SB24   Containing 8×1p (No. 43), 8×4p (No. 49) and
        12×5p (No. 50) . . . .   2·75

Quantities sold: SB23 29,872; SB24 29,608

1976 (29 JAN). *20p Stamp Sachet. Blue cover as Type* B **4**
Containing 3×1p (No. 138), 2×5p (No. 139) and 1×7p (No. 141)

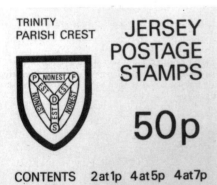

TRINITY
PARISH CREST

JERSEY
POSTAGE
STAMPS

50p

CONTENTS   2 at 1p   4 at 5p   4 at 7p

B **6** Trinity Parish Crest

1976 (5 APR). *Green cover* (SB25) *or magenta cover* (SB26) *as Type* B **6**

50p Booklet. Trinity Parish Crest
SB25   Containing booklet panes Nos. 138a, 139a and
        141a . . . .   2·25

£1 Booklet. St. Ouen's Parish Crest
SB26   Containing booklet panes Nos. 138b, 139a×2
        and 141a×2 . . . .   2·75

Quantities sold: SB25 85,210; SB26 64,609

1976 (2 NOV). *20p Stamp Sachet. Green cover as Type* B **4**
Containing 3×1p, 2×5p and 1×7p (Nos. 138/9 and 141)

1977 (29 SEPT). *20p Stamp Sachet. Brown cover as Type* B **4**
Containing 3×1p, 2×5p and 1×7p (Nos. 138/9 and 141)

1978 (28 FEB). *Orange-red cover* (SB27) *or pale blue cover* (SB28) *as Type* B **6**

£1 Booklet. Grouville Parish Arms
SB27   Containing booklet panes Nos. 138b and 140a
        ×4 . . . .   2·50

£1 Booklet. St. Saviour Parish Arms
SB28   Containing booklet panes Nos. 138b and 142a
        ×3 . . . .   2·50

Quantities sold: SB27 43,446; SB28 45,015

1978 (1 MAY). *30p Stamp Sachet. Violet cover as Type* B **4**
Containing 2×1p, 2×6p and 2×8p (Nos. 138, 140 and 142)

1979 (13 AUG). *30p Stamp Sachet. Purple cover as Type* B **4**
Containing 2×1p, 2×6p and 2×8p (Nos. 138, 140 and 142)

POSTAGE STAMPS
JERSEY

£1.20

CONTENTS 8 at 1p 8 at 8p 8 at 8p

B **7** Jersey Post Office Headquarters, Mont Millais, St. Helier
(*illustration reduced. Actual size 90×65 mm*)

1979 (1 OCT). *Bistre-brown on buff cover as Type* B **7**. *Stapled*
SB29   £1.20 booklet containing Nos. 138b, 140a and
        142a each ×2 . . . .   3·25

Quantity sold: 82,738

1980 (6 MAY). *Black on red cover as Type* B **6** *showing St. Helier Parish Arms. Stapled*
SB30 £1.40 booklet containing Nos. 138b×3, 141a
×2 and 143a×2 . . . . 3·25

Quantity sold: 29,900

1980 (6 MAY). 20p *Stamp Sachet. Black on red cover as Type* B **4**
Containing 4×1p, 1×7p and 1×9p (Nos. 138, 141 and 143)

1981 (24 FEB). *Black on blue cover as Type* B **6**, *but* 82×65 *mm, showing De Bagot crest. Stapled*
SB31 £1.32 booklet containing Nos. 250a×2, 252a,
256a and 259a . . . . 4·25

Quantity sold: 49,486

1981 (24 FEB). 20p *Stamp Sachet. Black on blue cover as Type* B **4**
Containing 2×3p and 2×7p (Nos. 252 and 256)

1981 (1 DEC). *Black on green cover as Type* B **6**, *but* 82×65 *mm, showing Poingdestre Arms. Stapled*
SB32 £1.20 booklet containing Nos. 250a, 251a,
256a and 259a . . . . 3·50

Quantity sold: 43,434

B **8** Jean Martell
(*illustration reduced. Actual size* 155×80 *mm*)

Martell Cognac

1982 (7 SEPT). *Multicoloured cover as Type* B **8**. *Booklet contains text and illustrations on labels attached to panes and on interleaving pages*
SB33 £3.08 booklet containing Nos. 293b, 295b and
297b each ×2 . . . . 8·00

Quantity sold: 54,654

1983 (19 APR). *Black on orange-red cover as Type* B **6**, *but* 82×65 *mm, showing Bisson crest. Stapled*
SB34 £1.32 booklet containing Nos. 250a, 251a,
257a and 260a . . . . 3·25

Quantity sold: 29,393

1983 (19 APR). 20p *Stamp Sachet. Black on turquoise-green as Type* B **4**
Containing 2×½p, 1×8p and 1×11p (Nos. 249, 257 and 260)

1984 (3 JAN). 30p *Stamp Sachet. Black on pink cover as Type* B **4**
Containing 2×9p and 1×12p (Nos. 258 and 261)

1984 (27 APR). *Black on rose-lilac cover as Type* B **6**, *but* 80×65 *mm, showing Robin crest. Stapled*
SB35 £2.16 booklet containing Nos. 252ba×2,
258ab ×2 and 261ab . . . . 6·75

Quantity sold: 38,782

1985 (15 APR). 50p *Stamp Sachet. Black on light green cover as Type* B **4**
Containing 1×1p, 3×3p and 4×10p (Nos. 250, 252b and 259)

B **9** Cross of Lorraine
(*illustration reduced. Actual size* 155×80 *mm*)

300th Anniversary of Huguenot Immigration

1985 (10 SEPT). *Multicoloured cover as Type* B **9**
SB36 £3.60 booklet containing Nos. 370a/5a . . . . . . 9·00

Quantity sold: 31,042

1986 (1 APR). *Black on carmine cover as Type* B **6**, *but* 81×65 *mm, showing Messervy crest. Stapled*
SB37 £3.12 booklet containing Nos. 251ba, 259ba
and 263ab, each ×2 . . . . 7·50

Quantity sold: 23,729
Withdrawn: 31.3.91

B **10** Post Office Emblem

1986 (1 APR). 50*p Stamp Sachet. Black and orange-vermilion cover as Type* B **10**
Containing 1×2p, 2×4p and 4×10p (Nos. 251*b*, 253*a* and 259)

1987 (6 APR). *Black on blue cover as Type* B **6**, *but* 81×65 *mm, showing Fiott crest. Stapled*
SB38   £3.60 booklet containing Nos. 253*ab*, 260*ba* and 264*ab*, each ×2 . . . .   8·25

Quantity sold: 23,647
Withdrawn: 31.3.91

1987 (6 APR). 50*p Stamp Sachet. Black and orange-vermilion cover as Type* B **10**
Containing 1×2p, 1×3p, 3×4p and 3×11p (Nos. 251*b*, 252*b*, 253*a* and 260)

B **11** Vikings
(*illustration reduced. Actual size* 168×80 *mm*)

900th Death Anniversary of William the Conqueror

1987 (16 OCT). *Multicoloured cover as Type* B **11**. *Booklet contains text and illustrations on labels attached to panes and on interleaving pages*
SB39   £5.50 booklet containing Nos. 422*a*/7*a* . . . . . .   22·00

Quantity sold: 30,107
Sold out: 4.88

1988 (17 MAY). *Black on bright green cover as Type* B **6**, *but* 81×65 *mm, showing Malet crest. Stapled*
SB40   £3.84 booklet containing Nos. 253*ab*, 261*ab* and 265*a*, each ×2 . . . .   9·00

Quantity sold: 16,566
Withdrawn: 31.3.91

1988 (17 MAY). 50*p Stamp Sachet. Black and orange-vermilion cover as Type* B **10**
Containing 1×2p, 3×4p and 3×12p (Nos. 251*b*, 253*a* and 261)

B **12** Chouan Rebels
(*illustration reduced. Actual size* 155×80 *mm*)

Bicentenary of the French Revolution. Philippe D'Auvergne

1989 (7 JULY). *Multicoloured cover as Type* B **12**. *Booklet contains text on labels attached to panes and on interleaving pages*
SB41   £6 booklet containing Nos. 501*a*/6*a* . . . .   15·00

Quantity sold: 31,052
Sold out: 7.8.89

B **13** Flags of Jersey and Great Britain
(*illustration reduced. Actual size* 108×63 *mm*)

'Stamp World London 90' International Stamp Exhibition

1990 (3 MAY). *Multicoloured cover as Type* B **13**
SB42   £4.20 booklet containing Nos. 470*a*, 474*a* and 478*a*, each ×2 . . . .   8·50

Withdrawn: 30.6.96

B **14**

1990 (3 MAY). 50p *Stamp Sachet. Multicoloured cover as Type* B **14** *showing* 18p *stamp* (*No.* 478)
Containing 2×4p and 3×14p (Nos. 470 and 474)

B **15** Elizabeth Castle
(*illustration reduced. Actual size* 108×63 *mm*)

1991 (12 FEB). *Jersey Scenes. Multicoloured cover as Type* B **15**
SB43   £4.80 booklet containing Nos. 471*a*, 475*a* and
480*a*, each ×2 .... 11·00

Withdrawn: 30.6.96

1992 (25 FEB). £1 *Stamp Sachet. Multicoloured cover as Type* B **14** *showing design of* 22p *stamp* (*No.* 480)
Containing 1×2p, 2×16p, 3×22p (Nos. 467, 476 and 482)

B **16** William Mesny on Horseback
(*illustration reduced. Actual size* 155×80 *mm*)

Jersey Adventurers (3rd series). 150th Birth Anniversary of William Mesny

1992 (25 FEB). *Multicoloured cover as Type* B **16**. *Booklet contains text on labels attached to panes and on interleaving pages*
SB44   £5.50 booklet containing Nos. 573*b*/8*a* .... 11·00

Withdrawn: 30.6.96

B **17** Jersey Post Logo

1992 (25 MAY). *Covers as Type* B **17**. *Panes attached by selvedge*
SB45   £1.12 booklet (scarlet on white cover)
containing No. 474*b* ....   2·75
SB46   £1.28 booklet (bright yellow on scarlet cover)
containing No. 476*a* ....   3·50
SB47   £1.76 booklet (scarlet on bright yellow cover)
containing No. 482*a* ....   4·25

Withdrawn: 30.6.96

1993 (26 JAN). *Covers as Type* B **17**. *Panes attached by selvedge*
SB48   (£1.36) booklet (bright yellow on green cover)
containing pane No. 601*a* ....   3·25
SB49   (£1.84) booklet (scarlet on flesh cover)
containing pane No. 605*a* ....   4·00
SB50   (£2.24) booklet (white on bright new blue
cover) containing pane No. 609*a* ....   5·00

Face values quoted for each booklet are those at which they were initially sold. The price of No. SB48 was increased to £1.44 and that of No. SB50 to £2.40 on 10 January 1994. No. SB48 was sold at £1.52 from 4 July 1995. On 10 March 1997 No. SB48 was increased to £1.60, No. SB49 to £1.92 and No. SB50 to £2.48.

B **18** Invasion Map
(*illustration reduced. Actual size* 162×98 *mm*)

50th Anniversary of D-Day

1994 (6 JUNE). *Multicoloured cover as Type* B **18**. *Booklet contains text and illustrations on panes and interleaving pages*
SB51 £5.68 booklet containing Nos. 659*a/b*, 661*a* and 663*a*. . . . . 20·00

Sold out: 12.94

B **19** 'Greetings From JERSEY'
(*illustration reduced. Actual size 152×75 mm*)

Greetings Stamps

1995 (24 JAN). *Multicoloured cover as Type* B **19**. *Pane attached by selvedge*
SB52 £2.24 booklet containing pane No. 684*b* . . . . 4·50

B **20** Crowd Celebrating
(*illustration reduced. Actual size 162×97 mm*)

50th Anniversary of Liberation

1995 (9 MAY). *Multicoloured cover as Type* B **20**. *Booklet contains text and illustrations on panes and interleaving pages*
SB53 £7.06 booklet containing Nos. 700*a*, 702*a*, 704*a* and **MS**706*a* . . . . 14·00

B **21** Mont Orgueil Castle, Gorey
(*illustration reduced. Actual size 164×97 mm*)

Tourism

1996 (8 JUNE). *Multicoloured cover as Type* B **21**. *Booklet contains text and illustrations on panes and interleaving pages*
SB54 £8.32 booklet containing Nos. 752*a/b*, 754*a* and 756*a*. . . . . 16·00

B **22** Island Sports
(*illustration reduced. Actual size 163×98 mm*)

7th Island Games, Jersey

1997 (28 JUNE). *Multicoloured cover as Type* B **22**. *Booklet contains text and illustrations on panes and interleaving pages*
SB55 £8.72 booklet containing Nos. 812*a/b*, 814*a* and 816*a*. . . . . 17·00

FREE ILLUSTRATED
CHANNEL ISLAND & ISLE OF MAN
MAIL ORDER LISTING

- Produced twice yearly and used by thousands of collectors worldwide.
- Packed full of popular material from one of the world's largest stocks.
- Includes a number of rare and specialised items.
- Contains illustrations (many in colour), accurate descriptions and SG catalogue numbers throughout.
- Features a useful checklist and a pull out mail order form in the centre pages.

CHANNEL ISLAND &
ISLE OF MAN COLLECTORS CLUB

Our team of experts maintain detailed records of your collection and are therefore able to offer you further stamps to help you complete it. Members will receive:

- A monthly or quarterly selection of stamps specially selected within your own pre-set spend limit.
- Free stamps worth £75 when you spend £75 per month or to the value of £50 if you spend £150 per quarter.
- Free album supplements will be sent to you each year to keep your collection up to date.
- Regular savings on all the stamps we send you, generously discounted from our normal retail and catalogue prices.
- Special offers on a whole range of other Stanley Gibbons catalogues, albums and accessories.
- Interest free extended payments help you spread the cost of your stamps.

For your free illustrated mail order listing and details of our
Collectors Club phone 0800 731 8052

Stanley Gibbons Mail Order
399 Strand, London, WC2R 0LX. England.
Tel: 0171 836 8444 Fax: 0171 836 7342
e.mail mailorder@stangiblondon.demon.co.uk
internet: http://www.stangib.com/

BY APPOINTMENT TO
HER MAJESTY THE QUEEN
STANLEY GIBBONS LTD
LONDON PHILATELISTS

● OUR NAME IS YOUR GUARANTEE OF QUALITY ●

THE GREATEST RANGE OF BRITISH ISLANDS ALBUMS

We offer probably the world's largest range of high quality albums to both display and protect your stamps. A very special range of tailor-made albums have been developed for today's discerning collector with supplements produced each January to keep you right up to date.

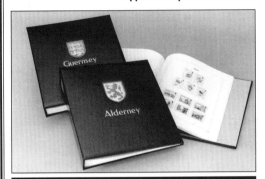

STANDARD ALBUM

The best value album currently available
- Large page size and high capacity.
- Houses all Islands in just two volumes.
- Navy blue canvas peg fitting binder.
- Embossed with the Islands crests.
- Luxury slipcase.
- Selected stamp illustrations.

Alderney, Guernsey, Jersey & Isle of Man Set

Item 5286	Volume 1 (1969-1990)	£59.95
Item 5294	Volume 2 (1991-1996)	£44.95

STANLEY GIBBONS

• THE COLLECTOR'S CHOICE •

Stanley Gibbons Publications, 5 Parkside, Christchurch Road, Ringwood, Hants BH24 3SH England
Tel: 01425 472363 Fax: 01425 470247
e.mail sales@stangib.demon.co.uk

ONE COUNTRY ALBUMS

Ideal for the straightforward collection
- Five detailed and easy to use seperate volumes.
- Features SG catalogue numbers.
- Padded leather finish 22 ring maroon PVC binders.
- High quality leaves with illustrations.
- Includes self-adhesive album title sheet.

Item 5524	Guernsey Vol.1 (1941-1994)	£24.95
Item 5526	Guernsey Vol.2 (1995-1996)	£14.95
Item 5526	Jersey Vol.1 (1941-1994)	£24.95
Item 5526	Jersey Vol.2 (1995-1996)	£14.95
Item 5256	Isle of Man (1958-1996)	£32.50

LUXURY HINGELESS ALBUMS

The ultimate in quality, convenience and style
- Four detailed volumes.
- Navy blue leatherette hingeless binders.
- Embossed with the national crest.
- Expertly arranged leaves containing illustrations.
- Clear protective mounts affixed in place.
- Features Issue dates, face values and colours.
- Each album housed in a matching slipcase.

Item 5549	Guernsey (1969-1996)	£74.95
Item 5550	Jersey (1969-1996)	£74.95
Item 5292	Alderney (1983-1996)	£29.95
Item 5286	Isle of Man (1973-1996)	£74.95
Item 5549(so)	Complete Set Offer	£229.95

Available from all good stamp shops, our showroom at 399 Strand, London or by mail order - phone 0800 611622 for our free colour brochure.

FREE 1997 SUPPLEMENTS
with all these albums

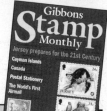

LUXURY ALBUMS FOR DISCERNING COVER COLLECTORS

Stanley Gibbons cover albums are designed to meet the needs of today's first day cover collector and postal historian alike. Each of the high capacity luxury padded binders is handmade to exacting standards, gold embossed on the spine and supplied complete with polypropylene leaves which do not crease or tear easily and give substantial protection against ultraviolet light. All leaves also contain black insert cards and extra leaves are available in packs of ten.

Choose from:

Items 3510 **New Pioneer £8.95**
A high capacity single cover album either in red, green or black PVC with 20 leaves. (holds 40 covers)

Item 3525 **New Classic £14.95**
A compact deluxe single cover album available in black, blue and red with 20 leaves and two index leaves. (holds 40 covers)

Item 3588 **Malvern £12.95**
A classic fully padded 4-ring double cover album in blue, green, red or black. Contains 20 double leaves and 1 single pocket leaf. (holds 78 covers)

Item 3550 **SG Major £24.95**
A luxury peg fitting album with padded deep red or blue cover and 25 double pocket leaves and two index leaves. (holds 100 covers)

Available from our London showroom at 399 Strand and by Mail Order - Phone 0800 611622 for our free colour brochure

STANLEY GIBBONS

Stanley Gibbons Publications
5 Parkside, Christchurch Road, Ringwood, Hants BH24 3SH England.
Tel: 01425 472363 Fax: 01425 470247
e.mail: sales@stangib.demon.co.uk Internet: http://www.stangib.com/